Childhood Practice

Sara Miller McCune founded SAGE Publishing in 1965 to support the dissemination of usable knowledge and educate a global community. SAGE publishes more than 1000 journals and over 800 new books each year, spanning a wide range of subject areas. Our growing selection of library products includes archives, data, case studies and video. SAGE remains majority owned by our founder and after her lifetime will become owned by a charitable trust that secures the company's continued independence.

Los Angeles | London | New Delhi | Singapore | Washington DC | Melbourne

Edited by

Mike Carroll & Mary Wingrave

Childhood Practice

A reflective & evidence-based approach

Los Angeles | London | New Delhi
Singapore | Washington DC | Melbourne

Los Angeles | London | New Delhi
Singapore | Washington DC | Melbourne

SAGE Publications Ltd
1 Oliver's Yard
55 City Road
London EC1Y 1SP

SAGE Publications Inc.
2455 Teller Road
Thousand Oaks, California 91320

SAGE Publications India Pvt Ltd
B 1/I 1 Mohan Cooperative Industrial Area
Mathura Road
New Delhi 110 044

SAGE Publications Asia-Pacific Pte Ltd
3 Church Street
#10-04 Samsung Hub
Singapore 049483

Editor: Delayna Spencer
Editorial assistant: Bali BirchLee
Production editor: Nicola Marshall
Copyeditor: Jane Fricker
Proofreader: Sharon Cawood
Indexer: Author
Marketing manager: Lorna Patkai
Cover design: Wendy Scott
Typeset by: C&M Digitals (P) Ltd, Chennai, India
Printed in the UK

Library of Congress Control Number: 2022945134

British Library Cataloguing in Publication data

A catalogue record for this book is available from the British Library

ISBN 978-1-5297-7777-2
ISBN 978-1-5297-7776-5 (pbk)

At SAGE we take sustainability seriously. Most of our products are printed in the UK using responsibly sourced papers and boards. When we print overseas we ensure sustainable papers are used as measured by the PREPS grading system. We undertake an annual audit to monitor our sustainability.

Contents

List of figures

List of tables

Selected acronyms

We have used a variety of acronyms throughout the book which are given in full when first introduced. Listed below are selected acronyms that appear in several chapters.

CCEA   Council for the Curriculum Examinations and Assessment

CP   Childhood Practice

CPD   Continuing Professional Development

DfE   Department for Education

DfES   Department for Education and Skills

ECEC   Early Childhood Education and Care

ELC   Early Learning and Childcare

ES   Education Scotland

EY   Early Years

EYFS   Early Years Foundation Stage

GIRFEC Getting it Right for Every Child

NCE   Non-compulsory Care and Education

NSPCC   National Society for the Prevention of Cruelty to Children

OECD   Organisation for Economic Co-operation and Development

Ofsted Office for Standards in Education, Children's Services and Skills

OSC   Out-of-School Care

SG   Scottish Government

SP   Scottish Parliament

SSSC   Scottish Social Services Council

UK   United Kingdom

UKG   United Kingdom Government

UKP   United Kingdom Parliament

UN   United Nations

UNCRC   United Nations Convention on the Rights of the Child

UNESCO   United Nations Educational, Scientific and Cultural Organization

UNICEF   United Nations International Children's Emergency Fund

About the editors

Dr Mike Carroll is a retired Senior Lecturer in Education at the University of Glasgow. Mike was formerly the Director of the MEd Professional Learning and Enquiry. Mike contributed to a range of master's-level programmes for serving teachers, with a particular interest in the development of leadership at all levels in the school. As a retired member of staff, Mike continues to contribute as an Associate Tutor involved in supporting students on school placements as well as working as an Education Consultant contributing to Teacher Induction Programmes. Mike co-edited the successful *Understanding Teaching and Learning in Primary Education* text published by SAGE.

Dr Mary Wingrave is a Senior Associate Tutor, and she supports the Associate Tutors who work in both Initial Teacher Education and undergraduate studies at the University of Glasgow. Previously, she was the Director of Initial Teacher Education and Undergraduate Studies and was also the Director of the West Partnership. In this role, she worked with local authorities in the West of Scotland, and with other universities, to support the school placements of initial teacher education students. The focus of Mary's teaching has been in the area of the non-compulsory sector where she developed and led the BA and MEd in Childhood Practice Programmes. Her areas of focus are leadership, early years, and the professionalisation of the non-compulsory childcare and education sector. Mary was involved in the revision of Scotland's key national policy document for the non-compulsory education and childcare sector, the Standard for Childhood Practice.

About the contributors

Dr Cynthia Abel is a registered early childhood educator from Ontario, Canada. Currently she is employed as the Deputy Registrar and Director of Registration with the College of Early Childhood Educators (Ontario). In this role, Cynthia leads the team responsible for developing and assessing the entry to practice requirements for those wishing to practise the profession; and works with post-secondary institutions to ensure pre-service training meets the established requirements in a manner that reflects the current needs of the sector. Prior to taking on this role, she spent many years with both the local and provincial governments, working extensively in the children's mental health and early years policy areas in increasingly progressive positions. Cynthia holds a Master's of Leadership Studies from Royal Roads University, British Columbia, Canada and a Doctorate of Education from the University of Glasgow, Scotland. Her research interests include workforce development and collaboration within human service systems.

Jillian Barker is an Associate Tutor at the University of Glasgow and is currently completing the Doctorate in Education (EdD) at the University of Glasgow. Alongside this, Jillian currently works within the private Out-of-School Care sector and has gained over 10 years' experience directing and managing private establishments. Through this, Jillian gained her SVQ Assessor Qualification and contributed to the formation and delivery of teaching materials and projects for assessment. Her career, along with her academic journey at the University of Glasgow, has led to research interests in concepts of children and childhood, gender stereotypes and assumptions, leadership in early learning and childcare, theories of play, and raising professional awareness, particularly within the Playwork sector.

Elizabeth Black is Programme Leader for the MEd/PGD in Childhood Practice at the University of Glasgow. She joined the University in January 2017 from a professional background in early learning and childcare, having worked with children and young people aged 0–14 in various practitioner, leadership and management roles within the private and voluntary sectors. She has worked in early years in England, Scotland and the Czech Republic and benefited from a study placement in the Netherlands. Her undergraduate study of social policy informs her understanding of Childhood Practice as a policy-driven field. Areas of research and scholarship interest include early numeracy, modern apprentices' professional identities, and (within higher education) the development of feedback literacy and useful assessment practices. As a co-convenor of the Scottish Educational

Research Association Early Years Network, she enjoys fostering opportunities for practitioners and academics to interact.

Mark Breslin is a lecturer of Health and Well-Being and Initial Teacher Education at the University of Glasgow, Scotland. Mark has taught for over 20 years across all spheres of education from early level through to higher education in both England and Scotland. He has had many leadership and managerial roles throughout his career working within education. Mark supervises Postgraduate Taught Master's students during their dissertation phase and is also an advisor of studies for undergraduate students. He is also an original member of Education Scotland's Health and Wellbeing Improvement Team, helping to develop Scottish Government policies and practice within Scottish schools. Mark specialises in areas related to the mental, emotional, social and physical wellbeing of children within education. His current research interest is mental health in Scottish schools, where he has a focus on developing teacher confidence on issues related to mental health and emotional wellbeing.

Jana Chandler is a lecturer at Borders College and an Associate Tutor at the University of Glasgow. She also sits on a board of directors for a charitable organisation delivering early years provision and family learning in Midlothian, Scotland. Jana has worked for nearly 20 years within the early years sector before transitioning to further and higher education. Her experience encompasses working in the private and voluntary sector, both in the UK and abroad. Completing her degree in Psychology and later Master's in Education, she is now at the final stage of obtaining her Teaching Qualification in Further Education. Jana is keen to complete Doctoral research in the future. Her research interests include children's rights, sustainability and digital education.

Dr Jennifer Farrar is a lecturer at the University of Glasgow in children's literature and literacies with a background in secondary English teaching. Her research interests include teachers' engagement with themes of migration and diversity; the critically literate potential of metafictive texts, family literacies and home–school relationships; pedagogies for literacy teaching; and initial teacher education. Jennifer has supported several school and community-based projects involving picturebooks. Her most recent publications have focused on the extent of student teachers' knowledge and use of children's literature in the classroom; the relationship between challenging picturebooks and literacy studies; and the status of critical literacies within policy and curriculum across the United Kingdom's four home nations. Jennifer is Programme Leader of the PGDE Primary and Secondary, an intense one-year route into the teaching profession, and enjoys working with a wide range of university students, from undergraduate to doctoral level.

Dr Jacqui Horsburgh is an Associate Tutor in Leadership and Management in Education at the School of Education, Glasgow University. She has taught and held leadership roles in a range of day and residential educational settings. She is an international educational consultant working with different project teams in Scotland and Sub-Saharan Africa to achieve outcomes related to educational improvement for learners in schools and teacher education establishments. As the HMIE (Scotland) Lead Inspector for Primary Education, she worked with practitioners across the country to evaluate and improve educational provision. Her research interests include the education of care-experienced children. She has published a book, *Improving Outcomes for Looked After Children* (Emerald, 2022), of case studies and self-evaluation tools to support practitioners to improve outcomes for care-experienced children.

Joe Houghton received a Master's of Education in Childhood Practice from the University of Glasgow in 2021. His early career, however, began in the very different field of music, as a professional oboe player. Completing a degree in Music from the University of Cambridge in 1992, Joe then studied the oboe at the Royal Academy of Music followed by the Conservatoire de Musique in Geneva. In 2012, after 14 years as principal oboe with the Orchestra of Scottish Opera, a very different career path presented itself and he is now, along with his wife, the co-founder, co-owner and manager of two busy Out-of-School Care settings. Playwork and a deep respect for the intrinsic value of play under-pin practice at both settings. Joe's MEd dissertation reflects this focus through seeking to explain perceived differences in the way children play between the two Out-of-School settings, one rural, the other more urban.

Susie Marshall works as a lecturer in Mathematics Education at the University of Glasgow, where she teaches on the Initial Teacher Education programme and postgraduate courses in Inclusive Education. She has been closely involved with the Childhood Practice pro-gramme, teaching both undergraduate and postgraduate courses. She is also a primary mathematics consultant for the Numicon Approach, leading Professional Development in schools and early years settings. Susie began her career as a primary teacher and has taught across all age ranges, both in Scotland and England. She was Deputy Head of a primary school for seven years, where part of her responsibilities involved supervising the Foundation Stage and working closely with staff to enhance children's learning. Susie's areas of interest include developing young children's mathematics through play, the use of concrete-pictorial-abstract representations to further conceptual understand-ing, and promoting reasoning in mathematics.

Dr Margaret McCulloch has recently retired from full-time work as a lecturer in the School of Education, University of Glasgow, but continues to teach and assess on a part-time basis, as well as managing a group of Associate Tutors. She has developed, led and taught courses across the School's Initial Teacher Education programmes; currently her main area of teach-ing is with international students and practising teachers across the UK who are studying on the Master's programme in Inclusive Education: Policy, Research and Practice, focusing on issues of curriculum, learning and teaching, as well as teaching on the EdD and supervising doctoral students. She is a Fellow of the Higher Education Academy. Previously, she worked for many years as a primary teacher, specialising in Support for Learning, before becoming an Inclusion Development Officer, and has extensive experience of working collaboratively with parents, teachers and colleagues from other professions.

Dr Christine McKee completed her BA (Hons) in Hispanic Studies at the University of Strathclyde, following which she completed her PhD on the concept of the nation in Bolivia at the University of Hull in 2001. Christine completed her PGCE after which she taught Modern Languages in England for 10 years, finishing as an Advanced Skills Teacher before returning to Scotland. Due to personal circumstances, Christine began to focus her research on attachment theory and trauma and has contributed to Adoption UK's work in this regard. She is now a Trustee for the charity Scottish Attachment in Action and is working to enhance awareness of attachment and trauma across the educational sector. Christine worked as a Support for Learning Assistant prior to joining the University of Glasgow as a lecturer in Teacher Education in 2016.

Marie McQuade is a lecturer in Childhood Practice at the University of Glasgow. Prior to joining the University, Marie worked as a Policy Manager for the Scottish Government, spending time in the Early Learning and Childcare, and Mental Health Directorates, developing and delivering government policy commitments. Marie has considerable experience delivering professional learning services to early years, education, and out-of-school care practitioners with a specific focus on high-quality practice, family learning and leadership. Earlier in her career, working across a variety of early years services and settings, including local authority, private and third sector, Marie supported the development and management of projects to deliver improved outcomes for children and families. Whilst working in the sector, Marie completed the MEd in Childhood Practice with a research focus on early career leadership and mentoring. Current research interests include high-quality school-age childcare, mentoring, and leadership development. Before joining the education workforce, Marie gained her Bachelor of Arts in Communication Studies from Glasgow Caledonian University and spent a number of years as a television producer in music television and other media outlets in Asia and Europe.

Ruth Myles is an Associate Tutor for the School of Education within the University of Glasgow, and the Registered Manager within a third-sector children's respite centre, supporting children and young people with additional and complex health and support needs. Ruth has worked in a variety of social and educational care settings, in both practice and strategic development roles since 2007. Ruth is a qualified manager with a Master's degree in Childhood Practice, experience in child protection, children's rights, and childcare, with a focus on inclusion and support for children and young people with additional and complex support needs.

Craig Orr is currently a lecturer in Childhood Practice at the University of Glasgow. Having worked in a variety of roles in Childhood Practice over many years, including the early years, play and youth work sectors, Craig has extensive experience of both policy and practice. Whilst working in the sector, Craig also completed a BA(Hons) degree in Childhood and Youth Studies through the Open University, before progressing on to the MEd in Childhood Practice at the University of Glasgow. Craig is currently completing a PhD in Education at the University of Glasgow, exploring Collective Impact approaches to cross-sector collaboration. The project aims to investigate such approaches from a bottom-up perspective, supporting participants through a process of structured reflection. By mapping the structure of their professional networks, Local Coordinators within the Children's Neighbourhoods Scotland programme examine the cultural and historical factors that support or hinder effective collaborative practice.

Dr Irene Pollock is the Deputy Head at Casa Montessori Nursery, the Learning Services Manager at Forth Valley College, and the External Examiner for the Montessori Partnership. She is also an Associate Tutor in the School of Education at the University of Glasgow, working with both the BA and PGD Childhood Practice programmes, as well as supervising Master's students across the School. Dr Pollock was in the first cohort to graduate with an MEd in Childhood Practice; her dissertation focused on developing the academic writing ability of BA Childhood Practice students. She recently completed an MSc in Psychological Studies, exploring how emotional literacy is supported in Scottish schools. Irene's previous publications have included research for the Scottish Book Trust and investigations into Gaelic-medium early years and primary education.

Kristina Robb is an Associate Tutor at the University of Glasgow. She also leads learning for Modern Apprentices and the wider workforce in Early Learning and Childcare in Midlothian and is an SQA External Verifier. She has previously held leadership positions in both early years and out-of-school care settings, lectured in FE and written nationally recognised qualifications. Her research interests, developed from her undergraduate focus on play as a vehicle for learning, now encompass a passion for creating professional learning opportunities, enabling authentic environments, loose parts, and the development of STEM and creativity in early years. She has presented at national and international conferences on STEM in the early years after winning a Scottish Government ELC Innovation Award in 2020. Kristina's current projects include developing STEM and numeracy professional learning and resources, and a suite of online training specifically for the Scottish ELC and OOSC sectors.

Julie Robinson works as a teacher educator at the University of Glasgow School of Education. She is involved in the field of Initial Teacher Education, convening, lecturing and teaching on a range of courses within the undergraduate MEduc Degree and the Postgraduate PGDE programme. Her areas of focus here include educational theory, educational inquiry and interdisciplinary approaches for learning and teaching (aligning with her initial undergraduate Master of Arts degree in Geography). Julie has had particular teaching focus here too, in the field of Primary Mathematics and Numeracy. Julie also teaches on the MEd Master's in Educational Studies programme and is a lead supervisor for Master's level dissertations, with a specialist focus on Primary Mathematics and Inclusive Education. She is a school experience tutor, working with school partners and university colleagues within a community of practice to support, mentor and assess students whilst on school placement for their teaching qualification.

Tracey Stewart is an Associate Tutor at the University of Glasgow, School of Education. She teaches within both the Childhood Practice MEd/MSc and the Inclusive Education MEd/MSc programmes, is a Lead Reviewer on the Ethics Committee and is a Dissertation Supervisor on the Educational Studies MEd/MSc programme. She has previously worked with children and families for over 10 years as a manager within the Scottish Voluntary Early Learning and Childcare sector and mentored many staff. This role also involved coordinating with local authorities and advocating the voluntary sector agenda. Having earlier worked for several years in Human Resources in the Middle East, she is a keen advocate of diversity, and her research interests include both gender equity and intersectionality within early years education.

Dr Kelly Stone taught English language, literature and literacies in primary and secondary schools in Scotland and Canada before becoming a lecturer in primary education (early literacies) at the Moray House School of Education and Sport, University of Edinburgh where, until 2020, she taught across undergraduate and postgraduate programmes in Initial Teacher Education. Her research was primarily concerned with issues of equity and social justice, and specifically with critical literacies and the use of children's literature as a platform for social justice and sustainability. She was involved in a number of research studies which focused on educational, health and social inequalities.

Martin Winters is a lecturer at Glasgow Clyde College, specialising in Childhood Practice, Early Education and Childcare qualifications. Part of this role involves working with students participating in the Enhanced Vocational Inclusion programme run by Glasgow City Council. This programme provides alternative access to education for secondary pupils experiencing a range of circumstances creating possible barriers to learning. Martin also contributes to the ongoing work of the College in developing flexible approaches to learning and teaching which are responsive to the changing needs and circumstances of learners at different levels of education. Martin recently achieved his Master's in Education (MEd) at the University of Glasgow, focusing his research on the use of mobile technology in Childhood Practice settings. Prior to this, Martin was a Child Development Officer, supporting children and families in Glasgow.

Acknowledgements

We would like to thank our editors at SAGE, particularly Delayna Spencer, who was involved in the production of this book from the very start. Throughout the period of writing, Delayna was a constant source of intellectual and emotional support, providing invaluable guidance to help shape the UK-wide focus of the book. We also thank the production team, particularly Nicola Marshall and Jane Fricker, for their help and support in pulling the final manuscript together.

We are very grateful to our colleagues in the School of Education at the University of Glasgow who contributed to the book despite the competing demands they face in their personal and professional lives.

A highlight in writing the book was the contribution made by a number of our postgraduate students. Through their networks of professional connections, we were provided with an invaluable source of observation and dialogue, giving rise to numerous interesting questions that have challenged our thinking and helped to refine our ideas.

Finally, we would like to acknowledge the contribution of our families in providing us with the time and space to make this book possible. We are deeply grateful for their forbearance; in them we take great pride.

Acknowledgements

Part I
Policy and legislative context of non-compulsory care and education (NCE) in the UK

Part I

1
Legislative and policy frameworks: practice and implementation

Craig Orr and Mary Wingrave

Key ideas

This chapter will explore:

- The non-compulsory care and education (NCE) landscape.
- Changes to policy and legislation which have contributed to changes in the NCE sector.
- Elements of consistency and confusion within the NCE sector.
- The need to support staff as part of the change process.

Introduction

In this chapter, we will introduce the term Childhood Practice and outline the landscape of the services and provision it covers. Childhood Practice is a uniquely Scottish title and is one that specifically relates to those who work in the non-compulsory care and education (NCE) sectors. While this chapter will predominantly focus on the Scottish context, other chapters in the book will present a broader UK perspective of policy and legislation from across the UK.

In Scotland, NCE provision ranges from playgroups and crèches, through to nurseries and out-of-school care settings. Providers come from the private, local authority and third sectors, with each offering both part- and full-time NCE. Given the range of different providers and services, leaders and mangers are required to consider and take account of a range of national legislation, policies and guidelines. As the policy landscape continues to develop, it is important that leaders and managers within NCE take due account of their legal obligations. Yet, not all of these legislative measures apply to all settings, leading to some confusion as to what should be prioritised and considered. This chapter will explore some of the legislative and policy frameworks in Scotland, and will make some reference to those implemented across the UK, focusing on those that are applicable across NCE settings. In addition, consideration will be given to some of the difficulties staff and managers face when required to implement, revise and update practice due to the ongoing professionalisation and expansion of the NCE sector.

Childhood Practice and the non-compulsory education sector

Childhood Practice (CP) is a uniquely Scottish umbrella term that covers all forms of NCE which provide services for children and young people that are, unlike school settings, not mandatory. This term was introduced in Scotland at the turn of the millennium and is distinctive as it incorporates both early years and out-of-school care (OSC). Therefore, in this chapter, we use Scotland as an example of how NCE can be developed, as currently no other country in the UK has initiated a policy strategy for both early years and OSC, in terms of staff development and provision for children.

CP seeks to blend the dual importance of both care and education in the development and learning of children and young people. However, at times fragmentation exists as services are provided by a range of groups including local authority (LA) and private, voluntary and partnership providers (Wingrave, 2015). Whilst the sector covers many types of settings, the two biggest contributors to NCE in Scotland are the ones that will be discussed in this chapter, namely Early Years and OSC services.

Early years

Across the UK, all governments have introduced initiatives to provide funded childcare in the early years sector. In England, 30 hours over a minimum of 38 weeks is provided (UK Government, 2015) whilst the childcare offer in Wales, from autumn 2017, provides 30 hours' free provision to eligible working parents of three- and four-year-olds for up to 48 weeks a year (Welsh Government, 2016). In Northern Ireland, parents of all three- and four-year-olds are still entitled to receive 2.5 hours per day, 5 days per week, for 38 weeks over the academic school year, September to June. However, the Northern Ireland Government has introduced the Children and Young People's Strategy 2020–2030 for Northern Ireland (Northern Ireland Executive, 2020a), where there is a commitment to focus and provide early intervention in the early years. In Scotland, in 2017, the Scottish Government (SG) committed to the further expansion of Early Learning and Childcare (ELC) to fund provision of 1,140 hours per year for all three- and four-year-olds and eligible two-year-olds (SG, 2017a). This is equivalent to 30 hours per week, bringing possible contact hours to the equivalent hours of those in the primary school sector.

The move towards providing expansive childcare in the early years is reflective of advice from the Organisation for Economic Co-operation and Development (OECD), in the first of its Starting Strong documents in 2006, recommending that governments support and regulate early years programmes (OECD, 2006). Bakken et al. (2017) also advocate that investment in early years childcare will result in pre-school education being of economic benefit both in the short term, in supporting children entering compulsory schooling, and in the long term as an investment which will shape and develop the economy. McKendrick (2021: 4–5) identifies similar drivers for the provision, or wraparound care services, for school-aged childcare, such as tackling child food insecurity, supporting parents to sustain their engagement with the labour market and improving the wellbeing of children and young people, specifically through socialisation and play.

Out-of-school care

In recognition of these societal benefits, the Scottish Government (2021a) announced its plans to develop the expansion of childcare provision to include funded wraparound care before and after school, and during holidays for the lowest income families. The CP sector in Scotland includes more than early years services and encompasses OSC services, which provide childcare for children and young people in the compulsory education sector before and after school, with many providers also offering full-day provision during holiday periods.

The Scottish Government has been promoting the development of OSC services and initiatives such as the Access to Childcare Fund (Children in Scotland, online), leading to the publication of a Draft Framework for OSC in Scotland (SG, 2019), alongside a public consultation. From this, the Scottish Government has supported several pilot projects, exploring innovative models of school-aged childcare, including rural island provision, childminding provision and organised activities (SG, 2021a). Given the focus on such projects, it is clear that wraparound childcare provision for school-aged children in Scotland is high on the political agenda.

———— THINKING POINT 1.1 ————

What would you consider to be the benefits of Childhood Practice services to:

- children?
- families?
- society?

Policy and legislative developments in the non-compulsory education sector in Scotland

Since the turn of the millennium, many changes have taken place in the NCE sector in Scotland; many of these are as a result of international recommendations and increasing interest in the NCE sector. The Scottish Government is committed to improving NCE services with a plethora of policies and changes to legislation. The introduction of the Scottish Social Services Council (SSSC) in 2001 was set up in response to the Regulation of Care (Scotland) Act (Scottish Parliament, 2001), with responsibility for registering those who work in social services and for regulating education and training. Part of this strategy was to recognise the professional status of early years leaders (Scottish Executive [SE], 2004) and according to the SSSC, '[f]or the first time, social service workers would have to meet a set of national codes of practice that would bring professionalism and consistency as well as setting out for the people of Scotland the standards they could expect from the people working with and caring for them' (SSSC, 2015: 5). The Register of Social Service Workers in Scotland opened on 1 April 2003 and introduced three levels of registration for workers in day care (SSSC, 2003). The requirement for NCE staff registration and the increase in meeting new regulations have been supported by the introduction of the Codes of Practice for Social Service Workers and Employers (SSSC, 2016a) and the Standard for Childhood Practice (SSSC, 2016b; Quality Assurance Agency for Higher Education [QAA] Scotland, 2007).

First published in 2003, then revised in 2016, the Scottish Social Services Council (SSSC) Codes of Practice for Social Service Workers and Employers (SSSC, 2016a) provides a tool for staff in all social care services in Scotland to reflect on and continually improve their practice. They also provide guidance for those who use social services, clearly describing the standards that can be expected from the workers who support them (SSSC, 2016a). Similarly, clarity and support for service users have been further developed in recent years with the establishment of the Health and Social Care Standards (SG, 2017b). Replacing the variety of National Care Standards (SE, 2002), the Health and Social Care Standards (SG, 2017b) were introduced to provide better outcomes for everyone using health, social care or social work services in Scotland. Within these standards, human rights underpin the five main principles of dignity and respect, compassion, inclusion, responsive care, and support and wellbeing (SG, 2017b). Both the Codes of Practice (SSSC, 2016a) and the Health and Social Care Standards (SG, 2017b) apply to all care services in Scotland, including care home services, adult support services and the day care of children services. However, for those within the NCE sectors, including early years and OSC, an additional set of professional standards was introduced.

The Standard for Childhood Practice

The SSSC registers all staff in NCE services and employers are legally required to check that their staff are registered within six months of employment. There are three levels of registration: Support Worker, Practitioner and Leader/Manager. Those who lead and manage a service are required to meet the Standard for Childhood Practice (SSSC, 2016b), which has established a professional status for those who lead and manage NCE settings, but who are not qualified teachers. In Scotland, the journey to upskilling the workforce has been to ensure that 'managers have the same regulatory requirements and there are no differences in the status of their awards. It ensures better outcomes for children' (SSSC, online). Effectively, all managers of NCE settings in Scotland must achieve, or be working towards, a degree-level qualification in Childhood Practice, regardless of whether they manage an early years setting or OSC service.

Starting Strong IV (OECD, 2015: 84) notes that 'staff qualifications, obtained through initial education or professional development, contribute to enhancing pedagogical quality', which is ultimately associated closely with better child outcomes. Walker et al. (2011) noted that NCE can have a positive impact on children's learning, with significant long-term benefits. Sheridan et al. (2009) further commented that key to this is the quality of childcare from highly qualified staff who can create a positive pedagogic environment which constructs positive learning experiences resulting in long-term benefits for children. The requirement for leaders and managers to gain the Childhood Practice Award at a minimum of a graduate-level qualification has helped to realise this ambition. However, whilst these changes go a long way to upskilling the workforce, the Nutbrown Review in 2012 cautioned that there was a lack of parity with those in the compulsory education sector (Nutbrown, 2012: 8). One of the biggest differences between the sectors, according to Barron (2016), is a lack of equality in terms of pay and conditions, and opportunities for promotion for NCE staff. This issue is not limited to the Scottish context and will be discussed further in Chapter 16.

Traditionally, NCE had been viewed as a separate, and often a less skilled sector, from compulsory education; this was in part due to its non-compulsory nature (OECD, 2000), the differences in staff qualifications and the plethora of job titles used. The introduction of the Early Years Framework I and II (SG, 2008a) contributed to changes in the provision of NCE and the position of its workforce by focusing on the qualifications, responsibilities and professional status of early years practitioners. Arguably, the Early Years Framework (SG, 2008a) helped to relocate the NCE sector, placing it within the mainstream education agenda. Along with these changes, the Scottish Government introduced a continuous framework with the Curriculum for Excellence (SG, 2008b), which for the first time addressed the educational needs of children from age 3 to 18. The combination of the Early Years Framework (SG, 2008a), the Standard for Childhood Practice (SSSC, 2016b; QAA Scotland, 2007) and the introduction of the Curriculum for Excellence (SG, 2008b) all contributed to a repositioning of NCE as complementary and essential in the care and education of young children.

THINKING POINT 1.2

1. Why was it beneficial to regulate and expand the early years sector?
2. What were the benefits to: children, parents, society?
3. Why do you think the NCE sector has grown as a result?

Whilst the ongoing developments of the legislative and policy arenas within NCE can often appear daunting, it is important to recognise that these changes do not happen in isolation but instead are reflective of, and related to, larger social policy considerations and developments. Some of these related areas will be explored and discussed in greater detail within this book. For example, the next chapter, 'Safeguarding and protecting children: from policy to practice', will explore the role of the NCE sector in relation to safeguarding and child protection, including consideration of national guidance and the legal responsibilities of those working with children, young people and families. Chapter 3 will go on to examine the importance of diversity and inclusion within NCE, as McCulloch and Stewart examine the ways in which legislation, such as the Equality Act 2010 (UK Parliament, 2010), can support and develop practice. Following this, Chapter 4 will explore children's rights, with due regard to the United Nations Convention on the Rights of the Child (UNCRC) (UN, 1989), and the ways in which NCE leaders and managers can ensure a rights-based approach to service development. In Chapter 16, a broader UK-wide examination of NCE will be presented, with a focus on the professionalisation of those who work in this sector. This examination will discuss the ambition of all four countries in the UK to provide funded early years childcare provision, and outline the emerging development of OSC. This commitment made by each nation has resulted in various comprehensive, progressive documents being developed to guide practice.

Confusion and misalignment

As outlined above, Scotland has made progressive changes to the delivery of early years education and care and has committed to providing wraparound care for the lowest income families. Arguably there is a recognisable lag in the production of guidance documents specifically for the OSC sectors, and there are several documents targeted at both the early years and school-aged childcare sectors (ES, 2020; SG, 2017b). Developments such as the Draft Framework for OSC in Scotland (SG, 2019), and the associated consultation, demonstrate a commitment to provide professional guidance specifically for staff working with older age groups of children, although this is still in the formative stages. Along with a continuing professionalisation of the workforce, the plethora of documentation targeted at the NCE sectors can present a challenge for many practitioners, leaders and managers. Wingrave and McMahon (2016) suggest that despite the drive towards professionalisation, the NCE sectors are still largely perceived as low-status occupations in comparison to the compulsory education sector. Roles that are all too often viewed as nothing more than 'playing with kids' often involve additional responsibilities, due to the 'pervasive bureaucratization' of the NCE sectors (Mooney and McCafferty, 2005: 229).

Supporting a changing landscape in NCE

The NCE sector is not alone in attempting to navigate the current landscape of legislative and policy implementation and change. In examining the array of curricular guidance documents in Scotland, Humes and Priestley (2021: 182) noted that the 'confusing welter of documentation' led to greater uncertainty and varied interpretations as to how these were to be enacted across the compulsory education sector. However, unlike the formal education sector, staff within NCE are faced with low expectations in relation to policy implementation, reflective of the pervading perceptions of a low-pay, low-status occupation (Wingrave and McMahon, 2016). Given such perceptions, staff within NCE often struggle to adapt to the seemingly overwhelming raft of legislation, policies and documentation from government. For leaders and managers within such settings, this can present challenges in implementing strategic changes. One of the primary challenges for leaders and managers within NCE, when new legislation, policies or documents are introduced from government, is in supporting staff with the transition. This includes ensuring all staff are aware of, understand and are on board with the implementation of the new policy and the development of their practice.

Much has been written about the ways in which leaders and managers can support their staff through the process of change, including developing an awareness of common responses to change initiatives (Fullan, 2004; MacBeath, 2003; Kotter, 1995). Alongside this, frameworks have been developed to support the implementation of legislation, policy and guidance, such as the traditional SWOT analysis (Strength, Weaknesses, Opportunities, Threats). Considered an important tool for strategic planning, the SWOT analysis technique helps identify internal and external factors when seeking to adopt new strategies. The aim of such analysis is to identify the internal strengths and external opportunities that can support strategic change, along with the internal weaknesses and external threats that need to be mitigated. Although acknowledging that the SWOT analysis technique is generally popular, Ghazinoory et al. (2007) claim that there are certain issues with such analysis. Of these, the authors specifically argue that the technique does not account for uncertain factors, fails to prioritise factors, and often produces too many strategies. Within the NCE sector specifically, these issues are further complicated as staff may lack the necessary knowledge, skills, or confidence in policy implementation. Therefore, it is important for leaders and managers within such services to consider how best to bring staff on board with such developments, and how best to support them through the period of transition.

Practitioners: policy and legislation

Practitioners in NCE are familiar with policy documents and in the last 20 years there has been a constant creation, implementation and updating of policy documents aimed at the sector. These policies have the express aim of improving outcomes for children and their families and seek to improve practice. However, there is often confusion about the difference between policy and legislation (Norwich, 2014). Both policy and legislation provide direction and legal requirements in relation to practice, to practitioners, in how to support children and young people. They also regulate and seek to provide consistent approaches and practices to those who work in and benefit from the service.

In principle, laws see each person as equal, and no-one's social standing should put them in a better position than another (Nussbaum, 1993). Legislation is the law and is a legal commitment that is enforceable. Legislation emerges from the parliamentary process and has been voted on by government, which should reflect the promises made to the country's population at the time of their election. Policy, by contrast, is the documentation which arises from legislation and is the enactment and interpretation of what the legislation aims to achieve. A policy will seek to outline the values and the mechanisms that will effectively implement the legislation, and to help an organisation achieve its long-term goal (Cerna, 2013).

When policy which relates to the NCE sector is implemented successfully, it allows procedures to be put in place to achieve best practice and positive outcomes for children and families (Cerna, 2013). A top-down application is where management is required to implement policies which have been created by others. DeLeon and DeLeon (2002: 484) point out that this can result in those implementing the policies at a practice level not understanding all the elements of the policies, and they may implement their own logical inclinations based on their experience. Thus, a top-down approach results in tactical rather than strategic implementation. It is therefore advised that when policy is implemented, it is necessary to apply a bottom-up approach with staff. DeLeon and DeLeon (2002: 478) argue that a bottom-up approach seeks to enable those implementing the policy to be active in determining practices and in interpreting how it can be implemented in their own setting; they argue that this approach is 'more realistic and practical'. The more opportunities and support staff are given to be involved in the implementation of policy, the more committed they will be to the change. This in turn will develop a sense of collegiality which will provide opportunities for successful change implementation within a setting. However, Hargreaves (2005) notes that little work has been undertaken to consider how staff respond emotionally to the change process. Changes in practice to accommodate new policies can challenge personal principles and practices, resulting in negative emotions, as they can result in uncertainty and the questioning of professional identity. It can be argued that the examination and recognition of emotions can raise an awareness of staff's interpretation to change (Karami-Akkary et al., 2019). According to Oreg et al. (2011), staff's emotional responses can determine how change is achieved and the associated value and sustainability of new practices.

Drivers, Opportunities, Emotions and Strategies (DOES) analysis

We now present a tool that we believe can be used with staff in the change process. The DOES (Drivers, Opportunities, Emotions and Strategies; see Figure 1.1) combines the areas for examination in traditional change models, which include obstacles as well as opportunities and drivers, with the recognition that emotional responses need to be considered. The DOES analysis can be used as a starting point in the change process. The aim is to allow staff an opportunity to discuss and recognise not only practical changes but also their emotional response to these changes. The staff are encouraged to express both positive and negative emotions as, according to Ford et al. (2008), challenge or resistance to the change process is a persistent and recurring theme when implementing change. Often, they claim, resistance is blamed on staff's unwillingness to embrace progress or change. Daus et al. (2012) believe that the emotions provoked by change can severely impact the ultimate realisation of the project. Thus, as DeLeon and DeLeon (2002) suggest, staff should be given an opportunity to air their reactions and feelings, allowing both staff and management an opportunity to work together to mitigate these. Further, this provides all staff an opportunity to be involved, to evaluate and discuss obstacles which may be encountered, and which in the long term could derail the implementation of the change. Salvato and Vassolo (2018: 1739) advise that staff should be encouraged to share their responses in order 'to achieve ambitious, long-term goals within highly dynamic environments and contested decision-making processes'. Oreg et al. (2011) claim that change will not be sustained if staff's emotions are not respected. The more opportunities staff are given to share their voice and responses to the implementation of policy, ultimately the more committed they will be to the change. Talat (2017) argues that the success or failure of a change project can rest on the emotional responses of a team and that it is in fact a key resource in the change process. Dasborough et al's. (2015) work on change management found that if staff were given an opportunity to discuss both their positive and negative emotions to change, the responses became less concentrated over time, thus allowing the change process to be embraced.

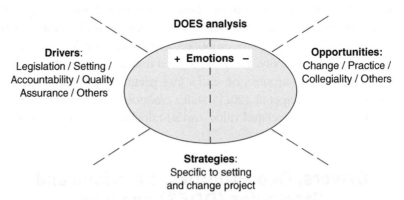

Figure 1.1   Drivers, Opportunities, Emotions and Strategies (DOES) analysis

Here we present a 'View from Practice' which highlights the change and how the DOES analysis can support a setting's examination and consideration of the effects of the change. Emotions, both positive and negative to the change process, are recognised along with the drivers for change, the obstacles that can prevent the change taking place and some of the possible strategies that can be adopted to support the required change.

—————— VIEW FROM PRACTICE ——————

Staff concerns related to expansion in hours

In 2017 an expansion of Early Provision was announced by the Scottish Government. As part of this expansion, there was a doubling of the hours children and families were entitled to, from 600 to 1,140 hours per year, from August 2020. This has implications for the staff and their ability to ensure that there is enough staff cover and space for the increase in enrolment. The manager has brought the staff together to discuss their concerns.

By allowing staff to express their responses, it is possible for policy change to be implemented collegiately as well as allowing the management team to be aware of concerns which could derail the policy implementation. By recognising and discussing the drivers of the change, staff can understand and discuss the impetus behind the change. While they may still not agree with the change, they are provided with information that can otherwise often get lost in the implementation process. Throughout the process, emotional responses are recognised as both positive and negative, thus accepting and respecting the initial resistance. By discussing the obstacles, it is possible to achieve a balance by examining the strategies that can mitigate these concerns. By providing space for concerns to be voiced and roles and responsibilities to be assigned, successful implementation can be supported. It should be noted that the use of the DOES analysis is not *a one off* but should be used and revisited throughout the change process. This allows staff to revisit their concerns, re-examine and update the status of the initiative.

—————— THINKING POINT 1.3 ——————

Carry out a DOES analysis examining the likely staff concerns related to the expansion in hours from 600 to 1,140 hours per year.

Summary

In this chapter, we have explored some of the legislative and policy frameworks, across NCE settings, with a particular focus on Scotland, and the changes that have taken place which have arguably altered the NCE landscape. There has been an acknowledgement of the range of different providers and services that are required to implement policies in childcare settings. We have suggested that key to the success of the dissemination and implementation of these changes is the support and recognition of staff, who must implement and change or adapt practice as a direct consequence. We recommend that in order to support changes to policies and legislation, all staff need to be involved in the process so that new policies and legislation can be successfully implemented. The DOES analysis has been proposed as a tool which can support this endeavour. As the policy landscape continues to develop, it is important that leaders and managers within NCE take due account of their legal obligations and the need to encourage staff to embrace new initiatives.

END-OF-CHAPTER QUESTIONS

1. What do you consider to be the biggest changes to legislation and policy since entering practice?
2. How have you responded to the shifting policy landscape? What have been the challenges and benefits?
3. How would you use the DOES analysis to support staff in your setting?

2
Safeguarding and protecting children: from policy to practice
Ruth Myles and Jana Chandler

Key ideas

This chapter will explore:

- Definitions of safeguarding and child protection.
- Different types of child abuse.
- Key issues related to safeguarding and child protection.
- The current landscape for child protection and the impact of COVID-19.
- Safeguarding and child protection in practice, considering national policy, legislations, frameworks and practice guidance.
- Communication, partnership and multi-agency working.

Introduction

This chapter sets out to explore the issues related to safeguarding and child protection. Firstly, the terms safeguarding and child protection are briefly considered. Next, the meaning of abuse and an overview of the types of child abuse are provided. Following this, some of the current legislation and policies related to safeguarding are outlined. Three case reviews that led to changes within legislation, policy and guidance related to safeguarding are also considered, drawing on a UK-wide perspective. The current climate of child protection is also discussed, taking into consideration the recent global pandemic and the impact this had on child abuse issues worldwide. An indication of how the principles of safeguarding and child protection underpin practice documents and frameworks that inform everyday practice is presented, whilst also highlighting the importance of partnership, multi-agency working, and communication with families and children. Throughout this chapter, a series of thinking points are presented to engage the reader in reflective thinking on their practice. For consistency, the term child/children is defined as anyone under the age of 18.

Defining safeguarding and child protection

Safeguarding in its simplest form sets out the processes adopted to aid the protection of children. It refers to actions taken to support the wellbeing of children and relates to wider activities encompassing child protection (National Society for the Prevention of Cruelty to Children [NSPCC], 2022a). Within statutory guidance (Department for Education [DfE], 2018a; Education Scotland [ES], 2018a; NSPCC, online-a), safeguarding has been defined as:

- protecting children from maltreatment;
- preventing impairment of their health or development;
- ensuring that they are growing up in circumstances consistent with the provision of safe and effective care; and
- taking action to enable all children to have the best outcomes.

Child protection is part of the safeguarding process, otherwise known as the act of protecting a child from abuse (ES, 2018a). It can be explained as activities carried out to protect children who are perceived to be at risk, vulnerable or suffering from significant harm resulting from abuse (Scottish Government [SG], 2021b).

Definition and types of abuse

Children often do not disclose abuse; therefore, it is imperative practitioners are aware of the 'warning signs' and know what to look out for (DfE, 2021a; SG, 2021b). According to Allnock and Miller (2013), children do not report abuse for a number of reasons:

- fear that no one will believe them;
- concerns that the abuse will worsen if the abuser finds out, threats from abuser(s);
- guilt, shame and embarrassment;
- for the child the abuse may have been normalised;
- there may be no-one in their life for them to tell;
- a sense of loyalty to their abusers (Blizard and Bluhm, 1994);
- hope that it will stop; and
- worry about the consequences – what will happen to them if they tell.

Having an understanding of these factors can prepare practitioners to identify and be aware of the potential risk factors for children. When safeguarding and child protection are considered, many will think about what behaviours would warrant concerns, specifically thinking about child abuse and the form that child abuse can take. Therefore, having clear knowledge and understanding of child abuse is necessary. There are many definitions that can constitute abuse. The National Guidance for Child Protection in Scotland (SG, 2021b: 12) states that:

> Abuse and neglect are forms of maltreatment. Abuse or neglect may involve inflicting harm or failing to act to prevent harm. Children may be maltreated at home; within a family or peer network; in care placements; institutions or community settings; and in the online and digital environment.

Whilst the NSPCC (2022b) defines child abuse as:

> Child abuse is when a child is intentionally harmed by an adult or another child – it can be over a period of time but can also be a one-off action. It can be physical, sexual or emotional and it can happen in person or online. It can also be a lack of love, care and attention – this is neglect.

Despite the differing definitions, they both focus on protecting children from harm. There are no specific circumstances that can lead to abuse, nor is there a specific set of individuals who can be the cause of abuse. Children can be subject to abuse within their home by family, friends, in their community or education/care setting (SG, 2021b; Lindon and Webb, 2020; DfE, 2018a; Powell, 2011).

Abuse can take many forms, some of which are detailed below:

- Emotional abuse – ongoing emotional maltreatment of a child, which can have a severe and persistent negative effect on the child's emotional health and development.
- Physical abuse – physically hurting a child and causing them harm, such as broken bones, bruises, cuts and burns.
- Neglect – ongoing failure to meet a child's basic needs, such as being left hungry, thirsty, dirty or without proper clothing, shelter or health care.
- Child sexual abuse – forcing or persuading a child to take part in sexual activities, involving both physical contact or non-contact activities which can happen both online and offline.
- Grooming – when someone builds a relationship, trust and emotional connection with a child online, via text, social media or email for the purpose of manipulating, exploiting and abusing them.
- Non-recent/historic abuse – when an adult was abused as a child.
- Bullying/cyber-bulling – behaviours that hurt someone, such as name calling, hitting, pushing, spreading rumours, threatening or undermining someone.
- Witnessing domestic abuse – witnessing controlling, coercive, threatening, violent or abusive behaviours, usually in the home.

(NSPCC, 2022c)

The United Nations Convention on the Rights of the Child (UNCRC) (UNICEF, online-a) states that 'without discrimination, children have the right to be protected from all forms of abuse, neglect and exploitation'. Enforcing authorities must take the measures to promote and protect children's rights. The introduction of the Children Act 1989 (UK Parliament [UKP], 1989), which was implemented in 1991, can be viewed as 'the most comprehensive and far-reaching reform of childcare law which has come before Parliament in living memory' (Lord Chancellor, 1988, cited in Harding, 1991: 180). It shone a light on social care legislation in relation to child protection and safeguarding and brought forth multiple changes to law, with the intention of bringing private and public law together to create clear guidance (Bridgeman, 2017). Some of the legislation and policies that followed on safeguarding and child protection in the UK are outlined in Table 2.1. Importantly, safeguarding is a key priority, as evidenced through the UNCRC (UNICEF, online-a). The UNCRC was ratified by the UK in 1991, with all devolved countries taking steps to show a commitment to the protection of children's rights. Within Scotland, there is a desire to incorporate these rights through the UNCRC (Incorporation) (Scotland) Bill into Scotland's law (Humanist UK, 2021; UNICEF, 2021a), meaning that children's rights would be legally protected within Scotland. In Wales, the government formally adopted the UNCRC as the basis for policy making and has enshrined it in law under the Rights of Children and Young

Persons (Wales) Measure 2011 (Welsh Government, 2022a). In England, children's rights are protected through the Human Rights Act 1998, although the UNCRC contains additional rights that are not otherwise protected by this Act (Children's Rights Alliance for England, 2022). Similarly, the UNCRC underpins several policies and legislations in Northern Ireland, including the Children's Services Co-operation Act (NI) 2015 (UKP, 2015) and the Children and Young People's Strategy 2020–2030 (Northern Ireland Executive, 2020a).

Table 2.1 Legislation and policies related to safeguarding and child protection in the UK

Key policy and legislation	Scotland	Northern Ireland	Wales	England
The Children (Northern Ireland) Order 1995 (UKP, 1995a)		X		
The Education Act 2002 (UKP, 2002)			X	X
Children Act 2004 (UKP, 2004)	X	X	X	X
Safeguarding Board Act (Northern Ireland) 2011 (UKP, 2011)		X		
Children and Families Act 2014 (UKP, 2014)			X	X
Children and Young People (Scotland) Act 2014 (Scottish Parliament (SP), 2014)	X			
Working Together to Safeguard Children 2018 (Department for Education, 2018a)				X
Keeping Children Safe in Education 2021 (Department for Education, 2021a)			X	X
Getting it Right for Every Child (GIRFEC) (SG, 2012a)	X			
National Guidance for child protection in Scotland 2021 (Scottish Government, 2021b)	X			

——————— **THINKING POINT 2.1** ———————

1. What is your experience of supporting the protection of individuals?
2. What are some of the policies and legislation relevant to your working context?

Key issues relating to safeguarding and child protection

In this section, some of the major child protection incidents and their impact on legislation and policy in the twenty-first century are considered. In recent years, there has been an increased emphasis on safeguarding and child protection, specifically in relation to early intervention and prevention. Powell (2011) indicates that whilst child abuse can be prevented if vulnerable children are identified, and early intervention is available, abuse can often remain hidden. Many past failures show that there appear to be common themes when failing to protect children from harm.

Examples of past failures

The UK has seen several widely published child protection failures. In 2000, Victoria Climbié's life and death at 8 years old was widely reported: moving from her home in the Ivory Coast to France before coming to the UK, which her parents believed would provide Victoria with a better education, only to be killed by her great aunt and partner. Victoria's death sparked concerns across the UK and led to Lord Laming's report (Laming, 2003). The inquiry into this failure to protect Victoria highlighted many assumptions and failures made in the care provided for Victoria. Some of these included: the failure of social workers to follow up visits after admissions to hospital; an apparent lack of awareness of child protection procedures, with the director of the social services dismissing concerns raised; and medical practitioners assuming that marks on Victoria's body could be caused by her black heritage, suggesting that a child growing up in Africa may be expected to have more marks on their bodies. Lord Laming's report (Laming, 2003) made over 100 recommendations for change to child protection processes to avoid repeating the same mistakes that led to Victoria's tragic death. Some of the key recommendations included:

- Authorities to have a committee for children and families with members from police, council and health services.
- A national agency for children and families to be established.
- Social services directors to ensure staff have adequate training.
- Senior managers should periodically inspect case files and social workers should check information from all child protection agencies before doing home visits.
- All allegations must be followed up and specialist services must be available 24 hours a day.
- Health professionals who suspect a child is being harmed should consider taking an account from the child directly, regardless of consent from a parent/guardian (Batty, 2009; BBC News, 2003a).

The report (Laming, 2003) called for a reform to services, specifically in relation to better information sharing and multi-agency working. This led to the Westminster government implementing the Children Act 2004 (UKP, 2004) to improve the child protection system in England and Wales. In Northern Ireland, the Safeguarding Board Act (Northern Ireland)

2011 (UKP, 2011) was introduced, outlining a duty to cooperate to safeguard children at risk. In Scotland, this led to a child protection review, resulting in the establishment of the Commissioner for Children and Young People, the development of a Children's Charter and later the Framework for Standards, the principles of which underpin the Children and Young People (Scotland) Act 2014 (SP, 2014; Kendrick, 2004).

Similarly, in 2001 Caleb Ness died at 11 weeks old at the hands of his father. Caleb spent the first few weeks of his life in hospital due to addiction to drugs from his mother. The father had previous convictions for drug addition, drug dealing and violence whilst also being on the child protection register. A 260-page report into the death of Caleb was commissioned and completed by Edinburgh City Council. The inquiry identified faults at almost every level in every agency involved in Caleb's care (BBC News, 2003b), including social work, police, housing and health care. One of the key findings was a lack of awareness of individual roles and responsibilities, and information not being passed on, resulting in vital information not being shared (SP, 2003). In response to this inquiry report, Edinburgh Lothian Borders Executive group issued 35 new child protection guidelines, including calling for a review of the accuracy of record keeping for at-risk children, and for more adequate child protection training. This report also called for the need for inter-agency assessments to be completed across the board to better identify gaps in communication (SP, 2003).

Despite the very public cases noted above and the recommendations from the reviews, a few years later, Holly Wells and Jessica Chapman, both aged 10, were killed by Iain Huntley, their school caretaker (BBC News, 2003c). In response to this failure, the Home Secretary called for an independent inquiry. The Bichard Inquiry (Bichard, 2004) found a number of flaws in the system, including a failure to carry out vetting procedures by police forces; a failure to communicate and share information between police and social work; and no adoption of a multidisciplinary or multi-professional approach. By not sharing information and agencies failing to work collaboratively, the information was missed, leading to mistakes which resulted in the deaths of Holly and Jessica. This inquiry resulted in recommendations for police, social work and education. One of the key recommendations was in relation to the vetting and registration of staff working with children and vulnerable adults. In Scotland, individuals working with children and vulnerable adults are required to register with the Scottish Social Services Council (SSSC, 2022a) and must be part of the Protecting Vulnerable Groups Scheme (PVG) (Disclosure Services, online). For employees in England and Wales, this process is similar, where vetting and registration with the Disclosure and Barring Service (DBS) (UK Government [UKG], online) is required. Similarly, in Northern Ireland, an Access Northern Ireland disclosure (NI Direct Government Services, online) is required for anyone working with children or vulnerable adults in paid or volunteer work.

These three cases of failure in child protection practice happened within a short time frame and led to inquiries resulting in several recommendations, some of which have been discussed. These examples are only a small number of the failures in child protection that are utilised in childcare, education or protection courses at all levels of study and practice today.

THINKING POINT 2.2

What learning points can you take away to inform your safeguarding and child protection practice?

Current landscape: child protection and the impact of COVID-19

In the UK, children who are either considered to be suffering from or at risk of abuse, neglect or significant harm can be identified and then placed on either the Child Protection Plan (England) or Child Protection Register (in Northern Ireland, Scotland and Wales, as appropriate). Information from these sources can then be utilised to create overall statistics. For example, in the UK a total of 58,772 children were identified as being on the child protection registers detailed above (NSPCC, 2022d). The number of children who are or have experienced abuse if not reported is indeterminable. As already indicated, abuse is often hidden (Powell, 2011), and may go unnoticed by adults who do not recognise the signs of abuse. Research obtained via UNICEF (2020a) indicates that approximately 1 billion or one in two children worldwide will be exposed to abuse. In 2013, the NSPCC started an annual report that gathers and analyses data from sources across the UK to evidence the child protection landscape of that time. The latest report was completed in 2020 and specifically considers the abuse of adolescents and includes rising data on the impact that the COVID-19 pandemic has had on children's safety in the UK (NSPCC, 2020a). Key findings from this report highlighted that the police recorded higher levels of physical, sexual and online abuse against adolescents than younger children; the number of adolescents in care is higher than for younger children; however, numbers of adolescents subject to a child protection plan or on a child protection register are lower than younger children. Furthermore, the report indicated that risks associated with abuse have intensified through the COVID-19 pandemic. Romanou and Belton (2020) explore the risk of abuse and neglect to children in isolation and lockdowns imposed due to the COVID-19 pandemic. For some families, lockdown, working from home and home schooling brought a chance to reconnect and bring a level of closeness to their family;

however, for others, these circumstances added to stress levels, creating a negative impact on the family dynamics (Teo and Griffiths, 2020).

In terms of children's wellbeing, the global COVID-19 pandemic has had a devastating effect that is ongoing and far reaching, with potential long-term impacts (Sserwanja et al., 2020). As a result of children being out of school, family's loss of income and employment, which leads to economic insecurities, rates of child maltreatment have increased. Caron et al. (2020) explored the impact of COVID-19 and national lockdowns on children and found that for the period from March to May 2019, on average roughly 136 supervision orders were reported; however, for the same three-month period in 2020, at the height of the COVID-19 pandemic, there was a drastic decrease in supervision orders, with only 24 reported. They argue that this is a result of the COVID-19 lockdowns that led to school and childcare setting closures, hence child abuse being largely undeterminable. In one week, England reported approximately 1.5 million children being absent from school, predominantly for COVID-19-related reasons (BBC News, 2021). With closures of schools, isolation and lockdowns resulting in children not being seen by educators or childcare practitioners, there is a risk that vulnerable children have been or will be missed (Office for Standards in Education [Ofsted], 2020).

Considering this issue in an international context, research in the US echoes that of Caron et al. (2020), suggesting that a delayed response time in relation to child abuse and a lack of education systems monitoring children lead to abuse not being reported (Thomas et al., 2020). This implies that lockdown(s) and the lack of face-to-face education have led to a decrease in reported abuse; however, evidence suggests that abuse rates have in fact increased (Thomas et al., 2020). Furthermore, Sserwanja et al. (2020) discuss changes in child abuse in Uganda during the COVID-19 pandemic, with their research indicating a rise in violence against children. Prior to COVID-19, the Ugandan child helpline received an average of 100 calls per day; however, when lockdown measures were put in place there was a rise to 1,369 calls per day during April 2020. Furthermore, Save the Children (2021) suggest that the COVID-19 pandemic has turned trafficking online. As a result of this, it is harder to track down gangs pursuing children for sexual exploitation, prostitution, drug smuggling or forced labour. Destination Unknown (2020) suggests that despite the travel ban, child trafficking continues, stating that desperation in families due to the COVID-19 crisis and aggravated economic inequalities are forcing desperate actions.

The research compiled by these organisations and others reflect Seddighi et al.'s. (2021: 176) suggestion that '[e]mergencies and natural disasters escalate the risk to weakened child protection systems and disruption of preventative mechanisms'. By understanding the challenges and risks brought by COVID-19, it is possible to mitigate these and ensure children are kept safe while at home, online particularly, as restrictions start to ease.

—————————————— **THINKING POINT 2.3** ——————————————

1.   Consider any children within your setting who you were concerned about due to lockdown or
     on their return to your service. Why the concern?
2.   What support or provision did you put in place to ensure their engagement?

Safeguarding and child protection in practice

The landscape of safeguarding and child protection is evolving and over recent years
there has been a greater focus on implementing effective legislation, policy and practice
guidance to streamline safeguarding principles. Many laws and legislation apply to child
protection, and different countries have their own policies and practice guidance. For
the purpose of this section, the focus will be on UK policies and guidance. Please refer
to Table 2.1, as these documents are all centred around children's wellbeing and in turn
child protection and safeguarding.

Every Child Matters (UKG, 2003) states five key outcomes for children and young people, supported by the Children Act 2004 (UKP, 2004), including:

- being healthy;
- staying safe;
- enjoying and achieving;
- making a positive contribution; and
- achieving economic wellbeing.

This is also reflected in Scotland's national policy, GIRFEC (SG, 2012a). Created with
children's rights in mind, the policy principles reflect the UNCRC (UNICEF, online-a) and
respect the parental rights under the European Convention on Human Rights (ECHR)
(Council of Europe, 2013). Similarly, in Wales, the national practice and principles framework for all those working with children is 'The Right Way' (Children's Commissioner for
Wales, 2017). This approach has children's rights in mind. More recently, Northern Ireland
have created a 10-year Children and Young People's Strategy. This incorporates local and
national legislation and sets forth recommendations on how to improve the wellbeing of
all children (Northern Ireland Executive, 2020a).

In line with relevant frameworks, statutory guidance and legislation, each local authority will have a local child protection board or equivalent. The role of this board is to
create policies and procedures to be adopted in practice, such as local safeguarding and
child protection policies. Similarly, as set out in legislation previously discussed within

this chapter, there is a responsibility for each organisation and service provider who provide both direct and indirect support to children, to have their own policies and procedures related to safeguarding and child protection. However, policy and guidance cannot solely be responsible for protecting children, with a need for practitioners to work alongside the general public to stand up against abuse and recognise the signs of abuse when faced with them (SG, 2021b).

Many organisations will have what is known as a Safeguarding Officer (SO). This role can also be referred to as Child Protection Lead, Designated Safeguarding Officer, Designated Safeguarding Lead, named person for child protection, or Safeguarding/Child Protection Coordinator. The position of SO will be a nominated practitioner with experience, knowledge and appropriate training in child protection. Depending on the size of the organisation, the role can be managed by one individual, split between staff or, in some cases, the responsibility of a safeguarding team (NSPCC, 2020b).

Some aspects of the SO's role are:

- Taking the lead role in designing and implementing policies and practice guidance.
- Supporting child protection training and the development of staff.
- Ensuring that information about a child around whom there have been concerns is appropriately shared and followed up in a timely manner.
- Offering advice and guidance to colleagues on how best to navigate safeguarding concerns.
- Ensuring maintenance of accurate records.
- Ensuring that the correct processes are followed.
- Ensuring effective communication with all parties involved.

(Lindon and Webb, 2020)

Being aware of who your SO or safeguarding team is and where to locate the policies and procedures for your setting, is vital.

——————————— **VIEW FROM PRACTICE** ———————————

Role of safeguarding officer in responding to concerns raised by nursery staff

John is a quiet, reserved 4-year-old, who lives at home with his parents. He has been attending the setting for six months, having moved from another nursery due to the family relocating. There was little transition information from John's previous nursery. His attendance is poor, with frequent

(Continued)

unexplained absences. There is a lack of communication with the parents, with frequent changes to mobile details without informing the service and limited response to email and written letters. When John does attend, the main contact is his elderly grandmother, who does not live locally. Since joining the nursery, the Speech and Language Therapy (SaLT) team has become involved to provide John with additional support.

Staff have raised concerns in relation to John's engagement and interaction with his peers, as he prefers to spend time on his own and struggles to form relationships. When staff encourage John's participation in group activities, it often leads to distressed behaviours. Similarly, SaLT has observed that John has made limited progress due to his frequent absences and the lack of support from his parents. Following child protection policy, and procedures within the setting, these concerns have been reported to the safeguarding officer (SO) and recorded. The SO has tried to address the concerns with his parents. The SO has also communicated these concerns with other professionals involved in John's life, in the first instance the health visitor who, in Scotland, is the named person for children under the age of 5. Contact has been made with John's SaLT worker, to make her aware that concerns have been raised with the health visitor. Following these processes ensures communication and transparency between other agencies and partners to support John.

Communication, partnership and multi-agency working

There is no one-size-fits-all pattern or process to ensuring the safety and wellbeing of children. However, from case studies discussed previously in this chapter, along with the frameworks, guidance and legislation already highlighted, communication and partnership working are crucial. When supporting children, it is important to build relationships, and the best way to do this is through communication, including that with children, parents/carers, colleagues or health and other professionals.

Article 12 of the UNCRC (UNICEF, online-a) highlights the importance of children's participation in matters that affect them (see Chapter 4). Falch-Eriksen et al. (2019) highlight that often children feel that their voices are not being listened to, suggesting effort needs to be made to ensure the effective implementation of Article 12 in relation to child protection services. It is also widely acknowledged that effective communication between multiple agencies is best practice (Bichard, 2004; Laming, 2003) and this is further evidenced in practice framework documents, such as Every Child Matters (UKG, 2003), GIRFEC (SG, 2012a), The Right Way (Children's Commissioner for Wales, 2017) and Children and Young People's Strategy 2020–2023 (Northern Ireland Executive, 2020a), all of which highlight the importance of multi-professional working, communication and partnership. Similarly, the need for strong communication and engagement between your setting and families is fundamental to meeting the needs of children. By establishing communication, you build relationships and trust with families. Parental engagement is essential to supporting children: through this engagement, practitioners can find solutions, seek support for families, and offer guidance and interventions if required (Platt, 2012).

Summary

This chapter has considered the terms safeguarding and child protection, whilst also considering abuse more closely, and in a wider policy context. A brief overview was presented of some historic incidents in relation to failures in safeguarding and child protection, and their impact on today's policy and legislation developments in the UK. Consideration was also given to the effect of the COVID-19 pandemic on child protection. Along with an overview of the role that legislation and policy play in safeguarding and child protection in practice, the importance of the role of SO was highlighted as well as that of communication and partnership working. Within today's society, safeguarding and child protection are fundamental to everyday life. For practitioners, the act(s) of safeguarding are often unconsciously carried out, therefore it is imperative that practitioners are aware of the principles, frameworks and legislation involved in safeguarding and child protection.

END-OF-CHAPTER QUESTIONS

1. What are the strengths in safeguarding and child protection practice within your setting/local authority?
2. What do you perceive as the greatest challenges in safeguarding and child protection?
3. How do you currently embody safeguarding and child protection in your daily practice?

3
Diversity, equity and inclusion in early years

Margaret McCulloch and Tracey Stewart

Key ideas

This chapter will explore:

- The key concepts of diversity, equity and inclusion.
- The legal and moral drivers towards creating a welcoming and inclusive space for all.
- The range of factors which can be affected by unconscious bias and stereotyping.
- Key issues relating to practice which can support the learning and development of all.

Introduction

It can be argued that early years pedagogy is, by nature, nurturing. Practitioners are aware of the varying social and emotional needs of the young humans in their care who are separated from their primary caregivers for the first time, and of the significance of forging trusting relationships. Children are expected, through interactions with others, to learn the foundational literacy skills of listening and talking, the basic numeracy skills of order and a fair share, and the foundational language of maths. In addition, they learn social skills around sharing resources and attention from both staff and peers. But what is 'socialisation' if not the art of 'inclusion? Children are learning how to be included and therefore how to include others – and they are learning this through the actions, both explicit and implicit, of the adults around them. They are learning what behaviours are encouraged or discouraged, who is allowed to use space and make noise, who is expected to be quiet, who receives positive attention and who receives negative attention. Therefore, through the adults' actions, they are learning who is valued and included and who is not.

Research has identified the inequities that exist in UK educational, personal and social outcomes because of aspects of diversity, for example gender, race, levels of affluence, culture and (dis)ability (Hutchinson et al., 2019; Demie and McLean, 2016; Clifton and Cook, 2012). International legislation and national legislation and policies have highlighted the range of ways in which discrimination and inequalities have existed in the past and must now be addressed. The Organisation for Economic Co-operation and Development (OECD, 2020a: 4) suggests that 'investing in early childhood education and care and ensuring universal access to quality services is not only one of the most effective ways to reduce inequities, it is also one of the most *efficient*'. It is vital that we take account of both policy and existing knowledge as we seek to create inclusive environments for all young children in early years settings; however, just as importantly we must also examine our own values and consider how these impact on our thinking and our practice.

Practitioners must be aware of their own unconscious biases and the way their actions – intentionally or not – may influence the children in their care. In this chapter, we offer thinking points around a range of issues relating to diversity and inclusion to raise awareness of the impact that the environment (physical, social and emotional) can have on children and to help practitioners, specifically focusing on those in the non-compulsory care and education (NCE) sector, engage in the most inclusive practice possible, ensuring that their own assumptions do not hinder the limitless opportunities that should be on offer to all the children in their care.

THINKING POINT 3.1

1. When you first meet a child or parent, are you aware of creating a mental 'first impression' of them? Consider the information you use to form your impression.
2. Think of situations where your first impression may have changed over time. What caused this change?

Defining the key concepts

Diversity – it is important to realise that this is not the same as 'difference'. If we talk about people being 'different' from us, or a child being 'different' from other children, we are implying that there is a norm which they do not meet in some way. If, on the other hand, we recognise diversity as **being** the norm, that is, we are all unique individuals with unique experiences, traits and behaviours, we can then value differences rather than using them as a source of division. Responsive planning in early years allows opportunities for practitioners to recognise and utilise diversity amongst learners in positive ways.

Equity – is not the same as equality. Equality can imply everyone getting the same, the same treatment, the same opportunities. Equity, however, is a more nuanced idea, that is, for things to be equitable, everyone should get what they need to be able to attain the same outcomes. This may mean some seeming to get 'more' or 'less' than others. For example, some children may require more time in conversation with adults to develop language skills than others; some may require more support with physical activities than others. Treating everyone 'the same' is not necessarily, in the long run, going to allow everyone to reach equitable outcomes.

Inclusion – is a highly contested concept and inclusion within education settings potentially even more so. However, there are three key principles of inclusive pedagogy (Black-Hawkins, 2017) which will underpin this chapter and link closely with the concepts noted above. Inclusive pedagogy requires:

1. A move from focusing on differences amongst children to making learning and outcomes accessible to everyone. Responsive planning allows this principle to be followed in early years settings.
2. A 'rejection of deterministic beliefs' (Black-Hawkins, 2017: 22), with a belief instead in transformability. That is, practitioners need to be aware of the potentially limiting effects of different types of conscious or unconscious bias, or assumptions based

on family circumstances and recognise that they can be making a daily difference to the child's life.

3. The development of ways of working with and through other adults. Working in partnership, both with professionals and parents, is addressed more fully in Chapter 21. If we are to keep the 'child at the centre', we must look at the aspects in their world that shape them and also take advice, as appropriate, from relevant specialists.

The wider context of current legislation and policy

Over the past few decades, there has been an increasing focus on the importance of upholding human rights and of enshrining these within legislation. UK national and devolved governments have gradually amended and rewritten legislation and policy as they have recognised that areas of discrimination remained. Perhaps the most significant recent legislation was the Equality Act (2010) (UK Parliament [UKP], 2010), which pulled together existing anti-discrimination legislation and put new duties on all to prevent the discrimination, harassment and victimisation of people according to one or more of nine protected characteristics. The characteristics that are protected by the Equality Act 2010 are: age, disability, gender, gender reassignment, marriage or civil partnership (in employment only), pregnancy and maternity, race, religion or belief, and sexual orientation. 'The Act also provides for protection against discrimination by association, which provides protection for people who are discriminated against because someone close to them falls under the definition of one of the protected characteristics' (Local Government Association, 2022). In an educational setting, there is a particular responsibility for practitioners to recognise and avoid potential discrimination in respect of both children and their families.

In 1989, the United Kingdom government signed the United Nations Convention on the Rights of the Child (UNCRC) (UNICEF, online-a). The Convention is based on four principles: non-discrimination; best interests of the child; life, survival and development; the right to be heard (UNICEF, online-a), and 54 articles. Article 2 emphasises that the Convention 'applies to every child without discrimination, whatever their ethnicity, sex, religion, language'. Successive Education Acts and other child-focused legislation in all of the four nations in the UK have incorporated elements of the principles and relevant articles, although it is recognised that there are sometimes challenges in implementation (Hogg, 2019).

Each of the four home nations has its own history of Children Acts, through which we can trace the development of the way society conceptualises its responsibilities towards children and their families. For example, the Children and Young People (Scotland) Act of 2014 (Scottish Parliament, 2014) incorporated into legislation some key policy principles under the heading of Getting it Right for Every Child (GIRFEC) (Scottish Government, 2012a). This states that every child has the right to be 'safe, healthy, achieving, nurtured, active, respected, responsible and included'. These wellbeing indicators can be seen to reflect the principles of the UNCRC.

Education for All (UN, online-a) is a global policy which drives national legislation and guidance. Building on the earlier internationally agreed Salamanca Statement (UNESCO, 1994), which had a strong focus on the inclusion of young people with disabilities in mainstream establishments, Sustainable Development Goal (SDG) 4 includes reference to early childhood development, gender equity and inclusion (UNICEF, 2015), recognising a broader definition of inclusion which moves beyond thinking only about (dis)ability as a potential exclusionary factor. Thus, our responsibilities as early years practitioners to every child in our care are outlined by a framework of legislation and policy to which we must adhere, as well as the related moral principles of non-discrimination and human rights on which that legislation is based. These principles also extend to our relationships with families and caregivers and it is vital that, as thinking professionals, we recognise the need to 'hunt for assumptions' (Brookfield, 2017) and biases that we may unconsciously hold which impact on the way we respond to and interact with others. The following 'View from Practice' will help to examine and discuss some of the issues of diversity, equity and inclusion which arise for us as practitioners.

--------- **VIEW FROM PRACTICE** ---------

Unconscious gender bias in the nursery

Sally is an early years practitioner with eight years' experience within a large local authority city centre setting. Twins Amira and Assan, aged 4, have recently joined the nursery, having moved from the other side of the city; they are Pakistani and speak Urdu at home and spoke English in their previous nursery. Sally has been observing their interests and has been facilitating their blossoming friendships with other children in the setting. Yesterday Amira and Ellen had spent a great deal of time playing with the nursery's toy animals, whilst Assan and Paul had enjoyed using the marble run together. This morning Amira has brought a cuddly soft unicorn toy into nursery and she and Ellen are engaged in an elaborate vet role play in the home corner of the main playroom. Meanwhile, Assan has brought a small beanbag covered in Pakistani national flags and is enjoying a game of throw and catch with Paul; the boys are using one side of the playroom and counting their throws 'One, two to you'. The ball-throwing game is getting noisier and several times the ball has landed in the 'vet area'. Amira and Ellen are becoming angry and are throwing the ball back hard. Sally intervenes, giving both girls a hug and saying, 'it is OK, if we move the vet's operating theatre to the floor, the ball won't bother you and we can all share the space'. Sally is aware that

(Continued)

ball throwing is not usually condoned within the playrooms but is reluctant to interrupt, when Assan and Paul are clearly making each other laugh; when she first saw the ball, she was also wary of forbidding it in case her actions appeared racist.

Some 20 minutes later, the two boys have ceased their ball-throwing game and moved to the art area, where they are painting flags. Sally observes this extended interest and is pleased that Paul seems keen to share his play experiences with Assan; they are already talking about what they will do later in the garden. Meanwhile, Amira and Ellen have successfully 'fixed' the unicorn and are teaching it 'how to fly'. Ellen throws the unicorn to Amira, but it misses and bumps her face instead. Amira is crying. Sally gives her a hug and says to Ellen, 'it is OK, it was an accident, but let's not throw things in nursery, you can do that later in the garden, how about we teach the unicorn to gallop on the rug?'

THINKING POINT 3.2

1. What was Sally's main concern in this scenario?
2. How has Sally's intervention affected the boys' and girls' use of space and choice of resources?

Gender equity

Today's practitioners are increasingly aware of the need to treat boys and girls equitably to prepare for a more equally skilled and confident future workforce, and to avoid the potentially limiting effect of traditional gender delineation amongst activities. Much has been made of the need to ensure that boys access nurturing activities – small-world resources, role play and arts and crafts – to ensure they develop a well-rounded set of skills and interests as well as early literacy skills (Tyler and Price, 2016; Browne, 2004). Girls are now more likely to be encouraged to participate in construction and problem-solving activities, which help to build a foundation of spatial awareness and estimation skills necessary to support numeracy.

But while care can be taken to direct both boys and girls to a range of activities, there are other more subtle ways in which messages about expectations of behaviour based on gender can be sent. From the 'View from Practice', we can see how the adult, perhaps subconsciously, allowed the boys to occupy and dominate the greater amount of space, whilst the girls were expected to compromise their play; later, when they were throwing the unicorn, they were again encouraged to occupy the space to a lesser degree. Staff need to remain vigilant in recognising their own subconscious bias.

Again, the well-intentioned actions of the practitioner are perpetuating a way of being for each gender – namely that boys can be louder and girls should have less of a physical presence. The 'View from Practice' also helps demonstrate the often unconscious ways adults accept aggression in boys but not in girls, soothe girls and actually do not allow them to be angry, thus potentially hindering their ability to regulate and learn affective/ emotional skills. As advocates of equity, we as practitioners must constantly challenge our own behaviours to ensure we are allowing all children to express themselves fully.

Cultural equity

As the 'View from Practice' suggests, practitioners can be overly concerned not to seem racially biased – allowing the ball because it had a nation's flags depicted on it – rather than treating children fairly. However, as noted above, equity is not about giving everybody the same support; it is about giving appropriate support. Practitioners need to be sensitive to the emotional support a new child may need, particularly if English is not their first language and communication may be problematic. What is fundamental to a child feeling included is a sense of belonging and of being treated fairly. Remembering the second principle of inclusive pedagogy (Black-Hawkins, 2017), staff need to take care that assumptions are not made regarding a child's prior experiences or abilities. In relation to culture, it is too easy to make assumptions and generalisations based on limited knowledge. Research by Reid et al. (2019) suggests that while family is a vital context for learning, children's development is a dynamic process, impacted by experiences in different cultural environments; in addition, they found 'more diversity in child-rearing practices and developmental outcomes *within* cultural communities than *between* them' (Reid et al., 2019: 979). What remains at the heart of early years practice is the concept of relationship building and the importance of establishing mutually respectful communication channels between families and practitioners so that all feel involved, welcomed and part of the setting. This is important to ensure shared understanding between the family's expectations for their children's learning and the expectations of staff in relation to developmental norms. In practical terms, we would suggest:

- Where possible, staff who speak the same language could be appointed as the child and family's key person; however, it is important to remember that for language acquisition the child should be immersed in English language conversations and that 'cliques' of children or staff should not inadvertently be created.
- The use of resources and books that embrace diverse cultures will support all children in developing an understanding that there are many ways of organising domestic life and relationships.

- Take opportunities that arise naturally to discuss cultural differences in a respectful and inclusive way. This helps children to understand that their own situation is unique and that the situations of others are also valid and valuable, and no more or less 'right'.

THINKING POINT 3.3

1. Identify any assumptions that you may hold about those from different cultural backgrounds.
2. What impact might these assumptions have on how you interact with different children and their families?

The role of staff and adults

As noted in the introduction, the staff team are crucial role models in influencing children's attitudes to others. The existence of a cohesive and mutually respectful team also impacts on parental engagement and helps to develop a sense of trust, that 'this is us' ethos which is vital in creating a nurturing and safe space for children and families (Vuorinen, 2021). However, the opportunities to role-model simple turn-taking, for things as mundane as tea breaks or lunch, show children that adults too must take turns and share resources. We can also show children that it is possible to agree to disagree and that together we can find an acceptable outcome for all by ensuring a polite and respectful atmosphere, where all members of staff are clearly encouraged to have and to voice an opinion. In addition, staff and children need to be listened to, for example when staff and children are mind-mapping ideas for room layout or engaged in activities. The way in which parents and other visiting adults are treated will also impact upon children's impressions of inclusivity.

Additional support

It is generally accepted in child development theory that there are considerable ranges of age between which children may develop any specific developmental skill (see Chapter 5). As children begin their educational journey in the early years setting, it is vital that, while recognising that children will develop at their own pace, practitioners are aware of expected 'norms' of development. They need to recognise and be responsive when interventions may be required to support a child further. For some children, there may be a mild case of shyness, or a period of quiet absorption as they adapt to a new language; for others, however, there may be more specific neurodiverse conditions such as attention deficit hyperactivity disorder (ADHD) or autism spectrum disorder (ASD), or particular learning difficulties. Difficulties with hearing or sight may also be identified. There may also be some children whose skills are more advanced than many of their peers and for whom more challenging activities need to be provided.

Concerns about progress, and the potential involvement of other professionals, can be difficult for parents, but through skilled observations and professional judgement, staff can support them on their journey of acceptance as they adapt to the needs of their child. For some parents, a 'label' can be a welcome explanation, a shorthand way of explaining to the world the needs of their child. For others, however, it may be seen as limiting and deficit-laden, something 'missing', and thus it is important to foster inclusive practice that demonstrates to parents, carers and all children the need to support individual children as learners at their own pace.

In relation to practitioners, research suggests that human beings' natural tendency to categorise others leads to stereotyping (Stangor, 2012). Stereotypes attached to different labels can lead to expectations of certain types of behaviour, or views that some children 'cannot do' certain things. They may also make us feel that we are not able to work with some children (Gibbs et al., 2020). There are many studies which demonstrate that the beliefs of educators impact on their practice (Thornton and Underwood, 2013). It is really important that we use what we know about any assigned 'labels' as an insight into the child's potential needs. We must adapt to each child's individual learning behaviour and recognise that we can use the different skills in our repertoire to support children in different ways.

Following Black-Hawkins' (2017) first principle of inclusive pedagogy, careful responsive planning can ensure that learning opportunities are arranged in a way that makes them accessible to all, with appropriate support as required, tailored to individuals but without singling anyone out as 'different'. For some children, the early years setting can be a socially and emotionally challenging environment. Practitioners should look on social-emotional and behavioural needs as a learning difficulty, a need to be supported, in the same way as they would support a child with a hearing impairment, by adapting practice, not the child, seeking ways to differentiate activities in order to contextualise them and engage all learners. Everybody in the room should be engaged in an activity that is meaningful to them and this may require the provision of a significant range of opportunities. By offering children agency and interacting with them as individuals, practitioners can scaffold learning at the child's pace in ways that are meaningful to them. Practitioners are encouraged to appreciate their impact on the child, to recognise that through their interactions they are adding value to the child's experiences and affecting their future, demonstrating their transformative impact (Black-Hawkins, 2017).

Many strategies to assist in learning engagement and minimise low-level disruptive behaviours, for children with a specific diagnosis or simply different ways of learning, can be gleaned from collaborative work with specialist staff from other organisations and from sharing best practice amongst colleagues; this is the third principle of inclusive education

(Black-Hawkins, 2017). Through sharing experiences and insights across the team, staff can help children equip themselves with self-calming strategies. By accepting the Nurture Group principle that 'all behaviour is communication' (Bennathan and Boxall, 1996), we can respond in a way which recognises that there is a reason for any particular behaviour. Talking about strong emotions and appropriate responses is relevant to all children and thus having discussions about these issues as part of the development of health and wellbeing for all is crucial. For example, a child with ADHD may need a fidget toy or movement to help them stay focused at story time. If this scenario is explained to other children in the frame of 'what Jamie needs' then a more accepting environment will be created. Even better, they could all have access to a fidget toy if they wanted. Similarly, if there are strategies – certain songs or actions – that help calm a child, these can be taught to all the children, so that they are equipped to 'help' each other. If transition times are challenging for some children, a regular routine which prepares all the children for movement or a change of activity can be used. Through helping children regulate their own and each other's disruptive behaviours and building a 'learning community' (Morris et al., 2013), staff are fostering a healthy emotional climate in the playroom which better equips the children for future, more formal education. Evidence from research into the development of 'nurture corners', and the use of nurture principles, suggests that both children and families can benefit from this approach (Glasgow Centre for Population Health, 2014).

Physical equity

National disability legislation requires that all learning environments should be accessible to all. Since 2010 all buildings should have been physically accessible, and we should all be well aware of the need, and legal requirement, to have materials and resources easily accessed by everyone. What must be given paramount consideration is the adaptation of activities to ensure that those with physical or emotional difficulties can be fully included. This is an area where the expertise and knowledge of specialists should be welcomed: for example, in the use of pictorial signs for those with hearing impairment or ASD, and sensory stimulation for those with visual challenges. Again, these are strategies that benefit all and show an inclusive approach.

Continuing professional development (CPD)

Chapter 17 covers in depth the need for practitioners to be reflexive, to reflect upon what does and does not work and to be responsive to the needs of the other humans around them. This also includes the need to be aware of one's own attitudes and behaviour and to challenge unconscious bias (Brookfield, 2017). Ongoing CPD both in ways to enhance practice and to raise awareness of others' needs is vital in the quest to sustain inclusive environments. There is evidence that engaging in professional development around issues of inclusion results in teachers developing a more positive attitude to inclusive practice (Holmqvist and Lelinge, 2021). Workforce development is held by the OECD (2021: n.p.) to be one of the most important drivers towards 'fostering quality in children's everyday interactions'. Maintaining an interest in ongoing research and self-development will ensure a staff team who feel equipped, knowledgeable and therefore prepared to support all the children in their care and to know when to seek additional specialist assistance.

Summary

In this chapter, we have outlined the legal and policy drivers towards inclusive early years settings. We have suggested that through their ethos of active learning and child-led play, early years settings have the potential to be inherently inclusive. Children are, for the most part, free to choose what they do, where they do it and with whom. Adults are there to scaffold their learning through building on their interests; time spent on individual planning and building relationships with the children offers clear opportunities to address each child's individual needs.

Our main concern is around the role of the practitioner. It is through our words and actions that children learn who is important and who and what are valued. It is crucial that we demonstrate through what we do and say that everyone matters, that no-one is more or less valued and that we respond positively to each child and adult. In order to do this, we must be prepared constantly to work at checking our conscious and unconscious biases to ensure that we do not, even inadvertently, limit the learning or self-esteem of any child.

END-OF-CHAPTER QUESTIONS

1. Provide examples of how the UNCRC and its main principles – protection, provision and participation – have impacted on your setting's ethos.
2. What types of children's behaviour do you find yourself commenting and reflecting on the most with your colleagues – positive behaviours or challenging ones? Which children do you feel take up the most of your time? How does this make you feel when interacting with them?

(Continued)

3. Think of activities you have been involved in that have been accessible to a wide range of children. What adjustments can you make for children who need more support and those who need more challenge?
4. Think of ways in which staff can demonstrate openness and support to families/carers.

4
Children's rights and the UNCRC
Jana Chandler and Ruth Myles

Key ideas

This chapter will explore:

- Key milestones in establishing the United Nations Convention on the Rights of the Child (UNCRC).
- Challenges in implementing the UNCRC.
- The UN Committee monitoring process.
- Children's autonomy and participation rights.
- Realising children's rights in practice

Introduction

This chapter outlines the key milestones in the development of the United Nations Convention on the Rights of the Child (UNCRC) (or the Convention) (United Nations, online-b). This is followed by a reflection on how the UNCRC stands up to some of the challenges of the twenty-first century. The role of the United Nations (UN) Committee on the Rights of the Child (United Nations, online-c) in monitoring processes is considered, whilst also exploring some of the implications of the Convention's implementation on children's autonomy. The issues in the legislative implementation of children's rights at political and practice level are discussed, concluding with suggestions for the effective implementation of children's participation rights in early years.

Key milestones in establishing the UNCRC

Almost a century ago, the first Declaration of the Rights of the Child was drafted. In 1924, Eglantyne Jebb, founder of the Save the Children Fund and a pioneer of children's rights, convinced the governments assembled in the League of Nations to adopt it unanimously (Kerber-Ganse, 2015; Fuchs, 2007). The aftermath of the First World War had a devastating effect on the health of children and the young through famine, poverty and disruptions to family lives (Donson, 2014), resulting in placing children and the young onto the political agenda at a national and international level. There was an urgent need for governments to establish provisions to which children were entitled. This movement was committed to protecting children, schooling and commitment on action against child labour (Alaimo, 2002).

The Second World War was similarly a time of major upheaval for children (Venken and Röger, 2015; Waugh et al., 2007). Notwithstanding, the end of the war led to the establishment of the UN General Assembly in 1946 (United Nations, online-d) and continued discussion regarding the enforcement of children's rights, also discussed by Fuchs (2007). In 1959, the General Assembly adopted the Declaration, recognising amongst other rights, children's rights to education, play, a supportive environment and health care (United Nations, 1959), asserting that each child has a right to a 'happy childhood' (Kosher et al., 2016: 15). The Declaration was characterised by the view of children being vulnerable, with no mention of or support for the child's rights to participation (Cohen, 2002). It did not require ratification by national parliaments or promote the entitlement of children's rights (Kerber-Ganse, 2015).

The next two decades lost sight of children's rights due to opposing views between countries about their enforcement, governmental responsiblity, cultural differences in parental duties, and also non-governmental organisations (NGOs) directing their focus on separate child-related issues, including child welfare and education (Fuchs, 2007). However, on the 20th anniversary of the Declaration in 1979, the UN designated it the International Year of the Child, which also provided an opportunity for the proposal for a new treaty. Whilst the drafting began that year, it was not until November 1989 that the General Assembly adopted the Convention on the Rights of the Child (UN, 1989) as it is recognised today. Janusz Korczak (1878–1942) was an advocate for children's rights and autonomy, directly influencing the genesis of the treaty. The modern children's rights movement derived from the acknowledgement that every child is entitled to be respected as a human being (Kerber-Ganse, 2015), recognising children's freedom of expression, interests, desires and privacy (Molloy, 2019; Thomas, 2013, cited in Feldman, 2016). With the adoption of the UNCRC, children's rights have become a significant field of study, with the Convention often key to debates about children being the bearer of rights (Reynaert et al., 2009) and the concepts of childhood (Hart, 1991). This led to a shift from the emergence of children's rights and their need to be protected (Hart, 1991) to raised awareness of children's rights to participation and their right to have a voice (Kosher at al., 2016), and the development of a framework that would allow children's active participation in society. As highlighted by Coppock and Gillett-Swan (2016), the way children are considered, conceptualised and enacted changed, accepting children not just as 'becomings' but as 'beings' (Qvortrup, 2009).

THINKING POINT 4.1

1. What have been some of the events contributing to the development of the UNCRC?
2. Two of the discourses prevailing within the UNCRC include:
    - The need to protect children
    - For children to have the freedom to express themselves in the matters affecting them

Which discourse do you tend to engage with and what do you think influences this?

Challenges for the UNCRC implementation

November 2019 marked the 30th anniversary of UNCRC. The 54-article Convention is the most comprehensive and widely ratified treaty, endorsed by all countries except for the USA (Together [Scottish Alliance for Children's Rights], 2022). By ratifying the Convention, governments made a commitment to fulfil their obligations to implement the UNCRC under an internationally legally binding agreement that sets out the civil, political, economic, social and cultural rights of every child, regardless of race, religion or abilities (UNCRC, 2003). This is a huge landmark achievement for children's rights, recognising children as autonomous human beings with innate rights (Bentzen, 2019). At a global level, children's rights are however implemented by governments to differing degrees. UNICEF (online-b) evidenced that the progress made over the past three decades remains uneven. Whilst conditions have improved for many children around the world, there are still many that face poverty, violence, war or disease, with persistent challenges and new threats to the effective implementation of children's rights still remaining.

The UK ratified the Convention in December 1991. Whilst international treaties are not generally incorporated directly into domestic law (Department for Education, 2010: 4), which some of the devolved governments took this step. The Welsh Government incorporated the UNCRC through the Rights of Children and Young Persons (Wales) Measure 2011. Although Hoffman (2019) explains that the Measure does not fully meet the recommended incorporation model, as it does not ensure UNCRC rights enforcement by the courts, it still makes a significant contribution in integrating the rights into Welsh law. More recently, the UNCRC (Incorporation) (Scotland) Bill was passed unanimously by the Scottish Parliament in March 2021. Once becoming a law, public authorities would be legally required to respect and protect the rights in all the work that they do; however, this has not been without its challenges from the UK Government. Whilst the Supreme Court does not object to the intention behind the Bill or the Scottish Parliament's ability to incorporate the UNCRC, it raised concerns about parts of the Bill that require amendment so the Bill does not exceed the powers of the devolved government (Together, 2021). There have been other developments furthering children's rights in the UK, such as the establishment of the Children's Parliament in Scotland, Youth Parliament in England and Wales, Youth Forum in Northern Ireland, Children and Young People's Commissioner in all devolved nations and the Children's Rights Alliance in England (CRAE). Indeed, Fuchs (2007) highlights the role NGOs play in local, regional and national change in the field of children's rights.

Yet, implementing rights into domestic law, whilst it shows that the States Parties (UN Member states) take measures to implement the UNCRC to the maximum extent, also requires effective enforcement mechanisms. Lundy et al.'s (2012) research study on the legal implementation of the UNCRC in 12 countries provides a valuable insight into effective and impactful ways to embed children's rights into domestic law. Interestingly, the study highlighted that there is 'no one right way' to incorporate the UNCRC, yet the process adopted to implement it and the result, where it becomes translated into the systems at national level, are of a high value in realising children's rights (Lundy et al., 2013).

Whilst most of the rights are related to child protection (Kosher et al., 2016), efforts are being made, with an increase in social and public commitment to children's rights, to promote children's participation. This balance remains one of the fundamental challenges (Lansdown, 2006). The negative assumptions associated with children's capacity and the power relationship between adults and children contribute to this and will be discussed when considering children's autonomy. The issue of tokenism in children's participation persists, and the global pandemic and climate change are pertinent issues that, one could argue, once again have brought increased attention to the notion of children's rights.

Firstly, the matter of tokenism has been discussed by numerous scholars and is usually considered a 'tick-box' exercise that does not take children's views seriously, and as such does not inform meaningful change (Lundy, 2018; Tisdall and Bell, 2006; Sinclair, 2004; Tisdall and Davis, 2004; Hart, 1992). The UNCRC (2009: 29) in paragraph 132 'urged States Parties to avoid tokenistic approaches which limit children's expression of views, or which allow children to be heard but fail to give their view due weight'. Article 12 recognises children's rights to express their views and be taken seriously in all matters affecting them. Indeed, there is a widely held view that children's participation is a key objective to improving children's rights (Council of Europe, 2021; OECD, 2006, 2001; Hart, 1992).

Considering the idea of tokenism in early years raises concerns about participation due to a misunderstanding of the term, particularly with the assumption that one must do as children wish. Shier (2001: 113) explains that listening to children's voice 'does not imply that adults must implement what children ask for' but there is an obligation to give due weight on all matters affecting them. Indeed, the understanding of children's participation varies, and requires an ongoing dialogue between children and adults. One may also question babies' participation, particularly as their routines and experiences are mostly determined by their parents and others that care for them as they lack autonomy. Yet, from birth they can express themselves using sounds and body movements, hence letting their needs, likes, dislikes and intentions be known. As Lansdown (2006: 142) argues, the dialogue between the child and adult needs to be based on 'mutual respect and power sharing', with children having the power to shape the process and the outcome. Thus, it could be said that the pedagogical approaches adopted in practice can support or hinder children's participation, for example child-led versus adult-led approaches.

THINKING POINT 4.2

1. Consider whether you have adopted a tokenistic approach in your practice. How could this be changed to adopt an approach that considers children's participation more meaningfully?
2. If not, in what ways does your approach facilitate the implementation of the UNCRC?

Climate change and the global COVID-19 pandemic further raised awareness of children's participation and the need for government to take children's views seriously. To elaborate, Neenan et al. (2021) pointed out that children have not been adequately included in conversations related to climate change, with their participation in decision making being rarely more than tokenistic. Prior to the COP26 climate change summit, the survey published by UNICEF UK and Votes for Schools noted that 81% of children did not feel they had been listened to, leaving them anxious about their future (BBC Newsround, 2021).

Neenan et al. (2021) outline the need for children to make a meaningful contribution on the matters affecting them by including them. In recent years, the presence of young activists who exercise their right to express their views and are the voice of their peers, including Greta Thunberg, instil children's agency and the need to create spaces for their meaningful participation.

Additionally, the global COVID-19 pandemic has had a devastating effect on children (Meredith, 2021). Human Rights Watch (2021) produced reports about the potentially far-reaching and long-term negative impacts due to children being out of school, the loss of job and income for many families and economic insecurity. Whilst UNESCO (2020) recommended that countries adopt solutions to assure children's continuity of learning, the longstanding inequalities have been highlighted, with some children not having access to the internet or the technology needed. Governments worldwide took emergency measures in response to the pandemic, yet many failed to take account of children's rights. The research carried out by Croke and Hoffman (2021) examined the impact of emergency measures and the application of a child rights impact assessment by government, highlighting the negative impact of these measures on children's rights. Amongst numerous other recommendations, the report stressed children's participation in decision making so that 'their views are accounted for in times of public emergency' (Croke and Hoffman, 2021: 16).

Tisdall and Bell (2006) explain children's participation demands political change. Indeed, without urgent child-centred policy measures, it would be difficult to stand up to the challenges and new threats infringing children's rights, such as those discussed above. Tobin (2015) explains that adopting a rights-based approach enables the development of more effective and sustainable policies that relate to children and young people. Whilst the challenges highlighted above would benefit from closer exploration, the authors hope it will aid practitioners' understanding of some of the issues and encourage further enquiry.

Monitoring process for the UNCRC

In 1992 the UN Committee on the Rights of the Child was set up, consisting of 18 independent experts elected by States Parties. The Committee oversees the process of implementation and amendments of the UNCRC by countries that ratified it through reporting progress. Within this process, the Committee has three main roles: reviewing the progress, issuing guidance and hearing individual complaints. To elaborate, the Committee identifies areas where the country is doing well and where it needs to improve or if it is in breach of rights. It examines the reports submitted and procures a set of concluding observations and recommendations. Since 2014, individuals can also submit complaints regarding specific violations of their rights. Further information regarding this process is outlined by the UN Office of the High Commissioner on Human Rights (OHCRC) (Treaty Bodies, online).

Each government is required to submit a periodic report on the measures adopted to implement the UNCRC. Yet, as noted by Lundy et al. (2012), the Committee cannot force States Parties to submit these reports. Additionally, not all engage regularly in the reporting system (Freeman, 2020). Hence, there are variations in the UNCRC implementation. In the UK, commissioners in devolved nations have a core role in monitoring implementation of the UNCRC, holding the government accountable and ensuring consistency in its implementation at times of political change (Lundy et al., 2012). In other countries, this responsibility can also be delegated to regional governments.

One of the implications in the monitoring system is that the Convention does not prescribe the way or the means by which it needs to be implemented. Hence, it is open to interpretation with different legal or non-legal mechanisms for the realisation of children's rights. Legal measures of incorporation include direct, indirect, or sectoral incorporation (Lundy et al., 2012). The UN Committee favours direct incorporation, where the UNCRC is fully incorporated into domestic law at either legislative or constitutional level. This is the step that Wales and Scotland have taken, as indicated earlier. Indirect incorporation means that there are other legal mechanisms in place that give the UNCRC some effect in the domestic legal order. Sectoral incorporation means that the state transposes the relevant provisions of the UNCRC into relevant sectoral laws. In other words, the treaty provisions related to education are incorporated into the related education laws. On the other hand, non-legal measures include processes that countries use to progress the implementation of the UNCRC. Lundy et al. (2012) provide a more detailed overview of these measures, some of which include the establishment of children's commissioners or ombudspersons, the development of national strategies and action plans, child impact assessment processes or children's rights training.

Engaging in the review process can and does lead to policy reform and improvements in practice (Kilkelly, 2001), and the reporting system encourages debate leading to policy change to implement the UNCRC. However, it has also been observed that the Committee does not have an effective mechanism to enforce the UNCRC at national level (Lundy et al., 2012). Reynaert et al. (2009: 527–8) noted that the approach of standardised 'setting-implementation-monitoring' generalises thinking about children's rights. It does not encourage questioning or problematising the norms in policy and practice, nor consider the context, including 'children's living conditions, their social, economic or historic context, or diversity among children themselves' (Reynaert et al., 2009: 527–8). The responsibility nonetheless lies with government (Woll, 2001). The States Parties must take their commitment to implement the UNCRC seriously for children's rights to be realised, through constructive engagement with monitoring processes and measures to support effective UNCRC implementation. This echoes the Convention's requirement of the States

Parties to undertake all appropriate measures – legislative, administrative, social and educational – to implement the rights of children, as stated within numerous UNCRC Articles (for example, Articles 2, 4, 19, 26 or 38).

Children's autonomy

The notion of children's rights is concerned with balancing the need for children to be protected (see Chapter 2) and their entitlement to active participation. Whilst having the right to be protected, they should not be prevented from exercising their rights (Freeman, 2020). The legislative nature of the UNCRC outlines the significance of children's engagement in Article 12, which gives children the right to express their views and to have those views taken seriously in all matters affecting them. However, the UNCRC acknowledges that the way children exercise their rights and express their views on all matters affecting them changes with their age and maturity. Still, the States Parties have an obligation to create opportunities for children to be heard and to take the necessary actions in response to their views.

In a political context, Freeman (2020: 45) explains that decision making would be 'swifter, cheaper, more efficient, and more certain' if children lacked their rights. Yet, he observes that it was adults who presented children with the UNCRC (Freeman, 2020). Whilst the accountability for implementation lies with governments, the choices and values of professionals and the political elite should not exclude children and young people in the decision-making process. However, this is a complex task. Whilst political change is needed to realise children's rights, James and James (2001, cited in Reynaert et al., 2009) argue that children's participation in policy making can paradoxically lead to a reduced opportunity for children to be relatively free from adult control. Adopting a tokenistic approach will arguably not aid children's autonomy. In the same way, children denied opportunities to engage in decision-making processes will not provide them with opportunities to build experience and competence, the lack of which, as pointed out by Lansdown (2014), justifies their exclusion. Interestingly, Archard (2015) discusses the need to protect children's developing competence, suggesting that justifications are needed for restrictions to their freedom and autonomy in terms of maximising their future choices.

Over the years, children's meaningful participation has nonetheless caught the attention of numerous academics (Freeman, 2020, 1998; Lundy, 2018, 2007; Kosher et al., 2016; Lansdown, 2014; Tisdall et al., 2006) and this has influenced a breadth of activity at a global level. Examples of children exercising their rights are demonstrated through children and young people's activism, campaigning for issues which are important to and affect them, such as those associated with climate change (UN, 2013). Children have also been attending conferences at local, national and international levels, such as the Children's Rights Summit in 2016 in Ireland or taking part in Child Friendly Cities Summits worldwide (UNICEF, 2020b). NGOs, such as Children's or Youth Parliaments, have an important role in advocating for children's rights and creating initiatives and resources and engaging in research to ensure children's voice is being heard on matters that affect them. Reports on children's experience of learning and school life are a good example of this (Children's Parliament, 2017). Other initiatives such as the Rights Respecting Schools Award (UNICEF, online-c) empower children and place children's rights at the heart of their policies and practice. Granting children's rights evolves around the extent that children act in an autonomous way, which gives weight to their decisions (Veerman, 1992).

According to Dearden (1972, cited in Veerman, 1992: 19), autonomy is 'a learning task set by a particular ideal of human development' to reflect moral societal principles. The tension between adults and children is one of the key challenges in realising children's participation. Just as adults, children are considered human beings, yet perceived differently. It is this difference that can restrict children's autonomy. To illustrate this point from a practice perspective, if one were to adopt only an adult-led pedagogical approach, this could potentially hinder children's opportunity for autonomy. On the other hand, child-centred anthropology focuses on children's voice and agency to be taken seriously, hence promoting autonomy. This is not intended to criticise the pedagogical approach but to highlight challenges when considering children's autonomy.

Adopting a rights-based approach places equal value on process and outcome. This powerful approach posits the rights of all persons to participate in societal decision making (Kosher et al., 2016). This is so that children's interests are served meaningfully. Understanding children's autonomy and capacity more broadly will arguably be a positive step in realising children's rights.

—————————— VIEW FROM PRACTICE ——————————

Responding to children's right to express themselves

Jack is nine months old and has been attending the nursery setting for seven weeks. He has settled in well, with transition from home going smoothly. He enjoys exploring both the indoor and outdoor environment, showing signs of contentment and bonding with his key person.

Although Jack is familiar with daily routines in the setting, he does not enjoy the sleep routine, getting distressed when he is taken to the sleep room. The key person has been communicating with the family with the intent to replicate his home routine as much as possible in the setting. Still, Jack keeps getting distressed. After further reflection, the staff team engaged in closer observation of Jack. Creating an opportunity for Jack to take the lead with the sleep

(Continued)

routine, they observed that Jack seeks his knitted blanket at certain points of the day, with a preference to settle in the story area with a member of staff before falling asleep. Following on from observations, the staff team have created a rest space for Jack within the story area, creating a coracle using soft cushioning.

For older children, different ways can provide opportunities for children to express themselves. Providing a safe and comfortable space, children can be given opportunities to express their interests and views using resources such as floorbooks. Asking meaningful questions about the theme or topic of interest can be a good starting platform for children to participate and engage in construction of their learning, with practitioners respecting their autonomy and adopting a children's rights framework for pedagogy.

Realising children's rights in practice

As pointed out thus far, the realisation of children's rights not only lies with international monitoring and review, but the actions that governments take (Lundy et al., 2013). To realise children's rights, the principles of the UNCRC need to be translated into governmental structures and national legislation. In addition, Veerman and Levine (2000) point out the necessity to act at regional and local level to achieve the objectives of the UNCRC as it needs to inform everyday practice. Freeman (2020: 47) explains that through social practices we can advocate for children's rights so it is 'morally right that people will wonder how they can ever have thought otherwise'. Yet, adults, researchers, policy makers and professionals 'grapple' with the task to realise the UNCRC in 'real world' practices (Coppock and Gillett-Swan, 2016: 369).

Implementing children's participation rights in practice

Perhaps one of the most important mechanisms, beyond those noted above, is to raise awareness of children's right to participation amongst those working with children. There is also a need to acknowledge that these rights must be interpreted in conjunction with other rights in the UNCRC. Disseminating knowledge among children and young people to raise their awareness about all their rights is required. Article 42 of the Convention states that all children, young people and adults should know about the UNCRC, regardless of their age. Daly et al. (2006, cited in Reynaert et al., 2009) explain that knowledge on children's attitudes towards their rights is an important step in respecting children as citizens and to protect them from violations of their rights. Sharing the knowledge with other adults is incorporated within this Article, thus including parents and carers and other professionals can be another positive step in realising children's rights (Reynaert et al., 2009).

Adopting a child-centred anthropology is perhaps key, where children's voice should be given due weight. Reflecting on practice and questioning how well it embeds children's participation rights can be achieved by considering the relevant theoretical frameworks. Hart's (1992) 'ladder of participation' has been perhaps the most influential model when planning for participation. Yet, as pointed out by Shier (2001), these models should not be used to tick off the questions presented within the model but as a tool for discussion to explore what needs to be done. Whilst there are other models of child participation (Creative Commons, online), Lundy's (2007) model of child participation proposes a way of conceptualising Article 12. It consists of four elements of 'must do's', outlined below:

- Space: safe and inclusive for children to be given opportunity to express their views.
- Voice: provide children with appropriate information and facilitate them to express their views.
- Audience: ensure the views are listened to.
- Influence: the views are listened to and acted upon, as appropriate.

An example of how this model can be applied in the classroom environment has been considered by Harmon (2018), exploring how children can be active participants in decision making on issues of religion. There is a growing body of literature that may also be helpful to consider when reflecting on how children's participation is being embedded within practice (UNICEF, 2021b). Correia et al. (2021) suggest that child participation in practice considers the relationships practitioners have with children and the way they empower children and develop a shared understanding about their needs, experiences and perspectives. It is about adopting an approach that encompasses meaningful children's participation.

Summary

The UNCRC is the most comprehensive document on the rights of children. Whilst governments are accountable for implementing the Convention, its implementation varies due to limitations within the current monitoring system and differing implementation mechanisms. Considering children's participation is key when realising children's rights. Whether it be at political or practice level, children being viewed as autonomous and participating in decision-making processes that affect them should be meaningful. Raising awareness about children's rights and considering participation models may be good starting points in the realisation of children's participation rights.

END-OF-CHAPTER QUESTIONS

1. Identify areas of strength and development to implement children's participation rights.
2. Why do you think the areas of strength are important aspects of practice?
3. In terms of areas of development, in what ways can you enhance children's participation rights within your setting?

Part II
Contexts of childhood

5
Theories of child development
Mike Carroll

Key ideas

This chapter will explore:

- Behaviourist theory.
- Constructivist theory.
- Socio-constructivist theory.
- Attachment theory.
- Psychosocial development theory.
- Ecological systems theory.

Introduction

A number of different theories have been developed to help understand how children develop over time. A theory is an explanatory framework which helps explain known facts and enable practitioners to make predictions of future outcomes if a particular theoretical perspective were to be true. There are many theories of child development that help explain cognitive, emotional, physical, social and educational growth amongst children as they progress from birth through to early adulthood. This chapter will confine itself to examining several of the more prominent theoretical perspectives that help explain how children change and grow over time.

Behaviourist theory

Burrhus Frederic Skinner (1904–90) was primarily concerned with observable indications of learning. Skinner focused on observable 'cause and effect' relationships by examining the relationship between stimulus (S) and response (R) bonds or connections (Jordan et al., 2008). Appropriate responses from children are often acknowledged through a variety of praise systems (e.g. stickers, verbal praise, being given a special task or 'responsibility'). The assumption is that all children will strive to work towards achieving these rewards (or reinforcers). Those children who are unwilling to play the 'behaviour game' are classed as disruptive rather than as learners who are constructing a different meaning from the experiences with which they are provided (see Chapter 3 – 'problematic' behaviour as a learning need).

The Skinnerian perspective states that children learn best by being rewarded for 'right responses', or for responses that show evidence of having the potential to lead to 'right responses'. Skinner's general principle stated that if the response is followed by a reinforcing stimulus, the rate of responding will increase (Jordan et al., 2008). Skinner developed the 'law of positive reinforcement', which includes the notion that children can be 'trained' to replicate certain behaviours if they come to associate such behaviour with the receipt of a tangible reward. A positive reinforcement is any stimulus (reward) that when added, following a desired response, increases the likelihood that the response will occur (Jordan et al., 2008). A negative reinforcement is any stimulus (punishment) that when removed, following a desired response, increases the likelihood that the response will occur. The converse of this is an aversive stimulus which is an unpleasant or painful stimulus (punishment) which seeks to extinguish an undesirable behaviour. Skinner was opposed to the use of aversive stimuli as they were, in his opinion, not very effective (Jordan et al., 2008). The practitioner's role, within such a perspective, would be to facilitate the modification of the children's behaviour by introducing situations which reinforce children when they exhibit the desired responses.

—————————————— **VIEW FROM PRACTICE** ——————————————

Review positive behaviour protocols

In Scotland and Jersey (and, from March 2022, in Wales), the law no longer permits any type of physical punishment of children. Working in a private nursery physical punishment is an anathema to our professional duty of care towards the children; however, we took the change in legislation as an opportunity to engage staff in professional dialogue focused on positive behaviour protocols drawing on behaviourist principles.

We agreed to:

- Set clear and easily understood boundaries and routines.
- Be consistent in sticking to these as much as is possible.
- 'Catch children being good', providing praise and rewards whenever possible.
- Be specific in terms of what we see and hear that is good, using verbal and non-verbal language.
- Stay calm. Avoid making rash decisions and becoming angry.
- Defuse self before saying or doing anything. Create some space before talking/acting so as not to inflame a problematic situation.
- Focus on the behaviour. Take care not to communicate dislike for the child, it's the behaviour we dislike.
- Use quiet, private talk. Public shaming will only inflame the situation.
- Explain, using simple language, why the behaviour that we see and hear is not acceptable.
- Explain what we want them to do instead.
- Listen as well as talk. Focus on trying to understand things from their perspective.
- Help the child understand their feelings, using activities that help them to express themselves and calm down.
- Follow through on consequences, as agreed in nursery protocols, if the child does not respond.
- Heal the breach after the consequence, reassuring them that we love them and want to help them enjoy being in the nursery.

Constructivist theory

Jean Piaget (1896–1980) is best known for his work on the development of cognitive functions in children. Cognitive (constructivist) learning theorists argue that an understanding of the internal processes of the child is critically important. Constructivism is a metaphor for learning which suggests that knowledge is 'constructed' by the child. This differentiates it from views of education that presume that it is possible to transfer information directly into a child's mind. Constructivism asserts that real learning can only occur when the child is actively engaged in operating on or processing learning experiences facilitated by an adult through play and active experimentation.

Stages of cognitive development

Piaget asserted that thinking patterns evolve through a series of stages, linked to specific age ranges, in which cognitive structures become progressively more complex (Olson and Hergenhahn, 2009). Piaget (1960) postulated four stages of cognitive development which have influenced 'age-and-stage' thinking in policy documents linked to education:

- **The sensorimotor stage (0 to 2 years)**

  Towards the end of this period, the child, by exploring the world through sensory experiences and movement, begins to represent the world in terms of mental images and symbols through the acquisition of basic language.

- **The pre-operational stage (2 to 7 years)**

  The pre-operational stage is subdivided into pre-conceptual and intuitive stages:
  o   The pre-conceptual child (2 to 4 years) is unable to abstract and discriminate the attributes of a concept: inductive reasoning. Instead, they use what Piaget terms transductive reasoning, going from one specific instance to another specific instance, so forming pre-concepts.
  o   The intuitive child (4 to 7 years) considers only one variable of a situation at a time to the exclusion of all other aspects. In the Piagetian framework, this is called centring.

- **The concrete-operational stage (7 to 11 years)**

  The child begins to think hypothetically where two or more variables can be considered at once. However, there may still be a tendency to adjust the facts to meet the hypothesis. The development of logic structures continues to require concrete experience so that logic can be applied.

- **The formal-operational stage (11 years onwards)**

  During this period, the child starts to use abstract reasoning. Abstract hypotheses can be built along with the capability to hold some variables constant, while manipulating other variables in order to determine their influence. Analytical and logical thought no longer requires reference to concrete examples (Woolfolk, 2007; Spodek and Saracho, 1999).

Contemporary thinking suggests that individual children go through the stages at different rates (Edwards, 2003; Spodek and Saracho, 1999).

For Piaget (1960), the development of human intellect proceeds through a process of adaptation to the environment. The child makes sense of their environment through a series of schema (Spodek and Saracho, 1999), which is a cognitive framework or concept that enables the child to organise their knowledge and interpret new information. Adaptation becomes necessary when children are confronted with new knowledge, leading to cognitive conflict with existing knowledge. Two complementary processes help to resolve cognitive conflict: assimilation and accommodation (Olson and Hergenhahn, 2009). When a new experience is incorporated alongside existing knowledge, assimilation is said to occur. The child's thinking does not really change as a result of assimilation. When new experiences require an adjustment to take place in a child's thinking then accommodation is said to occur. Assimilation and accommodation act together to bring about cognitive equilibrium or internalisation of new learning (Olson and Hergenhahn, 2009).

Piaget (1960) suggests that practitioners should design learning activities that are practical and experiential in nature. Practitioners influenced by the constructivist perspective provide children with opportunities to experience learning as an active, social process of making sense of experience; as opposed to 'instruction' whereby children are given information (Olson and Hergenhahn, 2009), albeit that information remains important set within the context in which it is applied. Practitioners should engage children in learning activities (hands-on, minds-on) through creating stimulating environments containing centres of interest such as the 'shop corner' to stimulate a culture of inquiry.

Socio-constructivist theory

Lev Vygotsky (1896–1934) focused on the socio-cultural context of cognitive development and, in particular, the role of language in development (Vygotsky, 1962). The Vygotskian perspective asserts that children's development is affected by the social environment or culture in which they live (Spodek and Saracho, 1999). In simple terms, this culture is responsible for teaching children not only what to think, but how to think. Children come to understand through collaborative social engagement. So, for Vygotsky, development occurs on the social level within a cultural context, with learning being essentially an active and interactive process (Edwards, 2003). The child internalises the mental processes initially made evident in social activities and moves from the social to internalise this at an individual level. Internalisation is the process whereby the social becomes the psychological: from the interpsychological plane (between you and others) to the intrapsychological plane (inside yourself) (Jarvis, 2005). Knowledge is not handed on, nor is it discovered by the child, but rather it is part of a process of co-construction. This co-construction takes place through problem-solving activity that enables children progressively to access the world of knowledge that is initially beyond them, but of which they are a part.

Vygotsky rejected the Piagetian idea that learning must wait for development to take place (Spodek and Saracho, 1999). Vygotsky (1978) asserted that children are capable of learning within a zone of proximal development (ZPD). The ZPD is the difference between actual development, as determined by independent problem solving, and the level of potential development, as determined by problem solving under adult or more able peer guidance (Woolfolk, 2007). This gives rise to the notion of the more knowledgeable other (MKO) as someone who supports children towards higher levels of attainment than they would be capable of working alone. Learning and development therefore are a social and collaborative activity. It is up to children to construct their own understanding in their own minds, supported through social interaction. The practitioner has a crucial role to play in this by designing appropriate activities and experiences which involve social interaction and discussion. For Vygotsky (1978), the child's ongoing interaction with the social world will lead to the development of an ever more complex view of reality; along with the development of their language skills, which become the primary tool of intellectual adaptation.

The critical importance of language to the process of social interaction led Vygotsky to research the connection between how children learn and how they acquire language. According to Vygotsky, language is used in different ways as the individual is shaped by culture. Vygotsky (1962) identified three stages of language development:

Social speech (up to age 3): is external communication used to talk to others. A young child learns that saying 'please' and 'thank you' usually provokes a positive response from caregivers.

Private (egocentric) speech (from 3 to 7): directed at the self to support 'thinking out loud' as part of problem solving or the child explaining what they are doing.

Inner speech (from 7 onwards): takes on a self-regulating function and is transformed into silent inner speech (talking to self without the need to make this audible) and verbal social speech (McCaslin et al., 2011).

Language is used as a tool to enable children, working collectively, to negotiate a change in their thinking. Children learn best through problem-solving activity, supported by more knowledgeable others, including the practitioner (Spodek and Saracho, 1999). The support provided is called scaffolding, a term developed by Wood et al. (1976). Scaffolds can include focused questioning, prompts, hints and think-aloud time (Hartman, 2002). This support should only be provided when the child requires assistance to bridge the gap between actual and potential development (ZPD). This support does not alter the nature of the task but rather enables the child's participation through graduated assistance (Hodson and Hodson, 1998). Crucially, this support is temporary and should be gradually removed as the child achieves success. Consequently, practitioner–child interaction becomes a dynamic process, with the practitioner constantly gauging when support is needed, the nature of support required, how much support is needed as well as considering when and how to progressively remove the scaffolding.

THINKING POINT 5.1

1. Consider whether it is possible to scaffold a child's learning and if so, how is this accomplished in your establishment?
2. Do you recognise Vygotsky's stages of language development? If so, consider the ways these stages manifest themselves amongst the children in your care.

Attachment theory

John Bowlby (1907–90) and his collaborator Mary Ainsworth (1913–99) developed attachment theory, which suggests that the child's attachment with their primary caregiver develops during the first 12–18 months of life (see also Chapter 8). This theory suggests that the child has an innate (i.e. inborn) need to attach to one main attachment figure (i.e. monotropy), usually the mother. Attachment may be defined as 'an affectional tie that one person or animal forms between himself and another specific one – a tie that binds them together in space and endures over time' (Ainsworth and Bell, 1970: 50). This is seen as an evolutionary trait which helps children to survive; the ability to cry, scream, smile or crawl helps to keep caregivers close to the young child. These attachment (proximity-promoting) behaviours are initially directed at a primary caregiver or a few caregivers. By the time the child is eight months old, they start to exhibit distress when their caregiver(s) leaves their presence – separation anxiety (Bowlby, 1960). In attachment theory, there are three stages to displays of distress (Bowlby, 1960 and Robertson, 1970, cited in Alsop-Shields and Mohay, 2001), which include:

- **Protest:** a child will scream, cry, and display anger on the departure of the primary caregiver. If they are able, they may well cling to the caregiver in order to prevent them from leaving or struggle to release themselves when another person holds them.
- **Despair:** a child may appear to be outwardly calm; however, they internalise the feelings of being abandoned, causing the child to withdraw and refuse comfort.
- **Detachment/Denial:** the child begins to re-engage with their environment and interact with objects and other caregivers. On the return of the primary caregiver, the child will display emotion.

By the time the child becomes a toddler, they will have internalised their attachment relationships, which, according to attachment theory, provides the child with a view about their own self-worth and whether they can depend on others to meet their needs. According to Bowlby and Ainsworth, early interactions with a caregiver result in the emergence of patterns of attachment. There are four patterns of attachment (Ainsworth and Bell, 1970), which include:

Ambivalent attachment

The child exhibits distress when being separated from their caregiver and continues to exhibit the same behaviours on the return of the caregiver, even when there is an attempt to comfort the child. The child is not secure in the knowledge that their caregiver will provide comfort and reassurance as and when required, possibly as the result of inconsistent parental availability. Displays of emotional anxiety and anger towards their caregivers are typical coping strategies.

Secure attachment

Children exhibit distress when being separated from their caregivers and, conversely, welcome the return of the caregiver or are quickly comforted if upset. When the child is hurt or concerned by something, securely attached children will seek comfort from their caregivers – their 'secure base' (Ainsworth and Bell, 1970: 53). The child is secure in the knowledge that their caregiver will provide comfort and reassurance, as and when required.

Avoidant attachment

Children with avoidant attachment are relatively calm when separated from caregivers and tend not to display any reaction on their caregiver's return. These children tend to distance themselves from dependence on others to reduce emotional stress. This may be indicative of a disengaged caregiver and possibly abuse or neglect.

Disorganised attachment

This pattern was added later by Main and Solomon (1986) to help incorporate children with a disorganised attachment style with no predictable pattern of attachment behaviour. Children with this form of attachment are often unable to cope with separation distress, tending to oscillate between aggressive behaviour and social isolation. The pattern of disorganised attachment may well be the result of inconsistent behaviour from caregivers (Kennedy and Kennedy, 2004).

Attachment theory provides insights as to how the emotional, social and/or physical interactions that occur between a child and their primary caregiver(s) can affect the child's emotional development (see Chapters 7 and 8). However, attachment theory only acts as a rough guide rather than a predictor of future outcomes for any given child (see also Chapter 8).

THINKING POINT 5.2

1. Consider whether the four patterns of attachment are evident amongst the children in your care.
2. Consider whether the absence of a mother can be overcome by a relationship with other adults who provide the child with care, intellectual stimulation and social experiences.

Psychosocial development theory

Erik Erikson (1902–94) postulated eight phases of psychosocial development (Erikson, 1963a), based on how children socialise and how this affects their sense of self. Psychosocial links the psychological needs of the individual (i.e. psycho) with the often conflicting needs of society (i.e. social) (Erikson, 1963b). Each phase represents a crisis that requires resolution; the nature of the resolution achieved will influence progress during the next phase. McLeod (2018) provides an overview of the first four of the phases of psychosocial development that affect children, which include:

Trust vs mistrust (infancy: 0–12 months): in this phase, infants who are nurtured and loved by their caregivers develop a sense of trust which will have a positive effect on other relationships. Infants who are mistreated tend to become anxious, insecure and mistrustful. Children whose care has been inconsistent, unpredictable and unreliable tend not to have confidence in the world around them or in their abilities to influence events.

Autonomy vs shame (early childhood: 12–36 months): toddlers start to develop a sense of personal control with respect to the development of physical skills (e.g. walking, dressing themselves) as well as beginning to assert their independence and develop their unique personality, making tantrums and defiance commonplace. The child's sense of newfound control – autonomy – often exhibits itself with them frequently exclaiming NO! If the child is encouraged and supported to become more independent during this phase, they are likely to become more confident and secure in their own ability to survive in the world. A sense of shame and doubt may result if the child is made to feel incompetent or is punished for failing to undertake basic tasks (e.g. during toilet training, dressing themselves).

Initiative vs guilt (pre-school: 36–60 months): children during this phase begin learning about social roles and norms, often linked to active play. They will begin to develop their imagination, cooperate with others, lead as well as follow and broaden their skills. Adults who facilitate active play and allow children to make their own decisions are likely to enable the child to develop self-confidence. If the child is not given scope for independent action or is subjected to critical scrutiny, they may develop a sense of guilt, feeling that they are a burden to others and as such become fearful, unwilling to lead others and become dependent on adults' guidance. During this phase, children become inquisitive as their thirst for knowledge grows, with adults treading carefully around the 'dreaded' WHY? If adults dismiss or ridicule the child's questions then the child may develop a sense of guilt for 'being a nuisance'.

Industry (competence) vs inferiority (primary school age): during this phase, the child is transitioning from free play to more formal play with rules and regulations. The child is also building important relationships with peers and adults as well as beginning to feel the pressure of academic performance. A child who has experienced successful resolution of earlier psychosocial phases is more likely to be industrious and this should promote learning, particularly if the adults, and their own friends, support them in achieving their goals. A child who has not successfully met the challenges encountered in the early phases of development is likely to develop feelings of inferiority and doubt their abilities.

Although not based on empirical evidence, many find that they can relate the various phases of the life cycle to their own experiences. The model is useful as it provides insights into the influence of social relationships on development. A weakness of the model is that Erikson does not provide any real insight as to what kinds of experiences enable individuals to successfully resolve psychosocial conflicts and thus move from one phase to another. Despite this, the phases of psychosocial development do provide a useful overview of how an individual's personality develops.

Ecological systems theory

Urie Bronfenbrenner (1917–2005) believed that a child's development emerges from the interaction of the child and their environmental context. For Bronfenbrenner (1977), human development involves an individual being influenced by, as well as influencing, their environment. The environment is called an ecological system. Bronfenbrenner (1977) suggested that the environment of the child consists of five interrelated systems and that the influence of one system on a child's development depends on its relationship with the others. Bronfenbrenner (1977) organised these systems as a set of nested structures (i.e. like a matryoshka doll) in terms of the impact they have on a child. Guy-Evans (2020) provides an overview of the five systems of Bronfenbrenner's ecological systems theory as consisting of:

The microsystem

This is the environment that is closest to the child and includes the things and people who have direct contact with the child in their immediate environment, such as parents, other family members and childcare workers. The microsystem is where face-to-face interactions take place and is the most influential system affecting the child (Bronfenbrenner, 1977). Relationships in this system are bi-directional, which means how people treat the child will affect how the child treats them in return. Nurturing relationships, particularly with their parents, is likely to have a positive effect on the child's development; whereas neglectful parenting (relationships) is likely to have a disastrous impact upon development.

The mesosystem

The mesosystem describes the relational linkages between the people who formed the microsystem (Bronfenbrenner, 1977): for example, the relationship between the parent and the day care worker will have an impact on the child. Each time a child enters a new setting (e.g. joins a club), the microsystem is widened, or diminished when the opposite happens (Bronfenbrenner, 1977). The theory suggests that where good relationships exist, this should have positive effects on the child's development; conversely, troubled relationships are likely to have an adverse impact on development.

The exosystem

The exosystem consists of formal and informal social structures that have an impact on elements of the microsystem and in so doing indirectly affect a child's life even though they may be external to the child's experience. A caregiver's work commitments are often quoted in this regard as these can have an impact upon the amount of time they have to interact. The loss of a job or a prolonged absence of employment can also have an impact on the child. More recently, there was widespread concern as to how the decisions by government during the COVID-19 pandemic would affect children's development.

The macrosystem

This is the wider environment which involves cultural elements that affect a child's development, such as the role of women in society, socio-economic status, the role of religion in society, legal and political systems and ethnicity. The macrosystem is the 'overarching belief system or ideology' (Rosa and Tudge, 2013: 247) which exerts an indirect influence on the child's development as it influences all other systems that have a more direct impact on the child: for example, a child living in poverty would experience a different development trajectory than a child living in a wealthier family.

The chronosystem

The chronosystem adds the element of time and the influence on development as a result of change and constancy that occur over the course of an individual's lifetime caused by events and experiences (Bronfenbrenner, 1989). These events may stem from the external environment (e.g. going to day care, parents separating) or within the individual (e.g. becoming ill, entering puberty) (Rosa and Tudge, 2013: 249). A change in family structure brought about by bereavement may have differential impacts depending on the child. Major life transitions (e.g. parental divorce) can, and often do, have an impact upon development as 'they alter the existing relation between person and environment, thus creating a dynamic that may instigate developmental change' (Bronfenbrenner, 1989: 201).

Bronfenbrenner and Ceci's (1994) paper marked a further transformation in thinking with the addition of person factors, which they differentiated in terms of demand (i.e. age, gender, etc.), resource (i.e. intelligence, caring parents, etc.) and force (i.e. motivation, temperament, resilience, etc.), that interact with the individual's context over time to influence development. Time includes ontogenetic time set within the specific historical time through which the individual lives (Rosa and Tudge, 2013). Bronfenbrenner's theory provides us with insights as to the influence of social environments on human development. This theory suggests that the environment in which a child grows up can have a positive or negative impact on every facet of a child's life. If we can identify those elements that have a negative impact upon a child's development, we can put in place compensatory measures. There is a note of caution, in that the theory developed by Bronfenbrenner can lead to overly simplistic assumptions that development can be impaired for those with adverse or weak ecological systems. This may be true for some but not all as many can still develop into well-rounded individuals without positive influences from their ecological systems.

—————— **THINKING POINT 5.3** ——————

1. For a child in your care, map out the various aspects of the first three ecological systems that may have an influence on the child's development.
2. For the same child, consider the compensatory measures that may counteract any negative influences identified in the first three ecological systems.

Summary

No single theory can be said to provide a comprehensive overview of the factors influencing child development. Childhood Practice professionals may find it useful to adopt an eclectic approach in their use of theoretical perspectives by using different facets of these theories to help inform their understanding of the contextual issues encountered in their practice. Building on data gathered through observation, and professional dialogue with colleagues, the child and their caregivers, theory can help inform the analysis of care and learning situations in order to arrive at a deeper understanding of the contextual issues encountered. Using theory linked to the data gathered from practice can often highlight the limitations of certain theoretical perspectives as well as enable practitioners to develop new approaches to practice.

END-OF-CHAPTER QUESTIONS

1. Why is an understanding of child development theories important?
2. Is development universal or diverse? If we have the same kind of experiences, will we develop in the same way or will a diversity of experiences result in similar, but not identical, patterns of development?
3. Is development episodic, taking place at periods of rapid growth, or is it a more gradual process?

6

Contemporary perspectives of children and childhood

Mary Wingrave and Jillian Barker

Key ideas

This chapter will explore:

- Childhood as a social construct.
- Changes in understandings of childhood.
- The complexity of defining childhood.
- Historical changes in society towards children.
- Current practice and approaches to supporting children.

Introduction

Traditionally, many viewed childhood as a temporary state and children as adults in wait-ing, who will contribute to society and the economy in adulthood (James and James, 2004). Peleg (2013: 526) further contributes to this perception, describing the 'human becomings' concept of children, where children are viewed as passive actors, vulnerable, lacking agency and needing protection. However, contemporarily, childhood is considered a distinct stage and children's lives should be considered as having significance for them in the here and now, not simply viewed as what adulthood might hold for them. In this chapter, we discuss children's need to engage and be active contributors in their lives. We consider the need for adults to be responsive to children's ways of thinking and being. Contemporary understand-ings of childhood which challenge traditionally structured perceptions of 'adults in waiting' and approaches to how children can be supported to live and develop as active members of society will be presented. Specifically, consideration of policies in the United Kingdom which frame not only attitudes towards children but are often underpinned by economic drivers to get women back to work whilst aiming to prepare children for the future, will be examined. As part of this discussion, the role of the United Nations Convention on the Rights of the Child (UNCRC) (UN, 1989), which was adopted by the United Nation's General Assembly in 1989 and supports governments in the creation of policies, will be examined as a tool that can sup-port the needs of children in society. Finally, we suggest that while children do need protection and guidance from society, they also need to be involved in the shaping of their world.

Childhood as a social construction

James and James (2004) argue that childhood as a social phenomenon is separate from the biological examination of child development. A biological perspective on childhood, as discussed in Chapter 5, often identifies universal and general findings that can be applied to aspects such as when most children will walk, develop language or learn to undertake particular tasks (Piaget, 1964; Gesell, 1934). In contrast to this, a social con-structive view presents childhood as created by a society which has specific rules and expectations that can be modified or developed depending on how society changes and evolves over time. This social concept of childhood can be viewed as being change-able: elements such as gender, ethnicity and class provide different experiences (Ryan, 2008; West et al., 2008; James and James, 2004). Frones (1993) suggests there is not one, but many childhoods, formed through varying cultures, social, economic, natural and human-made environments, thus producing varying childhood experiences.

Children are born into society, which has existing practices and traditions. As the child grows, it learns to participate, reproduce and contribute to these (Bourdieu and Passeron, 1977). This suggests that children should be viewed as autonomous agents, who not only learn from their environment but also contribute to the creation of meaning in their society. 'Children's social relationships and cultures are worthy of study, and not just in respect to their social construction by adults' (James and Prout, 2015: 4). Whilst a change in perspective is evident, it could be argued that rather than a paradigmatic shift of childhood occurring (Ryan, 2008) there has been an ongoing shift in society's view, which has resulted from research involving children to elicit an emic or insider perspective, thus allowing a deeper view of childhood to be understood. James and Prout (2015: 2) claim that the twentieth century was the 'century of the child', where a new paradigm regarding the changing perspectives of childhood emerged.

Changing perspectives of childhood

Childhood as a social construct can be seen as a ubiquitous concept in its structure, potential and recognised period – when it starts and finishes – changing according to the societies that both create and recreate it. Wyness (2006) advocates that the study of childhood can highlight and challenge wider social issues. Montgomery (2009) comments that childhood has been conceptualised in a variety of ways across time and in societies and that there are many inconsistencies in how children's roles and status have been understood. Montgomery (2009) observes that human young are unique in the amount of time they take to become physically independent in relation to other animals, as they are hyper-dependent on adults for nurture and care. Children also have the capacity to learn to adapt to the values and cultures of the environment into which they are born. However, this dependency upon adults also results in the acceptance that children are excluded from full participation in the adult world (Montgomery, 2009). James and James (2004) argue that childhood is a cultural component of many societies, but it is not a universal one: '[c]omparative and cross-cultural analysis reveals a variety of childhoods rather than a single and universal phenomenon' (Jenks, 2002: 78). Therefore, viewing childhood as a social construct offers an examination and understanding of children's lives, its complexity and the role of children in its construction. It should however be noted that children's participation in the construction of their own world takes place with the recognition of their subordination to adults. Furthermore, the child's understanding of what it is to be a child is impacted upon by their interaction with adults, who also have preconceived ideas about what it is to be a child (Abebe, 2019).

Understandings of childhood

When examining the concept of childhood, perspectives and understandings of what it is to be a child vary, with some claiming that it is a natural period associated with biological development and others suggesting that childhood did not always exist (Hendrick, 2015). Aries (1962) claims that attitudes towards children were progressive and evolved over time with economic change and social advancement, until childhood as a concept came into being in the seventeenth century. De Mause (1995) argued against this view, stating that childhood has always existed and that it is parents and their practices that have changed. Whilst Aries (1962) played an important role in highlighting childhood as a concept, many theorists do not agree with his perspective. However, his work does provide a broad framework which recognised that childhood is socially constructed and, for many, his work remains the foundation of childhood study programmes. It could be said that Aries started the conversation, but his views have been challenged and built upon.

As noted by Prout (2011), contemporary childhood recognises that there is no standard view of childhood. As such, childhood representations need to reflect diversity, complexity, and the overlap between theories. As such, we present a conceptual framework that has application for those in educational practice and, as shown later in this chapter, can be used to plan for the education and care of children. Figure 6.1 outlines where concepts interlink, drawing from many theorists and researchers, including Wells (2021), James and Prout (2015), Wyness (2015), Ryan (2008), James and James (2004), and Opie and Opie (1969).

The *Authentic Child* views the child as their own author and recognises that the child has innate qualities, which if nurtured correctly, will come to the fore. The concept is derived from the Greek word meaning 'author' – '*authentikos*'. According to Gianoutsos (2006), Rousseau believed that children were born good and that if allowed to develop and grow according to natural instincts, their natural-born goodness and purity would be preserved. Diaz et al. (1992) also proposed that through the adult's promotion and nurturing of self-control and unconditional love, the child's natural goodness comes to fruition. Approaches promoted by the likes of Montessori, Steiner and Reggio Emilia recommend that the child can develop at their own pace and contribute to their own development, that the natural child, the best version of the individual, will emerge. The concept of the *Authentic Child* promotes the child's natural ability and goodness, which is unique and will develop at different rates depending on the child.

The *Developing Child* can be viewed using a scientific lens to present a pattern or logic to the universal child (Skolnick, 1975). According to McLeod (2020), established norms for development can be broadly applied to all children in the same order. It is claimed that the basic building blocks and the process of development are broadly universal. Gesell's observations, according to Oliveira (2018), claim that there are norms which describe developmental milestones. Piaget's (1964) stages of development and reasoning presume that children 'work' through each stage before moving onto the next. Piaget's (1952) theory is based on biological stages and that progress is based on the belief of when the child is developmentally ready. Piaget explains that the child develops biological maturation

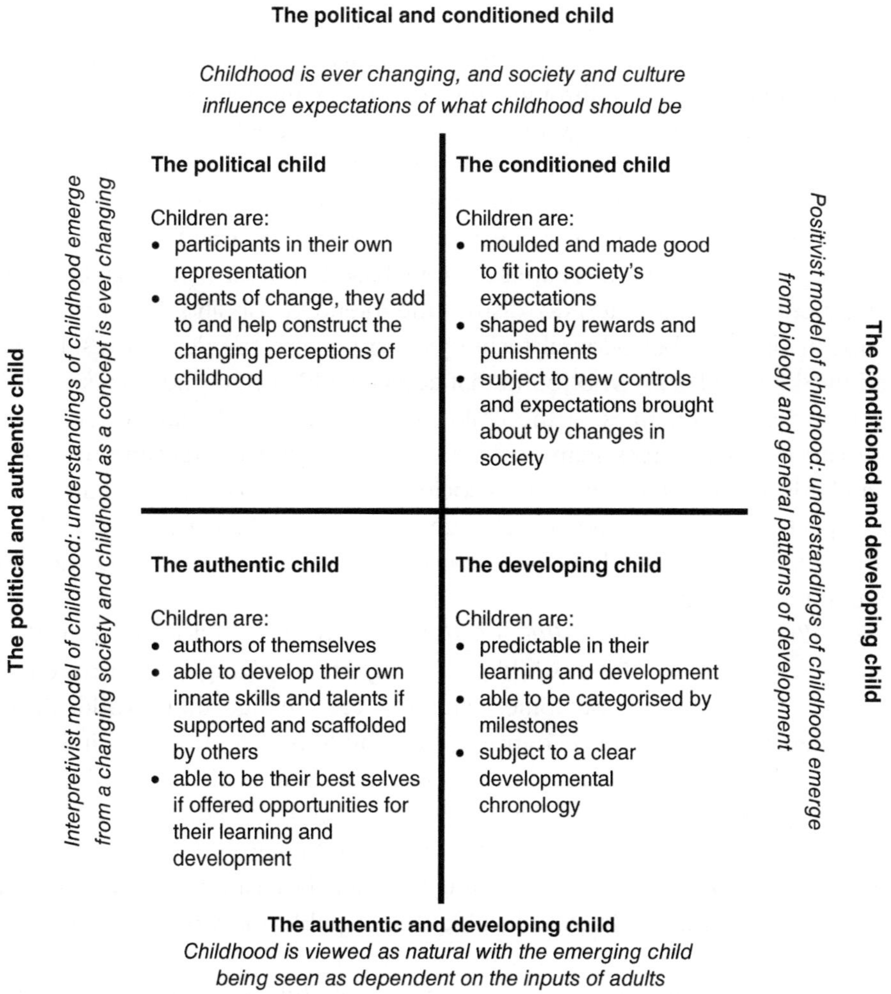

The political and conditioned child

Childhood is ever changing, and society and culture influence expectations of what childhood should be

The political child

Children are:
- participants in their own representation
- agents of change, they add to and help construct the changing perceptions of childhood

The conditioned child

Children are:
- moulded and made good to fit into society's expectations
- shaped by rewards and punishments
- subject to new controls and expectations brought about by changes in society

The authentic child

Children are:
- authors of themselves
- able to develop their own innate skills and talents if supported and scaffolded by others
- able to be their best selves if offered opportunities for their learning and development

The developing child

Children are:
- predictable in their learning and development
- able to be categorised by milestones
- subject to a clear developmental chronology

The political and authentic child

Interpretivist model of childhood: understandings of childhood emerge from a changing society and childhood as a concept is ever changing

Positivist model of childhood: understandings of childhood emerge from biology and general patterns of development

The conditioned and developing child

The authentic and developing child
Childhood is viewed as natural with the emerging child being seen as dependent on the inputs of adults

Figure 6.1 Concept of childhood map

and environmental experiences in stages to construct their own view of the world around them. However, Piaget's work has been questioned, specifically in regard to when some children develop competence, suggesting that children's cognitive development is not necessarily linear (Carpendale and Lewis, 2021; Lefrancois, 2000; Weiten, 1992). A further criticism is the specifically Western view taken by Piaget where he generally ignores environmental and cultural influences (Gray, 1994). Whilst there are criticisms of the staged model of development, the study of it has fuelled further exploration of developmental psychology and has influenced educational practices which provide a framework for many curricular models (McLeod, 2020).

The *Conditioned Child* recognises that the adult can employ certain controls which will determine the type of child they wish to produce. Known as operant conditioning, controls are exerted primarily through rewards and punishments (Skinner, 1972). This builds from John Locke's ideology of the child being created by the adult and that the child will reflect the morals and ethics of the adult who controls the conditions. Bandura (1986) suggested that when positive and negative reinforcement of behaviours occurs, children will start to assume similar behaviours. However, Siann (1994) argues that children are not passive and can evaluate situations based on their own cognitive reasoning and consequently can, and often do, disrupt the intended conditioning.

The notion of using behavioural techniques to acquire the desired results was also explored by Skinner (1972), who found that adults could control the child's environment which would lead to changes in the child's expectations or behaviours. Conditioning therefore can be used across many spheres of social life to determine the social outcomes, and it is important to note that as society's expectations of behaviours and beliefs change, expectations of the child also change. According to Leonard (2016), education is key in the preparation of children for adulthood and specifically in preparation for their contribution to the economy.

The *Socially Constructed or Political Child* is where the child is active in their own representation (Hendrick, 2008). Children are agents of change; where their choices and decisions can influence outcomes, children can change their world. Supporting children's agency is also about recognising that children have a right to influence their lives. Children have their own perspectives of what their world should look like, and an increasing participation of children in all aspects of life helps to shape concepts of what it is to be a child (Smith, 2011). In this view, children are no longer seen as passive subjects preparing for adulthood, 'becomings', rather they can be viewed as 'beings' in the here and now who are knowledgeable and capable individuals (Christensen and Prout, 2005).

Different understandings contribute to notions of childhood and have implications for practice and planning. In the following 'View from Practice', it is possible to see how the different perspectives of childhood interplay to provide a targeted approach to supporting a child.

VIEW FROM PRACTICE

Planning for Josh

Josh is 10 years old and is a happy child. There is significant delay in his language and he cannot always express himself, so he often resorts to tantrums. It is clear that Josh is at times frustrated and can be reluctant to use language to express his needs. Cognitively, Josh does not show any significant delay and is able to complete age-appropriate tasks and to understand and complete tasks when given instructions. No specific condition has been diagnosed beyond his language delay. Mum and dad are supportive and are content to work with the school and the out-of-school care service to establish routines and approaches which will support Josh's development.

It is possible to use Figure 6.1 to encourage a holistic view of the child to be taken in order to help staff plan for Josh (see Figure 6.2).

The social actor/political child	The conditioned child
Josh will not be pressurised to use language • Staff/children should not speak for him • Makaton symbols can be used to support his ability to express his needs or emotions • Josh should be encouraged to make choices for himself: if he is unable/unwilling to use language, strategies should be put in place to allow Josh to make choices using pictures or concrete objects	Use praise to help Josh feel self-worth and for him to be rewarded for his efforts and control • Use praise when Josh tries to use new words • Reward Josh's efforts to communicate with staff and children • Use praise when Josh does not lose control and tries to either use words or other means to communicate
The authentic child	The developing child
Accept where Josh is at and provide opportunities for him to develop at his own pace • Exposure to appropriate language around Josh so he has opportunities to hear language without pressurising him to use it • Exposure to hearing and engaging with developmentally-appropriate stories and books which are accessible to him and encourage emersion in language • Appropriate play opportunities to encourage socialisation with peers	What is the expectation of language for a 10-year-old? • Provide opportunities for Josh to play with other children to help encourage language, to communicate and express ideas • Encourage Josh to develop his vocabulary through 1:1 play sessions targeting specific language • Story time and shared reading opportunities where Josh is encouraged to make choices from age-appropriate reading materials

Figure 6.2 Planning for Josh

─────────── **THINKING POINT 6.1** ───────────

1. Why do you think it is necessary to adopt a variety of approaches to ensure that Josh's needs are met?
2. What difficulties do you think practitioners and teachers will encounter when they encourage Josh to participate in activities?
3. What additional outside agency support mechanisms could you use to support Josh's language and behavioural development?

Historical perspective on compulsory education in the UK

In the 'View from Practice' scenario, Josh is viewed in a holistic manner which aims to promote a childhood where children are healthy, encouraged to participate and protected. However, Cunningham (2020) suggests that how childhood is viewed by society and the political and economic conditions of that society will impact on understandings. One major change to perceptions of childhood occurred during the Industrial Revolution (1750–1900), where children arguably moved from being economic assets, as contributors to the labour workforce and home finances, to the recipients of compulsory schooling at the end of the nineteenth century (Hendrick, 2015). The introduction of compulsory education and of targeted legislation for children resulted in children becoming even further separated from adult society (Pilcher, 1995). It could be argued that separateness and distinction have shaped and been shaped by many of the policies created to protect and control children. Here we link the changing perceptions of childhood to the introduction of policies in the UK.

History of policies impacting on children's lives

Children during the Industrial Revolution were viewed as part of the workforce and there was an expectation that they would work alongside adults performing key roles (Cunningham, 2006). However, a movement within Parliament to regulate factory conditions led by Anthony Ashley-Cooper and Michael Sadler in the early 1800s, highlighted the dangers of industrial machinery causing serious injuries and unregulated practices which often involved incredibly long working hours, for both children and adults.

The campaigning led to The Factory Act (1833) being passed by the UK Parliament to improve conditions for children and set out guidelines for children working in factories (UK Parliament [UKP], 2022). This key piece of legislation changed the lives of working children and led to the introduction of further policies and legislation (UKP, 2021a). The Act restricted child labour for children over 9 and those up to 13 years of age to a maximum of nine hours labour per day. In 1891, the Factory and Workshop Act (UKP, 1891) was consolidated and extended safety regulations alongside raising the minimum age of employment to 11 years old. Policies such as these and those introduced since have served not only to protect children but have also defined the parameters and requirements of childhood (Gillard, 2018).

With the continuing expansion of industrialisation came the development of public education provision (Carl, 2009). The Factory Act 1833 (UKP, 2022) introduced two hours' schooling each day for children. With the growth of industry and changes in permitted working hours for children, support for public education grew. Education Acts were passed across the UK, resulting in widespread education (UKP, 2021b). The first significant piece of legislation in England and Wales was the Elementary Education Act in 1870 (UKP, 1870); in Scotland, where education was always a devolved matter, compulsory education was introduced in 1872 (UKP, 1872). Northern Ireland, which until the early 1920s was part of Ireland, was subject to a national system of primary education which was not compulsory. Northern Ireland's first Education Act was in 1923 after partition as a result of the Lynn Committee (Biaggi, 2020).

It was not until the end of the nineteenth century that the UK mandated that all children aged 5 to 10 years old had to attend school (UKP, 2021b). In 1899 the compulsory attendance age was raised to 12 (UKP, 2021b, 1899). Robinson (2010) argues that education was delivered and constructed along the lines of a factory model: children entered in 'batches' which were age dependent. Children's education was often delivered on a large scale with as many as 75 children being in one class (Barrow, 2013). Children were the recipients of knowledge, and the teaching style didactic (Banning, 2005). In terms of childhood, these approaches focused on the staged model and the conditioned model where expectations of the child were universal and fixed regardless of the individual child's needs.

Alongside developments in education, there was a growing interest in the safety of children, culminating in the introduction of the Prevention of Cruelty to, and Protection of, Children Act 1889 (UKP, 1889) when arguably the modern concept of childhood was created with further laws that protected children. In 1933, the Children and Young Persons Act (UKP, 1933) combined all child protection laws into one piece of legislation, resulting in the raising of the minimum working age to 14 and setting guidelines for the employment of school-aged children. Attitudes towards childhood were becoming more compassionate and the need to safeguard and protect them became a focus at a legislative level (National Society for the Prevention of Cruelty to Children [NSPCC], 2021). This compassionate view of childhood is still evident in contemporary UK policies, where children are viewed as vulnerable, a separate category from adults that require special attention (UNICEF, online-d). Having outlined the developing policy landscape in the UK, we now explore policies which illustrate how children are viewed within contemporary documents as these reflect current perceptions of childhood.

Contemporary child-centred UK policies

The Plowden Report stated, '[a]t the heart of the educational process lies the child' (Central Advisory Council for Education [CACE], 1967: 9). This view promoted the child-centred approach to education which arguably still exists today. Many policies promote children's best interests and needs and these are at the forefront of curriculum and policy making. James and James (2004: 17) acknowledge the interplay between children, adults and perceptions, and recognise the importance of viewing children as individuals rather than as a collective. Qvortrup (1994) suggests that childhood changes with each generation, with parents' childhoods being different from that of their children with corresponding changes in law, policies and social practices. Arguably, contemporary policies have the common goal of promoting and prescribing what is best for the child; however, Woodhead (1996) suggests that what is best for the child is culturally constructed, variable, and often only from a white, Western perspective, supporting the claims that one childhood does not exist.

In 1991, the UK ratified the United Nations Convention on the Rights of the Child's (UNCRC) charter (UN, 1989), with the goal to incorporate all aspects of a child's life and their rights within the UNCRC, as discussed in depth in Chapter 4. The right for all children to be in education regardless of ability resulted in the four countries in the UK examining their own policies. In Scotland, the Standards in Scotland's Schools etc (Scotland) Act 2000 (Scottish Parliament [SP], 2000) expanded education to funded pre-school. Northern Ireland declared that the Education and Libraries (Northern Ireland) Order (Northern Ireland Assembly, 2003) seeks to promote the welfare of children. The consolidation of the Education Act in 2002 (UKP, 2002) in England and Wales required local authorities to promote and safeguard the welfare of children. Lord Laming's report in 2003 (Laming, 2003), which investigated the missed opportunities by authorities in a child abuse case, led to further developments in each country across the UK, creating many of the child protection and welfare policies to be used in both compulsory and non-compulsory settings. The aim was to enshrine the rights of each child and encourage collaborative working between all adults in children's lives to promote their wellbeing. Responsibility for educational and social policy across the UK is devolved to national governments and there is no one UK approach. Table 6.1 sets out the four nations' child protection legislation and contemporary legislative documents.

Table 6.1 UK legislative documents

	England	Northern Ireland	Scotland	Wales
Initial Child Protection Acts	The Children Act 1989 (UKP, 1989)	The Children (Northern Ireland) Order 1995 (Northern Ireland Assembly, 1995)	The Children (Scotland) Act 1995 (UKP, 1995b)	The Children Act 1989 (UKP, 1989)
Contemporary Child Protection and Wellbeing legislation/acts	Children Act 2004 (UKP, 2004) after Victoria Climbié murder, amended by the Children and Social Work Act 2017 (UKP, 2017)	Children's Services Co-operation Act (Northern Ireland) (Northern Ireland Assembly, 2015)	Children and Young People (Scotland) Act 2014 (Scottish Parliament, 2014)	Social Services and Wellbeing (Wales) Act 2014 (National Assembly Wales, 2014)
Supporting documents for child protection, rights and wellbeing	Working together to safeguard children (Department for Education [DfE], 2018a)	Children and Young People's Strategy 2020-2030 (Northern Ireland Executive, 2020a)	Getting it Right for Every Child (Scottish Government [SG], 2012a)	A plan for All Children and Young People 2019-2022 (Children's Commissioner for Wales, 2019)

All four countries have introduced protective legislation for children. In Scotland, Getting it Right for Every Child (SG, 2012a) is a social policy document that seeks to protect children with evidence of the developing child and the authentic child, insofar as they acknowledge that different approaches are required for different ages. England's Working Together to Safeguard Children (DfE, 2018a) sets out a clear framework for a child-centred approach to safeguarding and promoting the welfare of all children. These documents show evidence of the authentic and social child, where adults listen and work with children, taking their views seriously. The Welsh legislation of Children and Young People: Rights to Action (Welsh Assembly Government, 2004) also demonstrates clear evidence of the need to listen to and include children and young people, evidencing the socially constructed and authentic child. The Welsh Plan for All Children and Young People 2019–2022 (Children's Commissioner for Wales, 2019) indicates the use of a nationwide survey of pupils and teachers to gain an understanding of how children and young people experience the principles of a children's-rights approach in their education, evidencing the socially constructed and authentic child. Northern Ireland's Children and Young People's

Strategy 2020–2030 (Northern Ireland Executive, 2020a) seeks to promote children's wellbeing and provides outcomes and focus areas based on evidence collected from stakeholders, children and young people's consultations. Within this strategy, there is evidence of the authentic child, the developing child and the socially constructed child through the inclusion of children's representation.

All governments in the UK have taken steps to promote and listen to the voices of children, with each country creating a Children's Commissioner and a forum where children's voices are heard, further evidencing the authentic and social child's agency. However, further work would be beneficial to securing true child agency with the inclusion of opportunities for children to contribute to the protective legislation and policies, as there is little evidence of the inclusion of their voices beyond the initial consultations before publication. Children may connect through many methods of communication, and it is important to recognise that the phrase 'children's voice' assumes a collective view which seek views from all children, from initial consultation to beyond publication – one that would present children's perspectives that are not purely superficial (Murray, 2019). In addition to the protection of children, curricular focus has taken centre stage in educational developments, and how children learn and contribute to their society is considered essential to the delivery of education.

———————————— THINKING POINT 6.2 ————————————

Consider the legislation and documents you use in practice:

1. How evident is it that children are consulted, and their view taken seriously (UNCRC Article 5/12) when decisions are made about their lives?
2. Consider whether it is necessary that adults make the final decision about children's safety.
3. Examine the above model (see Figure 6.1) and consider which child is more evident? Why do you think this is the case?

UK curricula

Each country in the UK has its own curriculum and approaches with supporting policies; here we examine each country's approach through the lens of our diagram (see Figure 6.1), considering how children are represented in each to maximise their educational experience. Each country uses the following curricular policies outlined in Table 6.2.

Table 6.2 UK curricular documents

Country	Document	Age range of document	Age of compulsory education
Scotland	Curriculum for Excellence (Scottish Government, 2008b),	Ages 3 to 18 years old	4.5-16
England	National Curriculum (DfE, online)	Ages 5 to 16 years old	5-16 You must stay in full-time education, start apprenticeship or 20 hours working/volunteering while in part-time education/training until 18
Wales	National Curriculum for Wales (curriculum currently under review)	Ages 3 to 16 years old	5-16
Northern Ireland	Curriculum (CCEA, online)	Ages 3 to 16 years old	4-16

Table 6.2 illustrates the similarities in age ranges for compulsory education across the UK and, with the exception of England, notes the age range of the curricula being applicable to children before compulsory education. Attitudes have changed since the introduction of compulsory education, with contemporary practices identifying and aiming to meet the needs of all children (Davis, 2018). The original factory model of education appears to have been rejected in favour of a more child-centred and child-led learning environment and curriculum, as evidenced in the Plowden Report (CACE, 1967). The political and authentic child concepts in the above curricular documents are promoted where the individual child is recognised. Children's views, ideas and choices are encouraged, and the child is included in the planning of their learning. Generally, there has been a move from previous didactic models of education, but echoes remain, such as lesson delivery being underpinned by specific outcomes derived from predetermined key stages of curricula. Fixed notions of the developing child are still evident, as all the curricula have key stages directly related to the age of the child. There remains an expectation that children achieve a developmentally age-appropriate level. For example, England's National Curriculum (DfE, online) promotes key stages, outlining what should be taught at each stage of schooling, with an assessment of children's performance carried out at the end of each stage. Similarly, the Northern Ireland Curriculum (Council for the Curriculum, Examinations and Assessment [CCEA], online) is divided into key stages, reflecting the achievement of milestones and building blocks of curriculum. In addition, in Scotland and Wales there is clear evidence of societal conditioning where expectations of conformity to behaviours and attitudes are clearly indicated in Scotland's four capacities (Education Scotland, online-a) and the four purposes in Wales (Welsh Government, online).

Comparing the above curricula, it could be suggested that children's academic achievement and performance are the focus of all curricula; however, each document views the child in slightly different ways and all four concepts from the model can be found within each curriculum. Whilst the authentic and political child elements aim to recognise and view children as agents of their own learning, the evidence of the developing and socially constructed child suggests adults are fundamentally responsible for what children learn.

Summary

Views of childhood have changed and will continue to change as each child continues to contribute to the reimagining of childhood well into their adulthood. Figure 6.1, whilst not exhaustive, demonstrates that childhood is not a singular concept, rather it captures the complexity and intertwining of various concepts which continue to change as society changes. Laws, policies and approaches to supporting children's educational development will continue to incorporate societal changes and in doing so will construct and reconstruct contemporary perspectives of childhood.

END-OF-CHAPTER QUESTIONS

1. Why is it difficult to define childhood?
2. Why is it important to your practice to understand childhood?
3. What changes have you experienced in practice which reflect the changing approaches to involving children in their learning?

7
Personal, social and emotional development

Marie McQuade and Irene Pollock

Key ideas

This chapter will explore:

- Non-compulsory care and education (NCE) settings offering a range of opportunities for personal, social and emotional development (PSED).
- Practitioners at all levels being responsible for children's development.
- Collaborative working with families/carers and other agencies as a way of promoting good practice.

Introduction

The role of practitioners in personal, social and emotional development (PSED) is evident across a range of non-compulsory care and education (NCE) settings. Government policy, guidance documents, change initiatives and targeted interventions aim to reduce inequalities, address lifelong outcomes, and reduce the poverty-related attainment gap. This chapter will explore how practitioners and families work together to support children's holistic development, develop family resilience, and build the foundations of warm attached relationships. The centrality of children's relationships with a key worker or trusted adult, as well as relationships with the child's family/carers, forms the basis of a collaborative working approach that provides the best outcomes for children and families. This chapter considers the benefits of high-quality NCE in supporting children's development, including the value of a highly skilled and knowledgeable workforce, and will highlight specific challenges that may emerge for practitioners when promoting children's PSED.

What is personal, social and emotional development?

Personal, social and emotional development is the development of the necessary skills and abilities for children to understand their feelings, develop independence, build relationships and develop self-esteem. These factors are considered key to healthy, secure development and children's wellbeing. The importance of warm attached relationships in children's brain development and the value of positive interactions in ensuring positive life outcomes (Conkbayir, 2021) are recognised by both theorists and policy makers, as discussed below. When practitioners view childcare through the lens of relationship-based practice, the child is automatically placed at the centre of their practice as professionals work together to support the child's holistic development.

Personal, social and emotional development is considered to be a foundation for success, happiness and positive outcomes for children (Dowling, 2014). Children's wellbeing is supported by encouraging them to build positive relationships, develop self-awareness and control, interact effectively and embed positive self-image (Dowling, 2014). Key to PSED is the importance of strong attached relationships with consistent key adults. Children who experience these positive relationships are more likely to develop resilience as they grow up (Education Scotland [ES], 2020). Attachment, as defined by Bowlby (1969), is the deep emotional bond that connects a child and an adult (see Chapter 5 for an outline of attachment theory). In 1979 Bowlby argued that children can have multiple close relationships and build firm attachments with a range of adults by the time they are 18 months old. These strong attachments can lead to high self-esteem, trusting relationships, empathy, confidence and resilience, and provide a base for the development of PSED; in contrast, children who do not experience these relationships can struggle with executive function skills later in life (Dowling, 2014). Physical contact and emotional closeness build attachment and stimulate brain development (Perry and Pollard, 1997). Practitioners who work with young children have a key role as a close, trusted and attached adult for young children in the setting. This important attachment will subsequently support the child to build other trusting relationships, develop their self-confidence and manage their own behaviours (Manning-Morton and Thorp, 2006).

THINKING POINT 7.1

1. Review whether and how you set aside meaningful times and spaces where you can spend time being close with and getting to know your key children.
2. In what ways do you speak sensitively and in a consistent way when communicating with children? How could this affect your attachment relationships?
3. Consider the ways in which you develop a 'triangle of trust' (Goldschmied and Selleck, 1996), working closely with parents/carers and valuing their understanding of their child and the home learning environment they provide.
4. How could you use daily routines to deepen key worker/child relationships, for example during nappy changing or nap times?

National policy approaches

Getting it Right for Every Child (GIRFEC) (Scottish Government [SG], 2012a) is the Scottish approach to ensuring all children develop and reach their full potential. The focus of the policy is to improve outcomes for all children by meeting their individual and unique needs. GIRFEC is a rights-based approach, interlinked with the United Nations Convention on the Rights of the Child (UNCRC) (UN, 1989), and dependent on successful partnership working between parents/carers and all services that support children and young people (see Chapter 21). GIRFEC focuses on children's development using the wellbeing indicators. These indicators provide a framework for measuring wellbeing in terms of children being Safe, Healthy, Achieving, Nurtured, Active, Respected, Responsible and Included (SHANARRI). The approach provides a consistent and shared language for professionals and requires that children and young people are agentic and involved in decisions that will affect them. GIRFEC encourages all children's services to foster an early intervention approach, promoting the wellbeing and individual needs of the child in order to avoid crisis interventions in their futures (Rose, 2012).

Scotland's GIRFEC framework is augmented by the early learning and childcare guidance Realising the Ambition (RtA) (ES, 2020), which centres on the learning environment for the youngest children, highlighting what children need to grow, develop and learn. Realising the Ambition focuses on the interactions, experiences and spaces, both indoors and outdoors, that best support a child's learning and development; the document highlights the practitioner's role in developing these environments. It maintains a focus on babies, toddlers and young children, and shows how the quality of interactions children have with sensitive adults will fundamentally impact on not only their experience of childcare, but also on their emotional resilience, wellbeing and development. This document works in tandem with the national Curriculum for Excellence (SG, 2008b), which features the health and wellbeing experiences and outcomes which children are expected to achieve throughout their time in education and childcare from ages 3 to 18.

In England, the Early Years Foundation Stage (EYFS) (Department for Education [DfE], 2021b) is the framework that supports practitioners to deliver the outcomes and experiences required for children from birth to 5. The EYFS focuses explicitly on PSED, breaking it down into three key aspects:

- **Self-confidence and self-awareness**

  The first aspect highlights the expectation that children be supported to develop confidence in who they are, in how they express themselves and in what they can achieve. Practitioners should provide children with the understanding that they are cared for as individuals and that their contribution is valued.

- **Managing feelings and behaviour**

  Managing feelings refers to how adults support children to understand their own and other people's feelings and how they learn to moderate and manage these. Children need the support of sensitive and attached adults to help them to navigate their emotions.

- **Forming relationships**

  The final aspect concerns how children learn to build positive relationships with both peers and adults. Practitioners can support children to empathise with others and to see situations from another point of view. By supporting the development of this aspect, practitioners can help to scaffold children's friendships and, by modelling high-quality and sensitive interactions, can support children to develop personally, socially and emotionally.

Wales and Ireland take a similarly focused view on the importance of PSED through the delivery of key policies and curricula, including Northern Ireland's Curriculum Guidance for Pre-School Education (Department of Education [NI], 2018) and the Welsh Foundation Phase Framework (Revised) (Welsh Government, 2015). In addition to the focus on PSED within curricula and guidance documents in all four UK nations, legislation and government policies have been enacted that aim to reduce inequalities and support the closure of the poverty-related attainment gap (Sosu and Ellis, 2014). To this end, a range of targeted interventions are made available to those who most need support. Practitioners are key to the delivery of these policies and, through building relationships and understanding the communities in which they work, will ultimately positively influence outcomes for the children and families in their services.

Early intervention and prevention policies in particular are a current priority across the UK nations, aiming to identify those at the highest risk of poor outcomes and provide direct and, where possible, preventative support to children and families. Effective early intervention programmes aim to prevent problems and challenges from occurring, or to address them quickly before the challenge becomes insurmountable (Allen, 2011). By offering early support, negative outcomes such as low educational attainment or poor physical and mental health can be avoided or lessened. Early intervention and prevention approaches are also known to help build resilience and the skills to help address future challenges.

Evidence from a range of studies shows that high-quality childcare can make a significant difference to children's lives, particularly when they are growing up in more disadvantaged circumstances (Scobie and Scott, 2017). The Growing Up in Scotland (SG, 2015) study is a significant longitudinal research project tracking the experiences of a large number of children in Scotland through their early years and beyond, while the OECD's (2021) Starting Strong VI report is subtitled 'Supporting meaningful interactions in early childhood education and care' and includes data from 26 countries, including the UK. Such studies provide critical information that helps inform the development of children's services, government policies and can help practitioners in all fields to understand national and local trends.

One aspect of enabling effective interventions for PSED is financial. In 2019, for example, the European Commission (EC) noted the positive impact of affordable care for school-aged children as a lever for reducing poverty and enabling access to the labour market for parents (EC, 2019). In England, Wales and Northern Ireland, children aged 3 and 4 are offered 30 hours of free childcare per week (NI Direct Government Services, 2022; UK Government, 2022; Welsh Government, 2022b). More targeted support in Scotland, in addition to existing funding streams for pre-school children, is the offer of funded early learning and childcare to 2-year-olds who are most likely to benefit from early access. This policy aims to support children's development, including social skills, language and literacy, while providing parents with the opportunity to enter or re-enter work, training or study (SG, 2017a).

———————————— VIEW FROM PRACTICE ————————————

Early years setting for eligible 2-year-olds

Following the expansion of funded hours in 2021, the service manager has brought together the nursery team for a staff meeting to discuss the extension of their service to eligible 2-year-olds. Drawing on documents such as RtA (ES, 2020) as well as local guidance and published research, they work together to produce an analysis that will help them plan for changes that may be needed to support the wellbeing needs of the younger group of children (see Table 7.1).

Table 7.1   Early years settings and 2-year-olds

What do 2-year-olds need to feel happy and safe?	What kind of practitioners do 2-year-olds need?
Support from responsive and skilled adults	Consistent and responsive
Environments that are the correct scale for them to be independent	Understand and are trained in working with children from birth to 3
Access to suitable spaces for sleep and rest when they need it	Familiar with guidance and documentation supporting younger children
Safe environments, free from clutter	Understand the importance of schematic play
Warm and stable relationships with a consistent key worker	Know how to create nurturing environments
Nurturing relationships	Offer opportunities to make friends and build relationships
Support to manage their feelings and emotions	Listen and pay attention
Regular routines	Offer praise and encouragement to help support emotional regulation and development
Consistent social groupings	
Opportunities for play indoors and outdoors	Meet the needs of the individual, understanding that children develop in different ways
Opportunities for risky play within safe boundaries	Help to involve parents in their children's learning
Pretend play to reflect their homes, wider environment and culture	Well-tuned to children's non-verbal communications
Opportunities for sensory play	Give them time and space to wallow in their play and exploration
Support to understand and communicate their feelings and needs	Enjoy language, rhyme, music and stories

———————————— VIEW FROM PRACTICE ————————————

Learning through play in prisons

Learning Together Through Play is a programme which provides prisoners with opportunities to improve attachments with their children so that relationships are more likely to stay strong, leading to more positive outcomes for the children (Early Years Scotland, online). Early years practitioners work directly with fathers and mothers to support early attachment and bonding and to build an understanding of their children's development, including the importance of play. Alongside the learning sessions, families attend play sessions which provide opportunities for prisoners and their young children and families to interact, to improve attachment and confidence, and to play and learn together. Most of all, these services provide valuable opportunities for children to feel that they have a bond and relationship with their father or mother while they are in prison. Almost all parents involved say that access to the programme improves and strengthens their relationship with their child and family.

THINKING POINT 7.2

1. How is children's wellbeing assessed in your setting?
2. What could 2-year-olds (if applicable) benefit from in your setting?
3. What challenges might practitioners face in developing high-quality and effective environments for 2-year-olds or for children with imprisoned parents?

Challenges of promoting personal, social and emotional development

As outlined above, relationships with caregivers are an important factor in PSED. Particularly for young children who are not yet verbal, sharing information with caregivers allows both the setting and the caregivers to provide the best care possible (Barnes et al., 2016). For older children as well, a free flow of information between the setting and the home allows for early intervention if any issues arise, for example around bullying or a change in a child's behaviour. However, for some settings, particularly those that cater to working parents/carers such as out-of-school care provision or private nurseries that offer full days, engaging caregivers can be more challenging. These settings may have very minimal contact with parents/carers due to their busy schedules. Further, raising concerns around emotional development can be a sensitive topic, not well suited to a hurried conversation as the caregiver leaves for or returns from work. Restrictions in contact due to the COVID-19 pandemic have encouraged all settings to reconsider how they engage with parents/carers.

---------- **VIEW FROM PRACTICE** ----------

School-aged childcare

Low Income Families Together (LIFT), a school-aged childcare organisation in Scotland, discovered through engagement with families that a lack of childcare was having a significant impact, particularly single parents who had no-one to help with after-school care. Childcare was mostly required for one or two hours while parents worked. Local schools finish around 3.30 pm and there was little after-school care available to support families. The charity decided to trial a flexible childcare after-school programme with a cost to parents of just 50p.

Provision of a safe environment resulted in improved mental well-being. Staff understood that children who have challenging behaviour might benefit from a more relaxed childcare service, allowing them to spend time with friends, meet new people and build their confidence. Children felt ownership of their space as they were encouraged to take the lead in decision making and programme delivery of the service. Children planned for outdoor activities, including football and games, as well as arts and crafts. In future, the setting hopes to introduce homework help sessions to further support their families.

Another potential challenge for practitioners in supporting PSED is a lack of cultural awareness. While equality and diversity training is a part of many qualifications (National Occupational Standards, online), such training may be superficial, for example focusing on religious beliefs or dietary requirements (Ashurt, 2019). Practitioners should not assume that Western values such as independent thought are shared by all families (Cousin, 2011). For example, in cultures with more power distance, children are taught that it is disrespectful to make direct eye contact (le Roux, 2002) or to contradict an adult (Oetzel et al., 2003). A practitioner who is not aware of these characteristics may wrongly assume that the child is autistic or that the child lacks confidence in stating their preferences. Another aspect of cultural differences may be in how acceptable it is for boys to express their emotions. Collectivist cultures tend to emphasise self-control, and therefore discourage crying (Jellesma and Vingerhoets, 2012). A final example of potential conflict can occur within cultures, such as working-class families finding it unacceptable for children to dress up in clothes of the opposite sex (Freeman, 2007). All of these issues demonstrate the importance of not only being aware of a child's cultural heritage, but of also considering how the child's experiences at home may influence their development and behaviour in NCE settings.

Although some elements of a child's PSED will be related to their experiences outside of the setting, such as the cultural differences discussed above, practitioners must also be aware of the ways in which some aspects of development are affected by a range of additional support needs (ASN). In early years settings, children will often not have a formal diagnosis, but practitioners should be alert to difficulties in socialising, a lack of flexibility, or unusual use of language. A good awareness of 'normal' PSED is required in order to identify when children's development may be lagging (ES, 2020). As discussed below, close links with health visitors can help. As outlined in Scotland's GIRFEC approach (SG, 2012a), children may also experience temporary disruptions to their development, for example as a result of illness, a bereavement or the arrival of a new sibling. All of these occurrences, as well as other issues such as child protection concerns, may cause a regression in both a child's physical and emotional development (McDonald et al., 2012).

Whether children's PSED needs are the result of a temporary situation, or whether they are related to an underlying condition, practitioners need to be confident in providing Additional Support for Learning. Trauma-informed practice provides a range of useful tools to help both children/young people and practitioners to develop resilience (Nicholson et al., 2018; see also Chapter 8 in this volume). Language assistance, whether this is increasing children's emotional vocabulary (Emotion Works, 2021) or providing key phrases for children to use (Haines, 2000), is widely applicable. Boardmaker symbols or other tools can be helpful for non-verbal children (Cafiero, 2012). Additional techniques that may be required could include anger management strategies such as the 'Take Five' breathing technique (Wiltshire Council, 2020) or the use of social stories to navigate tricky situations (Karkhaneh et al., 2010). The child with PSED difficulties should not, however, be the sole focus. It is essential to have age-appropriate conversations with the other children in the setting to develop their understanding and to support their interactions (Mowat, 2015).

All of the above suggestions for effectively addressing PSED rely on staff with appropriate training and the soft skills (SG, 2012b) to build relationships with children, parents/carers and other stakeholders. However, sourcing training to meet children's needs can be an additional challenge, with issues such as availability, relevance and cost (both of courses and of cover to allow staff to attend) all contributing to a lack of suitably qualified staff. This issue is compounded by high levels of staff turnover, particularly in out-of-school care settings (Siraj and Kingston, 2015). Staff turnover not only affects the expertise available, but also requires the establishment of new relationships. Unfortunately, children's ASN in relation to PSED can often be a source of burn-out for staff (Colton and Roberts, 2006). In addition to the interactions with children themselves, practitioners need the confidence to raise concerns about PSED with parents/carers.

--- **THINKING POINT 7.3** ---

1. What training or professional learning have you identified that would support your PSED practice?
2. How could children with ASN be better supported in your setting?
3. Can you identify any potential cultural barriers for the families that access your setting?

Collaborative working to promote PSED

As with many aspects of the NCE sector, relationships are central to supporting children's PSED. The key relationship is between the practitioner and the child or young person. However, a range of other relationships are also essential for the most effective support. As discussed above, working with families/carers allows for holistic development. A whole-family approach also encourages family resilience, which can set the foundation for the family to tackle challenges even after the child has left the setting (Khanlou and Wray, 2014). In order for the practitioner and setting to offer this support, a trusting relationship must be established. This process takes time, and requires multiple positive interactions (Knopf and Swick, 2007). Given the time pressures on families and settings, and the restrictions arising from the COVID-19 pandemic, careful planning is necessary to enable these interactions.

Parents/carers may also be struggling with their own social and emotional wellbeing (White, 2017). Parental support classes, such as Triple P (Sanders and Mazzucchelli, 2017) and Incredible Years (Saunders et al., 2020), are aimed at developing parents' skills as well as providing them with tools to engage more effectively with their children. However, encouraging parents/carers to access such classes is a sensitive topic and must be approached cautiously in order to increase the likelihood of attendance (Lindsay et al., 2011). Practitioners must be careful to avoid patronising families or suggesting deficiencies, as this may undermine their relationship.

However, practitioners can support families to promote PSED through the implementation of effective family learning approaches (ES, online-b). Family learning is a process whereby practitioners encourage and support family members to work and learn together, with a focus on intergenerational learning. This can enable parents and carers to learn skills to help support their children's development.

———————— VIEW FROM PRACTICE ————————

Family learning

We decided to try the Peep Learning Together Programme (Peeple, online) to help increase parental engagement and help support transitions between local early years settings and our school. The early years practitioner based in the nursery was trained to deliver the programme, where parents and children enjoy activities and discussions together that are focused on aspects of children's learning and development. Peep sessions develop understanding, raise awareness and show how sharing books and stories, singing and rhymes, talking and playing together can help strengthen relationships and develop children's communication skills. Parents say that their involvement with the Peep Learning Together Programme has had a positive impact on their relationship with their child and, in addition, has improved their understanding of the impact they can have on their child's learning. Staff also reported the value of establishing relationships with families and how this helped support both parents and children in the transition to school.

Collaborative working thus extends beyond relationships with families to include a range of public and third-sector organisations. The benefits of collaborative working are discussed in depth in Chapter 21; this section will discuss specifically how involving other organisations supports children's PSED. It is useful to consider three categories of organisations that are relevant for PSED: health, education and the third sector. Nurseries will have the most contact with health visitors, while for referrals and for children of school age the child's GP is involved. For the most serious concerns, Child and Adolescent Mental Health Services (CAMHS) will be accessed; however, this service has long waiting lists, with 27.5% of children waiting more than 18 weeks following referral (Public Health Scotland, 2021). Educational psychologists, who may be associated with CAMHS or with the local authority, can provide expert advice to the setting.

With regard to education, schools may be involved with NCE settings as children transition from nursery, as partners for out-of-school care services including childminding, or if the setting provides a service such as respite care. Regular communication with teachers or auxiliary staff about children's challenges and support needs allows for continuous care. A wide range of third-sector organisations support children's PSED. For example, Who Cares? Scotland (2022) provides targeted support for care-experienced children and young people; this population is more likely to have attachment difficulties and benefits particularly from continuity (Stein, 2008). The Child Poverty Action Group (2022) seeks solutions for children living in poverty across the UK, ensuring that their basic needs are met so that the children are better able to attend to PSED (Saitadze and Lalayants, 2021). Finally, many third-sector organisations in the UK are targeted at particular ASN that may affect PSED, such as the National Autistic Society (2022), the ENABLE Scotland (2021) group for learning disabilities, and I CAN (2021) for speech and language difficulties. While the NCE setting may not directly work with these organisations, having an awareness of their work allows practitioners to provide signposting for parents/carers.

Collaborative working, although a commitment of time (Rodd, 2013), means that practitioners do not need to be experts in every area (see also Chapters 17 and 21). While their relationships with the children are the most direct for supporting PSED, and their knowledge of individual children is essential for creating care plans, practitioners are not expected to fulfil every need. Practitioners' own awareness of their professional relationships is also important for modelling (Siraj-Blatchford et al., 2002: 32). Working within playroom teams is also beneficial for both the practitioner and child, as engaging with a range of adults helps to develop relationships and promotes resilience, while children who have attachments to multiple caregivers are better able to adapt to change (Rolfe, 2004).

Summary

To conclude, this chapter has illustrated the importance of personal, social and emotional development for children and young people. It has considered government policy approaches, as well as elements of pedagogy within NCE settings, that may influence this aspect of development. A focus on early intervention and targeted approaches in all four countries has been highlighted. Challenges to good practice are considered, and the importance of effective collaborative working discussed. It is possible to conclude that highly effective practitioners can have an impact on ensuring the best outcomes for young children, enabling young children to deepen and broaden their learning and develop confidence, curiosity and creativity. Parents and carers are undoubtedly the most important influences on children's lives. However, it is clear that practitioners in NCE have the opportunity to support the family as well as the child, and that they play a key role in promoting children's PSED through relationship building, modelling good practice and offering targeted support when necessary.

END-OF-CHAPTER QUESTIONS

1. What organisations that promote PSED does your setting work with in health? In education? In the third sector?
2. What existing relationships could be developed further?
3. How could you enhance the opportunities for collaborative working in your setting to support children's PSED?

8

Attachment-focused and trauma-aware early Childhood Practice

Christine McKee and Mark Breslin

Key ideas

This chapter will explore:

- Attachment theory and patterns of attachment.
- The role of the professional caregiver in building relationships and attachments with children.
- Trauma and adversity in childhood.
- The impact of adverse childhood experiences (ACEs) on development.
- Whether poor outcomes are an inevitable consequence of ACEs.

Introduction

Noddings (2012: 777) suggests that creating 'a climate in which caring relations flourish' should be the objective of all involved in education and that this should underpin all we do: 'When that climate is established and maintained, everything else goes better' (Noddings, 2012: 777). She is not alone in supporting a narrative which prioritises compassion, nurture and the building of relationships to support children's wellbeing. Indeed, Scotland's national guidance for early years states that the focus of early learning and childcare (ELC) should be to support children to 'form a secure and emotionally resilient attachment base' (Education Scotland [ES], 2020: 14). The professional standards required by the General Teaching Council for Scotland (GTCS) (2021: 5) include the need to understand 'the importance of positive and purposeful relationships to provide and ensure a safe and secure environment … within a caring and compassionate ethos'.

Knowledge of child development, understanding how attachment theory informs this as well as appreciating the impact of early adversity on children are all becoming key areas of concern for educationalists across the world (see Chapter 5). Ellenbogen et al. (2014) examine how quality ELC in Canada may promote resilience in maltreated children, while in the US Shirvanian and Michael (2017) consider how attachment-based childcare can improve the lives of children. Trauma-informed education is given considerable attention in Australia (Tobin, 2016; Riley, 2013; Australian Childhood Foundation, 2010), while the Attachment Aware Schools (AAS) project in England is reporting some success with regard to pupil outcomes (Kelly et al., 2020; Rose et al., 2019).

This chapter will seek to explore the key theories and evidence supporting this focus on relational-based strategies and interventions in early education. We will consider attachment theory (Bowlby, 1969) and its significance for education practitioners. An examination of what is meant by 'trauma' and adverse childhood experiences (ACEs) (Felitti et al., 1998) will follow before we discuss what the latest findings from neuroscience add to practitioners' understanding of children.

Attachment theory

Attachment theory first emerged in the 1950s when John Bowlby started to draw attention to the impact of disruption to the relationship between a child and their primary caregiver, usually the mother, in the early years (Bretherton, 1992). The main tenet of the theory, which was further developed in collaboration with Mary Ainsworth in the following decades, focused on the child's need to have a close and consistent relationship with a primary caregiver who attunes and responds sensitively to their needs, or as Crittenden (2017: 438) expresses it, 'the universal innate propensity of humans to form protective and comforting relationships'. Bowlby based his findings on observations he made of children who had been separated from their mothers (Page, 2018) and concluded that the healthy social and emotional development of children was directly related to the stability of this primal attachment relationship. The 'secure base' which such a relationship provides is crucial to the child's developing sense of trust and safety as well as their sense of self and others (Geddes, 2017). It is this secure base which gives the developing child the confidence to explore the world, to eventually form new relationships (Page, 2018) and, in time, a readiness to learn (Shirvanian and Michael, 2017).

Essentially, if we are fed when hungry, given warmth when cold, comforted when distressed, we learn that we are both loved and worthy of love. Conversely, if we are neglected, abused and dismissed we learn that we cannot rely on others (in spite of our fundamental need for survival) and we learn distrust and fear. It is this 'internal working model' (Bowlby, 1980, 1973), this 'emerging sense of the self and who others are' (Geddes, 2017: 39), which can heavily influence behaviour as the child grows up, attends nursery and goes to school (Ainsworth, 1979). Charlwood and Steele (2004) summarise a number of studies which found that securely attached infants are more compliant, sociable, empathic and less dependent on their teachers than insecurely attached children. In pre-school settings, those who are securely attached display 'optimal patterns of peer relations and adjustment' and achieve more academically when they go to school (Charlwood and Steele, 2004: 62). In contrast, those with an insecure attachment may struggle with impulse control, behave aggressively and demonstrate 'antisocial behaviours, emotional dependency and difficulties in relating to peers' (Charlwood and Steele, 2004: 62). Practitioners will undoubtedly observe the outward expression of much of this in their daily lives as children navigate their way through the relationships they encounter during their time in education.

Attachment patterns

The work of Ainsworth (1979: 932) identified different 'attachment patterns' in children depending on how reliably and consistently their needs had been met by their caregiver (Page, 2018). These patterns sought to categorise the typical behaviours of children with similar early relational experiences. The four principal categorisations will be considered in turn: secure, avoidant, ambivalent/resistant and disorganised attachment (Geddes, 2017).

The securely attached child has developed in an optimal environment with a carer who has met their needs lovingly and consistently. This child's internal working model tells them that others are available and that the environment in which they find themselves is manageable (Baldry and Moscardini, 2010). They are typically confident, cooperative and engaged in learning. They are socially competent and trusting, they play well together and can process distress in the knowledge that they have a secure base upon which to fall back (Geddes, 2017). It is no surprise then that this is linked to success in education as secure attachment 'liberates children to explore their world' (Bergin and Bergin, 2009: 142).

Those with avoidant attachment patterns will appear self-reliant and indifferent to a relationship with their teacher. They will not seek help but suppress emotions in an act of defence against the rejection they have felt from their inconsistent caregiver (Baldry and Moscardini, 2010). They may view others as potentially hurtful and as such their environment as threatening, caught as they are between 'their biological drive to contact the attachment figure and anger toward the attachment figure' (Bergin and Bergin, 2009: 143).

Ambivalent attachment is often illustrated by persistent attention-seeking behaviours (Geddes, 2017) which can frustrate and overwhelm education practitioners. Emotions may be exaggerated in order to gain proximity to the attachment figure and yet the child appears unable to be soothed when such proximity is achieved. Their chronic need to protect themselves from what they perceive as a chaotic and unpredictable environment can result in incessant controlling or hyperactive behaviour (Geddes, 2017; Baldry and Moscardini, 2010).

In the case of disorganised attachment patterns, the child's early environment may have been frightening. This has left them with 'no coherent method for dealing with stress' (Baldry and Moscardini, 2010: 5) and their behaviour can be aggressive and dysregulated. They may have little trust in their teachers, can be hyper-vigilant and respond with defiance (Geddes, 2017). In cases of insecure attachment, Geddes (2017: 42) highlights that these behaviours are often the different means by which children get noticed as she states 'in the absence of a capacity to communicate distress in words, it is behaviour through which vulnerable children communicate their distress, for behaviour is a form of communication'. These children are often defending themselves against powerful patterns of thought and employing different mechanisms for coping in a world in which their needs have not been adequately met. In Crittenden's words (2017: 440), 'we humans, from the first moments of life and in all contexts, have the capacity to organise around the threats that we experience so as to survive and thrive'. So if behaviour is viewed this way, as a means to minimise threat, as an attempt to survive, as communication of a need for protection and nurture, then perhaps, as practitioners, we begin to respond with empathy and, importantly, with increased effectiveness.

————— THINKING POINT 8.1 —————

Think of some of the behaviours you may have witnessed in educational or childcare settings. If all behaviour is communication, what do you think the child was communicating?

The role of the professional caregiver

Awareness of attachment patterns is only part of the equation, though, as another important aspect of attachment theory is the recognition that others beyond the mother can become attachment figures for children (Rose et al., 2019; Ainsworth, 1979) and hence, it is hoped, that their internal working model is open to change (Geddes, 2003). As research into teacher–child relationships expands (Verschueren and Koomen, 2012), the suggestion that 'the teacher is imbued with attachment potential' (Geddes, 2003: 233) seems reasonable. Some suggest that considerable improvements can be made as caregivers build relationships and attachments with children (Baldry and Moscardini, 2010). Bergin and Bergin (2009: 155) highlight that very young children are more likely to develop a secure relationship with their teacher but that slightly older school-aged children may also establish a powerful relationship with their teacher if the latter behaves in 'ways that disconfirm the insecure child's internal working models'. In addition, it cannot be denied that the multiple responsibilities of the early years worker (to care, teach, protect, nurture, assess, evaluate, amongst others) (Whitters, 2020) mean that this role in particular lends itself to the development of such a relationship.

The behaviour of all who care for and educate children, then, is crucial for the social and emotional health of the children in their charge. With attachment theory in mind, the need to be 'responsive and sensitive' (Page and Elfer, 2013: 556) becomes more pertinent. It could be argued that the key person approach favoured in many early years settings across the UK is indeed an attachment-focused system (Elfer, 2006). If relationships are truly prioritised within this system, then we may agree; but as Page (2018) suggests, practical difficulties often impact negatively on the effectiveness of this policy and reality is frequently more nuanced than policy may assume. Issues include shift patterns and the difficulties of ensuring continuity as well as consistency of approach within settings, and the emotional exhaustion of carers (Page and Elfer, 2013; Elfer et al., 2011). Others argue that the key person approach limits children's opportunities for socialising with other staff and peers (Elfer, 2006). That said, one Scottish nursery's ambition to put 'attachment' into action in their setting included restructuring staff rotas so that staff worked condensed hours over fewer days, ensuring that more consistency was in place for the children (Cherry, 2021). For Ellenbogen et al. (2014), the difference between high- and low-quality day care is substantial in terms of its impact on the healthy development of children, and they suggest that children receive care from no more than four adults, be in groups of no more than 15 and that carers should avoid being too controlling.

Returning to Noddings (2012), the concept of 'professional love' (Page and Elfer, 2013) merits attention as it is this which, it is theorised, enhances children's emotional and cognitive development (Page, 2018). Defined as 'a legitimate discursive interlocutor which recognises and affirms the existence and importance of loving relationships between professionals and young children' (Page, 2018: 138), it is this that is needed in order to embrace approaches which focus on relationships. While we may shy away from a discourse which revolves around love, perhaps it is a 'pedagogy of love' which is needed (Page, 2018: 136). In Scotland, the importance of high-quality interactions within the context of a safe emotional space is reiterated throughout the latest national practical guidance for early years professionals and we are reminded to be 'mind-minded', that is, 'to think of children as having thoughts, feelings and plans that we need to respond to and respect' (ES, 2020: 32). In Finland, care and education are given equal status (Page, 2018), as a fundamental aspect of the role of the nursery teacher includes building close affectionate relationships with children to the extent that trainees are taught about 'caregiving' as well as teaching and learning (Horppu and Ikonen-Varila, 2004).

In recognition of the idea that a secure base/strong attachment is 'the dimension that underpins all others' (Baldry and Moscardini, 2010: 8), examples of how education professionals are putting these theories into practice are beginning to emerge. While there is not space here to examine all aspects of nurture, it is an approach which is founded on attachment theory. Nurturing approaches have been successfully and extensively promoted in establishments across Glasgow, not just at targeted groups of children but as whole establishment policies (March and Kearney, 2017). As a result, attendance has increased and exclusions have decreased (March and Kearney, 2017). In an attempt to improve their pupils' ability to self-regulate and meet their emotional needs, three primary headteachers in Scotland implemented 'teddy bear policies' (Zeedyk, 2020). This involved placing teddy bears all over their school and using them in creative ways to boost children's sense of emotional safety. In England, Attachment Aware School projects have been implemented with many of these including training for staff, the development of new policies around behaviour management and transitions as well as making alterations to physical spaces and closer collaboration with parents (Kelly et al., 2020). All of these point to a shift in narrative within which a holistic view of the child matches a desire to view disruptive behaviour as an expression of need, a narrative in which we are asked to consider not what is wrong with our children but what has happened to them.

──────── VIEW FROM PRACTICE ────────

Taking steps to alter a child's negative image of self

Joseph was three-and-a-half when he was adopted so had been with his adoptive parents for just over a year by the time he started school. He was a lively boy with plenty of energy. At school he struggled to sit still and was often in trouble for walking round the class, shouting out and disrupting learning. His teacher gave him a 'behaviour chart' to bring home every night. Each section of the day was stamped with a sad or a happy face depending on his behaviour. Joseph did not seem to care how many happy faces he achieved; indeed his teacher reported that he often seemed to act out in order to get a sad face. Input from a therapist later helped Joseph's parents and teachers understand that much of his behaviour was instinctive rather than intentional and that viewing it through a lens of compliance or non-compliance was ineffective with him. Indeed, his apparent desire for sad faces may well reflect the negative image he has of himself, one which he feels comfortable with because this is the one he knows, one which he feels he needs to reinforce in order to feel safe. With this knowledge, Joseph's teacher stopped using the behaviour chart and instead began to focus on building his self-esteem.

THINKING POINT 8.2

When considering the use of the word 'trauma', what do you think of? How would you define it?

Trauma and adversity in childhood

It is important to clarify what is meant here by the term 'trauma'. Natural disasters, wars and major life events are perhaps what first come to mind when thinking about trauma but this constitutes only a superficial understanding of the concept. Single incidents like these which are shorter in duration are considered simple trauma (though this is not intended to belittle it) while complex trauma refers to multiple, ongoing incidents which are usually experienced interpersonally (NHS Education for Scotland, 2017). Examples of this may include abuse, bullying and domestic violence. Developmental trauma is that which causes rupture of the attachment relationship between a child and their primary caregiver, potentially resulting in profound developmental impairment or delay (Tobin, 2016; Australian Childhood Foundation, 2010). Given the malleable nature of the child's rapidly developing brain, they are even more vulnerable to such trauma, which may include neglect, abuse or living with family violence. These can be the most stressful experiences of a child's life as the interpersonal nature of such trauma 'undermines the very resource that can help children recover – the stability and predictability of their connections with others' (Australian Childhood Foundation, 2010: 13).

NHS Education for Scotland (2017: 7) suggests that recognising and responding to trauma is 'everyone's business' and as such it is this view that informs the framework for the Scottish workforce. Experience of trauma is widespread (Tobin, 2016) and what this means for education practitioners will be discussed below. First, let us consider the evidence that has brought trauma and adversity to the forefront.

Adverse childhood experiences (ACEs)

ACEs can be defined as 'those experiences which require significant adaptation by the developing child in terms of psychological, social and neurodevelopmental systems, and which are outside of the normal expected environment' (Lacey and Minnis, 2020: 117). Ten such adversities were the focus of the first ACE study, which was carried out in the US during the 1990s. These were categorised under three broad headings: abuse, neglect and household dysfunction (Felitti et al., 1998). Participants' total out of 10 became their ACE score and findings suggested a correlation between a score of four or more and various mental and physical health conditions, social outcomes and health-harming behaviours. The commonality of ACEs has since been highlighted in a number of contexts and much attention has been paid to the impact of early experiences (NHS Health Scotland, 2019; Mersky et al., 2017). For example, 50% of the adult population of Wales is reported to have experienced at least one ACE with 13.5% experiencing four or more (Di Lemma et al., 2019). Those with four or more, according to Di Lemma et al. (2019: 8), are three times more likely to develop heart or respiratory disease and 16 times more likely to use substances like heroin.

Clearly, enhanced awareness of the impact of early adversity has the potential to alter societal views as we consider more what may lie behind certain behaviours and conditions. Through such a lens, we may shame less and seek to intervene earlier in order to prevent further adversity (NHS Health Scotland, 2019); we may view others with more compassion and begin to consider what we can do to mitigate the effects of adversity. That said, since the Felitti et al. (1998) study, many have criticised both the categorisation and the focus on scores. Lacey and Minnis (2020) caution against the over-simplification of the ACE approach and argue that there are issues with both the concept and the measurement of adversity. They are joined by others in suggesting that other adverse experiences should be equally considered, namely poverty, parenting style (Lacey and Minnis, 2020), social marginalisation (Davidson et al., 2020), bullying, discrimination and parental bereavement (Mowat, 2019). In terms of measuring ACEs, it is argued that considering them cumulatively means that each ACE is weighed equally, when in reality that is rarely the case. Similarly, it does not allow for the impact of each individual ACE to be adequately assessed (Lacey and Minnis, 2020; Mersky et al., 2017). On a more general level, there is a danger that the ACE approach over-emphasises deficits (Davidson et al., 2020) and that poor outcomes are considered inevitable, when, in reality, the resilience of individuals and the effectiveness of a myriad of interventions prove otherwise. We should avoid, then, 'deterministic messages' (Lacey and Minnis, 2020: 126) about ACEs as we seek to introduce policies and practices which respond to our awareness of their impact.

———————————— **THINKING POINT 8.3** ————————————

Consider whether knowing a child's 'ACE score' has an impact on how you as an education professional would treat that child. If so, why? If not, why?

The neuroscience of adversity

In spite of recent advances in neuroscience, we still know relatively little about the brain (Satchwell-Hirst, 2017). That said, several key principles of neurodevelopment are generally accepted and offer some interesting insights for practitioners. The work of Perry (2009) is significant here and he offers us three broad areas which are useful starting points: the fact that the brain develops sequentially from the bottom up; that brain development is use-dependent; and that healthy relationships have the power to both protect from and heal the wounds caused by trauma (Perry, 2009: 244).

The 'normal' human brain develops from the brain stem pre-birth upwards through the limbic system and finally the cortex (Australian Childhood Foundation, 2010). This vertical, sequential development begins with basic survival functions like the control of heartrate and blood pressure (brain stem). It is this part of the brain which responds to threat, real and imagined, throughout the lifespan (van der Kolk, 2014). The limbic system is our emotional centre and the store for our sensory unconscious memories. Trauma can have a substantial impact on this area of the brain. Finally, the cortex is our thinking brain where we reason and consciously process thoughts, memories and reflections (Australian Childhood Foundation, 2010). The significance of this sequential process lies in the fact that the development of each area is reliant on the healthy functioning and growth of the areas 'below' it. As Perry (2009: 242) explains, 'the organisation of higher parts of the brain depends upon input from the lower parts of the brain', therefore if trauma occurs during the early months of life (or even pre-birth) when the lower regions of the brain are particularly sensitive to disruption then there is the risk of a 'cascade of dysfunction' (Perry, 2009: 242) as the child's brain develops.

Let us explore this in more detail. Bessel van der Kolk's (2014) seminal work *The Body Keeps the Score* elucidates the true impact of early trauma on the child's developing brain. Where the mind may not remember what has happened, the physiological changes which occur in the body as a result may have long-lasting consequences. These may include 'a recalibration of the brain's alarm system, an increase in stress hormone activity, and alterations in the system that filters relevant information from irrelevant' (van der Kolk, 2014: 3). When a child finds themself facing adversity, where there is a perceived threat to their survival, that part of the brain which is responsible for survival (the brain stem) will respond (Lyons, 2017). Fight, flight or freeze reactions will be initiated in a highly effective evolutionary attempt to adapt and remain alive. However, if that adversity or perceived threat is prolonged and a sense of safety is not achieved, the child may remain in this heightened state of alert even when in a 'safe' environment. The brain's smoke detector (or stress-response system) may remain hypersensitive to stimuli which are not in fact life-threatening – a loud noise, for example, or a new teacher (van der Kolk, 2014). The prefrontal cortex, that part of the brain which eventually determines whether the 'smoke' is life-threatening or a simple case of burnt toast, does not get the opportunity to turn on and do its job (van der Kolk, 2014). As Perry (2009: 244) states, '[t]he neural networks involved in this adaptive response will undergo a "use-dependent alteration" and normal development is hampered'.

Gerin et al. (2019) characterise the changes in the brain as 'developmental recalibrations' which are 'adaptive within the context of maltreatment and confer short-term functional advantages' but which also 'incur long-term costs … as the individual may not be optimised to cope with the demands of more normative environments' (Gerin et al., 2019: 312). Neuroimaging confirms that the typical links that the normally developing brain makes between the amygdala, which responds to danger, and the regulatory frontal cortical regions, which assess the degree of danger, are less clear in the brains of maltreated children (Gerin et al., 2019). We begin to understand, then, how children with such histories may struggle with the busy, often unpredictable social and educational environments in which they find themselves; how they may be unable to connect with their key worker, learn effectively or form trusting relationships (Cozolino, 2013). We may also begin to appreciate that interventions must begin with regulation of the child's body via 'patterned, repetitive neural input' (music, movement, breathing, for example) in order to soothe (Perry, 2009: 243) before reasoning with their mind.

How the brain is used, then, will determine how it develops. Recent discoveries in neuroscience illustrate that new pathways can be formed in the brain, highlighting its neuroplasticity or capacity for change (van der Kolk, 2014). This is indeed a message of hope. There is recognition that the presence of at least one supportive carer provides a buffer against developmental trauma (Scottish Adverse Childhood Experiences Hub, 2017), therefore the significance of the role of education practitioners and caregivers cannot be overestimated. Furthermore, 'supportive, encouraging, and caring relationships stimulate students' neural circuitry to learn, priming their brains for neuroplastic processes' (Cozolino, 2013: 17). Poor outcomes across the lifespan are not inevitable if we prioritise relationships and aim to build resilience, self-esteem and emotional regulation skills (Di Lemma et al., 2019).

Summary

So, in essence, we circle back to Bowlby and his theory of attachment. His views from decades ago on the internal working model and its capacity for change are echoed in recent findings from neuroscience as we recognise the fundamental need that human beings have for connection with others. We survive and thrive in the context of our relationships with others: 'we are not only wired to connect, but we are also wired to attune to, resonate with, and learn from others ... we are also wired to need others to treat us with care and compassion' (Cozolino, 2013: 13). If we are to be truly attachment-focused and trauma-informed in our settings then it is this focus on compassion which must predominate. Safe physical and emotional environments, a focus on wellbeing, asking what has happened to children, and interventions which support self-regulation are all necessary (ES, 2018b). Supporting parents in their role is crucial as is early identification of adversity (Di Lemma et al., 2019). Opportunities to 'positively re-experience physiological sensations' through movement and meditation may also help (Tobin, 2016: 12), as would encouraging children to recognise and name their emotions. Above all, though, it is the 'presence of familiar people projecting the social-emotional cues of acceptance, compassion, caring, and safety' which calms the troubled minds of the children in our care (Perry, 2009: 246).

END-OF-CHAPTER QUESTIONS

1. How might we adapt our behaviour policies to take account of developmental trauma?
2. What strategies may we use to build children's self-esteem?

Part III
Early learning

Part III
Early learning

9
Creating learning environments
Elizabeth Black and Jacqui Horsburgh

Key ideas

This chapter will explore:

- Learning environments as interactions, experiences and spaces.
- Some key aspects of physical indoor and outdoor spaces.
- The impact of social and cultural interactions within learning environments.
- The impact of organisational climate and cultures on learning environments.
- The guiding influence of pedagogy on learning environments.
- The role of leadership in creating high-quality learning environments.

Introduction

In this chapter, we discuss the importance of creating stimulating learning environments in the non-compulsory care and education (NCE) sector. Effective leaders need to take account of the interplay between different aspects of the environment to provide meaningful and engaging experiences for children and young people (Kokko and Hirsto, 2021). This chapter will adopt a socio-cultural viewpoint (see Chapter 5) to assist readers in reflecting on their provision and their own skills in leading the development of a multi-faceted learning environment.

We recognise that some practitioners identify play as the key aim of their work with any learning being incidental to this goal. Although terms such as 'learning environment' and 'pedagogy' may seem incompatible with this understanding of play, here we use these terms in their broadest sense, as it is our belief that in any childcare setting children and adults will be learning through their various interactions. Therefore, everything that happens in the setting has the potential for learning, positive or negative, and the setting as a whole is by default a learning environment. The way in which different organisational elements interact to influence the experience of children within the setting is captured in Figure 9.1.

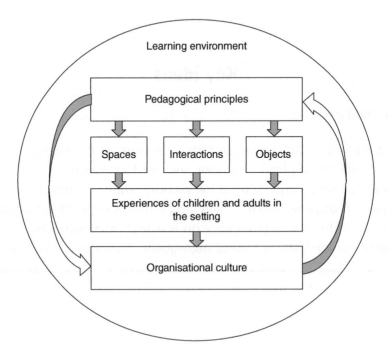

Figure 9.1   Organisational elements evident in creating a learning environment

Physical environment

We will argue in this chapter for the central importance of interactions and principles for defining an effective learning environment; however, the physical environment can shape how these occur as these are often aspects over which settings have least control, whether due to budgetary constraints, architectural features or geographical location. This section will consider three key considerations for learning related to the physical environment.

Using the outdoors

A wide range of benefits for children and adults of being outdoors have been identified (Kemple et al., 2016). The understanding that outdoor spaces provide opportunities for much more than noisy physical play can also be seen in projects trialling resources to support collaborative outdoor learning and play in primary schools (Sydney Playground Project, 2017). Although historically advocated by childcare pioneers such as Froebel, amid growing concerns about childhood obesity and mental health, there has recently been a renewed focus on this aspect of provision across the UK, with an emphasis on the use of outdoor spaces as everyday learning environments now central to practice guidance documents (Welsh Government [WG], 2022c; Early Education, 2021; Education Scotland [ES], 2020; Council for the Curriculum, Examinations and Assessment [CCEA], 2018) (see also Chapter 15).

While many settings benefit from reliable, accessible outdoor spaces suitable for regular use, or are fully outdoors, there are others for whom this is a daily challenge. For example, there might be a lack of access to large grass surfaces or green spaces in urban locations, or perhaps a setting is a converted building, where staircases, hallways and doors present challenges to accessibility. Finally, there are the challenges presented by parents/carers, staff and children themselves in relation to being outdoors, sometimes even for short periods: concern about accidents, getting cold, wet or dirty, or a lack of appreciation of the opportunities for learning (Kalpogianni, 2019; see also Chapter 15).

Arranging the space

Whether outdoors or indoors, the placement of people and movable objects also impacts on the way that the space encourages or hinders learning, as Lyttleton-Smith (2019) relates in her analysis of gendered play encounters. Later in the chapter, we will return to the idea of the adult role in a learning environment; however, in relation to use of space, it needs to be decided whether adults will be based in certain areas or free to move with children, this having implications for the way in which learning can be supported. Architectural features of the space can restrict sightlines and communication between adults; this is particularly important should an emergency arise.

Large pieces of furniture can be attractive and very useful; however, the positioning of tables and chairs or large play equipment (such as a climbing frame, tent, sand tray) can quickly limit the flexibility of the space. Practical aspects such as appropriate flooring for messy activities, and routes through the space need to be considered as well as pedagogically informed choices, such as spaces to play unobserved, or for groups to be together. Increasing recognition has been given to the potential impact on all children of colour, sound and texture within a learning environment: the calming benefits of neutral and natural tones; colour contrasts to aid visibility; and the long-term impact of continuously high volumes (Parks, 2018; Linting et al., 2013).

Finally, there is the importance of the smaller objects: plastic and wooden toys, board games and puzzles, open-ended loose parts (Casey and Robertson, 2019), ICT resources, construction and art materials. Adults may set out with various ideas about how these resources might support learning, whether as open-ended 'invitations', 'proposals' or 'provocations' (Kashin, 2019) for completely 'open' play (Lester, 2008: 55), or for more closely adult-directed activities; however, when allowed, children frequently reimagine and combine resources to support their own play aims. Taking into account children's ages and the type of setting, key questions to focus on include:

1. How are children involved in choosing new resources and those available each day?
2. To what extent, if at all, is the space set up before children arrive?
3. How are children supported to identify and access resources that they cannot see?

Multi-use spaces

A final aspect of the physical environment that we will consider here relates to the affordances and restrictions of multi-use spaces. Many settings are fortunate to have dedicated areas for different activities; however, the adaptation of spaces for meals and rest/quiet times can pose a challenge. Creating a rolling snack station can have practical and pedagogical benefits as most of the play area can be kept in use; however, where the majority of children are eating a lunchtime meal, the challenges of creating the temporary space needed for all to eat simultaneously can undermine the benefits of learning to self-serve and calm, sociable mealtimes (Department of Health and Children, 2020; WG, 2019; Care Inspectorate, 2018; Action for Children, 2017). The particular layout of individual settings will often determine solutions. For some practitioners, every day involves creating and dismantling their setting. In addition to peripatetic services, the space may belong to another organisation, for example where an out-of-school service operates within a school building, or an early years setting uses a church hall. While this provides plentiful opportunities for rearranging the layout of resources, the time required and sense of transience can undermine the opportunities for children to feel ownership of their space, or to store projects in-progress from one day to the next.

The third category of multi-use spaces can be seen in wild or open outdoor area. Fully or regularly outdoor services will have well-established routines, risk assessments and contingency plans. For establishments beginning to explore the use of wild spaces, a clear definition of boundaries and expectations for children is necessary just as it would be when using a new indoor space. While increased opportunities for risky play are an advantage of the outdoors, managing the expectations and concerns of staff, children and parents/carers is important for ensuring that the learning opportunities afforded by wild spaces can be explored in full (Kalpogianni, 2019; Health and Safety Executive, 2012; Davis et al., 2006).

THINKING POINT 9.1

1. What advantages or challenges does your setting have in terms of the physical space's:
   a. Accessibility?
   b. Location?
   c. Architecture?
2. How do these impact on opportunities for learning? Who is included? Who is excluded?

Social environment

However well designed the physical space is, its use will only be optimised when consideration is given to how social interactions take place in that space. This section considers the importance of high-quality interactions within the learning environment, assuming the premise that learning is socially constructed. Socio-cultural theories of learning focusing on the importance of social interaction for supporting different aspects of learning have been developed from the work of Vygotsky (1978). He posits that cognitive development arises from social interaction and suggests that for this to happen there has to be guided learning within the zone of proximal development (ZPD) where interaction with a 'skilled tutor' supports different aspects of learning (see Chapter 5).

Sharing knowledge

Vygotsky identified how the environment in which a child grows up influences the ways in which they think and what they think about. Significantly, the 'tutor' does not have to be a teacher but rather someone who has more experience in the task than the learner, so could be undertaken by a range of people including practitioners holding different roles, parents or children and young people themselves. This highlights the ways in which the concept of pedagogy in childcare settings has the potential to move beyond the traditional notion of learning being predominantly adult led. For example, Pellegrini and Blatchford (2000) suggest that peer-to-peer interactions can provide a more motivating context for learning as they are more horizontally organised and there is likely to be less of a power differential.

Building on the work of Vygotsky, Rogoff (2003) notes the need to account for other types of engagement that might support different aspects of learning, such as that which takes place in childcare settings where adults have opportunities to engage with children and young people on a one-to-one basis for longer periods than may be possible in school contexts. In addition, childcare settings are able to offer varied opportunities for learning to be undertaken as a joint venture where all participants share responsibility. Bal et al. (2012: 4) posit that 'part of the process of becoming educated is becoming socialized to the cultural ways in which knowledge and skills are pursued, understood and performed'. Rogoff (2003) introduces the concept of 'guided participation', highlighting ways in which support for children and young people is underpinned by the values and practices of the community in which they are being cared for.

Guided participation enables learning to take place in its widest sense and may involve a range of interactions to support learning and development. One aspect of this process is bridging meaning through social referencing. This occurs between people as they modify their perspectives on a situation so that they can come to a common understanding, or when individuals try to grasp an understanding of social situations from the expressions of others (Rogoff, 2003: 285). Kluczniok and Schmidt (2020) concur, emphasising the importance of using varied modes of communication including not only facial expressions but also gestures. This may be of particular importance for very young children or for those who find verbal communication difficult (Rose and Rogers, 2012: 59–60).

Being together

Using social interaction effectively to support learning and development requires skilled planning on the part of practitioners. Consideration needs to be given to how activities could be organised in order to maximise the high-quality interaction between different players in different contexts; there is a need to think strategically and identify complementary group sizes, tasks and interaction types, and to build effective learning experiences. Although at times in childcare settings group work may be adult-led, to achieve a level of social interaction where children and young people are learning with and from each other, the balance of ownership and control of the tasks needs to move towards the learners themselves, and increasingly responsive approaches to planning (Rose and Rogers, 2012: 122). Childcare settings are multifaceted and within them we find various sets of relationships, rules and dynamics that either promote or impede learning and social development. When planning activities to develop effective group work, practitioners need to identify and develop a shared understanding of how these facets impact on social interaction (see National Council for Curriculum and Assessment [2015] for some useful strategies and examples).

Emotional support

When considering the quality of interactions in supporting learning and development, there is a need to explore the development of relationships. As individuals interact with each other, beliefs, values and expectations are shared and developed. Forming and maintaining good personal, social and working relationships is particularly important in relation to the development of wellbeing in childcare settings: Birth to Five Matters speaks of a 'triangle of trust' between child, family and the key practitioner (Early Education, 2021: 30). Ranson and Urichuk (2008) note that in the years prior to schooling parent–child relationships play a significant role in children's social-emotional development. However, interpersonal relationships outside the family can also have a considerable influence on children's development – particularly in relation to self-concept (Houston, 2019; Pianta et al., 2003) – and impact on a range of outcomes, including motivation to learn, behaviour and cognitive skills (Cornelius-White, 2007; Allen et al., 2006).

Pianta (2001) and Pianta et al. (1995) describe three important aspects of such relationships: closeness, conflict and dependency. Important elements of closeness were identified as warm interactions and open communication. Conversely, conflict was related to negativity and discord, and dependency to the extent that children become over-reliant on adult figures. Page and Elfer (2013) have highlighted the emotional challenges for practitioners in building and maintaining positive types of key worker relationships, particularly with the youngest children. They note the importance of leaders understanding the implications of attachment for both children and practitioners (see Chapters 5 and 8).

THINKING POINT 9.2

1.   How are adults and children grouped within your setting/area?
2.   What types of interactions do you observe between adults, between adults and children, and between children throughout the day/session?
3.   Who is included? Who is excluded?

Cultural environment

The social interactions described above are influenced by and express the organisational culture. Organisational culture defines the unique qualities of an organisation and can be a further driver or barrier to achieving an effective learning environment. While shared meaning, understanding and sense-making are central to a coherent vision for practice, there are often different value-systems within a setting whose beliefs, values, norms, symbols and traditions all influence the culture (Kiley and Jensen, 2003). Evidence of beliefs and norms often comes from the verbal and non-verbal behaviours that practitioners demonstrate while engaging with a range of stakeholders, rather than formal documents, as Tembo (2021) identifies in his analysis of black early years practitioners' experiences of working in predominantly white settings. Symbols might be displays of success or learning walls, for example; traditions may be captured in annual concerts or sports day events: common ideas that define the behaviour of the practitioners in an establishment.

The culture of a setting will not only be shaped by the goals of the setting but also by the deeply held values and previous experiences (of care, education and professional development) that shape practitioners' interactions with stakeholders. Social pedagogues label this process 'Haltung' (Eichsteller and Holthoff, 2010, cited in Smith, 2012), calling on individual practitioners to reflect on the interconnectedness of 'head, heart and hands'. Organisational culture is a central factor determining perceptions of the setting and the behaviour patterns of all partners, especially practitioners and children. Therefore, culture is a phenomenon that affects the quality of human relationships in childcare settings while also being affected by the quality of these relationships, and the learning environment as a whole becomes a representation of that culture.

A cohesive culture

Where there is a cohesive culture, practitioners will engage in practices that are consistent with the culture of their community. Practices and activities should be dynamic and regularly reviewed, as goals may change over time. For example, if an establishment claims to be inclusive then you would expect practitioners to use inclusive, non-discriminatory language and clearly demonstrate the ways in which they value diversity in their practice and beyond the setting. In terms of activities, where an establishment places an emphasis on promoting artistic and creative skills, practitioners would plan for children and young people to participate in a range of art, dance and music activities. One way of generating culture is to focus on the aims of the establishment. Thus, strategic leaders would support and reinforce behaviours aligning with the aims and would challenge and change those that conflicted.

VIEW FROM PRACTICE

Different child/adult experiences in nursery spaces

Rikki arrives with his parent, Jack, at Southside Centre for Rikki's first visit. They are faced with a large plain door with a door entry system to one side and wait for some time before someone lets them in. Once admitted, they enter a bright reception area featuring colourful posters with motivational quotes and a considerable amount of information about the staff and centre. Soon, a member of staff appears at a reception window, asking Jack about the purpose of the visit. The window is quite high, and Rikki cannot see who Jack is talking to.

The manager shows them into a playroom where they receive a warm welcome from the room leader. The room is very busy, with children engaging in a wide range of activities both individually and in groups of different sizes. Some children are playing outside, visible through an open door. The space outside is mainly concrete; however, it includes several planters, wall hangings and greenery. Staff are moving between the different groups, engaging in conversations with the children. The room leader explains that this is 'free choice' time, and the children will be gathering in key-groups later for story time.

Rikki is introduced to another practitioner and is led to join one of the groups while Jack talks to the room leader. Rikki is then encouraged to join a group for story time. As this is the end of the session, parents and carers arrive to collect their children, each one greeted by a member of staff and informed of what their child has been doing. Some remaining children return to quiet activities, waiting to be collected, and Rikki and Jack leave the setting.

THINKING POINT 9.3

Consider the experience of an adult and child entering your own establishment for the first time, in a similar way to Rikki and Jack. Can you identify any aspects that might promote or hinder learning relating to:

(Continued)

- The physical layout?
- Social interactions?
- Organisational culture?

The guiding influence of pedagogy

Leaders of practice need to reflect on the coherence between statements of vision and values, and the way in which the organisation actually manifests these: between the 'head, heart and hands' of the organisation. Ideally, the pedagogical principles claimed by a setting will be echoed in visible practices, interactions and use of the physical resources available to create a coherent organisational culture, but at times, practices may belie a more fractured vision (Kiley and Jensen, 2003). When analysing or reviewing a learning environment, it is crucial to ask what is understood by 'learning'. For some practitioners, this seems straightforward: learning refers to curriculum-linked outcomes or the meeting of specific developmental milestones. In contrast, Liu et al. (2017) argue that learning can and should be defined much more broadly than this as children learn constantly, through all kinds of activities. As outlined in the preceding section, it is our belief that in any childcare setting, children and adults will be learning through their various interactions, therefore everything that happens in the setting holds the potential for positive or negative learning, and the whole setting can be regarded as a learning environment.

Some practitioners may accept that children can learn through play, but, in basing their practice on the Playwork Principles (Play Wales, 2015), would view play itself as the only purpose of their activities. This contrasts with practitioners in early years or school settings who may identify promoting play-based learning as central to their role. So, the original question requires refining to establish whether a particular type of learning or alternative objective, such as play itself, is the intended outcome. Carpentieri (2012) identifies ways in which adult learning can also be promoted within childcare settings; therefore, a final addition to the question asks, who is identified as the learner within a given environment? Such definitions are significant as they will guide choices made about interactions, adult behaviours, type and availability of resources, layout and suitability of physical spaces.

Starting from the adults

Often, the definition of learning stems from guidance documents. For example, in Scotland, the Curriculum for Excellence defines learning experiences and outcomes for children from the age of 3 years accessing government-funded childcare, and similar guidance is provided across the UK (Department for Education [DfE], 2021b; WG, 2021a; CCEA, 2018; Scottish Government, 2008b). Although adults in any setting will inevitably impact on children's learning, where a response to curriculum outcomes or developmental targets of any kind is prioritised, greater adult direction of the environment to ensure that these intended goals are achieved is likely to be required: for example, the space may have labelled 'areas', such as a book corner or construction area, where different types of playful learning may be encouraged and activities with intended goals laid out. The role of the adult might be responsive but also interventionist, seeking to maximise opportunities to extend or direct learning towards the intended learning outcomes (see Chapter 13).

Starting from the child

Alternatively, some settings will actively aim to minimise the direction provided by adults, perhaps due to a focus on play-as-end-goal or through a 'responsive planning' approach where predetermined learning outcomes are not identified, and adults offer provocations and support for children to build on their interests (ES, 2020). Such a focus is found in the early years pedagogies of Reggio Emilia (Forman and Fyfe, 2012) and Froebel (Tovey, 2017) and in the Playwork Principles (Play Wales, 2015). When fully realised, this prioritisation creates learning environments that are wholly or mainly child-led, with access to choose resources, free-flow use of space and flexible deployment of adults as required.

Compromise

The purpose of contrasting these approaches is not to suggest that one is necessarily better than the other, but to support reflection on the principles underpinning choices in relation to the learning environment. It is also important to recognise that many settings may use a blend of approaches, for example drawing on adult-guided activities to support particular areas of learning. Effective practitioners need to take account of the interplay between different aspects of the environment to provide meaningful and engaging experiences for children and young people. The starting point for this reflection has to be the identification of a personal pedagogical perspective as this will define what is accepted as meaningful and engaging.

While reflection on principles underpinning practice is vital to an understanding of how to create an appropriate learning environment for your setting, there are likely to be practical constraints on what is possible, leading to the need for compromise. Some of these potential areas of compromise have been identified when discussing physical aspects of the environment; however, it is useful to consider to what extent these compromises impact on the ability of the setting to achieve its ambitions for children's learning.

Leadership of the environment

As can be seen from the preceding sections, creating a high-quality learning environment in childcare settings is a multifaceted process. Leaders working within such settings need to adopt a strategic approach and develop an understanding of how the different facets of the environment impact on the ways in which children and young people engage in tasks and activities (Jarzabkowski et al., 2007). Practitioners need to develop an understanding of all aspects of the work of their organisations and the ways in which these relate to each other. Four key leadership strategies can support a high-quality learning environment:

- scanning the environment;
- developing opportunities for knowledge exchange at different levels;
- establishing structures and processes which support the setting of priorities and the formulation of improvement strategies; and
- monitoring the implementation of initiatives as well as emerging strategic issues.

Scanning the environment involves keeping abreast of trends, issues, threats and opportunities and discerning mega trends. This requires that all practitioners, not only those with formal leadership roles, look within and beyond their establishment to identify aspects of good practice. It is also helpful to think about how trends beyond education impact on what you are aiming to achieve in developing the childcare environment, including developments in legislation, technology and the social and economic spheres. Effective use of this information for improvement will require having mechanisms in place to support stakeholders to share this intelligence and to collate and analyse it. This process will be achieved more easily in settings with a cohesive culture and where shared values underpin priority-setting processes. In monitoring the implementation of initiatives, it is important to take account of the interconnectedness of the different aspects of the childcare environment, such as ways in which the physical environment may impact on social aspects such as interactions between adults and children or children and their peers (see Chapter 20 for an outline of leadership in early childhood settings).

Summary

Working from an understanding of the learning environment as comprising interactions, experiences and spaces, this chapter considered the physical spaces in which learning takes place, before focusing on the social and cultural environments created within settings. The importance of reflection on practice as part of the effective leadership of learning environments is highlighted. We drew on socio-cultural and social pedagogical theoretical perspectives to analyse these interactions and identified the way pedagogical principles shape the choices made, supporting or hindering learning in any childcare setting. In adopting this lens, we emphasise the importance of taking account of individual needs and perspectives. Throughout, we have argued that it is the interplay of these elements that defines the learning environment (see Figure 9.1) and that, to ensure activities are meaningful and engaging for all children, a holistic understanding of these influences on learning is required.

END-OF-CHAPTER QUESTIONS

1. Whose or what learning is prioritised by the organisational culture of your setting?
2. How are the priorities evidenced in the physical environment, interactions and organisational culture of your setting?
3. In your own practice, what compromises do you make between principles and practicalities as you create a learning environment? Whose learning might be limited or blocked by these choices?

10
Early language and literacy development

Jennifer Farrar and Kelly Stone

Key ideas

This chapter will explore:

- Key features, including national policies, of literacy and language education in early years.
- How to audit literacy and language provision in a pre-5 setting.
- Children's literature and its role in supporting language and literacy learning.
- The potential of critical literacy in early years.

Introduction

This chapter outlines the crucial role early learning and childcare (ELC) educators play in supporting young children's literacy and language development. It considers recent developments in understandings about literacy and learning in early years, specifically in relation to the potential of children's literature and critical literacies as crucial tools for developing young children's key skills and dispositions as effective readers, writers and citizens. ELC educators are encouraged to review their provision to ensure the learning environments they construct fully acknowledge young children's complex proficiencies as language users, and to foreground inquiry and curiosity alongside questions of social justice and equity.

Literacy and language development

Children come to early years settings with a rich and diverse repertoire of literacies, a term that refers to 'the many ways in which learners actively make meaning' (Meyer and Whitmore, 2017: 3). From infancy, children receive and transmit messages laden with meaning using different modes. Young children use, for example, movement, drawing, music and visual stories to take from and contribute to what Harste et al. (1984) refer to as the *meaning data pool*, an ever-expanding fund of knowledge and experiences from which they draw to inform their responses and meaning making.

A central way that children make sense of their experiences is through talk, which might be guided and extended by an adult (Bruner, 1996), or through play and creative activities with peers (Hadley et al., 2020). Early years literacies use a range of modes, are collaborative, participatory, and bound to materials, spaces and places, as well as to the social and cultural contexts in which they take place (Rowe, 2010). In this way, literacies are understood as inherently social, plural, fluid and 'situated' within a particular context (Barton and Hamilton, 2003: 7). This contrasts with long-dominant views that conceptualise literacy as a finite and universal set of skills.

Literacies within formal learning contexts in early years and school settings can differ significantly from home literacies, in that there are different expectations, rules, boundaries and practices (Gee, 2012). Schooled literacies are not always attuned to the social and cultural literacy experiences that children have outside of school (Ladson-Billings, 2014), and can be narrow and prescriptive due to mandates and curricula that privilege one aspect of literacy, such as decoding, over others (Ellis and Rowe, 2020). This limits opportunities for meaning making using a range of modes, texts and socio-cultural resources. In addition, the dominance of developmental theories with their 'attendant assumptions' about what young children can and cannot do (Comber, 2003: 355) has also influenced the sorts of activities educators choose to make available within their settings. According to Comber (2003), a consequence of 'normative models' of literacy development, with biologically determined, universal stages, has led to a 'serious underestimation of what children do intellectually and socially' (Comber, 2003: 359). A challenging and key question this chapter explores, therefore, is how ELC educators can foster and extend young children's literacy development across and through multiple modes of meaning, while embracing the diverse cultural and social experiences they bring to educational settings. Later in this chapter, we look closely at a framework for learning and teaching that foregrounds four key roles in children's literacy development.

———————————— THINKING POINT 10.1 ————————————

1. Before reading on any further, pause to reflect on the types of literacy activities you choose to make available in your early years setting. Draw up a list of the literacy activities evident in your setting.
2. Look at the list and consider:
    a. What makes them 'literacy activities'?
    b. To what extent are the items on the list reflective of the diverse cultural and social experiences of the children in your setting?
    c. Who decides what literacy activities will be provided?

The literacy and language agenda

To some extent, answers to the question 'who decides what literacy activities will be provided?' can be found in the policy documentation that describes children's development and learning goals during their time within ELC settings. Across the four nations of the United Kingdom, different approaches are advocated, and priorities foregrounded in relation to young children's literacy and language development. As we noted in an earlier section, there are contesting theories and debates around literacy education that are underpinned by deeper arguments about the role and purposes of literacy within educational settings and, more broadly, children's lives. ELC educators can recognise these differing perspectives through a careful exploration of the approaches and pedagogies recommended as constituting 'what counts as literacy' by the statutory policy frameworks in their contexts. What follows here is a brief summary of literacy and language learning within UK national policy frameworks covering early years:

*   Scotland's Curriculum for Excellence (CfE) (Scottish Government [SG], 2009) places a central importance on literacy, numeracy and health and wellbeing, and teachers of children and young people aged 3–18 are responsible for developing and evidencing these three subjects across the curriculum. Organised around capacities and areas of learning rather than school subjects, the CfE aims to develop young people as successful learners, confident individuals, responsible citizens and effective

contributors (SG, 2009). The CfE sub-divides literacy into listening and talking, reading and writing and prioritises a focus on enjoyment and choice alongside the development of core tools and understandings about how language works.

- In England, the Early Years Foundation Stage (Department for Education [DfE], 2021b) has been developed as a statutory framework for all early years providers from birth to age 5. 'Communication and language' is identified as one of three 'prime areas' for all children to develop, while 'literacy' is highlighted as one of four specific areas requiring attention in ELC settings. Each area, whether 'prime' or 'specific', is linked to sets of 'Early Learning Goals', with expected, assessed literacy outcomes in relation to comprehension, word reading and writing (DfE, 2021b: 13).
- In Northern Ireland, the approach to early years education (Council for the Curriculum, Examinations and Assessment [CCEA], 2018) identifies seven key areas of learning, including a specific focus on language development. The curriculum guidance highlights children's prior learning and language use, including languages other than English, and foregrounds the role that play-based approaches, imaginative activities including drama, and exposure to books and stories should occupy within early years settings.
- The new Curriculum for Wales (Welsh Government, 2020), for all children and young people aged 3–16, is organised around four core educational purposes: to develop children and young people as ambitious, capable learners; as healthy, confident individuals; as enterprising, creative contributors; and as ethical, informed citizens. Languages, Literacy and Communication is identified as one of six areas of learning and experience, with four 'statements of what matters' used to frame what literacy and language learning 'look like' in schools and settings. This includes a focus on children's multilingual resources, developing understandings in and through language use, and the role of literature and imagination in children's development.

Frameworks for thinking about literacy, policy and for auditing your practice

Freebody and Luke's (1990) influential Four Resources Model is a learning and teaching framework that brings together four key capacities in literacy development – the functional, semantic, pragmatic and critical elements – which are considered equally important from the early years through secondary education and beyond. The four key roles (or resources) are:

- **Code breakers** recognise and use sounds, letters, spelling and structural patterns, including images, to understand and create texts.

- **Text participants** understand and compose meaningful texts, using personal meaning-making systems that draw from their cultural and social backgrounds.
- **Text users** know about and act on the cultural and social functions that texts perform in and outside of the school context, with an awareness of how to make meaning from different genres of texts.
- **Text analysts** recognise that texts are never ideologically neutral, that certain views are silenced when others are dominant, and that textual practices can be critiqued to uncover power structures and imbalances, and reconstructed.

Freebody and Luke (1990) did not intend the Four Resources Model to be used as a developmental stage model, where children are introduced to code-breaking in the early years and progress to critical literacy in secondary school. Instead, they argue that each of the four resources can be meaningfully engaged with at any age, including with young children. Their work also emphasises that each role is *necessary* for twenty-first-century literate citizens yet none of the four resources is *sufficient* in and of itself; in other words, learners should systematically and explicitly experience all four resources throughout their educational experiences of literacy learning.

In the 30 years since its publication, Freebody and Luke's (1990) influential, but printed-text focused model, has been further developed by other scholars, so it accounts for the broad range of multimodal, digital texts that twenty-first-century readers engage with on a daily basis. Serafini's (2012: 152) adaptation of the four resources explores the way 'reader-viewers' interact with visual images, structures and designs in conjunction with the written word. Under Serafini's (2012) expanded view, the four multimodal resources are:

- **Navigators**, who crack the print, design and visual codes of texts, such as concepts of print, directionality and sequencing, including non-linear structures and hypertexts.
- **Interpreters** actively construct meaning from written words, images and design by drawing from multiple perspectives, knowledge of other texts and life experiences.
- **Designers** actively make meaning but also design 'reading paths' through texts by selecting which parts of a text to consider and interpret, according to their interests and purposes (Serafini, 2012).
- **Interrogators** ask questions about how texts reflect the conditions of their production and their impact on audiences.

Taken together, as shown in Figure 10.1, Freebody and Luke's (1990) model, with Serafini's (2012) adaptations, offers educators a useful tool for auditing literacy provision within their setting to ensure a balanced approach. By discussing planning documents in relation to the model, educators can ascertain which resources dominate and which require some additional development. Doing so can ensure children get an opportunity to experience each of the resources through literacy activities that also build on their existing language and literacy practices. In addition, ELC educators could:

- Colour-code planning documents to highlight where each of the resources feature and where this may vary according to age and stage.
- Consider how each of the Four Resources are or could be included through meaningful and relevant opportunities to listen, talk, read and write, including mark making.
- Draw from existing strengths in staff teams to support the development of any missing resources. The tool could also be used to help gauge staff understanding of what each resource means and what it might 'look like' in specific settings and contexts.

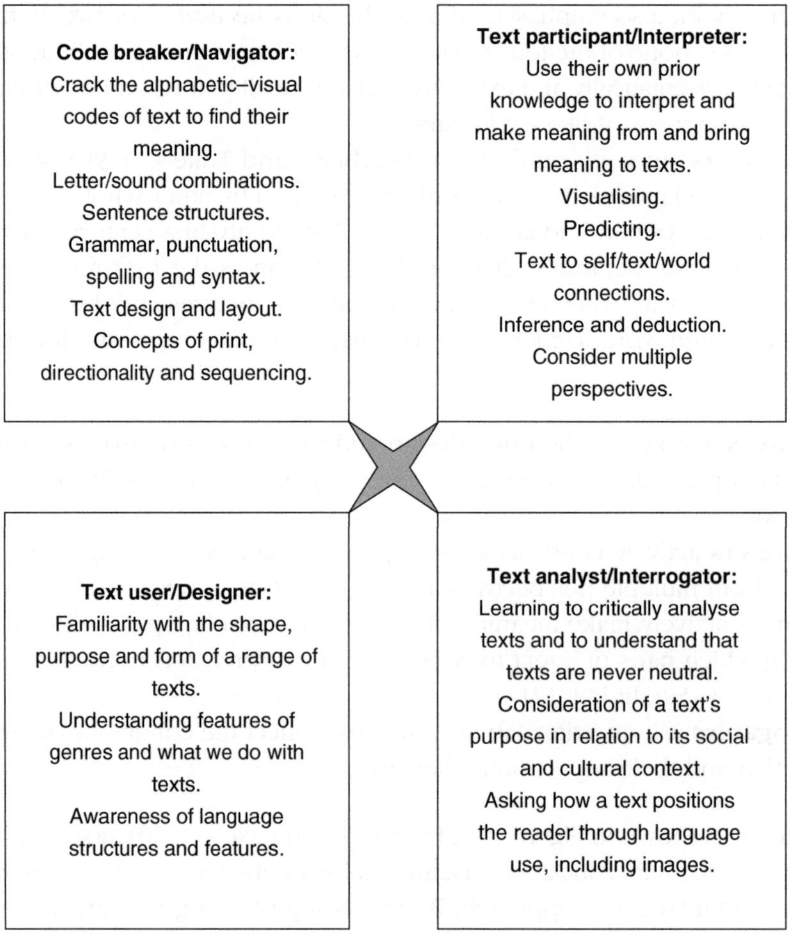

Code breaker/Navigator:
Crack the alphabetic–visual codes of text to find their meaning.
Letter/sound combinations.
Sentence structures.
Grammar, punctuation, spelling and syntax.
Text design and layout.
Concepts of print, directionality and sequencing.

Text participant/Interpreter:
Use their own prior knowledge to interpret and make meaning from and bring meaning to texts.
Visualising.
Predicting.
Text to self/text/world connections.
Inference and deduction.
Consider multiple perspectives.

Text user/Designer:
Familiarity with the shape, purpose and form of a range of texts.
Understanding features of genres and what we do with texts.
Awareness of language structures and features.

Text analyst/Interrogator:
Learning to critically analyse texts and to understand that texts are never neutral.
Consideration of a text's purpose in relation to its social and cultural context.
Asking how a text positions the reader through language use, including images.

Figure 10.1 The expanded Four Resources Model (Serafini, 2012; Freebody and Luke, 1990)

Literacy scholar Frank Smith (1988) used the metaphor of a 'literacy club' to describe the ways in which young children learn to be literate in their homes, early years settings, schools, communities and wider worlds. Under this view, the most effective literacy learning occurs when children are able to 'join the club' by participating in literate activities with people who already know how and why reading, writing, listening and talk are used in particular ways for particular purposes in everyday life. Continuing the analogy, Smith (1988) noted that:

> ... members occupy themselves with whatever activities the club has formed itself to promote, constantly demonstrating the value and utility of these activities to the new members, helping them to participate whenever they want but never forcing their involvement or ostracizing them for not having the understanding or the expertise of more practised members. (Smith, 1988: 3)

Smith's image also helps to illustrate the point that literacy is social by showing how more experienced members of the 'club' help induct younger members into the specific literacy practices they will need in order to join in as a member of society.

THINKING POINT 10.2

1. Referring back to your list from Thinking Point 10.1, what sort of literacy activities does your ELC 'literacy club' demonstrate, implicitly or explicitly?
2. Use the Four Resources Model (4RM) and Smith's metaphor to help you evaluate the literacy activities promoted in your setting.
3. Reflecting on the results of your 4RM audit, are there any resources that would benefit from development? How will you achieve this?

Taking a closer look: becoming a text analyst/interrogator

While all four of the expanded resources are important, in this next section we focus in on one in particular – the text analyst/interrogator. This is because the ideas that underpin this crucial, critical resource still remain relatively marginalised within discourses of early childhood education (Comber, 2003) yet are of great significance to literate citizens of any age, especially those growing up in an increasingly complex, interconnected, digital world. Such ideas, which are rooted in Paulo Freire's (1984) critical literacy pedagogy, emphasise becoming literate as an inherently political act, in which we become expert in particular communicative practices that reflect different ways of being and doing. Yet, as Comber (2001) notes, accepting literacy as political can be a challenge for educators, especially those in early childhood settings, given that it 'sounds almost dangerous' and given the contrast of this view with dominant perspectives of childhood innocence and age-related naivety (Comber, 2001: 168).

At its core, critical literacy is concerned with the ways that power is operationalised in and through language use and in the wider world. Young children are good at asking 'why' questions about issues that matter to them and are already very aware of 'what's fair, what's different, who gets the best deal' when they come to early learning and child-care settings (Comber, 2001: 170), and this is a strength on which educators can draw. Developing young children's capacities as text analysts helps to support their understandings of issues that matter most to them, while letting them see how inequity and injustice can be challenged, and more socially just alternatives imagined.

A growing body of research shows the potential of developing critical literacy practices with young children to 'help them question and change the way things are in texts and everyday life' (O'Brien and Comber, 2001: 154). Jennifer O'Brien (1994) was one of the first to show how young children (aged 4 upwards) responded as text analysts to representations of mothers in junk mail when compared to the 'real' mothers in their lives; Vivian Vasquez's (2014) work with 3–5-year-olds showcased their critically literate responses to the gendered stereotypes present in everyday texts, such as the toys offered to children in a McDonald's Happy Meal; while more recent work by Kelly Stone also explored the messages young children receive through social interactions and marketing about which toys are appropriate for them to play with, or otherwise (Stone, 2017). What all of these research projects have in common is a commitment to recognising the potential of young children to engage as critical citizens in issues relating to their lives.

O'Brien and Comber (2001: 156) created sets of questions to help early childhood professionals, families and young children move beyond the familiar in order to read texts carefully and critically. They can be used in relation to any text type – picturebooks, magazines, food packaging, adverts, films – whatever is being read. To get started, you could ask some of the following questions of the next text you read:

- What kind of a text is this?
- How can it be described?
- Where else have you seen texts like this?
- What do these kinds of texts usually do?
- Who is the text being produced for? How can you tell?
- Whose voices/perspectives do we hear in this text?
- Whose voices/perspective do we not hear in this text? Why might that be?
- How else could this text have been produced/written/drawn?

VIEW FROM PRACTICE

The literate citizen

When 4-year-old Jane first walks into her early years centre, her eyes are drawn to a new poster on the wall depicting a large illustration of the Earth, which has a sad face, a thermometer sticking out of its mouth, and a white bandage wrapped around its head. Jane spends a few moments staring at the poster, then asks Daniel, her key worker, why the Earth is sick. Daniel explains that they will be learning more during story time. But Jane's questions about the poster will not wait, and she begins to suggest some reasons why the planet is unwell. Jane tells Daniel about a Newsround feature that she watched about small plastic pieces causing harm to creatures living in the sea. She also knows that certain animals like polar bears are losing their homes because the ice is melting. Daniel tells Jane that she has remembered well, and that they will talk about it more later that morning.

During story time, Daniel reads *Hello, Mr World* (Foreman, 2017), in which two young children take on the role of doctors and ask Mr World what is wrong with him. The picturebook ends with a section on what climate change is, its effects on plant life as well as animal habitats, and actions children can take to help, such as switching off lights. Jane and a number of the other children actively engage with the story, listening attentively and adding comments that reflect their prior knowledge about climate change, and their emotional responses to the story about the sick planet. Jane remarks that the author has forgotten to include plastics in the book, which she knows are harmful to the planet.

When story time is over, Jane tells Daniel that they need to add something to the poster of the sick planet on the wall. Trying to find the word for the symbol she is thinking of, she looks through another book until she finds what she is looking for: a speech bubble. They need to write 'Help', inside it, and stick it to the poster, she says.

Jane demonstrates each of the four resources in this example from practice. When she first sees the poster, she is transfixed by the image in an effort to understand its meaning, and her need to do so is undeterred by Daniel's statement that they'll find out more later during story time. Although there are no words on the poster, Jane is a code breaker/navigator, using visual codes to unlock meaning from the poster.

She is a text participant/interpreter, using her prior knowledge gleaned from other texts – such as Newsround features and picturebooks – to interpret the meaning of the poster. She knows that the health of our oceans and seas is of vital importance to the overall meaning, as is the threat of extinction of species living on the planet.

As a text user/designer, Jane is attuned to how the poster of the sick planet makes her feel. During story time, Jane and the other children have the opportunity to explore their feelings about the issues related to climate change through the fictional character of Mr World, and also through the recommendations the book makes directly to them about their responsibilities to the planet. Text users are familiar with a range of text types, and Jane shows her understanding that

(Continued)

posters and other predominantly visual texts convey powerful meanings, just as picturebooks do, with the construction of a narrative using pictures and words over multiple pages.

Jane is also a text analyst/interrogator, critically analysing the picturebook by drawing on her previous knowledge to identify a gap in the story read aloud. Because she knows that plastics are central to the planet's health, she shows surprise that this is not part of Mr World's story. Similarly, she believes that the poster is missing a key piece of information: a speech bubble to send a message directly from the Earth, asking for help. In actively mediating the message by physically transforming the poster, Jane uses her knowledge about how meanings are made, and strengthened, across a range of texts.

Children's literature's potential in ELC settings and beyond

As Jane's example in the 'View from Practice' illustrates, children's literature has the potential to support young children towards multifaceted and complex responses to issues that matter to them. In this section, we consider how ELC educators can use children's literature to help enrich and enlarge young children's literacy learning, while providing a context for developing their understandings and experiences about words and their worlds (Freire, 1984).

Research has long shown that engagement with children's books can support the development of language and literacy skills. Teale and Sulzby's (1986) longitudinal study into storybook readings and adult–child interactions found an increase in emergent reading ability in contexts where storybook reading was embedded in the children's lives. Research by Wells (1986) identified a relationship between being read to during the preschool years with success in literacy on entry to school. In their more recent review of research related to children's literature and young readers, Arizpe et al. note that 'early encounters' with children's books can positively impact on literacy skills and general success in literacy attainment (Arizpe et al., 2013: 245).

According to Margaret Meek, children's books have such a positive impact on young readers because of the valuable 'lessons' they can impart about the 'nature and variety of written discourse, the different ways that language lets a writer tell and the many and different ways a reader reads' (Meek, 1988: 21). Taking this idea further, other scholars have shown that children's texts can teach important lessons about how different lives are lived. In a widely-cited and most helpful metaphor, Sims-Bishop (1990) visualised books as '*mirrors, windows and doors*' in order to describe the varied vantage points books can offer readers. Books can be mirrors, for example, when they 'offer views of worlds that may be real or imagined, familiar or strange' (Sims-Bishop, 1990: n.p.). Books can become mirrors when they reflect readers' lives back to them, and doors when they allow readers to enter, via their imaginations, the world created by the author. Sometimes this is with a view to taking action about the issue under exploration, just as Jane did in the 'View from Practice'. When looking at the potential of children's literature to develop intercultural understandings, Kathy Short (2009) proposes that children's books can help young readers to move beyond a surface-level 'tourist' approach to issues by inviting them to 'immerse themselves in story worlds, gain insights into how people feel, live, and think around the world. They also come to recognize their common humanity as well as to value cultural differences' (Short, 2009: 1). Another benefit of frequent exposure to children's books is the development of emotional literacy and empathy through vicarious engagement with a fictional character's feelings and experiences (Nikolajeva, 2013). Not only can this help young children make sense of other people's reactions and responses, but it can also support them towards understanding and acknowledging their own.

For ELC educators, the challenge is to ensure that the books made available to young children are rich and varied enough to act as windows and doors into new worlds and understandings, while also ensuring that as mirrors, they can reflect the lives of all the children in the group, including and especially those from socially marginalised groups.

THINKING POINT 10.3

According to Sheridan (2001: 109), being 'hooked on books' can support the development of literacy because it can motivate children to read for themselves, support developing understandings of what reading and writing are for, while also providing a crucial framework for experiences.

1. What do you do already to get young children 'hooked on books' in your setting? What else could you do?
2. Thinking of the books that are available to children in your setting, in what ways do they function as mirrors, windows and doors? Whose lives and experiences do they reflect?
3. Whose lives and experiences are not reflected and what can be done about this?

Summary

Readers growing up in the twenty-first century are bombarded with a bewildering array of complex text types on a daily basis. Young children come to ELC settings already well versed in a variety of literacy practices, including sophisticated understandings of oral storytelling and language use, playful and complex interactions associated with digital and multimodal texts and an acute awareness of what's fair and what's not

(Comber, 2001). ELC educators have an ethical responsibility to support young children's literacy and language development so they have the tools to make meaning from the diverse and challenging texts they will encounter.

Framed by understandings of literacy as a social practice rather than as a 'one-size-fits-all' approach, this chapter has encouraged ELC educators to use tools such as the Four Resources Model (Freebody and Luke, 1990) to review the types of literacy activities made available within their settings, with a view to addressing any gaps that emerge. In particular, we have highlighted the need for ELC educators to maximise the potential of the rich, critical resources that young children develop through their everyday experiences in their homes and communities and bring with them to their ELC educational settings.

We have also discussed some of the ways in which quality children's literature can support the exploration of issues that relate to children's lives, experiences and feelings, as well as issues pertaining to social justice and equity. By positioning young children as active and agentive, perhaps by using O'Brien and Comber's (2001) list of critical questions, or by reviewing the relevance and range of books made available to young children, we call upon ELC educators to continue to explore the wonderful world of children's literature.

END-OF-CHAPTER QUESTIONS

1.   What did you understand literacy to mean at the start of this chapter? What do you understand it to mean now?
2.   What texts have functioned as mirrors, windows and doors in your life? Can you think of any books for children and books for adults that fulfil these roles?
3.   What challenges do you foresee in trying to position young children as text analysts and critical reader-viewers in your contexts? How will you meet these challenges?

11
Early mathematical development

Susie Marshall and Julie Robinson

Key ideas

This chapter will explore:

- The theories of learning mathematics.
- How to develop mathematics through play.
- Foundational skills of mathematics.
- Developing aspects of number.

Introduction

The world is visual, the world is spatial. The world around us has form, shape, structure, depth, dimension, volume, symmetry, asymmetry, pattern. These natural attributes all need exploration, as without active and sensory engagement, the world around us is rendered all too abstract. Constance Kamii, under the tutelage of Piaget, researched extensively into how young children learn, develop, and make sense of the world. There is a distinctively mathematical resonance here. Kamii (1996: 100) highlights the critical nature of logico-mathematical knowledge in children's development – describing it as 'relationships created by each individual'. This succinct definition is so illuminating and such a vital one in helping to discern meaning; it is how the child sees, explores and discovers such relationships in the environment around them, it is how the child makes sense of patterns and connections between things, how they visualise the attributes of the world and environment noted above, how they form schema, how they 'classify'. The active verbs noted above are inherently sensory in approach. Fundamentally, these are competencies and they all come from within the child. It is the child who is at the core of all of this. Reflecting on the definition and traits of logico-mathematical knowledge, this sensory approach most certainly holds true. Surely then, it is through blending and nurturing both these sensory links and connections within the child from a young age, that a natural love and understanding of mathematics can be fostered. Hence, this chapter seeks to blend aspects of child and mathematics development, with naturally arising opportunities to capture and nurture a love of mathematics.

Theories of learning mathematics

Piaget's Theory of Cognitive Development (explored in Chapter 5) has much to inform for early mathematical development, particularly in the non-compulsory care and education (NCE) sector. In particular, the following terms are woven into the fabric of our writing:

- Assimilation – where children incorporate new information or experiences into what they already know, using existing knowledge to help make sense of new knowledge.
- Accommodation – Piaget's term for a learning process in which humans modify what they already know to make room for new information or experiences (Trawick-Smith, 2014).

These terms resonate powerfully within a play environment. Fuson (2009: 344) captures Piaget's approach to perfection, reminding us that 'children construct their own concepts and … these ideas develop along learning paths'. This is a wonderful mindset for practice – as practitioners we must involve the children and their senses, we must use experiences, resources and the environment around us, then build on this developmentally. Here we see links with logico-mathematical knowledge. Eliciting the mathematics from children's play to support the process of assimilation and accommodation will be developed in the next section.

Vygotsky (2004) approached cognition, thinking and problem solving from more of a linguistic, social and relational perspective. His work has much to support us in understanding social constructivism today and how children learn mathematics. Trawick-Smith (2014) recounts a familiar scenario, that of a young child engrossed in play, happily talking aloud on their own. Vygotsky recognised this as 'private' or 'self-directed speech' which 'helps children to guide their own attention and to organise ideas internally' (Trawick-Smith, 2014: 240). It is important to build on this natural capacity for 'private speech' by encouraging meaningful social interactions. Enabling language and dialogue to flourish whilst children play, experience, explore and engage creatively and actively with their environment supports logical thinking, reasoning and problem solving (Vygotsky, 2004).

Bruner (1966) offers us further theoretical grounding on which to build a supportive mathematical learning and teaching environment. Indeed, the Concrete-Pictorial-Abstract (CPA) pedagogical approach has its roots here (Chang et al., 2017). Bruner (1966) acknowledges the value of a sensory approach, too, advocating that a child's knowledge or learning journey, progression and development begin with lived and active experiences or with the engagement of tangible materials. Chang et al. (2017: 6) capture this, noting, 'The learning sequence of a new mathematical concept follows through a progression from an enactment on concrete objects or an experience, to perceptual images of both the enactment of the concrete object and experience, to the adoption of the mathematical symbol'. As Chang et al. (2017) highlight, this is resonant of Bruner's (1996) 'modes of representation' – enactive-iconic-symbolic. Bruner, they stress, valued knowledge being made visible and observable. Learning can evolve in so many subtle and nuanced ways from very early childhood, primarily through a play environment.

Developing mathematics through play

There is some debate about how best to develop young children's mathematics through play. Clements and Sarama (2017) advocate structured mathematics activities on the one hand, where the mathematics to be developed is planned for by the practitioner, and free play on the other, where children naturally enage with mathematics. Van Oers (1996) terms the former, structured mathematics activity, as 'mathematics made playful' and for the latter, free play, he highlights the need for 'mathematising play'. Play is the crucial and common factor.

Essentially, mathematising supports the children in reflecting on the mathematics in their play by giving language to their experiences (Clements and Sarama, 2017; Ginsburg, 2006).

Both mathematics made playful and mathematising play provide opportunities for scaffolding learning and for children to assimilate and accommodate new information (Clements et al., 2020). Indeed, there is a dynamic relationship between the two; there is evidence to suggest that structured mathematics activities increase the quality of young children's play (Hannula-Sormunen et al., 2020; Clements and Sarama, 2017; Ginsburg, 2006), whilst mathematical actions carried out in free play can support children in making sense of their mathematical learning (van Oers, 2010). The role of the practitioner is crucial; practitioners must respond to what children currently know and do not know. To do this effectively, practitioners must be cognisant of the developmental learning trajectories (Ginsburg, 2016: 942).

Mathematics made playful

In structured mathematics activities, mathematics is the starting point and can be developed in a range of playful ways (van Oers, 1996). Games might be played, initially modelled by practitioners to a whole group or explored within smaller groups to encourage children to play the games independently (Clements and Sarama, 2021). Mathematics opportunities can be planned for through literature and visual narratives/images, drawing on mathematical ideas from picture books (Uscianowski et al., 2019). Children can engage in baking activities, from which so much mathematics may be drawn (Ginsburg, 2006). Children should be encouraged to work with concrete materials as well as abstract ideas and these approaches can be scaffolded through the posing of story problems where the mathematics is contextualised (Carpenter et al., 2017; Ginsburg, 2006). Establishing daily routines rich in mathematics offers a wealth of mathematical discovery and enrichment, whether at registration (grouping and numbering and ordering), at snack time (favourite foods), when tidying up (sorting, classifying and categorising toys and equipment) or, indeed, learning mathematics outside (e.g. looking for shapes and symmetry in the natural and the built environment) (Early Childhood Maths Group, 2021a).

For practitioners to respond to and scaffold children's mathematical thinking and reasoning in such activities, open questions such as 'how would you help a friend to do it?' or 'can you show me how you did it?' are so valuable. Children should also be encouraged to show/represent their thinking using concrete materials and pictorial representations (Carpenter et al., 2017; Carruthers and Worthington, 2006).

Mathematising play

Whilst free play may incorporate many aspects of everyday mathematics, without interventions by practitioners to attach mathematical language and mathematise the children's play, there is potential for the full benefits of this approach to be lost (Ginsburg, 2006).

As well as organising rich environments that offer encounters with mathematics, teachers must look for opportunities to enable the reflection and development of children's mathematical thinking through their play (Hannula-Sormunen et al., 2020; Björklund et al., 2018; Anghileri, 2006).

───────────────── **VIEW FROM PRACTICE** ─────────────────

Seeking to mathematise children's free play

Skilled observation of children's play helps to capture mathematical opportunities that enrich and extend the focus of the mathematics through playful activties. Inspired by reading the book *Superworm* by Julia Donaldson, children compared the length of 'worms' in a mathematics-made-playful activity. Later that week, a practitioner observed that children were drawing worms with chalk in the outside area. The practitioner asked the children how they might work out whose worm was the longest. This led to the children moving their hands along each worm to work out the length of each one. The practitioner attributed mathematical language and thinking to this action, stating that they could work out how long the worms were by counting how many of their hands were the same length as the worm, and leading to a discussion about how they might work out whose was the longest. By mathematising the children's play in this way, the practitioner is laying the foundation for concepts of measure and equivalence.

In their study observing pre-school teachers, Björklund et al. (2018) explored different ways of mathematising play, concluding that four distinct lines of action emerged:

- **Confirming direction of interest**

  The practitioner shows interest by asking questions or repeating what the child has said. Open questions, such as 'how did that happen?' or 'are you sure?', can then be developed into mathematical reasoning.

- **Providing strategies**

  The practitioner makes strategies visible for mathematical activities occurring in play, for example touching one object at a time whilst counting (one-to-one correspondence).

- **Situating known concepts**

  The practitioners' questioning in play invites children to find a problem emerging from the play activity, such as when engaging in play about a birthday party, exploring the concept of space, by asking, how big would the room need to be to hold all the people we would like to invite to our party?

- **Challenging concept meaning**

    A concept emerging from the play is highlighted and the children need to explain their own meaning – for example, when a child is using a tall, narrow container to pour water, stating that they are using it because it is bigger than all the others. A practitioner uses this an opportunity to reflect on the properties of containers to help establish a shared mathematical understanding.

All four lines of action for mathematising play must be underpinned by sustained shared thinking between the practitioner and the child, where both parties have the opportunity to contribute, develop and extend their thinking (Björklund et al., 2018: 472).

─────── **THINKING POINT 11.1** ───────

Reflect on some occasions when you have mathematised children's play.

Foundational skills of mathematics

Executive function and spatial reasoning are highly intertwined with the development of mathematics (Clements et al., 2016; Diamond, 2016; van der Ven et al., 2012).

Executive function

Executive function (EF) is an 'umbrella term for the different cognitive skills that are needed to behave flexibly and adaptively in new situations' (van der Ven et al., 2012: 100). There is broad agreement in the literature that EF comprises the following skills: working memory (WM), inhibitory control (IC) and cognitive flexibility (CF) (Banse et al., 2021; Cameron, 2018; Diamond, 2016). WM involves recalling, holding and modifying new information, for example in a story problem where a practitioner may say that they have four apples and are given one more. In order for a child to find the answer, they have to cognitively hold the starting number (four) and update it by one. IC refers to the regulation of impulsive behaviours, such as mentally playing with ideas and giving a considered response. Both behavioural and cognitive responses are included. Finally, CF is the ability to switch attention to different aspects of a problem or to use a variety of strategies in problem solving, for example when sorting objects and changing the variables of classification, or when turning symbols, such as numerals, into meaningful representations

(Banse et al., 2021: 76; Cameron, 2018; Diamond, 2016: 11). When considering how to develop EF in young children, Cameron (2018) encourages us to approach EF as a whole, rather than focus on each skill individually.

There is evidence to suggest that scaffolding and a rich verbal environment can support the development of EF (Banse et al., 2021; Diamond, 2016). Importantly, mathematics can also nurture this progression (Clements et al., 2016). For example, Banse et al. (2021) describe a series of activities using a feelie box and a selection of shapes. In identifying a shape through the sense of touch and with the encouragement of the practitioner to then vocalise and describe the properties, the children are required to hold multiple pieces of information (WM). Then shifting cognitively from the feel of the properties to the name (CF), they regulate their responses and consider the properties of the shapes, whilst also resisting the urge to name the shape immediately (IC). As stated in an earlier example, if children are holding and integrating more than one piece of information, they are practising using their WM (Banse et al., 2021).

THINKING POINT 11.2

Reflect on opportunities for the development of executive function – an 'umbrella term for the different cognitive skills that are needed to behave flexibly and adaptively in new situations' – within your setting.

Spatial reasoning

As with EF, spatial reasoning is a fundamental component of mathematics learning and its importance to success in mathematics has been widely recognised. Spatial reasoning supports the recognition of patterns in subitising, aids one-to-one correspondence in counting and the understanding of a linear spatial representation of numbers in a number line. Mathematics activities, such as exploring measurement through blocks, can also provide opportunities to develop spatial reasoning (Clements and Sarama, 2021; Verdine et al., 2014; Gunderson et al., 2012).

Spatial reasoning is defined as 'the ability to recognise and (mentally) manipulate the spatial properties of objects and the spatial relations among objects' (Bruce et al., 2017: 146). This can be subdivided into two groups: spatial visualisation and spatial orientation. Spatial visualisation is the ability to imagine and transform two-dimensional and three-dimensional objects by composing and decomposing shapes or objects, or by transforming shapes. This includes symmetry and tessellation. Spatial orientation involves imagining the relationship between two or more objects, or between oneself and these objects from different perspectives; it involves considering position, direction and routes and perspective taking (Early Childhood Maths Group, 2021b; Uttal et al., 2013: 353).

The development of spatial reasoning

Developing spatial reasoning in isolation is often unsuccessful; instead it should be embedded across the setting, using naturally occurring experiences (Clements and Sarama, 2021; Levine et al., 2012). Initial development of spatial reasoning is grounded in movement, where children develop awareness of their own bodies, the environment around them and the interaction between the two. Children need many opportunities to be physically active in a variety of environments. This is fundamental in the later development of different perspectives in spatial orientation, and opportunities to develop pictorial representations of movements through maps can be used (Clements and Sarama, 2021; Early Childhood Mathematics Group, 2021c).

The use of gesture in explanations supports children's understanding of spatial relationships, both through modelling by the practitioner and by encouraging the children themselves to use gestures in their explanations (Clements and Sarama, 2021). Gestures such as pointing to a location or to an appropriate action in construction should be encouraged. It is important that language is used alongside gesture and the use of spatial language is particularly important. Properties of objects such as curved or flat can be reinforced; orientations or transformations such as flip or rotate can be highlighted; position and direction (between, next to…, etc.), too, can be articulated (Levine et al., 2012).

Uhlenberg and Geiken (2021) explored toddlers' interactions with contents and containers, observing them use a combination of actions such as filling, distributing contents and nesting containers inside each other; they concluded that toddlers were able to construct spatial relationships between and among the objects, for example choosing the right object to fit fully inside a container. Similar development in spatial reasoning can also be seen in the use of puzzles, where the additional use of spatial language by adults working alongside children was identified as an enhancing factor (Levine et al., 2012).

Pattern

Pattern is integral to mathematics, not least of all to counting, subitising and the understanding of tens and ones in our base ten number system. Mulligan and Mitchelmore (2009: 34) define mathematical pattern as 'any predictable regularity, usually involving numerical, spatial or logical relationships'.

Development of pattern

Borthwick et al. (2021) focus on three types of patterns that should be explored: repeated patterns, growing patterns and spatial patterns. The last of these includes subitising, which will be focused on in a later section under number. With both repeated patterns, where there is a core unit that is repeated, and growing patterns, where a pattern is increasing by the same unit each time, children should be given multiple opportunities to continue, copy and create, using a range of practical objects, as well as through using actions and sounds. Borthwick et al. (2021) highlight the value of using practical objects initially, as the unit of repeat or growth is more visible. Reflective questions should then be asked to draw children's attention to the organisation of the pattern, and to encourage them to look for mathematical similarities within and between patterns (Mulligan and Mitchelmore, 2009).

Number

One of the key aspects of children's developing conceptual understanding of number is their understanding of quantity, numerosity or 'how many-ness' (National Centre for Excellence in the Teaching of Mathematics [NCETM], 2021). Within counting, this is referred to as the cardinal principle, where the last number word used indicates the total number within the collection (Paliwal and Baroody, 2018). However, this ability to understand quantity does not appear to depend on counting alone. One way in which this is believed to be developed is the process known as subitising.

Subitising

The word subitising is derived from the Latin '*subito*', meaning 'to arrive suddenly' and indicates that people can see a small collection or array of objects and quickly distinguish the quantity (Clements and Sarama, 2021). Being able to recognise the quantity of dots on a dice face without counting each dot is an example of subitising in action. There is increasing awareness of the importance of subitising for number development; research has shown this can be so valuable for supporting young children's counting skills, highlighting that simply being able to subitise arrays of four is sufficient for constructing an understanding of the cardinal principle (Paliwal and Baroody, 2020). Indeed, there is also research that shows that the ability to subitise may be a predictor of later mathematics ability (Hannula-Sormunen et al., 2015; Benoit et al., 2004; Starkey and Cooper, 1995).

Development in subitising skills

Benoit et al. (2004) outline that the first stage of subitising is termed perceptual, where children notice differences between the quantity in arrays, where the arrays differ by only one item. At this point, verbal naming of the quantity is not required, simply stating whether the arrays are the same or different. A subsequent step is perceptual-verbal subitising, where the number words are used to express the quantity. When children are able to subitise more than five items, stating the quantity, the focus then shifts to conceptual subitising, where children are encouraged to notice the parts in the arrays and put them together for the whole. For example, children can see an array of eight as two arrays of four (Clements and Sarama, 2021). Subitising lays the foundation for other mathematical concepts, such as adding and subtracting, and can support children in assimilating subsequent learning about number operations.

Initially when subitising, the most important thing to consider is the size of the collection. From before the age of 2, children can distinguish between one and more than one, therefore the games and activities should initially be on collections of this size, before extending to three, then four and so on (Clements and Sarama, 2021). Collections should be of the same unit at first, comprising simple shapes such as dots; however this should be extended to include everyday objects, as well as exploring subitising in nature, for example with conkers or leaves.

In terms of organisation, the collections should begin in a line, not spaced too closely together, then progress to symmetrical orientations and rectangular configurations, dice or domino arrangements and finger patterns (Clements and Sarama, 2021; Benoit et al., 2004; Starkey and Cooper, 1995; von Glaserfeld, 1982). To support young children's development in subitising, it is vital that small number words are used frequently in everyday interactions between practitioners and children (Clements and Sarama, 2021). Paliwal and Baroody (2020) also advocate the use of a count-first approach to subitising, where practitioners model the counting of subitisable collections, and specify the total. Take children on a subitising walk and observe examples of small collections, for example trunks splitting into three branches (Wilding, 2020). The use of both examples and non-examples is also recommended – for example, when presenting collections of dots on cards, pointing to a collection that 'is not two' and those that 'are two' (Paliwal and Baroody, 2020). The relationship between subitising and counting is not one-directional, since subitising helps ground cardinality with the concept of quantity, and counting can also help subitising (Clements and Sarama, 2021).

Principles of counting

Gelman and Gallistel (1978) outline five counting principles. The first three of these are referred to as how to count, the fourth is referred to as what to count, whilst the final principle is an amalgamation of the first four:

- **One-one principle** – one number is given to each object in the set. This involves two processes: partitioning (separating) and tagging (naming, for example, one, two, three…) – partitioning those objects that have been tagged, and those that have not yet been, and tagging one item at a time.
- **Stable order principle** – the numbers are used in a repeatable order, in most cases involving knowledge of the number sequence.
- **Cardinal principle** – the number given to the final object represents the quantity of the set as a whole.
- **Abstraction principle** – the first three principles can be applied to any objects in a set and the objects do not have to be the same.
- **Order-irrelevance principle** – the order in which the numbers are given to each object is irrelevant, therefore it does not matter which of the objects receives the final number.

Cardinal principle

The counting principles above are learned gradually and the order in which these develop will vary between children (Sarnecka and Carey, 2008). The concept of cardinality is crucial; thus, it is vital to focus on this from an early age (Clements and Sarama, 2021).

Development of the cardinal principle

When focusing on how best to teach the cardinal principle, Paliwal and Baroody (2020) recommend initially using collections with quantities that children can subitise. Clements and Sarama (2021) also suggest that rather than presenting all the objects to be counted at the same time, the practitioner holds the objects behind their back. Each object is then presented one at a time and named with the appropriate number. Thus, when the child says the number two, they can only see two objects. Opportunities to draw children's attention to the purpose of counting should be grasped. Paliwal and Baroody (2018) advise for any collection to be counted, start by asking 'how many objects in this collection?' and answer, 'so there are x objects in this collection'.

Development of other aspects of counting

The knowledge of the number sequence can be termed as rote, verbal or procedural counting (Clements and Sarama, 2021; Martin et al., 2014) and links to the second principle – stable order. Crucially, Trundley (2008) highlights that children may not fully engage with the cardinal aspect of counting until they have knowledge of the stable order principle. This should be reinforced through songs and rhymes (Clements and Sarama, 2021). Detailed information about developing all principles of counting can be found in the book *Learning and Teaching with Learning Trajectories* (Clements and Sarama, 2019), but a key point to focus on is that children should have multiple experiences with number words.

Numerals

Number symbols or numerals can be used to represent a number word. Research states that the meaningful use of numerals can help children develop a concept of number (Clements and Sarama, 2021). However, there are concerns that focusing on knowing numerals may lead to practitioners imposing the standard symbols on children, which may dampen children's enthusiasm and not automatically lead to understanding (Carruthers and Worthington, 2006). The early identification or recognition of numerals begins with visual perceptual processes; however, it is the 'mapping' of the numerals that is key. Mapping involves children making connections between the numerals and the corresponding quantities (Kolkman et al., 2013; Neumann et al., 2013).

Connections between numerals and quantity

Gifford (2005) and Carruthers and Worthington (2006) encourage an emergent approach to such mapping, that encourages children to make their own mathematical marks. These marks could be early/emergent writing, pictorial representations or tally marks, for example, all of which enable children to construct their own understanding of abstract symbols or numerals based on experience with their own marks (Kolkman et al., 2013; Carruthers and Worthington, 2006; Munn, 1994). Endless opportunities can be found and encouraged within children's play, such as form filling at the vets or the use of shopping lists. Practitioners must seek opportunities for the children to explain the marks that they have made (Carruthers and Worthington, 2006). Alongside this should be rich materials that promote the use and discovery of symbols, with labels and signs on display for activities or equipment in the environment.

Summary

This chapter has sought to blend aspects of theories of learning mathematics and practice, outlining that play provides the ideal opportunity for logico-mathematical knowledge to thrive. Learning should be active, and this involves all the senses. Piaget reminds us to focus on what comes from within the child; Vygotsky champions social cognition with rich mathematical sharing of language and dialogue (mathematics talk) to support understanding; Bruner acknowledges the value of making knowledge and learning visible. And this all enables movement along a developmental learning trajectory, so that the abstract can become understandable, assimilated and accommodated. As practitioners, we must be able to capture and nurture all this by seizing opportunities for mathematics. Practitioners must use their senses, too, by observing, listening, and then responding to the children as they make sense of the world and the environment around them. The role of the practitioner is vital as their own knowledge has the potential to build confidence and transform children's mathematical learning journeys.

END-OF-CHAPTER QUESTIONS

1. Which theoretical perspectives in developing mathematics do the practices in your setting align to?
2. Reflect on the opportunities for both 'mathematics made playful' and 'mathematising play', and how to ensure an equal balance within your setting.
3. Consider ways in which practitioners can support the foundational aspects of mathematics (executive function, spatial reasoning and pattern) in addition to the development of number.

12
Digital learning in early childhood

Irene Pollock and Martin Winters

Key ideas

This chapter will explore:

- The relationship between technology, child development and learning.
- The role of practitioners in supporting opportunities for digital learning.
- Integrating technology within non-compulsory care and education (NCE) settings.
- Frameworks and principles for digital learning.

Introduction

Digital learning in early childhood is a subject explored from a range of perspectives in a growing field of research looking for answers to a number of questions. One significant question is: how can practitioners use digital resources and technology to effectively support and enhance learning experiences in Childhood Practice settings? Such settings include the range of provision and services in the non-compulsory care and education (NCE) sector. This chapter draws on a developing body of research to outline some key issues related to this topic and provide some possible answers to that question.

Digital learning

From the printing press to the internet, new technologies are often viewed by adults with a mix of optimism and concern over their impact on children (Nutbrown, 2019; Postman, 1994). In the context of NCE, optimistic views regarding new technology express ideas around the potential for it to transform learning environments and enhance learning opportunities (Miller et al., 2019; Yelland, 2015; Puentedura, 2006). However, concerns are also expressed over the potentially negative influence of technology on aspects of child development and learning (Dunn et al., 2018; Snider and Hirschy, 2009). Such views create uncertainty for practitioners around the use of technology to support learning, particularly during critical stages of development in the early years (Coban, 2020).

This tension can be linked to a range of issues related to the use of technology for digital learning, such as understandings of childhood (Postman, 1994), power relationships between children and adults (Lindahl and Folkesson, 2012), online safety (Quigley and Blashki, 2003), children's rights (Dunn et al., 2018) and children's agency in learning (Petersen, 2015). While a closer look at such topics is beyond the scope of this chapter, they shape the landscapes of learning where technology is becoming, or already has become, an integral part of children's experience of childhood and learning.

─────────────── **THINKING POINT 12.1** ───────────────

1. As a practitioner, what are some of your hopes regarding the use of technology to support learning?
2. What concerns do you have regarding the use of technology?
3. In what ways are your views shared by/or different from other practitioners in your setting?

The concept of digital learning draws on understandings developed by research to define, explore and clarify the role of technology in learning. Just as technology has developed at a rapid pace in recent years, so too have the concepts used to describe digital learning. Gilster (1997) describes ways of understanding digital literacy as the skills needed to access and evaluate information through digital resources. Developing this idea, in tandem with developments in technology, others began to explore concepts of multimodal learning (Wolfe and Flewitt, 2010) and digital fluency (Palaiologou, 2016). Such developments have helped to describe the variety of ways in which learners can employ different modes of interacting, not just with technology but also with others through technology to support their learning (Yelland, 2015). This approach of recontextualising traditional ideas about learning considers not just the process of how children can learn with and from technology but also the wider implications of learning through technology to develop digital competence (Lund et al., 2014; Janssen et al., 2013).

Digital competence (Falloon, 2020) in this context relates to:

- the knowledge and abilities required to use technology;
- flexibility to adapt those abilities to different learning tasks;
- awareness of socio-political factors related to the use of technology in society; and
- the ability to reflect on the purpose and value of technology in different learning environments and contexts.

Digital learning is defined here as a process of developing the contextually bound knowledge, skills and competencies required to support learning through technology (Falloon, 2020; Daniels et al., 2019; Manches and Plowman, 2017). A holistic and humanistic view of education (Petty, 2014) and child development (Bronfenbrenner, 1979) is essential to this understanding of digital learning. It places learners, not the technology used to support learning, at the centre of pedagogical approaches used to support digital learning.

Technology and child development

Research on the topic of technology use in childhood often begins by acknowledging the important role it plays in shaping children's experience of childhood, particularly in developed nations (Dunn et al., 2018; Lahikainen and Arminen, 2017; Snider and Hirschy, 2009). While technology may be viewed as an integral part of everyday life for children in such nations, Yelland (2015) suggests there is a disconnect between children's informal experiences of using technology (e.g. at home or during self-directed play) and the ways in which it is used to facilitate formal learning opportunities. Factors contributing to this disconnect have been highlighted in studies exploring practitioner perceptions of the role and purpose of technology in NCE settings, described in the section 'Technology in practice'.

—————————— **THINKING POINT 12.2** ——————————

1. Reflecting on your own observations of children using technology in different learning contexts, what do you notice about how technology is used in play?
2. What might this suggest?

Findings from a range of studies on the influence of technology use on child development indicate both potentially positive and negative outcomes. For example, Snider and Hirschy (2009) summarise a range of research findings to report on evidence indicating that overuse of technology can lead to: obesity through lack of physical activity; hearing loss; lack of concentration skills; disruption of adult–child relationships; and poorer outcomes in terms of a child's emotional development. Others, such as Zabatiero et al. (2018), also highlight concerns around social isolation caused by the use of technology. In contrast, other research highlights positive outcomes of technology use in childhood which can be linked to specific strands of development, including social development, such as:

- the development of prosocial behaviours (Ralph, 2018);
- social interaction through collaborative learning opportunities (Madanipour and Cohrssen, 2020);
- the development of creativity and problem-solving skills;
- improved mark-making ability;
- communication skills; and
- increased motivation for learning (Dunn et al., 2018).

Coban (2020) proposes there is a 'tipping point' in terms of technology use which changes it from a factor enhancing play, learning and development to becoming one that is potentially detrimental to a child's holistic development. Coban (2020) suggests that adults are responsible for facilitating a balanced approach in using technology to enhance opportunities for digital play and learning without impacting on critical stages of development.

Research on digital play (Marsh et al., 2016) provides a starting point to help adults develop understandings of children's perceptions and experiences of play and learning through technology and how this relates to their holistic development.

This understanding, according to Nutbrown (2019), can help practitioners view the process of integrating technology into learning environments as one centred around the learner. It shifts the focus away from practitioner concerns (e.g. lack of confidence, skill or knowledge about digital devices) and takes into account a learner's prior knowledge and experience. This perspective can help practitioners develop pedagogical approaches that will support the effective use of technology in practice as a tool for scaffolding digital play, learning and development.

For children, the use of digital technology in play across different learning contexts is, according to Dunn et al. (2018: 824), 'seamless, yet different'. Whether at home or in an educational setting, children appear to use technology as one resource among many to engage in play and do not share adult concerns over its use in the learning environment. Encouraging children's active participation in research on and the process of technology integration to Childhood Practice is key to challenging the 'polarised narratives' surrounding this topic (Dunn et al., 2018: 820). A crucial factor in determining the outcome of this process is the perceptions of practitioners on how technology can be used to support a child's holistic development and facilitate opportunities for learning.

VIEW FROM PRACTICE

Use of iPads in the nursery

Before the COVID-19 pandemic, we used technology in the nursery – it's part of the curriculum after all – but it was limited. The technology we had access to, like computers and cameras, would mostly be used by staff to record learning. Children were encouraged to develop computer skills but this was adult-led and supported most of the time because children found using the equipment we had, like the computer mouse and keyboard, difficult to get the hang of. Not long before the pandemic, staff members in my setting were given iPads. It was great to be given more up-to-date technology but a few members of the team weren't sure how to use them. Instead, the children often ended up showing us their potential since quite a few already had tablets at home.

During the pandemic, especially the first lockdown, we had to use technology and social media to stay in touch with families and children. Families would share information and pictures of what their children had been doing at home and staff would respond with activity and learning ideas for families. At the time, digital learning helped to bridge some of the gaps between home and nursery that in years gone by we would not have been able to have done in the same way. We used technology to support and strengthen our relationships with service users during a challenging time, not to replace them.

When returning to nursery, we started to make more use of the iPads we had been given. Staff spent lots of time exploring their potential and observing how children were using them.

(Continued)

Some children would have happily spent hours watching content on YouTube, so this was something we discussed and tried to limit. However, there were lots of other positive learning experiences to be had with the iPads and so this was our focus, finding interactive ways of using them with the children to support their learning. Relationships are the 'bread and butter' of our practice and digital learning needs to go hand in hand with conversations and ongoing communication.

Technology in practice

During the lockdowns resulting from the COVID-19 pandemic, educators at all levels were required to increase their use of technology in practice and to adapt their pedagogical approaches to continue supporting learners. Research on practitioner and learner experience during that time is still emerging (OECD and Education International, 2021; Doucet et al., 2020). However, the pandemic is likely to have encouraged many practitioners to engage with learning through technology in a way that they had not done, and in some cases not wanted to do, before the pandemic. This experience may have helped to address some of the key concerns and barriers around technology integration, to identify solutions to overcome such barriers and to challenge the existing beliefs of practitioners. The focus on using technology to maintain relationships and to continue supporting learning provided motivation for many to develop the technological skills, knowledge and pedagogical approaches needed to support digital learning. This process contributes to an ongoing shift away from pre-existing debates to consider not if, but how, technology should be used in practice to support digital learning (Lui and Audran, 2017).

The values, beliefs and personal experiences of practitioners are key factors influencing the integration and use of technology in NCE settings (Mertala, 2019; Miller et al., 2019; Ingleby, 2015). In addition, the personal and professional technological knowledge and skills that practitioners have can determine the extent to which technology is effectively incorporated into pedagogical practice (Aldemir et al., 2019; Miller et al., 2019; Quigley and Blashki, 2003).

Practitioner confidence and competence in being able to use technology to support digital learning is one possible barrier to successful integration into practice (Manches and Plowman, 2017; Wolfe and Flewitt, 2010). However, steps to overcome this by acquiring the skills and confidence required to use technology and digital devices, through practitioner education programmes for example, do not necessarily translate into the effective integration of such resources (Falloon, 2020). Even practitioners with high levels of confidence and skill in using technology in their personal lives can struggle to translate this familiarity into learning environments and their pedagogical practice (Fotakopoulou et al., 2020).

THINKING POINT 12.3

1. What are your views on children's use of technology for learning?
2. How confident are you in using technology to support opportunities for learning and digital play?
3. What key skills do you need to develop to support the use of technology for digital learning and play?

If practitioners are to avoid the potential outcome of technology being used by children only for passive consumption of media content, then issues such as practitioner confidence and understandings of how to effectively use resources to support digital learning need to be addressed. In doing so, the ineffective use of digital devices as babysitters or 'digital pacifiers' (Coban, 2020: 67) in practice can be challenged. Models for integrating and using technology in NCE settings, outlined briefly in the section 'Frameworks for digital learning' below, offer some suggestions to address such issues, as does the section 'Principles to support digital learning'.

To avoid the use of technology at all in NCE settings, or to rely on its use as a distraction or pacifier, is to undermine the role of technology and digital learning in children's lived experience of childhood. Educational policy and curricular frameworks also highlight the importance of technology in society by outlining educational goals for learners to develop the flexible digital skills and knowledge needed to support future economies (Burbules et al., 2020; Yelland and Gilbert, 2018; Wolfe and Flewitt, 2010).

The following curricula and associated documents from each of the four nations in the UK all contain some guidance on the role of technology in learning:

*   England: The Statutory Framework for the Early Years Foundation Stage (Department for Education [DfE], 2021b).
*   Northern Ireland: Curricular Guidance for Pre-School Education (Council for the Curriculum, Examinations and Assessment [CCEA], 2018).
*   Scotland: Scotland's Curriculum for Excellence (Scottish Government [SG], 2008b).
*   Wales: The Foundation Phase Framework (Welsh Government, 2015).

Such curricula, along with the many policies and frameworks offering guidance for practitioners to implement them in practice, often highlight the role of technology in children's lives and in supporting future economies. In recent years, this perspective on the role of technology in education has been developed to suggest that access to digital learning should be viewed as a human right which can support more opportunities for self-directed learning at all levels of education (International Council of Education Advisers [ICEA], 2020).

While such educational frameworks and policies may be arguably vague regarding the specifics of integrating and using technology in practice, there is no shortage of suggestions and clear guidance available to practitioners. The next section highlights examples of more detailed frameworks and models for integrating and using technology to support digital learning.

Frameworks for digital learning

Just as different tools can be required for completing different tasks so too are different frameworks required for integrating and supporting digital learning in a range of learning contexts and environments. There is no 'one-size-fits-all' approach, and nor should there be, according to Kimmons and Hall (2017: 34), who suggest an approach of 'informed pluralism' in practice. This approach supports an awareness and evaluation of the models and pedagogical approaches available to practitioners when using technology to support digital learning in different contexts. The models and frameworks described in this section can be used to consider the implications, possible outcomes and issues related to supporting digital learning.

Substitution, Augmentation, Modification, Redefinition (SAMR) (Puentedura, 2013, 2006)

This model categorises different ways in which technology can be integrated into practice to support digital learning. It can be useful for reflecting on and evaluating the pedagogical approaches used in this process, for example:

- Substituting a technological version, such as a tablet device and the use of drawing apps, for conventional resources such as paper and pencil.
- Augmenting traditional approaches to teaching and learning through the use of technology (e.g. game apps which help to develop mark making).
- Modification through more interactive and collaborative learning opportunities (e.g. use of camera or screenshots to capture digital drawings and create a story board).
- Redefinition by providing opportunities for creative and child-led learning experiences afforded by technology (e.g. the design of a character and creation of a story which could be enacted, captured and edited by children using recording equipment and the editing capabilities of devices).

Technological, Pedagogical and Content Knowledge (TPACK) (Mishra et al., 2009; Mishra and Koehler, 2006)

Each component of this framework describes the areas of knowledge that support practitioners in making effective decisions about the use of technology in practice to support digital learning. Traditional teaching approaches can tend to focus on the content of what is being taught, but the TPACK framework highlights the importance of considering the relationship between content knowledge, the practitioner's under-standing of pedagogy and the technology used to support this process. The framework provides a way for practitioners to consider the most effective use of technology and pedagogical approaches to deliver content knowledge at the right time and in the right context for learners.

The Teacher Digital Competency (TDC) framework (Falloon, 2020)

This framework incorporates the TPACK model to consider, in greater detail, the rela-tionships between technology, learners, practitioners and the learning environment. Social and ethical elements are also included to encourage the development of skills for learners and practitioners to use technology in sustainable, ethical and safe ways, for example by highlighting issues for consideration such as digital citizenship, human rights, agency in learning and digital wellbeing.

The competencies outlined in this framework provide guidance and suggestions for the selection of particular pedagogical approaches to effectively support digital learning. These include:

- the design of interdisciplinary learning opportunities and teaching approaches;
- the use of teachable moments and in-the-moment planning to develop learner interests;
- collaborative learning opportunities; and
- valuing a child-centred approach in all learning and teaching.

These represent a small sample of the models and frameworks available to practitioners looking for effective ways of integrating technology into their pedagogical practice to support digital learning. Such tools can provide a starting point for considering the 'how' and 'what' of technology integration in practice. In the next section, some key principles are outlined that provide a starting point to consider the 'why' of this process to support a critical reflection on the role, purpose and potential of technology in digital learning.

Principles to support digital learning

The principles outlined in this section are suggestions to support practitioners in developing an awareness and understanding of their role in the process of digital learning. The application of each principle in practice will of course depend on the context in which digital learning takes place and upon the individual needs of the learners and practitioners.

1. Recognition of prior digital learning

Not all children have equal access to digital resources. The 'digital divide' is a term often used to describe the separation between those with access to and use of technology in society and those without (van Dijk, 2020). Since gaining prominence in the mid-1990s, this concept has shaped the discourse around technology and equality of opportunity in Western society.

While some might critique the term for obscuring the complex, intersectional and changing nature of digital inequality across cultures (Holmes and Burgess, 2021; Gunkel, 2003), the term continues to inform understandings of such issues. Concerns about digital inequality and its possible impact on lifelong outcomes, highlighted throughout the COVID-19 pandemic, drive initiatives to reduce digital exclusion and inequality in society (Scottish Government [SG], 2021c).

Such efforts to equip more citizens with access to technology, the existing presence of technology in the homes of many, and its increasing presence in NCE settings, mean that a significant number of children are already equipped with a range of skills, understandings and experiences of using technology to engage in digital play and learning.

As practitioners, it is important to recognise this experience (and, in some cases, expertise) as it can be used to support a collaborative approach to enhancing digital learning opportunities. It is an important first step in practitioners developing technological knowledge with and alongside learners, in order to adapt pedagogical approaches that are responsive to individual learner needs and appropriate for the contexts in which learning takes place.

Some strategies to begin this process of recognising prior learning include:

- Conducting observations on the way in which children use and interact with technology in their play, with the aim of identifying digital play preferences and styles.
- Identifying apps and devices used in the home learning environment and how these align with resources available in the setting.
- Consultation with children to explore their ideas and feelings about technology.

- Developing an understanding of individual and changing learner needs to scaffold and support learning through technology, where and when appropriate, based on this understanding.
- Exploring issues regarding online safety and the appropriate use of technology with children, families and colleagues.

2. Promoting active participation

Authentic engagement in the learning process requires active participation, where children's views and ideas are heard and have real consequences. Digital learning opportunities should be supported by resources, experiences and technology, which promote this level of participation and foster a respect for others to do the same. Some ways of developing active participation in digital learning might include:

- Promoting opportunities for children to work together with technology to encourage positive interactions, supporting social relationships and collaboration between learners to achieve shared and individual learning goals.
- Considering and evaluating the types of apps and activities used in learning experiences. The use of 'open apps', which promote creative freedom of expression or collaboration with others to solve authentic problems, is preferred to 'closed apps', which have limited possible outcomes as they direct learners through prescribed stages or processes with little room for real choice and depth in learning (Lynch and Redpath, 2014).
- Providing opportunities to develop the physical and cognitive skills required to engage with and manipulate technological resources when engaged in digital learning: for example, activities to develop fine motor skills, hand and eye coordination, problem solving, research skills and symbol/letter recognition, among others.
- Evaluating digital learning experiences soon after they have taken place or as they are taking place (e.g. with the use of observation, conversations with learners). As part of the evaluation process, consideration should be given to the views, experiences and feelings of children taking part in digital learning opportunities, with a recognition of the social and emotional impact the use of technology can have on learners.
- Planning collaboratively for digital learning opportunities, with learners taking a role in the design of activities that support active participation in this process. Such activities might include those based on data collected from observations or consultation with learners, with consideration being given to the level of participation, for example using a model such as Hart's (1992) ladder of participation.

3. Use of the 4 C's – critical thinking, creativity, communication and collaboration (Burbules et al., 2020; National Educational Association, 2012)

If a central aim of education is to help learners develop the skills and knowledge needed to reach their potential and prepare them for an unknown future workforce, then a focus on developing transferable skills, such as the 4 C's, can provide an effective way of reframing the basic principles of early education to support digital learning. Each skill outlined in this final principle requires the ability of learners to engage with others, their learning environments and the available resources to develop solutions to authentic problems, for example:

- Critical thinking can be promoted through regular practitioner and learner evaluation of the resources, experiences and views of learners on the use of technology in the learning environment. It can also be supported using existing pedagogical approaches to develop a deeper understanding of the connections between different aspects of knowledge and learning, such as those outlined in curriculum design principles and in approaches facilitating the use of higher order thinking skills as outlined in Bloom's (1956) taxonomy.
- Creativity in this context relates to the ways in which learners can have the freedom to take the lead in their own learning. It is a process involving the connections made between new information and existing knowledge, as well as the ability to express new ideas and views. Creativity may be facilitated by carefully considered play provocations, offering child-accessible digital resources that do not require an adult's permission to use, and the provision of open-ended digital resources that can be used in a variety of ways by learners to express their own ideas and understanding of their learning experiences.
- Communication is a fundamental part of building responsive relationships, which help practitioners to understand, anticipate and meet the individual and changing needs of learners. Developing ways of communicating not only with learners, but also with families and colleagues, can be supported through the use of a digital learning journal in which the child's voice and contribution to its creation are clearly evident. This can be enhanced by using technology to capture learning experiences (e.g. photos or videos recorded by the learner) and the sharing of ideas, knowledge and approaches to supporting digital learning among communities of practice.
- Collaboration between learners and practitioners is important not only for the recognition of prior digital learning but also in providing opportunities for active participation and scaffolding. New technologies provide a range of opportunities for collaborative approaches to learning and teaching but these should complement

or enhance, rather than replace, the relationships and interactions between learners and practitioners in the learning environment. Opportunities for child-led collaboration among learners, focused on achieving shared goals, would support aspects of this and other principles outlined in this section.

Encouraging the development of these four skills when designing learning experiences, developing pedagogical approaches and engaging with learners – whether using technology or not – can support practitioners in reflecting on their role as well as the purpose and role of technology in digital learning.

Summary

This chapter has considered some of the key topics and debates around digital learning. In highlighting different ways for practitioners to reflect on and evaluate approaches to supporting digital learning in NCE settings, three key principles have been identified: recognition of prior digital learning, promoting active participation and the use of the 4 C's. These principles acknowledge the role of technology in children's lives, now and in the future, while emphasising the importance of relationships in the process of learning. Ultimately, NCE settings are not transformed or changed by technology itself, but can be transformed and improved by practitioners who are responsive to the changing nature of play and learning.

END-OF-CHAPTER QUESTIONS

1. In your own practice, how do you recognise the existing technological skills, abilities and experience of the learners you work with?
2. How does this knowledge inform your practice and approach to supporting play, learning and development?
3. What challenges are faced in your own setting in terms of using technology to support digital learning, and how can these be overcome?

Part IV
Perspectives on play

13
Playful pedagogy
Elizabeth Black

Key ideas

This chapter will explore:

- Definitions of play and playful pedagogy.
- Policy across the UK identifying play as key to children's learning, and evidence to support this connection.
- The difference between pedagogy which centralises the actions of adults, and play which centralises the experiences of children, therefore children's own definitions of play are crucial.
- The key features of play as choice, direction and motivation in order to understand children's experiences of play on a continuum.
- The role of a playful pedagogical approach in facilitating the engagement of children with activities across the continuum within each day or session.

Introduction

Many practitioners would describe play as being central to work with children and young people; however, there are longstanding associations and tensions between play and learning (Kuschner, 2012). Variation in practitioners' understandings of play as a concept and a practice has been noted (King and Newstead, 2019), with recently renewed calls for clear evidence to connect play and learning (Liu et al., 2017; Lillard et al., 2013) and an ever-growing range of research literature and explanatory texts seeking to address this issue. This chapter will highlight some key areas of tension in defining play, before discussing the role of pedagogical principles in guiding practitioners' approaches to play, noting that the childcare sector brings together practitioners from a range of playful traditions, and that not all would consider promotion of learning to be an appropriate focus of their practice. For those whose practice does focus on promotion of learning, the remainder of the chapter will explore ways in which play might be developed as a pedagogical approach, arguing that identifying the role of the adult in play is key to a clear understanding and effective use of intentionally playful approaches.

Defining play

There are many competing, and often contradictory, definitions and typologies of play offered by theorists; Loebach and Cox (2020) provide a useful overview, which establishes several areas of tension. Firstly, play is defined both as the child's work and the antithesis of work (Brown et al., 2018). As Brehony (2008) illustrates, adult fascination with understanding and responding to children's play is a centuries-old concern and play has frequently been associated with games and leisure activities, famously depicted in the sixteenth-century painting *Children's Games* (Orrock, 2012). However, the association of play with potential for learning is also historical, and key theorists such as Froebel, Piaget, Dewey, Vygotsky and Bruner identified play as a natural learning mechanism or process that can be promoted or utilised by parents and teachers (see Howard and McInnes [2013] for an overview of theories of play). Over time, these theories have been blended and assimilated by practitioners and parents into a broad general understanding of the benefits of play for children's learning, but where play is often presented in opposition to academic learning (Kuschner, 2012).

    The association of play with leisure and relaxation is reinforced in Article 31 of the Convention on the Rights of the Child: 'Every child has the right to relax, play and take part in a wide range of cultural and artistic activities' (UNICEF, online-e). Within the UK, the Playwork Principles, created in 2005, agreed an approach for practitioners working with children in various play projects and settings, defining play as 'a process that is freely chosen, personally directed and intrinsically motivated. That is, children and young people determine and control the content and intent of their play, by following their own instincts, ideas and interests, in their own way for their own reasons' (Play Wales, 2015: n.p.). Evaluation of progress towards meeting children's rights has highlighted a lack of access to appropriate play opportunities (International Play Association [IPA], 2013; Brown, 2008a) and, in the UK, has resulted in a plethora of policy statements and organisations promoting play across the four nations. The Playwork Principles definition has been influential and is frequently echoed within this guidance (for example, Play England, 2020; Scottish Government [SG], 2013a: 12; Welsh Assembly Government, 2002: 3; PlayBoard NI, online); however, within these documents, a further tension is established, with play required to be carried out for no external reason, to be 'non-essential' (IPA, 2013: 2), and yet simultaneously being acknowledged as beneficial for the child and wider society in various ways.

As the profile of play has been raised, gaps in the supporting evidence have been highlighted, and researchers are seeking to address these (Zosh et al., 2018). Contemporary findings are strengthening the rationale for play as a key pedagogical approach, central to health, emotional wellbeing and learning, particularly for the youngest children, within childcare and educational establishments, and also reinforcing calls to promote recreational play within childcare services, schools and in the community (Welsh Government, 2022c; Play England, 2020; SG, 2013a; PlayBoard NI, online). A final tension is established here, as this emphasis on play competes with a simultaneous emphasis on the focused teaching of academic skills to improve performance on national and international tests (Wood, 2015).

Given the variation in activities that have been claimed as or excluded from being play, this chapter will return to the broader definition of play as freely chosen, personally directed and intrinsically motivated. This allows the definition of play activities to be returned to children, in keeping with an understanding of the child as an active participant in their experiences (Howard and McInnes, 2013); however, as adults, practitioners need to decide what their role should be in children's play, requiring an understanding of these tensions inherent in definitions of play, and their own responses. The next section will consider how pedagogy focuses on defining the role of the adult.

Defining playful pedagogy

Pedagogy is a term drawn from ancient Greek, meaning literally to lead or guide the child (Papatheodorou, 2009), and in English-speaking traditions has become closely associated with the content, methods and purpose of teaching (Smith, 2021). This recurrent association of pedagogy with teaching can raise conceptual barriers for childcare practitioners, perhaps explaining the findings of Stephen (2010; see also O'Sullivan, 2019) that practitioners are uncomfortable using the term, struggling to describe their own pedagogical approach.

Taking the perspective that a conscious engagement with underpinning beliefs is crucial for any practitioner and building on ideas from social and relational pedagogical practices (Smith, 2021; Petrie et al., 2009), this chapter will define pedagogy as: practices that facilitate children's learning, development or wider wellbeing and the guiding principles that underpin these. This deliberately open definition allows that the practitioner's role may focus practitioners on the child's learning and/or development and/or wider wellbeing, providing space for an understanding of pedagogy as relevant to those focused on play opportunities or family support as well as early learning.

Returning to the Greek terminology, Papatheodorou (2009: 4) notes that "'guide" suggests that two (or more) people walk side-by-side and hand-in-hand along a route or path that has been walked before by one member of the group'; therefore, pedagogy can be understood as drawing on experience to know when and how to offer required support. Playful pedagogy can then be defined as the use of play or playfulness by practitioners to support the learning, development or wellbeing of children and young people. For some practitioners, this might mean that the Playwork Principles (Play Wales, 2015) are the underpinning framework for practice supporting creation of spaces for play. Chapter 14 focuses further on this approach, so the present discussion will explore the use of play or playfulness by practitioners viewing learning as an explicit intention of their practice.

THINKING POINT 13.1

1. What are your feelings about the terms 'play' and 'pedagogy'? Describe how these terms relate to your practice.
2. How would you explain the pedagogical approaches adopted within your setting?
3. What do you think the adult role should be in relation to play?

As Rogers (2011) notes, any discussion of pedagogy automatically recentralises the role of the adult, while the definition of play as non-essential and intrinsically motivated clearly centralises the child and their experiences within the setting (Goouch, 2009). Where settings are required to meet curriculum outcomes, or promote specific developmental goals, playful pedagogy seeks to recognise and maximise children's instinctive learning processes. The following sections will identify ways in which children are known to learn through play, before reflecting on how understanding play might inform more effective adult interventions.

Play as a learning experience

While it is commonly accepted that children learn from play, a lack of evidence supporting these claims has also been noted (Liu et al., 2017; Lillard et al., 2013; Trawick-Smith, 1989); however, there is a growing body of research into learning processes from neurobiology and psychology indicating support for play as an effective learning mechanism, and identifying aspects of play that encourage learning. This section describes themes in play as a learning experience.

The first of these is exploration and repetition: learning processes theorised by Piaget, Montessori, Froebel and others as key to the development of young children (Brown et al., 2018). While Hutt (1976, cited in Howard and McInnes, 2013: 40) explicitly excluded experimentation from play, others note that play is often observed to be a space where children try things out and appear to have less fear of trying something new (Howard and McInnes, 2013: 136). Having experimented, play also offers space for repeating the action, perhaps multiple times, in a way that adult-directed activities may not – a process referred to by Zosh et al. (2018: 3) as 'iteration'.

Secondly, play requires negotiation through the choice of who to play with (or to play alone) and the associated interactions. Choosing and playing in groups has been observed to involve complex, child-determined rules with opportunities for learning about leadership, ownership and agency (Wood, 2014; Pellegrini et al., 2002). For Vygotsky, this type of social interaction was central to learning (Fleer, 2021) and contemporary research supports the idea that humans are born with an instinct to communicate, and that this communication can reinforce and extend learning (Zosh et al., 2018; Paas and Sweller, 2012).

A third theme focuses on the physicality of play. The location of play activities (for example, at a table, on the floor) has been identified as an important characteristic (Howard and McInnes, 2013), with some evidence that table-top activities are less likely to be associated by children with playing than being on the floor. Referring to Montessori practice, Lillard (2017) notes significant confirmatory evidence for the choice of where to work as effectively supporting engagement. Additionally, play allows for exploration and repetition of large and small movements, supporting both physical development and skills in multimodal communication: combining the use of words, gestures, location, objects and movement (Cowan, 2020).

Finally, play is understood to promote emotional development and the restoration of balance (Brown et al., 2018). Lester and Russell (2008a) found evidence that increased resilience was a key outcome of play, while more recently Zosh et al. (2018) note ways in which play develops socio-emotional regulation. The opportunity for exploring emotional responses and imaginary situations appears to be key to these outcomes

(Howard and McInnes, 2013). An attribute of play cited in some definitions is that it is fun, and Liu et al. (2017) have identified that joyfulness might also provide motivation for learning.

Play as a teaching opportunity

In this section, teaching will be defined as adult intervention in the process of learning (Early Education, 2021) and the focus will be on ways in which practitioners might capitalise on playful approaches to achieve learning goals. Debate over the appropriateness of curriculum guidance for children in the early years is beyond the scope of this chapter, as is discussion of playful pedagogy specifically within primary school settings (Walsh et al., 2017); however, across the UK (and beyond), policy and guidance documents stress the value of play as a pedagogical approach for those working with children. Key messages are summarised in Table 13.1, which illustrates the way in which play has become not only the recommended, but the mandated approach to working with young children (Wood, 2015).

Table 13.1   Key messages in curriculum guidance relating to play

Country	Guidance type	Title	Age range	Play focus
England	Statutory	Statutory Framework for the Early Years Foundation Stage (Department for Education, 2021b)	0-5 years	Play is identified as important for learning: 'Play is essential for children's development, building their confidence as they learn to explore, relate to others, set their own goals and solve problems. Children learn by leading their own play, and by taking part in play which is guided by adults' (page 16).
England	Non-statutory	Birth to Five Matters (Early Education, 2021)	0-5 years	Substantial focus on play for supporting learning and wellbeing throughout: 'Adults must have a deep understanding of how play of different types supports children to develop and learn' (page 11).
Scotland	Statutory	Curriculum for Excellence (Scottish Government, 2008b)	3-18 years	Minimal focus on play, mainly identified as a format for learning (e.g. energetic play) and also reference to the value of play for active learning.
Scotland	Supplementary	Realising the Ambition (Education Scotland, 2020)	0-8 years	Emphasises play as central to learning for children up to the age of 8, drawing on Froebel and play research to centralise play as a mode for working with children across this age group: 'Child-centred play pedagogy requires us to take the lead from the children' (page 46).

Country	Guidance type	Title	Age range	Play focus
Wales	Non-statutory	Welsh Curriculum for funded non-maintained nursery settings (Welsh Government, 2022c)	3-4 years	Strong statements supporting play: 'Play is not only crucial to the way children become self-aware and the way in which they learn the rules of social behaviour; it is also fundamental to physical, intellectual and creative development' (page 15).
	Statutory and supplementary	Curriculum for Wales (Welsh Government, 2022d)	3-16 years	Guidance on curriculum design notes that play and play-based learning are 'essential' for learning, particularly for children up to the age of 5: 'Play and play-based learning supports holistic development across the curriculum. It should be valued by all practitioners as both an end in itself and as something that they should observe closely with the clear aim of seeing how it can enhance learning' (n.p.).
Northern Ireland	Non-statutory	Curricular Guidance for Preschool Education (Council for the Curriculum, Examinations and Assessment [CCEA], 2018)	3-4 years	Play is identified as a key activity: 'Learning through play is fundamental to children's social, emotional and educational development' (page 3).
	Statutory	Northern Ireland Curriculum Primary (CCEA, 2007)	4-11 years	Play is particularly a focus of the foundation stage for children aged 4-6 years: 'In the Foundation Stage children should experience much of their learning through well planned and challenging play. Self-initiated play helps children to understand and learn about themselves and their surroundings. Motivation can be increased when children have opportunities to make choices and decisions about their learning' (page 9).

Lester and Russell (2008a) conclude that policy outcomes are more likely to be met when children are able to play, and the previously discussed evidence supports an understanding of play as valuable to learning processes. Howard and McInnes (2013: 2) capture this in the idea of play as a loudspeaker 'maximising all of the learning processes that we know already are at work'; however, research findings repeatedly conclude that where specific academic learning goals are to be met, greater adult intervention is required to 'guide' (Zosh et al., 2018) or 'structure' (Walsh et al., 2011) play. This can be seen to place 'true' play in opposition to play for learning and some reservations about this approach will now be considered.

Limits to teaching through play

Howard and McInnes (2013) note that there is some evidence that even if activities are play-like, if they are perceived to be 'not play' by children, then the amplifying of learning does not take place to the same extent. Bruckman (1999: 75) uses the term 'chocolate-dipped broccoli' for activities where adults adopt a thin veneer of playfulness to mask their own learning agenda, and where the danger is that well-meaning adults close down play by imposing their own goals. Countering this are authors (Zosh et al., 2018; Trawick-Smith, 1989) asserting that the learning of some skills is best achieved through adult intervention in play: a context for learning chosen by the adult with a learning outcome in mind, or where the adult is actively involved in the play, but where play is directed by the child.

Although it is not necessarily a question of choosing one approach or the other, it is critical that practitioners have a clear understanding of their own and their setting's pedagogical principles; an awareness of whether play or learning is the end goal. If the setting prioritises free play as the route to a foundation for later academic learning, then less intervention is likely to be appropriate. Where academic outcomes are tracked, some adult intervention is more likely to be viewed as necessary to achieve progress. Using playful activities to maximise learning requires that the essence of play is retained (Zosh et al., 2018). Building on the definition of free play discussed previously, the following sections will therefore consider ways in which adults might design activities to foreground children's choice and direction and maintain a sense of intrinsic motivation.

Freely chosen

Drawing on the three defining characteristics of play discussed at the beginning of the chapter, the first aspect to consider is free choice. With the exception of some adventure play and wild outdoor settings, as soon as children enter a setting, they are likely to be entering into planned play, as the space is controlled by adults. Where children are involved in designing and choosing elements of the environment, they will have been invited to do so by adults. Immediately, then, the notion that play is freely chosen is restricted and adults will have to work to create ways in which children can experience choice.

Howard and McInnes (2013) note the value of establishing what children themselves understand to be play within any given context. Their research has found that activities adults perceive as play, that might look very similar to play, and be enjoyed by children, can actually be perceived as not play by children. They propose a method for gathering the views of children within a setting to determine what characterises play. Having developed an awareness of what children in the setting consider to be play, the adults can then create an environment rich with those opportunities. Given the findings of Lillard et al. (2013) in identifying the value placed on choice by children, free-flow spaces, accessible resources and self-chosen groupings are likely to be appropriate.

Invitations, provocations or propositions – where some kind of resource or stimulus is introduced to the environment based on children's observed conceptual interests and offered as an open-ended starting point – may be valuable approaches to support or extend learning while leaving the level of engagement and direction of development within the child's control. However, Forman and Fyfe (2012) observe that provocations based on superficial topics of interest are less likely to support learning, and Kashin (2019) cautions that the design of provocations must remain focused on the child's experience, rather than the adult's skill. The Playworlds approach, conceived of by Lindqvist (Fleer, 2021), draws on adult knowledge of children's interests to allow for the creation of a focused learning context, with opportunities for conceptual development through problem solving. Effectively, the adults concerned establish a context in which children choose to join in adult-initiated play.

Personally directed

The second defining aspect of play is that it should be personally directed. The nearness of adults during play has been identified as important for children's confidence in trying new things and, for the youngest children particularly, will be essential for safety; however, Howard and McInnes (2013: 124) identify the value of adults being 'proximal' while children are playing, rather than necessarily part of the game, and the constant presence and guidance of adults is sometimes seen as diminishing opportunities to play (Brown et al., 2018). Loebach and Cox (2020) note the restorative value to children of hiding or playing unobserved; therefore it seems that opportunities for children to be unobserved, alone or in groups, but aware of nearby adults in case of difficulty are key within a playful pedagogical approach.

Where adults only engage children to direct their activities, children have been found to identify the adult presence as a defining feature of not playing (Howard and McInnes, 2013: 57); however, there is substantial evidence that children can enjoy playing with adults, and that these interactions can offer some of the strongest opportunities for extending learning, and possibly extending the play as well. King and Newstead (2019) observe the importance of an attitude of playfulness in the practitioner for enabling children to see adults as play partners or collaborators rather than hijackers. Within the Reggio Emilia approach, Edwards (2012: 151) notes that the response of adult to child in play should be like catching and returning a ball, while Howard and McInnes (2013) illustrate the value of understanding the play cycle, within which adults' knowledge of play cues supports awareness of when to join in play and when to observe.

Having 'caught the ball' or responded to a cue, a practitioner can verbally scaffold and extend learning within the play, developing the kind of 'sustained, shared thinking' found to be effective practice (Siraj-Blatchford and Sylva, 2004). Zosh et al. (2018) also note discussion during play as a key part of 'guiding' children towards intended learning outcomes where children's own limited experiences would otherwise curtail their learning. To continue allowing children to direct the play, practitioners should frame their interjections in an open-ended manner that permits the child to engage or dismiss the proposed direction, for example thinking aloud with 'I wonder what...?' (van Oers and Duijkers, 2013), and be prepared to step out from the play when their support is no longer required (King and Newstead, 2019).

Intrinsically motivated

The third characteristic of play is that it should be intrinsically motivated. This would seem to be in direct opposition to any attempt to plan for specific learning outcomes, as frequently expected in government-funded childcare settings across the UK. Drawing on established early years philosophies such as Reggio Emilia and Froebelian practice, the notion of responsive planning can maintain a focus on observation of the child's interests, moving away from predetermined group plans towards a more individualised and child-led approach. There is some variation in the way in which responsive planning might be implemented, depending on the age of the children and the nature of the setting, although observation of children's abilities and interests is central (Ephgrave, 2018).

To meet the requirements for tracking progress against the specified outcomes, open-ended narrative methods of documenting learning might be adopted to create a record towards which child, practitioner and carers all contribute, where scribed comments, photographs and longer descriptions of learning can be linked to related outcomes (Carr and Lee, 2019). Within such approaches, the emphasis is on children articulating their own learning through discussion and working towards the ability to self-assess, rather than adults alone deciding what has been learned based on observable actions (Fyfe, 2012). Learning is understood to be process-driven rather than assuming that children will learn what adults teach them (Goouch, 2009). Crucially, practitioners need to recognise that children can learn from any interaction, whether positive or negative, and indeed, the opportunity for self-expression in play may lead to actions that exclude others or replicate other negative adult behaviours (Kinard et al., 2021; Lester and Russell, 2008a). The skill of the adult in playful pedagogy therefore becomes less about designing activities to achieve specified ends, and much more focused on the deep knowledge of individual children, responsive interactions, developmental processes, and possible learning trajectories within particular curricular areas (van Oers and Duijkers, 2013; Siraj-Blatchford and Sylva, 2004).

────────────── THINKING POINT 13.2 ──────────────

Thinking about the context of your setting:

1. How would you define learning opportunities for children?
2. How does this relate to the balance of play and other activities provided for children?
3. What do you see as the role of the adult in providing learning opportunities for children?

Play as a continuum of adult involvement

Whatever the context – free play, play-based learning, or more formal education – articulating play in terms of pedagogy recentralises the role of the adult. Pyle and Danniels (2017) highlight the adult role in evaluating play, noting the perceived purpose of the setting as key. Their research findings led to the description of a continuum of play-based learning, centred on the level of adult intervention, an approach also developed by Zosh et al. (2018). Figure 13.1 builds on this thinking, identifying three dimensions of adult interaction, each linked to one of the characteristics of play discussed above. While some practitioners might situate their practice exclusively to one extreme, the use of double-headed arrows is intended to show that in many settings, children's experiences of play may shift along these scales throughout a day or session.

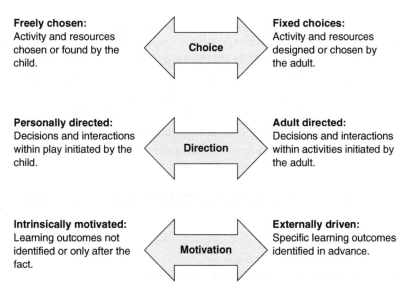

Freely chosen:
Activity and resources chosen or found by the child.

Choice

Fixed choices:
Activity and resources designed or chosen by the adult.

Personally directed:
Decisions and interactions within play initiated by the child.

Direction

Adult directed:
Decisions and interactions within activities initiated by the adult.

Intrinsically motivated:
Learning outcomes not identified or only after the fact.

Motivation

Externally driven:
Specific learning outcomes identified in advance.

Figure 13.1   Three scales of adult involvement in play

—————————— VIEW FROM PRACTICE ——————————

Moving between adult-directed and self-chosen play activities

After lunch, Evie enjoys some quiet time listening to a story read by a practitioner and looking at books by herself, before moving over to a group of her friends who are playing in the home corner. She watches from the doorway for a few minutes before drifting to the construction mat, where she helps build a castle from wooden blocks and giant plastic waffles. She engages in animated conversation with three other children, and they move to the home corner, bringing back some large fabric pieces and draping these over the blocks to make a roof, before crawling through the entrance and sitting inside for some time.

    Ash, another practitioner, has laid out a range of resources for mark making with paint in the art area. These include some sticks, feathers and leaves found by the children on a woodland visit earlier in the day, as well as various sizes of paintbrushes and sponges. He announces that there are three spaces at the table and Evie immediately crawls out from the castle and calls out to Ash that she wants to do painting. Evie spends a long time in the art area, using all the different mark-making resources, various colours of paint and several sheets of paper, layering the paint over and over again, covering the whole page until it is quite soggy and mixed into brown. As she paints, she talks to others at the table and to Ash about what she is doing, what is happening to her pictures and what she will do next. She is particularly pleased to find that a large pine cone she had found on the walk makes a stripy effect when rolled across her paper, and comments on this to Ash.

As demonstrated in the 'View from Practice', Evie moves smoothly between adult-directed activities (story time), through self-chosen play (construction), back to adult-initiated but open-ended activity (painting). Within this setting, adults may have identified specific learning outcomes to be achieved through collaborative play in the construction area, through access to a selection of books and through the mark-making-with-paint activity, among others. The practitioners might take advantage of any of their interactions with Evie to encourage conceptual development through sustained, shared thinking, but she can explore and construct her own learning throughout.

—————————— THINKING POINT 13.3 ——————————

1.   When do you think Evie is playing?
2.   What types of play does Evie engage in?
3.   What might she be learning and how might you find out?

Summary

Understandings of play are dependent on the conceptualisations of childhood and purpose(s) of work with children that are captured as pedagogical principles. A playful pedagogical approach focuses on adults adopting playful means to promote specific learning outcomes in their work with children, and as such, is most applicable to practitioners working within settings where meeting learning outcomes is prioritised. To integrate learning with play effectively and avoid presenting children with 'chocolate-dipped broccoli' (Bruckman, 1999) requires that children continue to experience playful learning as freely chosen, personally directed and intrinsically motivated. Drawing on the wealth of theory and research into play and children's learning, it is possible to identify ways for practitioners to maintain and develop the strong and trusting relationships that underpin effective play partnerships to enhance learning. Adults need to have a clear and reflective approach to their role in these playful learning partnerships, and an awareness of the ways in which children are experiencing activities. This chapter has argued that playful pedagogy requires adults to actively decentralise themselves within children's activities: to be aware of their own actions but prioritise children's interpretations.

END-OF-CHAPTER QUESTIONS

1. What do you think the role of play should be in children's learning? If play is used to meet adult-imposed learning goals of any kind, consider whether it is still really play.
2. The UK regulatory system is moving towards mandating playful pedagogy and guided play, while often also building towards standardised assessments of academic skills. In this context, how should early learning and childcare settings preserve children's right to play for relaxation and leisure?
3. In your own practice, how much choice, direction and intrinsic motivation are children able to exercise? Determine the extent to which this changes throughout the session.

14
Space to play
Joe Houghton and Kristina Robb

Key ideas

This chapter will explore:

- The history of Playwork.
- Theoretical understanding of Playwork.
- Practice as underpinned by the Playwork Principles.
- The Play Cycle.
- Playwork in the context of modern childhood.

Introduction

> [Playworkers must] not try to educate, teach, train, or therapeutically treat
> children in their time and space for play. (Wilson, 2010: 9)

The value of children's play has been debated in the spheres of psychology, sociology, children's geographies, education and care since the Greek philosophers. Regardless of the acknowledgement that play is common to children, its purpose and function have eluded an absolute definition (Burghardt, 2005). Our current understanding of play is influenced by these historical perspectives. Bruce (2012: 15) suggests that Froebel first 'took the natural play of children and gave it educational status', leading to our current early education frameworks. Playwork is a relatively new philosophy in comparison, developing after the Second World War in adventure playgrounds across Europe and the UK.

The notion of play as 'freely chosen, personally directed and intrinsically motivated' (Play Wales, 2015: 3) is not unproblematic and conflicting understandings of the purposefulness of play often lead to confusion. This chapter will seek to clarify the processes and language of play from a Playwork perspective and consider play in the context of Playwork theory and practice as underpinned by the Playwork Principles. We will connect modern Playwork theory and practice to the sociological study of childhood, exploring Wingrave and Barker's concept of childhood (see Figure 6.1).

A space for play(work)

Until the 1990s and the publication of the 'Colorado Paper' (Sturrock and Else, 1998), Playwork as a profession was not widely recognised, with minimal theoretical credence. Playwork was being defined by the mere fact that it was not education or 'playcare' (Sturrock and Else, 1998: 3). The roots of Playwork go back to as early as 1939 and were developed through the work of Sorenson and Lady Allen, who championed the idea of adventure playgrounds which had minimal adult supervision, encouraging children's autonomy and the freedom to lead play with tools and materials (Chilton, 2013; Brown, 2008b). Playwork is now a profession across the UK, working with mainly school-aged children with the primary focus being on the child's play agenda (Wragg, 2013).

The development of the theoretical foundations of Playwork have evolved from the work of Hughes (1996), Sturrock and Else (1998) and Brown (2008b). They are markedly different from the scope of previous studies of play which focused on pre-schoolers and the educational possibilities of play (King and Newstead, 2018). This development of theoretical work has helped establish Playwork as a profession and given credibility to the value of play outside the classroom. In 2005 the Playwork Principles Scrutiny Group (PPSG) consulted UK playworkers, crafting the Playwork Principles which 'establish the professional and ethical framework for playwork' (Play Wales, 2015: 2). The definition of play proved elusive and is described over several Playwork Principles (Play Wales, 2015) as a process rather than an action. This, perhaps, gives us the opportunity to be less invested in a definition and more observant of the different characteristics of the drive to play within various environments.

This process of play is described by Brown and Wragg (2015: 215) as 'a crucial developmental function and evolutionarily developed bio-psychological drive', while Bruce (1993: 237) suggests that in play children can 'wallow in ideas, feelings and relationships' and that it is the 'most meaningful situation for children'. Bruner (2006) and Nachmanovitch (1990) see play as the basis of human evolution and the process by which we learn and create. Hughes (2002) synthesised these ideas, developing a taxonomy of 16 play types, assisting adults to identify and support different forms of play. Hughes' (2002) play types incorporate various views of play from a biological, psychological and social perspective, naming play as ranging from widely understood descriptions, such as creative, to deep (risky and survival), and recapitulative (human evolution).

Tension exists between research into play as educational and the now established Playwork theory. That is not to say the playworkers do not regard play as educational; they view play as being at the heart of how a child learns and develops. It is the way in which play is utilised that is at the heart of the friction. This can be examined using Beunderman's (2010) reworking of Holden's (2006) value triangle, which describes the three I's of Instrumental value (play is valued for its learning potential), Institutional value (play adds value to the setting) and Intrinsic value (play is valued for itself). The differing tensions and values placed on these by institutions and individuals can lead to a disparity of thought in how educators and playworkers approach and value play.

This dichotomy can leave many of today's portfolio workers struggling to situate themselves in the landscape of play amid their own beliefs and experiences. Playworkers can find themselves with different expectations to other professionals and must rein in their natural inclination to teach or interrupt play with an adult agenda (Wilson, 2010). Playwork Principle 3 establishes the playworker's purpose: '[t]he prime focus and essence of playwork is to support and facilitate the play process' (Play Wales, 2015: 3). And while there are differences in approaches dependent on the space, provision, children and their needs, adults in a Playwork environment must commit to removing and negotiating the barriers to play, whether 'contextual, physical or attitudinal', and by valuing play for itself (Beunderman, 2010: 26).

─────────────────── **THINKING POINT 14.1** ───────────────────

1. What are your understandings of play in the context of your work?
2. In what ways have you seen a difference in values placed upon play in an educational and Playwork context?
3. How easy is it to enact the Playwork Principles in your setting?

───

Framing play

In their cataloguing of street play in the UK in the 1950s, Opie and Opie (1969: 10) observed that 'where children are is where they play'. Similarly, Ward (1978) observes that children will play everywhere and with anything. This supports Playwork's proposition of a child's innate motivation to play (Play Wales, 2015: Playwork Principle 1), driven by what Brown (2010: 147) considers an intrinsic ludic (playful) impulse, a vital essence of being human. The art of Playwork is practised in a range of settings, including adventure playgrounds, before school, after school and holiday clubs, parks and even play buses (Smith-Brennan, 2018: 60).

However, boundaries of play are considered to extend beyond the purely physical dimension of space. Sturrock (2003) refers to a more profound 'interpsychic' ludic ecology, which children access through free play, enabling them to explore the meaning of identity and self in relation to the world. This ecological understanding of the play space is mirrored by Lester (2018: 90), who suggests Playwork practice is concerned with co-producing *playspacetimes* which ignite rich possibilities of space through the production of 'playful meshworks of difference'. As Massey (2005: 9) suggests, space, with all its diverse possibilities, can be seen as a constantly constructed product of all the (macro to micro) interrelations and interactions within it.

Playwork practice, in line with professional National Occupational Standards (NOS) (NOS, online), is theoretically underpinned by the Play Cycle. Proposed by Sturrock and Else (1998), in their ground-breaking 'Colorado Paper', this cyclical process of play helps frame the innate play-driven impulses of the child. King and Newstead (2020: 109), reflecting the original 'Colorado Paper', present a newer, practice-friendly definition with clear consistent terminology. Retaining the original model, this revision breaks the process down into the pre-cue (metalude in original), play cue, play return, flow (loop and flow in the original), play frame and annihilation. Figure 14.1 shows a simplified visual representation of the Play Cycle unfolding within the bounded physical, emotional and psychological dimensions of the play space (Sturrock, 2003: 81). The unfolding cycle of play presented in Figure 14.1 follows the pre-cue of the child and is understood to come from 'a conscious or unconscious thought or idea within a child's inner world' (King and Newstead, 2020: 109). Once the play ends, 'annihilation' is used to describe this termination of play.

It should also be noted that Child A's play cue marks an invitation to the outer world to play and that Child B, as the responder, may just as easily be substituted by an adult, a group of children or even the environment itself.

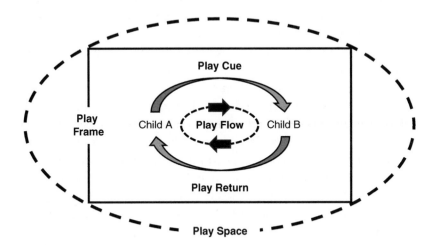

Figure 14.1   The Play Cycle (based on King and Newstead, 2020; Sturrock and Else, 1998)

Given that the playworker's primary objective is to support this play process, they must be mindful of their own impact on the play space. Appropriate intervention should afford children the space and freedom to determine and control what, why, when and how they play as these processes unfold (Play Wales, 2015). Sturrock and Else (1998: 23–4) assign a continuum of playworker intervention strategies to support 'play framing' – holding and containing the meaning of the play for the children (Sturrock and Else, 1998: 24). Hughes (2012: 217) is clear that in successful Playwork, the playworker must 'not lead play but facilitate', so that 'adulteration' (adult contamination) of the play and play space is avoided. Adulteration may arise from adults feeling a need to teach, educate or dominate the children's play or even compensate for 'unplayed' out material in their own lives (Sturrock and Else, 1998: 18). To help avoid adulteration, Wilson (2010: 10) suggests the practice-enhancing idea of the playworker wearing a metaphorical 'cloak of invisibility' to create an invisible yet active presence. Here, the playworker as facilitator is also required to create the necessary enriched environmental conditions for this play process to be effective (Brown, 2008b: 8–9). Underpinning this is the playworker's role in supporting what Brown (2003a: 53) terms *compound flexibility*: the idea that a flexible and adaptable environment leads to greater flexibility and adaptability in the child.

Strengthening this Playwork practice further is the practical application of the theory of affordances. The notion, first proposed by James Gibson in 1979, suggests that the affordance of an environment reflects how much a child can change it and directly relates to the performative potential it offers the individual through evolving psychological child–environment relationships (Gibson, 1979: 127). For Heft (1988: 29), affordances of the environment provide *functionally significant* properties in relation to the child, and he stresses the need to distinguish between potential affordances (qualities of the environment) and actualised affordances (individual relationships with the environment). Kyttä (2003: 55) believes that the way these affordances are actualised is determined through both individual and socio-cultural factors.

Extending this playworker repertoire, Brown's (2008b: 9, citing Sutton Smith, 1997: 231) discussion of 'adaptive variability' as a key function of play points to the need to create flexible environments which children can substantially adapt or control. Here, the provision of *loose parts* can be highly effective in promoting a child's autonomous creativity as well as facilitating potential affordances for actualised possibilities to emerge. In 1971, Simon Nicholson, an architect, first proposed his theory of loose parts, born out of a sense that children have been cheated out of a world of discovery and inventiveness. Succinctly summarised, his theory proposes that 'in any environment both the degree of inventiveness and creativity, and the possibility of discovery, are directly proportional to the number and kind of variables within it' (Nicholson, 1971: 30). In essence, loose parts apply to just about any object that can be moved, carried, rolled, lifted, piled or combined to enable the invention and creation of new structures and experiences (Wilson, 2010: 12).

For the playworker, however, it is also necessary to think beyond the purely physical layout and content of the play space to an environment that also supports the emotional needs of the child (Play Wales, 2021: 10). As Sutton-Smith (2003: 15) suggests, play acts as a form of emotional regulation, promoting the child's emotional capacity in everyday life. Playwork uses the term 'affective play space' to describe a space that enables children to freely express, experiment with and experience new and different feelings and emotions (Kilvington and Wood, 2018: 134–5). It is believed that emotional experiences become embedded in the architecture of young children's developing brains. This helps them understand their own feelings or emotions and those of others, to manage strong emotions, to regulate their own behaviour, to develop empathy and to learn how to establish and maintain relationships (National Scientific Council on the Developing Child, 2004: 1).

————————— THINKING POINT 14.2 —————————

1. Describe how you reflect on the play that you see in practice. How does the process of reflection enable you to determine links to the Play Cycle?
2. How can you ensure a play space that takes account of the children's needs and does not reflect an adult agenda?
3. In what ways do the constraints of your setting mean that the adult agenda is privileged over children's needs and what can you do to bring about change?

———————————— VIEW FROM PRACTICE ————————————

Multiple play frames in action

At a grassy outdoor space in an out-of-school care setting, 16 children, supported by three play-worker staff, are participating in a range of play experiences. Four boys and one girl are busy enacting a play-fight using make-believe swords and light sabres! Two boys play football using tyres for goal posts, while one girl chooses to chat to one of the playworkers about her weekend plans. One of the playworkers periodically joins in with the football – the two boys roll their eyes and shout in mock annoyance, yet seem humoured by the intrusion, returning to the game when the playworker withdraws. A group of eight children of varying ages are engaged with a large array of outdoor loose parts. They are working together to create a space rocket to transport them to the moon apparent in the late afternoon sky. Two older children drag a pallet into place for the all-important launch pad. An array of tyres, pipes, buckets, planks of wood, and crates are being considered, assessed and brought into the play. Serious negotiations (close to arguments at times) are taking place to find consensus for the design and materials required. Older children help younger children lift and move things into place. There is a buzz of excitement as the construction gets underway. The playworkers stay alert yet stand back, observe closely and remain on hand should additional resources be needed, or if something is too heavy.

———————————— THINKING POINT 14.3 ————————————

1. In the 'View from Practice', identify the various play frames and play cues and returns apparent in this play space.
2. How might these play frames relate to one another?
3. What are the roles of the adult in this play space? Are they similar to your own experiences or can you see differences?
4. Are there any interactions that might not support a Playwork agenda? How might you ensure that adults respect the children's play frames?

Modern Playwork and childhood

The concept of childhood map (see Figure 6.1) establishes a framework through which to view children and childhoods. This framework can be useful in situating Playwork within the wider theoretical landscape. We will examine each of these concepts in turn.

The political child

In the last century, the interconnectedness of modern global society propelled the lives of children to the fore with contemporary theorisations of childhood paralleled by developments within the modern children's rights movement (Freeman, 1998: 433). This amplified the child's participatory voice (Tisdall and Punch, 2012: 249), giving the child new political and agentic status countering the passive positioning of the child of socialisation and developmental science (Moran-Ellis, 2010: 188). The recognition of children's agentic rights supported calls from the 'New Social Studies of Childhood' (NSSC) to view children as social agents with a part to play in their own representation and social construction (James and James, 2004; James et al., 1998; Corsaro, 1997; Mayall, 1994; Qvortrup, 1994). This desire to bring children into view to combat their traditionally invisible status (Oldman, 1994: 43) marked an elevation of children's status from 'naturally incompetent' future-orientated 'human becomings' to a position as competent 'human beings' in the present (Qvortrup, 1994: 2).

Playwork's own contradictory tensions would appear to mirror some of the dualistic characteristics of this NSSC. On the one hand, an intrinsic view of child-led free play, seen by Brown (2010: 18) as the 'essence of freedom' existing for its own reward, energises the political agency of the child. On the other hand, the emphasis placed on play as a driver of socio-developmental benefits runs the risk of reducing the active political status of the child to a future-orientated 'becoming' (Qvortrup, 1994: 2). Highlighting this means-to-an-end 'rhetoric of play as progress' (Sutton-Smith, 1997: 9) only serves to reduce play to a simple tautology of freedom and purpose (Cook, 2019: 129). This further risks polarising the political agency of the child against traditional theories of development (Prout, 2005: 1–2).

Jans (2004: 37) makes a clear distinction between adult-based pedagogical future-looking interpretations of play and notions of play without obligation, where children are free to give active meaning to and experiment with their environment. This latter perspective appears to align with the process-driven Playwork ideal of facilitating intrinsically driven play, determined by children's own agendas (Play Wales, 2015). This would also appear to boost children's political status as 'agents of change' (see Figure 6.1), which for Corsaro (2012: 488) suggests a transformative power of play and interpretive internalisation of society and culture for the child which at the same time actively contributes to 'cultural production and change'. The rearticulation of Article 31 by the UN Committee on the Rights of the Child (UNCRC, 2013: 4–5) agrees, noting that through intrinsically motivated play children 'reproduce, transform, create and transmit culture' as a form of 'participation in everyday life'. Here, the child as social actor comes to the fore, not only as 'participants in their own representation' but also as drivers of change and perceptions of childhood (see Chapter 6).

Play environments are complex and in a Playwork setting, ultimately organised and ultimately controlled by adults (Russell, 2018: 48). Dimensions of power and political agency (child–child and child–adult) come into focus. Brown (2008b: 124–5) argues that Playwork Principle 2 (Play Wales, 2015) should be viewed more as an ideal and that it risks diminishing the inherent value and a reality of play which is 'chosen', but not necessarily 'freely'; 'directed', but not necessarily 'personally'; and 'motivated', but not necessarily 'intrinsically'. Children themselves also infringe on other children's freedom and choice (Brown, 2008b: 123) and as Sutton-Smith (1997) and the 'View from Practice' suggest, if children play in groups, then compromise and negotiation are to be expected.

This extends to the resource-bounded paradox of free play in a Playwork context, where adult-determined 'freedoms are limited, – and simultaneously supported – by resources that can be brought into play' (Russell, 2018: 48). Cook (2019: 130) concurs, arguing that the child's power in play relies on adults to simultaneously provide play contexts while at the same time refraining from disrupting the natural processes. Resolving this conundrum, Russell (2018: 49) suggests a subtle refocus away from the ideal of freely chosen play, to the co-production of relational space, where agency and power emerge from entanglements of intra-action.

The conditioned child

The NSSC seeks a 'permanent' status for the child to counter a more traditional 'transient' status as adult in the making (Wyness, 2006: 28). Pilcher (1995: 24) reasons that this positioning indicates a 'separateness' of incompetent child from competent adult. For Inkeles (1968: 76–7), this also reinforces a 'forward looking' social conditioning requirement for 'what a child must become to meet the requisites for the continued functioning of society'. The notion of the conditioned child as a blank slate, or 'tabula rasa', is often credited to John Locke (1996: 44) in the late seventeenth century, who viewed the child as being 'moulded and fashioned as one pleases'. This view of the child as a formless blank slate endures today (Duschinsky, 2012: 509). For Corsaro (2017: 8, citing Parson and Bales, 1956: 36), the persistence of these ideas sees the child not only as a novice but also as an 'untamed threat' in need of training, moulding and correction to become a fully competent and contributing member of society. This extends to shaping children through systems of reward and punishment (see Chapter 5), such as Skinner's (1938) historical theories of behavioural conditioning and reinforcement where, through 'operant conditioning', people become what they have been reinforced to be (Olson and Hergenhahn, 2009: 76).

Play's agentic promise to the child seemingly offers a counter-balance to this future moulding and conditioning; however, play's unique importance to the developing child inevitably widens play as a socialising force and as an object of political strategy and human flourishing (Foucault, 2009: 1). For example, the Play Strategy for Scotland ('Vision' and 'Action Plan') (Scottish Government [SG], 2013a: 1; 2013b: 1) attaches significance to 'play' as a key driver of Scotland's ambitions 'to be the best place to grow up', where children can achieve their full potential as healthy, productive members of society (SG, 2013a: 6). Lester and Russell (2008b: 13) make a strong case for play provision to focus on enabling children to enjoy (non-productive) play for its own sake rather than for instrumental outcomes. Furthermore, in relation to the educational outcomes of England's Every Child Matters (ECM) (be healthy, be safe, enjoy and achieve, make a positive contribution, achieve economic wellbeing) (Department for Education and Skills [DfES], 2004a), they reason that such play, by virtue of its 'flexible, unpredictable, imaginative, peer/self-directed' nature and '"as-if" behaviour', makes the realisation of these outcomes far more likely (Lester and Russell, 2008b: 24–5).

The developing child

The notion of the developing child is illustrated by Piaget's 'stages of development' theory; children learn actively through their play, adapting to the world around them (Flavell, 1963). The norms generated by research into children's development have given rise to a sequence that each child experiences in the same order (with some deviations) at differing times depending on the child and their environment (see Chapter 5). According to Bee and Boyd (2013), these can be viewed as being both of the child's circumstances, and of their own construct through play, integrating their internal and external worlds (Winnicott, 2005).

The Playwork context acknowledges that play, learning and development are linked; Brown (2008b: 8) states that 'children will learn and develop both while they are playing, and through their play'. Play opportunities therefore have a strong contribution to make in enhancing the experiences of children. The Play Strategy for Scotland: Our Vision (SG, 2013a: 12) identifies play as being 'a fundamental and integral part of healthy development'. The recognition of play as vital to the development of children is apparent in the Play Strategies of each country of the UK, with plans to expand play services across education and in communities to enhance children's opportunities for play. Reviews such as Scotland's Play in a COVID-19 Context (Play Scotland, 2021) reflect the need for play as central to the protection of children's rights and safeguarding their wellbeing in a time of change; however, there is a danger in this context of dismissing play as having the single purpose of a developmental tool while disregarding its other benefits (Sutton-Smith, 1997: 9). As a counterpoint, Playwork has potency in placing these other benefits at the heart of the process of play, supporting the developing child.

The authentic child

Rousseau's romantic child of the early eighteenth century (the 'authentic' child) was professed to develop naturally and grow according to their own natural instincts

(Bloom, 1987). Both Montessori (2002) and the Reggio Emilia approach echo this through the belief that children are connected to their surroundings and learn best from authentic experiences and participation in exploration (Gill, 2007; Edwards et al., 1998), resonating with Playwork theory.

Consideration of play from a Playwork perspective is premised on the notion that children need to play freely without adult intervention. The Playwork Principles (Play Wales, 2015) are more concerned with the process than any product of play in adult terms (King and Newstead, 2018: 125). Hughes (1996: 22–3) regards Playwork as 'child empowering', leaving the 'content and intent' of play to their natural inclinations, while Battram (2000) states 'through play we become human'. The role of adults in Playwork practice is not in directing children's learning but as providers and facilitators of rich fertile play environments from which children will inevitably learn (Shier, 2001: 115).

Children, as experts in their own play and following their own agenda, can be considered to fit the model of an authentic child in a Playwork context. The adult urge to intervene in play, to create a scaffold to support the child to develop (Wood et al., 1976) is one that conflicts playworkers. The decision to intervene or not is guided by Playwork Principle 8, which states that any intervention should enable play to be extended and balanced with the benefits of development and wellbeing of children (Play Wales, 2015). Sensitive intervention allows for the child to continue to lead the play and remain agentic, thus creating links to the socially constructed, political child.

Summary

This chapter begins by considering Playwork as an emergent profession over the last 80 years. It goes on to discuss the challenges faced by the playworker in providing an ideal of freely chosen play opportunities for the child, undertaken for their own sake, while seeking to maximise the developmental benefits for the child in a way that is free from adult agendas. The second part of the chapter explored the physical and psychic framing of play within the ludic ecology of the Playwork context. It looks at how the Play Cycle unfolds and how it can be framed and supported through appropriate intervention, affordances, loose parts and the provision of rich, affective play environments. Finally, the chapter explored the relationship with play and the new social study of childhood and brings into focus an underlying Playwork perspective to unlock the political agency of the child.

Playwork settings are in a unique position to enhance the voice of the child through play and strive to accommodate the child as master of their playful habitat; however, play brings benefits to the developing child, and this utility of play throws up wider adult and societal agendas to drive human flourishing (Foucault, 2009: 1) through the conditioning and developing constructs of modern childhood (see Chapter 6). While power relations between child–child and adult–child are problematic, the notion of a co-created environment of relational and material intra-active entanglements (Lester, 2018: 87) provides a possible solution to the dichotomic tensions associated with the agentic 'being' of the child and the assumptions of a future 'becoming' (Qvortrup, 1994: 2).

END-OF-CHAPTER QUESTIONS

1. Determine the extent to which the concepts outlined in this chapter reflect your experiences of children and play.
2. Is there one lens that stands out for you as the way you see or support children playing? Why this lens?
3. In what ways can the model outlined in Figure 14.1 help your theoretical understanding of Playwork practice?

15
Outdoor learning
Mike Carroll and Jillian Barker

Key ideas

This chapter will explore:

- Reasons for children's estrangement from outdoor learning.
- Developmental benefits associated with outdoor learning.
- Influential typologies of outdoor learning.
- The dimension of risk.
- Parental attitudes to outdoor learning.
- The practitioner's role in facilitating outdoor learning.

Introduction

There is 'growing concern about childhood obesity, with published statistics indicating that one in five children start school overweight' (Parsons and Traunter, 2020: 699). The dramatic increase in childhood obesity is a significant public health challenge as there are a number of associated health risks, including the development of cardiovascular conditions, high blood pressure, respiratory problems, asthma and the onset of Type II diabetes (Scottish Government [SG], 2018). A contributory factor in this health epidemic is that children are increasingly leading an indoor and sedentary lifestyle (Bates, 2020). Yanez et al. (2017: 58) describe this shift from the outdoors to indoors and increasingly online as leading to a 'wired generation'. This is a concern, as habits formed during childhood with respect to physical activity and sedentary behaviour tend to continue into adulthood (Tremblay et al., 2015). Given these concerns, curricular frameworks within the United Kingdom promote the benefits of outdoor play in both compulsory and non-compulsory settings.

Children's estrangement from outdoor learning

The increased availability and year-on-year improvements in digital technology along with the seductive qualities of social media (e.g. television, computers, electronic games, tablets, mobile phones) as well as parental safety concerns and expectations surrounding child protection are often cited as explaining this drift from time spent outdoors to increased time spent indoors (Tremblay et al., 2015). Arguably, child safety guidelines and child protection protocols have reduced exposure to harm; however, the 'precautionary principle' that underpins this has also led to the emergence of a risk-averse society that serves to limit children's experience of learning outdoors while also reducing their physical activity. However, the underlying assumption that the indoors is safer than the outdoors is questionable given the growing evidence of harm to children and young people through the use of social media (e.g. violence, cyber-bullying, online predators, pornography).

Louv (2005) suggests that children's estrangement from nature leads to higher rates of physical, emotional and mental illnesses, which he termed 'Nature Deficit Disorder'. Gray (2011) has lent weight to this finding that a lack of free play contributes to stress, increased anxiety and depression, a reduced sense of personal control and mental health disorders. Shifting the location of learning from indoors to outdoors can help realise improvements in four domains:

- Cognitive impacts – greater knowledge and understanding.
- Affective impacts – improved attitudes, values, beliefs and self-perceptions.
- Interpersonal and social impacts – improved communication skills, leadership and teamwork.

- Physical and behavioural impacts – improved fitness, personal behaviours and nature–society interactions (Dillon et al., 2005: 22).

Although UK curricular documents make mention of the outdoors (e.g. Learning and Teaching Scotland, 2010), third-sector organisations also provide learning opportunities outside the classroom (Department of Agriculture, Environment and Rural Affairs [DoAERA], online).

A plethora of terms

Zink and Burrows (2008, cited in Harris, 2018: 223) define outdoor learning as simply, 'that which is beyond the walls of the indoors'. Outdoor learning is 'an umbrella term for actively inclusive facilitated approaches that predominately use activities and experiences in the outdoors which lead to learning, increased health and wellbeing, and environmental awareness' (Institute of Learning [IoL], 2021: 1); thus, outdoor learning is 'facilitated' and leads to 'learning'. Outdoor play, sometimes referred to as active free play or self-directed play, is an active, unstructured process that is separate from formal outdoor learning. Thus, the outdoor environment provides children with space to move freely, with movement and play being described as 'one of the most natural and powerful modes of learning' (Wales Council for Outdoor Learning [WCOL], 2018: 3).

Practitioners often use a variety of terms to describe outdoor play when discussing outdoor learning. These can include terms such as 'self-directed play, unstructured play, free play, loose-parts play, active outdoor play and risky play' (Alden and Pyle, 2019: 240, 244). The adjectives used to describe the different forms of play are used to help inform our understanding. Alden and Pyle (2019: 240) suggest that although children's play is difficult to define and often misunderstood, it is 'generally defined by agency which is understood in terms of the child's freedom to choose play and the child's direction or control of play' (Hewes, 2014, cited in Alden and Pyle, 2019: 240). Goodhall and Atkinson (2019: 1696) indicate that the curriculum guidance for 3- and 4-year-olds (Department for Education [DfE], 2021b) specifies that outdoor learning involves a balancing act between adult-led and child-initiated activity, with practitioners making an ongoing judgement in relation to this balance (see Chapters 13 and 14). For our part, we define outdoor learning as active, unstructured physical activity that takes place outdoors, largely initiated by the children themselves with opportunities for adult-initiated support and activity.

Developmental benefits

Active outdoor play helps to support holistic educational development amongst children (WCOL, 2018). Several studies indicate that active outdoor play provides children with learning experiences across the physical, cognitive, social, communicative and emotional domains (Stack and Nikiforidou, 2021). Within the physical domain, space for movement is a vital component in order for children to develop and consolidate a range of key gross locomotor skills. Limited internal space within establishments acts as a constraint to developing these skills and, in addition, there is no guarantee that children have access to suitable space in their home location, particularly in urban environments; consequently, active outdoor play is more suitable than indoor play for the development of gross locomotor skills (Ihmeideh and Al-Qaryouti, 2016) such as 'walking, running, jumping, climbing, hopping, skipping, sliding and tricycling; manipulative skills such as throwing, catching, kicking, striking and bouncing; and stability abilities including bending, stretching, swinging, twisting and beam-walking' (Little and Wyver, 2008: 35).

Monti et al. (2019: 879) suggest that regular physical activity in outdoor settings has implications for children's health, with links to reductions in obesity rates (Tremblay et al., 2015). Exposure to physical activity through outdoor play sessions in the early years is linked to a healthier lifestyle in later life, which in turn reduces the risk of health issues arising out of a lack of physical activity (Parsons and Traunter, 2020). Maller et al. (2006) have identified a range of physiological benefits arising out of outdoor physical (play) activity, including improved recovery time from injury and illness; an improved positive outlook on life; and the ability to cope with stress, which in turn contributes to improved mental health (Parsons and Traunter, 2020). Outdoor play is also associated with the promotion of social skills and social functioning through facilitating peer interaction (WCOL, 2018). Outdoor play promotes pro-social behaviour as it provides children with greater freedom to interact with each other, and to make choices as to who they will play with (Harris, 2018: 224). Outdoor play also offers children opportunities for social and dramatic play which helps to develop their communication skills and build relationships with other children and adults (Canning, 2010).

Outdoor learning can help support children's personal, social and emotional development (Office for Standards in Education [Ofsted], 2008) through group work, team building and the development of social and communication skills. Monti et al. (2019: 879) argue that in addition to outdoor activities supporting growing social and communicative competence, they also offer opportunities for the development of negotiation skills through cooperative play. A study by Maynard et al. (2013: 213) found that outdoor play had a positive effect on children with emotional difficulties (i.e. withdrawn children became more confident) and social difficulties (i.e. boisterous or aggressive children became calmer and more focused, with a decrease in antisocial behaviours). Maynard et al. (2013: 221) also indicated that child-initiated activity in the outdoors led to different behaviours amongst children 'labelled' as underachieving in the classroom, such that their perception of self as an underachiever diminished and they were able to experience success (Nursery Resources, 2007).

Typologies of play

In any discussion of outdoor play, it is important to have an understanding of the different types of play albeit that much of the work in this field primarily relates to indoor play. There have been several attempts to differentiate play (see Table 15.1) in terms of cognitive and socio-emotional development (Turnbull and Jenvey, 2006). Parten (1933) identified six play subtypes based on the degree of social engagement evident during play. These subtypes can be grouped into three broad levels of social play: solitary (non-social), parallel (semi-social) and group play (social) (Xu, 2010). Parten (1933) further suggested that the six play subtypes followed a developmental sequence. Although this typology acknowledges the importance of social interaction during play and may help practitioners in non-compulsory care and education (NCE) settings to facilitate play experiences, it is not the case that children will go through Parten's sequence of subtypes (Xu, 2010). Furthermore, children can and do move between the different subtypes and this movement is often influenced by the situation they find themselves in: for example, interaction between a younger child and their sibling is more likely when compared with the child being in the company of unfamiliar children.

Parten's subtypes appear somewhat dated as they do not take account of 'cultural, environmental and social changes … [that] … may have an impact on children's social play behaviour' (Xu, 2010: 490). In addition, more recent developments in our understanding of play-based learning, for example symbolic play, fantasy/dramatic play and physical play, amongst others, are absent. Parten did suggest that there is a developmental dimension to social play which is echoed in the work of Smilansky (1968), who proposed a 'sequential, developmental hierarchy' between the four types of cognitive play and a child's intellectual development (Takhvar and Smith, 1990: 113). Critics of this typology indicated that many activities that are seen as 'playful' (e.g. rough and tumble play) are difficult to fit into the scheme (Takhvar and Smith, 1990). Furthermore, claims that Parten and Smilansky's typologies represent a nested developmental hierarchy are highly problematic and should be treated with caution (Takhvar and Smith, 1990).

Rubin (2001) developed a 'cognitive-social play matrix' with the cognitive play categories being nested within the social play categories, giving 15 possible nested behaviours (Rubin, 2001: 2). In addition, Rubin (2001) identified 'non-play' which included 'double-coded' subtypes (i.e. activity linked to more than one play category). Rubin's sequential typology primarily focused on examining how play, in indoor settings, contributes to social-emotional development. The main criticism of this particular typology is that some of the activities described as non-play are in fact commonly observed as forms of play (e.g. rough and tumble). Hughes' (2002) typology is more commonly known to practitioners in NCE settings as it was designed to assist playworkers in classifying play routines in order that they may support breadth and depth in the pedagogical strategies they deploy to enhance learning through play. Hughes (2002) identified 16 different play

Table 15.1   Selected typologies of play

Parten (1933)	Smilansky (1968)	Rubin (2001)	Hughes (2002)	Loebach and Cox (2020)
Social play	*Cognitive play*	*Cognitive play*	*Play types*	Physical
Unoccupied	Functional games	Functional games	Communication	Exploratory
Solitary	Construction	Constructive	Creative	Imaginative
Onlooker	Dramatic	Exploratory	Deep	Expressive
Parallel	Games with rules	Dramatic	Dramatic	Play with rules
Associative		Games with rules	Exploratory	Digital
Cooperative		Occupied	Fantasy	Bio
		Social play	Imaginative	Restorative
		Solitary	Locomotor	Non-play
		Parallel	Mastery	
		Group	Object	
		Non-play	Recapitulative	
		Unoccupied	Role	
		Onlooker	Rough and tumble	
		Transition	Social	
		Conversation	Socio-dramatic	
		Adult interaction	Symbolic	
		Out of room		
		Double-coded		
		Rough and tumble		
		Aggression		
		Anxious		

Loebach and Cox's (2020) subtypes:

Physical: gross motor, fine motor, vestibular, and rough & tumble. **Exploratory**: sensory, active and constructive. **Imaginative**: symbolic, socio-dramatic and fantasy. **Expressive**: performance and artistic, language and conversation. **Play with rules**: organic and conventional. **Digital**: device, augmented and embedded. **Bio**: plants, wildlife and care. **Restorative**: resting, retreat, reading and onlooking. **Non-play**: self-care, nutrition, distress, aggression, transition and other.

types with no suggestion that there are developmental phases underpinning the typology; it is simply a list of different types of play. Hughes' taxonomy has proved useful as a framework for playworkers and early years educators when planning, observing or participating in children's play activities, albeit that they do not necessarily cover all the ways children play. Several of the types of play overlap, for example socio-dramatic play, dramatic play and fantasy play. In addition, although the use of digital technology was still in its infancy, and as such was not incorporated, this now needs to be considered as young children use digital technology in a variety of ways (Marsh et al., 2016).

Loebach and Cox (2020: 6) have proposed a comprehensive new typology of nine primary outdoor play types, each with a number of sub-types (32 in total), that enable practitioners to 'effectively categorize children's activities in outdoor and naturalized play spaces'. They draw on five pre-existing play types: physical play, exploratory play, imaginative play, play with rules and expressive play. They have also introduced three new play types: bio play, restorative play and digital play. The final category of 'non-play' allows the observer to label activities normally considered not to be play. Loebach and Cox (2020: 25) argue that attempts to establish a 'hierarchy within the play types is counterproductive' as 'children do not necessarily develop physical, social, or cognitive skills along fixed, linear paths as once believed, and so a given play activity may not accurately reflect the developmental level or capacities of the child'. Ultimately, children's play activities are too diverse and complex to be captured by simplistic typologies; consequently, they suggest using more than one play type when describing any given play activity as this will provide a more realistic description of play activity.

Risk

Harper (2017) asserts that in modern Western cultures, particularly within urban settings, children may well be overprotected due to the emergence of a risk-averse society. Parental and societal attitudes are increasingly placing an emphasis on adult-structured activities which tend to reduce time spent on outdoor unstructured play (Clements, 2004). The 'precautionary principle' or 'protectionism' 'places children in a position of helplessness rather than strength' (Brown and Kaye, 2017: 1036) in order to minimise risk. Arguably, efforts to 'protect' children may in fact have a deleterious impact upon healthy child development through curtailing risk-taking during outdoor play (Tremblay et al., 2015). Risk aversion leads to a 'bubble-wrap generation' (Malone, 2007) of children who are being denied opportunities to develop 'psychological, social, cultural, physical and environmental competencies' (Brown and Kaye, 2017: 1035). Evidence clearly suggests that the 'overall positive health effects of increased risky outdoor play provide greater benefit than the health effects associated with avoiding outdoor risky play' (Brussoni et al., 2015: 6447).

The word 'risk' has become synonymous with 'hazard' and 'danger', implying a negative value judgement; consequently, risk-taking is increasingly interpreted with negative outcomes such as injury or death (Brussoni et al., 2015). Given these outcomes, parental concerns for their children's safety and wellbeing would be justifiable; however, conflating risk with hazard leads to children being denied opportunities to engage in play activity focused on enhancing learning and development (Little and Wyver, 2008). Brussoni et al. (2015) indicate that it is important to distinguish between 'hazard' and 'risk', with

Harper (2017) arguing that 'hazards' are potentially harmful whilst risks are potentially beneficial. When presented with a 'hazard', children cannot realistically assess the situation without guidance from a responsible adult. Risk, on the other hand, involves a child, during the course of outdoor play, being able to recognise and evaluate a challenge and decide on a course of action (Ofsted, 2008).

Outdoor risky play involves active, physical play with an inherent element of risk attached, including the possibility of physical injury (Shackell et al., 2008). The risk can be real or perceived (Brussoni et al., 2015). Outdoor play is thrilling and exciting (Brussoni et al., 2015) and can often expose the children to activities that they have avoided or have been prevented from trying (Harper, 2017). Sandseter (2009) identifies six forms of risky play, with each providing a differing experience of risk along with opportunities for child development. The main types of risky play include:

- **play at great heights** (danger of injury from falling as a result of climbing, swinging or jumping from height);
- **play at high speed** (danger of collisions with objects or other people as a result of swinging, sliding, running at speed);
- **play with dangerous tools** (danger of cuts, wounds and strangulation as a result of using knives, saws, ropes, etc.);
- **play with dangerous elements** (danger of injuries from falling from or into something such as trees, moving water, fire, etc.);
- **rough and tumble play** (danger of injuries from wrestling, play fighting and swordplay with someone); and
- **play with potential for child to disappear/get lost** (danger of becoming separated from adult supervision as a result of hiding, playing alone outdoors, exploring unfamiliar areas) (Sandseter, 2009).

The decision-making process involved when children decide for themselves whether or not to take a risk requires them to cope with feelings of fear and excitement leading to intense pleasure when they achieve success (Sandseter, 2010). With repeated exposure to the risks inherent in outdoor play, children become more adept in evaluating risk, which helps them develop their decision-making skills (Little and Wyver, 2008), resilience and self-reliance (SG, 2018). Given the growing culture to attach blame and engage in litigation when things 'go wrong', it would be unwise not to manage the transition of risk management away from adult supervisors to the children themselves. There is no specific legislation on play safety in the United Kingdom and that undertaking, as in England, a 'suitable and sufficient' risk assessment is the primary legal requirement (Shackell et al., 2008). Activities need to be scaffolded and inappropriate behaviours addressed so that children can be supported in developing sound judgement in assessing risks (Nursery Resources, 2007).

—————————— **THINKING POINT 15.1** ——————————

1. Consider the extent to which you incorporate the different types of risky play within your practice.
2. How would you rate each type of risky play in terms of the degree of risk? Provide a justification for your ratings.

Parental attitudes

Changing parental attitudes may also help explain the drift from time spent outdoors to increased time spent indoors as research has found that children can be sent to their caregiving establishments without weather-appropriate clothing so that they have to stay indoors (Copeland et al., 2009, cited in Olsen and Smith, 2017). Janssen (2015) outlines more fundamental shifts by which children's physical activity can be influenced by 'hyper-parenting styles':

- **helicopter parenting** – who attempt to protect their children from all dangers and solve all of their problems;
- **little emperor parenting** – who endeavour to satisfy all of their children's material desires;
- **tiger moms parenting** – who push their children to be exceptional in all domains; and
- **concerted cultivation parenting** – who schedule their children into several extracurricular activities to provide them with an advantage.

Hyper-parenting styles are often associated with significantly lower physical activity as increased adult involvement has resulted in the emergence of a 'backseat generation' (Karsten, 2005). Increasingly, children are taxied between locations to participate in enrichment activities without engaging with the outdoors. The concern is that such children will grow up to become 'de-natured adults' (Yanez et al., 2017).

The right of every child to 'rest and leisure, to engage in play and recreational activities appropriate to the age of the child and to participate freely in cultural life and the arts' is enshrined in Article 31 of the United Nations (UN) Convention on the Rights of the Child (UN, 1989). In Scotland, the government has enshrined children's right to play outdoors every day in its national Health and Social Care Standards (HSCS) (SG, 2017b: 7). Research that points to a deterioration in the quantity and quality of children's play represents a breach of children's rights and a failure to protect and provide for the right to play.

Furthermore, *Play England* (Shackell et al., 2008) highlights the importance of play being accessible for all children, disabled and non-disabled children.

―――――――――――― **THINKING POINT 15.2** ――――――――――――

1.   Consider whether the parenting styles listed above are representative of parents sending children to your establishment.
2.   Draw up a list of the advantages and disadvantages for children of each parenting style.

Practitioners' roles

The practitioner's role in facilitating outdoor play is somewhat fluid as practitioners constantly move between roles within any given experience of outdoor play. Alden and Pyle (2019: 242) identify three key broad roles for practitioners, namely those of gatekeeper, supervisor and playmate. Practitioners can be viewed as gatekeepers as they have decision-making power to allow or deny access to outdoor play. In addition, practitioners can exercise control over the types of play opportunities provided and the time allowed for play (Alden and Pyle, 2019). Children may well be provided with opportunities to explore risk; however, it is within the gift of the practitioner as to the extent to which this may be possible. Supervision takes place along a broad continuum from 'no supervision', 'informal supervision' (keeping an eye on things) on and off site to more 'formal supervision' by practitioners during activities (Alden and Pyle, 2019). The Scottish Playwork Principles (Play Scotland, 2022) recognise the link between supervision and risk by suggesting that playworkers keep their distance and choose an intervention style which enables children to extend their play, with adults only intervening when asked, or when absolutely necessary.

Within this broad continuum, the physical characteristics of the spaces within which activities take place (e.g. within or beyond a secure area, areal spread, line of sight, places to hide) introduce several elements that need to be considered; so our supervision strategy has further dimensions, which include:

- attention (extent of watching and listening);
- proximity (within versus beyond arm's reach); and
- continuity of attention and proximity (constant/intermittent/not at all) (Morrongiello and Schell, 2010, cited in Olsen and Smith, 2017: 1058).

For the practitioner, there is an inherent tension between supervision and Moore et al.'s (2021: 946) suggestion that outdoor play affords children the possibility of finding spaces 'to hide away from the constant gaze of adults and other children'. This links to the notion of agency, as it involves children taking control 'in constructing their own uninterrupted, symbolic or physical secret places' (Moore et al., 2021: 946). Encouraging children to engage in adventurous outdoor play does come with 'risks' as it will inevitably stimulate children's creativity, leading some to find ways to 'disappear from the practitioner's radar'. Outdoor space becomes an open-ended resource which children can transform for their own purposes. Nevertheless, it is important that practitioners and children know the boundaries of this space within which such play takes place. From the child's perspective, the absence of 'active supervision', within a supervisory framework, will allow them to pursue new experiences and 'venture' into their minds so that they can play with ideas and imagine different realities.

VIEW FROM PRACTICE

Developing forestry learning experiences

A Blueprint for 2020 (SG, 2017c: 10) called for 'a commitment to a minimum of one hour per week outdoors by encouraging all providers to have access to a stimulating outdoor play area for children, and, for full-time children, part of their day should be spent outdoors'. A local authority nursery, within an urban area, with no green space nearby that could be accessed by foot, especially with 3–5-year-olds, would have to access green space using a mini-bus. This raised the concern that while we are teaching children about respecting and looking after our environment, we are increasing our carbon footprint to do so. Nevertheless, we decided on an ambitious improvement plan to develop forestry learning experiences.

To take this initiative forward, we made contact with our local Forestry Commissioner, to find a green space where we could set up our 'Forest School'. In addition, staff visited a range of other settings to identify good practice. Staff were to be fully trained in forestry learning experiences. Although the Authority agreed to fund the training, it would be up to our Centre to purchase the numerous resources that would be required to facilitate the forestry learning experiences. It was anticipated that this would place a huge financial stress on the Centre's budget.

We sought input from children and parents, aware that an additional challenge to be overcome was that some children were reluctant to access the outdoors on a daily basis. It is 'too cold' or 'too wet' are often cited as reasons. The nursery purchased clothing for the children to access outdoor space. To win 'hearts and minds', we settled on using digital technology to record the children's learning experiences while at the forest. Photos of the activities were to be shared with everyone attached to the Centre to illustrate the valuable learning experiences and the fun the children have during the visit. Catch them having fun!

Practitioners may also act as children's playmates and adopt a 'backseat' approach in order to facilitate but not to direct children's activities, or engage in a directive dialogue arising from a child-initiated activity (Nah and Waller, 2015). The concepts of supervision and play facilitation do not appear to sit easily with each other. McNamara et al. (2017) suggest a shift away from the notion of supervision to one of guidance, placing practitioners in a supportive role on accepting invitations to participate in outdoor play. On entering into play, at the child's invitation, the practitioners' role involves scaffolding and extending play based on observing and following children's play cues (Alden and Pyle, 2019: 242). Practitioners remain well placed, through social interaction and knowing the children, to engage in developmentally appropriate conversations as well as offering social-emotional support, when required to do so. In the role of a more knowledgeable other (MKO), practitioners can scaffold children's current understanding, knowledge, skills and abilities in order to support them to develop (Vygotsky, 1978). The practitioner can support children, through active listening and open-ended dialogue, to find ways to solve problems, develop their skills and abilities, and find solutions to the socio-emotional issues that they may confront.

THINKING POINT 15.3

1. How would you describe your role in facilitating risky play?
2. Consider the impact of the regulatory focus on safety and supervision upon the children's experience of outdoor play.

Summary

This chapter suggests that there are a range of developmental benefits associated with outdoor play; however, research indicates that some children and their parents favour indoor play, which is increasingly virtual in nature, as opposed to the outdoors. The growth in sedentary lifestyles gives cause for concern with respect to increased instances of childhood obesity and associated health issues. Article 31 of the United Nations Convention on the Rights of the Child (UN, 1989) enshrines the child's right to play. Providing children with access to high-quality play in outdoor environments should be seen as a basic need for their health and wellbeing as well as enabling them to explore and make sense of the world. Government recognises that there are legitimate concerns surrounding health and safety, and the fears of litigation in the event of any accidents or injuries. However, exposure to well-managed risks will help children learn important life skills, including learning how to manage risks for themselves. Herein lies the challenge for practitioners.

END-OF-CHAPTER QUESTIONS

1. Why is an understanding of typologies of play important to the practitioner in NCE settings?
2. Consider the development benefits associated with outdoor play and how you go about ensuring that the children are exposed to developmental challenges.
3. Consider whether outdoor play is a policy imperative in your establishment. If it is, why is outdoor learning seen as important? If it is not a policy imperative, justify why this should be so.

Part V
Developing the non-compulsory care and education workforce

Part V

16

Professionalisation of the non-compulsory sector in the UK

Mary Wingrave

Key ideas

This chapter will explore:

- The importance and benefits of the non-compulsory care and education (NCE) sector.
- The development and changes in recent years to the NCE sector across the UK.
- Issues which may inhibit the recognition of the work done by those in the NCE sector.
- What still needs to be done to support the recognition of those who work in the NCE sector.

Introduction

At the of start of the millennium, many presumed that those working in the non-compulsory care and education (NCE) sector were generally unskilled babysitters (Mooney and McCafferty, 2005). However, during the last 20 years there has been a plethora of research which has highlighted the importance of the sector in terms of children's development, economic necessities (Organisation for Economic Co-operation and Development [OECD], 2015, 2006) and the need to invest in the upskilling of those in practice through the creation of relevant qualifications (OECD, 2017). In this chapter, I first discuss the importance and benefits of the two main services in NCE provision before outlining the current roles and expectations of the workforce, as there has been a move to standardise practice and professionalise staff. As part of this discussion, changes which have been introduced over the last 20 years, and which have arguably reshaped the NCE sector, will be examined. Consideration will be given to issues such as the status and pay that may be a factor which continues to inhibit the recognition of the work done by those in the sector (Goddard, 2020; Nutbrown, 2012). I also question whether a technical approach, through the introduction of qualifications and registration requirements, has resulted in achieving high-quality provision or whether it simply serves to regulate staff. Finally, I conclude this chapter with some tentative suggestions of what next for the sector.

The non-compulsory care and education sector

Non-compulsory care and education provision consists of services that children are not required to attend and incorporates facilities beyond statutory education services. NCE services aim to support working parents and provide care and education for children outwith compulsory schooling. These services can include, although are not limited to, those which relate to a variety of pre-school services, out-of-school care, Playwork and regulated childcare provision. Interest in NCE services has become a focus for many developed countries' educational and political agendas (Hillman and Williams, 2015). It is asserted that due to parental work commitments, care and education which go beyond the compulsory school day are needed to ensure a safe and caring environment for children (Sayre et al., 2014; Heckman and Masterov, 2007; OECD, 2006). Consequently, there has been both legislative and policy interest from the UK devolved governments which has resulted in the introduction of many forms of regulation to achieve high-quality staff and services for children. It is recognised that there are many types of provision which can be classified as NCE and are part of the support networks for children's education and welfare outside of compulsory education. In the UK, Scotland, England, Wales and Northern Ireland have created national standards which seek to articulate staff requirements in terms of the delivery of service for those who work with children. In the main, the early years sector, which includes crèches, playgroups and nurseries, and out-of-school care, which can include breakfast clubs, after-school care and holiday clubs, are the biggest providers; however, it is recognised that NCE is more complex and expansive than this and can involve many services which provide a variety of care and support for children. This chapter will focus on the two biggest contributors to NCE but recognises that all NCE service provisions and practitioners contribute positively to children's welfare and support parents' contributions to the wider economic agenda.

─────────── THINKING POINT 16.1 ───────────

1. Why do you think there is both educational and political interest in NCE?
2. Why do you think there has been an increase in need for families to access these services?
3. Can you think of the benefits of NCE provision?
4. Are there any drawbacks to the expansion of NCE provision?

Early years provision and benefits

Bakken et al. (2017) claim that, economically, pre-school education benefits both the compulsory schooling sector and the state as it is both a short- and long-term investment to shape the society of tomorrow (Heckman and Masterov, 2007). The OECD (2006) claims that early years provision not only supports parents by promoting children's development and wellbeing but that it helps determine children's prospects for lifelong learning. The UK Government (UKG) also asserts that '[p]roviding children with good-quality education and care in their earliest years can help them succeed at school and later in life' (UKG, 2015, n.p.). Thus, investment in early years services potentially provides a positive start to children's lives that will impact their personal future and the future economic infrastructures of the nation. It is acknowledged that early years provision is of benefit to both children's development and learning and to society generally through parents being able to contribute to the wider economy. While the benefits of early years provision are acknowledged, it is a devolved matter in the UK, meaning that different approaches have been taken by each country in the UK in terms of funding and investment in curricula development to support the delivery of provision.

All the UK devolved governments value and have made provision for pre-5 education and childcare; however, with the exception of Scotland, there appear to be no plans for all families in the UK to have access to provision at the same level as the compulsory education sector (see Table 16.1). Once families know their entitlement, parents can access pre-5 provision from a wide range of facilities, which can include: local authority or government establishments, private individuals, community groups, private organisations, commercial employers and partnership provision. However, there can also be issues with the availability of provision and some families may have to split their child's placement across more than one setting (Department for Education [DfE], 2018b).

Table 16.1 Provision of early years in the UK

Country	Children's age	Number of hours	Extended provision	Curriculum
England	3-4	15 hours a week for 38 weeks of year (570 hours)	For 3/4-year-olds whose parents meet the criteria up to 30 hours of free childcare for 38 weeks of the year	Statutory Framework for the Early Years: Foundation Stage (DfE, 2021b)
			Disadvantaged 2-year-olds have funded early years provision for 15 hours per week for 38 weeks of the year (DfE, 2018b)	
Northern Ireland	3-4	12.5 hours over 5 days a week during term time	Priority to identify resources to deliver extended, affordable and high-quality provision of early education and care initiatives for families with children aged 3 to 4 (NI Executive, 2020b: 9)	Curriculum Guidance for Pre-school Education (DfE (NI), 2018)
Scotland	3-4	30 hours a week during term time (1140 hours)	Eligible 2-year-olds can be provided with a funded place if they meet specified criteria (MyGovScot, 2021)	Curriculum for Excellence (Scottish Government, 2008b)
Wales	3-4	10 hours a week for 48 weeks of year	For families who meet household income requirements: • 3/4-year-olds, 30 hours a week for 48 weeks a year • Some 2-year-olds can have access to a maximum of 12.5 hours per week as part of flying start scheme (Welsh Government, 2021b)	Foundation Phase Framework (Welsh Government, 2015)

Out-of-school care provision and benefits

Whilst investment and consideration have been given to the pre-5 sector over recent years, the field of out-of-school care (OSC) appears to be less developed in terms of provision. Out-of-school care delivers sessions in the form of supervision and Playwork, both before and after school as well as providing full-day care holiday provision for primary school-aged children (4–12 years) in addition to holiday provision, where full-day care is required. While there has been rapid growth in the level of provision available, there remains limited understanding of how this type of provision impacts children developmentally or if a standard structure of delivery is required. Plantenga and Remery (2017) and Prochner (2000: 54) suggest that OSC is often viewed as a service that allows parents to give attention to their work commitments, knowing that 'their children were safe and happy', whilst tending to be viewed as less important when children are in receipt of compulsory education. Moloney and Pope (2020) express concerns about suggestions for OSC to provide opportunities for study classes and homework activities as this would result in provision simply being an extension of the school environment. Further, this focus would remove the positive importance placed on freedom and play which many children, who can be away from their home and family for up to 12 hours in a day, need to unwind and develop social skills. Kuperminc et al. (2019) also highlight that OSC staff are key to children benefiting from OSC programmes as they help to establish practices which promote positive relationships and community engagement. Klerfelt and Haglund (2014) argue that OSC could provide scope for practitioners to support and to address children's specific social and emotional needs. Given concerns from many sectors including health and education, regarding children's mental health, OSC could provide support and modelling to children with a focus on positive physical and mental health and wellbeing. Therefore, whilst differences in opinion exist in terms of the contributions to children's development and wellbeing that are made by OSC, there are many opportunities to support school-aged children beyond the delivery of a fixed curriculum. However, as noted by Plantenga and Remery (2017), the UK is not alone in finding it hard to define the role of OSC as very few European Union countries have an established structure for this provision. Riggs and Greenberg (2004) even suggest that OSC requires its own category within childcare and that there is still work to be done to clearly establish and develop the role of OSC within the UK.

In terms of provision and funding, most OSC settings rely on charitable funds, grants from government or statutory bodies, or investments from the set-up organiser for start-up funding (Out-of-School Care Alliance [OSCA], 2021). Scotland's First Minister, in September 2021, indicated a commitment to the expansion of OSC through the funding of wraparound provision (Bussey, 2021). Other governments have not yet committed to providing funding to allow every child the opportunity of OSC, thus arguably limiting its accessibility to all children; however, there have been some signs of funding being made available in England, through the Department for Education's National School Breakfast Programme (Tomlinson, 2020), which has reserved £11.8m to support this service.

It is perhaps issues around funding and multiple structures along with the lack of recognition and status of staff in NCE provision, that there is also a high turnover of staff in both early years and OSC sectors (Gaunt, 2021; Rolfe et al., 2003). It is not uncommon that practitioners move on to careers which offer better pay, conditions, career prospects and stability (Goddard, 2021; Bonetti et al., 2020). Over the last 20 years, as part of the focus and development of these key services, staff have also been required to comply with changing demands in terms of qualifications, employment requirements, child protection and the professionalisation of NCE staff. These changes can be viewed as increasing the recognition and status of the NCE sector and for many staff it can be seen as a move towards professionalisation of the workforce.

What is a professional?

Across the UK, each devolved country has taken some action to regulate staff who provide care in the NCE sector and for some there has been a move to professionalise some staff roles. As part of this endeavour, registration bodies, qualification requirements and legislation have helped to change some perceptions of the workforce (Wingrave and McMahon, 2016).

The term 'professional' is a concept that has had many different interpretations and applications (Hoyle, 2001; Bond and Bond, 1994). Frequently, the terms *professional* and *profession* are over-applied and are used interchangeably when describing many types of employment, thus leading to diminution of the term (Hoyle, 2001). Klegon (1978) identified three fundamental attributes of a professional: as someone who is required to follow ethical standards, be equipped to apply specialist knowledge and skills to benefit others and will, as part of ongoing development, continue to access research and learning to develop their specialist knowledge. May (2001) similarly recognised the importance of intellectual and moral commitment by professionals and noted that there were often specific organisational elements which define professional disciplines. Cruess et al. (2004) also proposed that professionals are governed by codes of ethics and are also regulated by those who have insight into the demands of the profession. Professionals are therefore accountable to others and are open to scrutiny. A recurring feature of the term professional is the association with a specialised body of knowledge and the acquisition of relevant occupational qualifications. In addition, qualifications require continual reinforcement in terms of the learning and skills of a workforce, so continuous professional development (CPD) is required (Choi and Kang, 2019). Thus, specific qualifications which relate to the complexity of the job and the ongoing requirement to engage in CPD provide a level of recognition that an employee is a professional (Wingrave and McMahon, 2016). A professional will be able to demonstrate that they:

- have specific, relevant, knowledge and skills, often in the form of higher-level qualifications;
- will engage in ongoing CPD to keep practice up-to-date;
- are subject to a set of standards which demonstrate a clear code of ethics and practice; and
- are a member of a professional regulatory body which sets professional standards and supports the profession through accrediting and approving related higher educational programmes and qualifications.

THINKING POINT 16.2

1. Who do you think of when you hear the term professional?
2. Why is it important that there are certain restrictions placed on entry to professions?
3. Consider the criteria listed above. In what ways do you consider yourself to be a professional or in the process of becoming a professional?

The development of the NCE sector as a profession

Osgood (2006: 5) claimed that the move to increase the professional status of those in childcare 'could lead to a strengthened position' for staff. All governments in the UK have introduced professional standards and inspection procedures in response to changes in legislation to secure high standards of practice across provision with graduate-led service managers. There are however some concerns related to a professionalisation agenda, as it could be viewed as an opportunity for government to apply controls and authority over the NCE workforce. As Day (2017) cautions, the introduction of professional standards could result in a professional identity being imposed by government through the setting of an ethical framework and prescribed moral purpose.

Inspection of services

Inspection bodies across the UK (see Table 16.2) were created under various pieces of legislation determined by the devolved governments. Across the UK, all care workers who provide more than two hours' care per day and on at least six days per year are regulated.

Table 16.2   Inspection of NCE in the UK

Country	Inspection body	Abbreviation
England	Office for Standards in Education, Children's Services and Skills	Ofsted
Northern Ireland	The Education and Training Inspectorate	ETI
Scotland	Care Inspectorate	CI
Wales	Care Inspectorate Wales	CIW

In Scotland, the Care Inspectorate (CI) was set up in response to the Regulation of Care (Scotland) Act (Scottish Parliament [SP], 2001). The aim was to improve provision and register services which provide paid care for more than two hours a day to children 16 years or younger. In addition, the Regulation of Care (Scotland) Act (SP, 2001) also resulted in the creation of the Scottish Social Services Council (SSSC) in 2001. The SSSC has the responsibility for registering those who work in social services and for regulating education and training in this field (Wingrave, 2015). The Care Inspectorate Wales (CIW) was created in response to the Care Standards Act 2000 (UK Parliament [UKP], 2000) with the aim to regulate and inspect settings in Wales. A uniform set of expectations for early years and childcare service were introduced for those providing more than two hours of care for children under 12. Further, the Health and Social Care (Community Health and Standards) Act in 2003 (UKP, 2003) gave legislative powers to CIW to allow them to inspect and review local authorities' social care services. In Northern Ireland, a key piece of legislation was the Children (Northern Ireland) Order 1995 (Northern Ireland Assembly, 1995), which resulted in the creation of the Health and Social Care Trusts (HSCT) who register and inspect services. The HSCTs updated their standards in 2018 with the publication of the Childminding and Day Care for Children Under Age 12 Minimum Standards (Amended 2018) (Department of Health NI, 2018). In 2000, the Childcare Partnerships (CCP) were introduced as a reaction to Children First: The Northern Ireland Childcare Strategy (Department of Health and Social Policy Unit: Northern Ireland [DHSS NI], 1999). The Northern Ireland Assembly sought to improve services in terms of the availability of childcare and the quality of delivery for children up to 14 years of age. In England, the Childcare Act 2006 (UKP, 2006) underpins childcare provision for children who are under 8 years for two hours a day and more, requiring registration with the Office for Standards in Education (Ofsted). Early years settings are required to be registered on Ofsted's Early Years Register and there is a legal requirement for staffing levels in services to conform to the Statutory Framework for the Early Years Foundation Stage (DfE, 2021b). However, since 2014, those who work in OSC and holiday play schemes in England are not required to register on the Ofsted Early Years Register or to employ staff with 'full and relevant' childcare or Playwork qualifications, although they can do so on a voluntary basis (Goddard, 2020). (A list of the NCE qualifications and regulatory bodies is set out in Table 16.3.) These inspection bodies have responsibility for ensuring that care services comply with requirements and any setting failing to fulfil the requirements can be de-registered and no longer allowed to provide the service.

Table 16.3 Staff registration and qualifications

	England	Northern Ireland	Scotland	Wales
Requirement to undertake continuous professional development (CPD)	Voluntary	Voluntary	Compulsory requirement for all registered staff. The Continuous Learning Framework (CLF) supports this	Voluntary
Regulatory body	Ofsted Early Years Register and the Childcare Register	Northern Ireland Social Care Council	Scottish Social Services Council (SSSC)	Social Care Wales
Set of professional standards	Early Years Professional Status (EYPS) in 2006	Social Care Council's Standards for Conduct and Practice	Standard for Childhood Practice (SSSC, 2016b) Codes of Practice (SSSC, 2016a) National Care Standards	National Minimum Standards for Regulated Childcare for Children up to the age of 12 years Codes of Professional Conduct

Across the UK, three levels of practice exist; although there is no consistency in terms of the names ascribed to equivalent status, each grade has qualifications requirements attached:

- **Support worker/Early years and childcare worker/Early years practitioner/ Early worker-playworker**

  Non-supervisory role: staff need to hold a Level 2 qualification or equivalent (National Qualification Framework/Scottish Certificate and Qualification Framework).

- **Senior playworker-practitioner/Practitioner: Early years or Playwork/Early years educator/Room supervisor/Team leader**

  Must hold a practitioner qualification – Level 3 or equivalent (NQF/SCQF).

- **Manager/Leader/Person in charge/Early years teacher status (EYTS)**

  Must hold or be prepared to complete a minimum of a degree-level relevant qualification.

In Scotland, specific qualifications for staff to meet the Standard for Childhood Practice (SSSC, 2016b) were created for staff to attain a degree-level Childhood Practice Award (CPA). The Care Inspectorate promotes the Health and Social Care Standards (Scottish Government [SG], 2017b), the Codes of Practice (SSSC, 2016a) and the Standard for Childhood Practice (SSSC, 2016b) and provides information regarding the quality of care and social work services. Wales, in their 2017 Childcare, Play and Early Years Workforce Plan (Welsh Government, 2017), is inclusive of both Playwork and early years education and childcare staff. In 2016 Social Care Wales, introduced the National Minimum Standards for Regulated Childcare for Children up to the Age of 12 Years (Welsh Government, 2016) along with a guide to Codes of Professional Conduct (Social Care Wales, 2021). In Northern Ireland, staff have to meet the Social Care Council: Standards of Conduct and Practice (Northern Ireland Social Care Council [NISCC], 2019). For those working in England, staff must meet the National Occupational Standards (NOS, online). In terms of qualification requirements, if the NCE provision has only children of Reception age or older, there is no requirement for staff to hold a Childcare or Playwork qualification, although staff are required to have the essential experiences and skills to work with children. However, if children younger than Reception age are being provided for, as in an early years setting or in OSC, staff must have a Level 3 qualification in the appropriate area (UKG, 2021). The Early Years Teacher role in England, while requiring the same educational requirements as teachers in schools, 'carries neither Qualified Teacher Status nor the same pay as schoolteachers' (Hillman and Williams, 2015: 19), therefore staff do not have equivalence with teachers with Qualified Teacher Status (Wild et al., 2015).

———————————— VIEW FROM PRACTICE ————————————

Workforce mobility and flexibility within the UK

Eddie is an early years professional working in a nursery in London. Currently, Eddie is the setting's manager and has completed a NVQ Level 3 in early years childcare. Due to family circumstances, Eddie needs to move to Edinburgh in Scotland and is concerned about what employment options will be available within the early years service. Eddie wants to apply for a manager's position in Edinburgh and wants to check the difference between requirements for working as a manager in Scotland compared to England.

Eddie observes that in terms of qualifications and experience it would be possible to meet the criteria for applying for a manager position in Scotland. Eddie's previous qualification is transferable from England to Scotland and would meet the practitioner-level registration with SSSC. However, in order to register as a manager in Scotland with the SSSC, Eddie will have to commit to undertaking the Childhood Practice Award at the Scottish Credit and Qualification Framework (SCQF) Level 9, the equivalent of an ordinary degree.

The ability to move within the UK is due to similar expectations in terms of qualifications and work role competencies, which encourages workforce mobility and flexibility. Qualification transferability is due to the Qualification and Credit Framework (QCF) adopted by England, Wales and

Northern Ireland in 2011 and the Scottish Credit and Qualification Framework (SCQF). Thus, Eddie will be able to transfer within the early years and meet employment requirements across the countries in the UK, although, as indicated above, he will still need to meet the registration requirements in Scotland and agree to undertake a degree-level qualification. (For a comparison of the required qualifications in the sector in the two nations, see Table 16.4.)

Table 16.4   Job comparisons between England and Scotland

	England: Nursery manager in London	Scotland
Qualifications	NQV3 or equivalent (can include Children and Young People's Workforce HND in an area of early years or degree in Childcare, Early Years or Child Development (QCF, online)	To work and register as a manager, it is necessary to hold a practice qualification (SVQ3 or equivalent) and hold or be prepared to undertake one of the following: • BA Childhood Practice • SQA Professional Development Award Childhood Practice (360 credits at SCQF Level 9) (SCQF, online)
Requirements	• Two years post-qualification experience in an early-years setting • Supervisory experience preferable	• SCQF Level 9 or BA Childhood Studies or be working towards relevant managerial qualification • Experience in an early-years managerial post is required
Salary	£23,614–£48,713 (for post advertised on Glassdoor (www.glassdoor.co.uk) in October 2021)	£25,000–£40,000 (for post advertised on Indeed (https://uk.indeed.com) in October 2021)

Across the UK, there has been a concerted effort to upskill and professionalise the NCE; however, in order that the profession can continue to improve and grow, the development of the workforce still needs to be reviewed. The main issue that appears to be impeding the recognition of and recruitment into the workforce is pay and conditions of service. While it is commendable that the UK has made moves to make the NCE sector a degree-level profession and there is a growing acknowledgement of the importance of the work in terms of experiences and outcomes for children, there is still a need to address pay and career progression.

Pay and progression in NCE

According to Akhal (2019: 5), who conducted a study in England comparing childcare workers' pay and conditions to those in the retail service, there has been a gradual decline in pay for those in NCE services. It was found that the monetary difference between those who worked in childcare and retail was the 'equivalence of £0.44 per hour'. This is despite the increasing demands on NCE staff to be qualified and with '74 per cent of the childcare workforce qualified at A-level or higher, versus 45 per cent of the retail workforce'; consequently, it is not surprising that many in childcare feel undervalued. The data highlighted concerns regarding retention of the workforce as it does appear unreasonable to ask staff to remain in a job where they have both responsibilities and educational requirements but no monetary recompense. Davis et al. (2014) acknowledged that the lack of a national pay scale or career pathway that other professions have in place makes progression for staff difficult. In addition to issues of pay, conditions and career progression, there are differences within the sector itself, and often those who work in local authorities are financially better off than staff who work in the private/voluntary sector. Further, Bonetti et al. (2020) claim that those working in local authority or public settings work fewer hours than staff working in the private or voluntary sectors. Akhal (2019: 17) found that low wages for childcare workers tend to be the biggest reason for staff to move out of the sector and that '44 per cent of childcare workers were claiming benefits in 2018 compared to 26 per cent of retail workers'. Additional requirements and responsibilities, as noted by Cooke and Lawson (2008: 6), 'often do not equate to extra pay, responsibility or professional development'. Nutbrown (2012) also acknowledged the disparity between compulsory and non-compulsory education sectors, in terms of both pay and status. Bonetti (2019) warns that for England a large percentage of the childcare workforce is rapidly approaching retirement age and there may be issues with a lack of new staff being trained to replace those retiring. The National Day Nurseries Association (NDNA, 2019) reported a similar concern in Scotland with private and third-sector provision, indicating that '71% of employers [are] struggle[ing] to recruit staff at practitioner level, 48% struggl[ing] to replace Lead Practitioners'. Having outlined the professionalisation of the service and considered the concerns facing those working in the NCE, I now consider what next for NCE services.

Continuing the professionalisation of NCE services

As a public good, NCE services should target gaps that support some children and families in the hope of decreasing negative long-term impact and improving subsequent educational outcomes. However, as Woodrow and Press (2018: 537) caution, 'new discourse in the way that childcare is perceived, is transforming it into a commodity for private benefit rather than as a public good'. It is necessary for governments to fully fund these services in order that all children have this opportunity and not just those families who can afford to access them. Further, there is a danger that these services are viewed as supplements to compulsory education and not as services offering particular and targeted childcare. The impact of how NCE services are viewed will influence the rewards for those who work in these services in terms of their career, pay and conditions. For many, a career in the NCE sector is hindered by the perceived low status and pay of the profession, and the non-standard hours associated with the work. In addition to the investments already in place, further commitment in terms of a clear pay scale which supports career progression for those entering the workforce and addressing the disparity in pay and conditions between those in the NCE sector and those with the same level of qualification in other professions such as teaching and nursing, would have significant consequences for the recruitment and retention of staff (Wingrave and McMahon, 2016). For staff entering the profession, there needs to be an ongoing commitment to gaining relevant qualifications and to professional development, which contribute to enhancing pedagogical quality and better outcomes for children (Osgood et al., 2017).

Summary

The last 20 years have seen many changes to the status and requirements of the NCE workforce. Arguably, qualifications and expansion have moved the services towards recognition and professionalisation; however, retention and pay remain the major barriers to the workforce. There is a danger that childcare services are viewed as supplementary to compulsory education and not as services offering particular and targeted childcare. Continuing investment and development of the NCE service are needed to promote the profession as a genuine career pathway which will attract a workforce who wish to remain and is held in high esteem as it is committed to providing recognised benefits for children.

END-OF-CHAPTER QUESTIONS

1. How important do you consider the NCE sector to be for children, families and society?
2. How successful do you think the various governments across the UK have been in professionalising the NCE sector?
3. What do you think needs to be done to attract and keep staff in the sector?

17
Professional learning and the reflexive practitioner
Irene Pollock and Tracey Stewart

Key ideas

This chapter will explore:

- Reflection as a constant individual activity, which feeds into group reflections to ensure ongoing evaluation and quality assurance.
- Individual and group reflection to assist identification of training needs.
- A variety of courses and resources to underpin and support continuing professional development.
- Selecting courses in order to maximise benefits to both individuals and settings.

Introduction

Within a context where the needs of children, local issues and legislation and guidance documents are continually changing, practitioners in non-compulsory education and care (NCE) settings must offer a responsive and reflexive learning experience, adapting to individual needs and situations. Both practitioners and children should be active participants in their learning. While learning can be defined in many ways, this chapter will emphasise that 'learning is that reflective activity which enables the learner to draw upon previous experience to understand and evaluate the present, so as to shape future action and formulate new knowledge' (Abbott, 1994, cited in Watkins et al., 2000: 4). Similarly, Kolb's (1984) learning theory asserts that reflective practice is necessary to facilitate genuine learning and development.

Being fully reflexive enables staff to see the links between problems and solutions, and also between actions and success. While there is no universal definition of the reflexive practitioner (Kelly, 2019), there is a reciprocal relationship between reflection and self-efficacy (Bandura, 1997). Reflection can be undertaken as individuals and in groups. By acknowledging their own ongoing learning needs and the benefits of training undertaken, practitioners are better equipped to respond to the needs of the children in front of them and to build professional confidence, skills and validation.

Sector guidance, as well as the requirements of regulatory bodies and registration organisations, emphasises a minimum amount of continuing professional development (CPD). This chapter will give an overview of the spectrum of CPD available, from mandatory essential courses and discretionary focused courses (e.g. Makaton, autism) to longer academic courses in educational practice such as pedagogical theory and leadership. The chapter will also ask you to reflect on the type of learner you are and what motivates you to learn, as a key component of reflexivity is self-awareness.

--- **VIEW FROM PRACTICE** ---

The reflective practitioner

Kim has worked in a 20-place voluntary sector nursery for eight years. During this time, she has attended various courses and she takes part in her local authority Practitioner Forums, where she is able to share experiences with peers from other settings. Kim is aware that her experience of children on the autism spectrum is limited. Previously, Kim worked with an external child psychologist to support an autistic boy who benefited from using a weighted blanket. She subsequently read widely on the sensory processing issues that some autistic children exhibit.

Kim has been observing a 3-year-old, Isabella, who recently joined the nursery. Isabella's mum, Rachel, describes her as 'bull in a china shop' and 'very cuddly'. Kim noticed that while Isabella seems keen to join in with other children's play, her rough way of climbing over them and of rolling across tables is irritating them. At mealtimes, Isabella's habit of chewing all her food with her mouth open is also upsetting others. Kim observed that Isabella often climbs into toy boxes or cupboards as she seems to need to 'feel' pressure all around her.

At the scheduled post-transition meeting, Kim carefully discussed with Rachel some of the behaviours she had observed. She explained that whilst it has only been a short time, she felt Isabella exhibits some sensory processing issues. As Kim herself is not an expert, she requested Rachel's permission to seek additional support from external agencies. Kim subsequently got in touch with the Local Health Board Occupational Therapy (OT) department and was offered the opportunity to attend a workshop along with Isabella's mother. The workshop proved to be highly informative, giving both Rachel and Kim several practical ideas that could be tried in the home and playrooms immediately.

Kim observed such positive results after attending the workshop that she contacted the OT department to ask for training materials. She shared these with all staff in her setting to improve practice. Kim also raised the issue at the next Practitioner Forum, suggesting that the local authority extend their annual training roster to include this highly informative and practical course.

THINKING POINT 17.1

1. How did Kim's previous knowledge influence her actions? Do you think it made her more confident in exploring possible avenues of support with Rachel? Explain why.
2. How would you feel in raising such issues with parents/carers?
3. Determine the extent to which individualised interventions can/cannot be adopted in your setting.
4. Kim used input from the psychologist, professional reading, and training to develop her practice. Which approaches are promoted in your setting? Would you rather attend a course or read up on a topic? Where would you find your reading?

The reflexive practitioner: individual reflection

Within an NCE setting, practitioners will be unconsciously engaging in reflexive practice as they respond to the needs of the children, for example by modulating speech or by offering resources and adapting activities to make them meaningful and challenging. With the recent increase in funded provision in Scotland, settings more frequently see a mix of attendance patterns, meaning that group and staff dynamics fluctuate. In all settings, there will be brief opportunities for professional exchanges of dialogue, for example 'hubs', 'pit stops' or 'daily huddles'. In these conversations, practitioners share information regarding the children and their responses to various events and activities, in order to ensure that a rich learning experience is offered to all (Brookfield, 2017).

It is often only at the end of the day that practitioners can privately ruminate on what they felt went well and what they may have done differently to further enhance the experience for those concerned (whether children, families, or staff).

Professional standards for all Scottish practitioners make reflective practice an expected component of daily practice (Scottish Social Services Council [SSSC], 2016b). In England, the Professional Association for Childcare and Early Years (2022) encourages self-evaluation as an ongoing professional requirement, reflecting the principles of Ofsted (2021). Practitioners, like the children in their care, are individuals with differing temperaments and preferences. In order to be a truly reflexive practitioner, a practitioner's own influence on any given situation must be acknowledged. Individual reflection has been defined as a constant critique of anything and everything (Cammack, 2012; Bolton, 2010) as well as deliberate thinking about a specific experience (Davies, 2012; Dewey, 1933). Models of reflection will be discussed later in this chapter. Practitioners who can recognise their own impact and who can realistically acknowledge their own responses and what they may have done differently are more likely to contribute constructively to group reflexive activities.

Group reflection

Group reflection can be defined as 'a state of learning which benefits the organisation' (Bleach, 2014; Schön, 1991). In order to offer a responsive, challenging and stimulating environment for children, the team within the setting need to exchange information on children's interests and development, as well as ideas for scaffolding their learning. Teams need to reflect on practice and consider what has worked well, what has not, and how best to reach the desired outcomes: as argued by Leeson and Bamsey (2015: 251), reflective practice 'should be regarded as an integral part of developing competent professionals in early years care'. During team meetings, the facilitator needs to 'develop a process that provides participants with support and encouragement that make meetings worthwhile' (Jones, 2005: 96).

Within Scotland, the early years national practice guidance Realising the Ambition (Education Scotland [ES], 2020: 9) aims to 'support improvement and quality by encouraging discussion, self-reflection and questioning about relevant practice'; that is, regular group reflection. In preparing for inspections by regulatory bodies (Education Scotland or Care Inspectorate in Scotland; Ofsted in England; Care Inspectorate Wales; or Local Authority Health Team and Social Care in Northern Ireland), staff are expected to be aware of the setting's self-evaluation and action plans. While Ofsted removed the Self-Evaluation Form from its pre-inspection requirements in 2018 (UK Government [UKG], 2018), it is still anticipated that staff are involved in and aware of their setting's ethos, achievements and development plans. Such awareness requires staff to come together regularly as a team to discuss and self-evaluate the setting as part of continual best practice, rather than simply holding an annual or quarterly event.

Most local authorities also conduct annual evaluations, both for their own settings and for partnership settings. Within Scotland, the current self-evaluation tool, How Good is our Early Learning and Childcare? (ES, 2016: 5), asks three main questions: 'How good is our leadership and approach to improvement?', 'How good is the quality of the care and learning we offer?' and 'How good are we at ensuring the best possible outcomes for all our children?' These questions have parallels in Annex B of the Welsh inspection guidelines (Care Inspectorate Wales, 2019). Ofsted's (2021) Early Years Inspection Handbook refers to using the setting's own analysis during inspection, while Northern Ireland's self-evaluation framework (Education and Training Inspectorate, 2017) provides questions similar to Education Scotland's. To answer these questions, a degree of reflexive dialogue is required amongst the staff team. In considering these questions, staff are given guidance on how to reflect – thinking and answering honestly about how and why practice is or is not creating the desired outcomes. Practitioners should reflect on positive occurrences as well as challenging situations.

Models of reflection

Many theorists have explored how educators think and learn about their practice. Arguably, the most influential of these is Schön (1991), who proposed that reflection occurs at multiple levels. He suggests that managing the complexity of professional practice requires the ability to think 'on one's feet' and use previous experience under new conditions. Schön's model can be viewed as having three levels:

- Knowing-in-action: educators automatically implement certain practices without thinking, based on previous experiences.
- Reflection-in-action: educators change their practice – often in response to a challenge – by consciously drawing on a range of strategies that they are familiar with to make adaptations straight away.
- Reflection-on-action: educators look back following an experience, thinking about what could have gone differently.

Practitioners may find it beneficial to consider when they have used these different levels, for example whether an automatic response negatively impacted the situation (Brown, 2003b) or if previous knowledge was applied to adapt appropriately. These types of questions can be addressed either individually or in a group evaluation exercise. As will be outlined later in this chapter, reflection should not be solely an in-setting activity. There are, for example, benefits from reflecting on your experiences and outcomes during professional development activities and courses.

Kolb (2015, 1984) suggests that reflection and learning are intertwined, and learning will occur while connecting experiences and knowledge. Kolb's Experiential Learning Cycle was devised as a way of interpreting reflective practice and presents reflection through four stages: do, reflect, think and plan. These stages require the practitioner to recall experiences from previous practice, think creatively to adapt the experience, and then experiment through trial and error. Building on these stages, Gibbs (1988) produced his own model, which offers a framework for examining experiences in six stages: description, feelings, evaluation, analysis, conclusion and action plan.

Influenced by the thinking within these models, the authors of this chapter offer a Reflexive Star Model (see Figure 17.1), which aims to show that reflection is an iterative process, with contributing factors having differing levels of impact depending on the situation. It is helpful to be aware of your own perceptions when reflecting: Do you always feel there was a lack of resources? Do you often react too slowly or too harshly? Do you tend to blame others, or yourself? Do you give credit or take credit? These types of questions help to develop a self-awareness of default emotional responses.

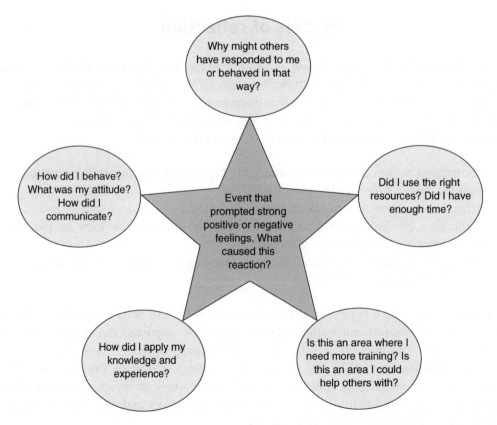

Figure 17.1   Stewart–Pollock Reflexive Star Model

Building self-esteem and the professional practitioner

The primary purpose of the NCE setting is the care and education of children. As discussed above, practitioners should be reflexive and responsive to the differing ways in which children develop and respond to the environment around them. However, practitioners must also be mindful of the need to offer intervention and support when necessary, and therefore must be confident in their knowledge of the anticipated developmental 'milestones' (ES, 2020). Many underlying support needs are first realised in early years settings, as indicated in the 'View from Practice' above. Families, as well as children, may require support as they adapt to the needs of the child. In order to start empathetic and tactful conversations with parents/carers, practitioners need to be confident in their own professional judgement.

Practitioners are not expected to be experts in all social and emotional behavioural areas, or medical conditions; however, they should be knowledgeable enough to be able to highlight why support may be required and what that support might look like (McKenna, 2020). Such knowledge comes from experience, as well as through CPD, which also allows staff to validate what they do and why. Staff, when completing children's documentation, must show an awareness of the child by reflecting upon the child's learning and their possible next steps; however, to do this well, staff must also be aware of their own learning and their own training needs. The following section will discuss CPD in greater detail.

THINKING POINT 17.2

1. In your setting, how often do you undertake reflection as a group exercise?
2. How do you feel when asked to contribute to the evaluation of your setting's work? How do you feel when asked to reflect on your individual contributions?
3. Determine the extent to which these activities make you feel empowered or threatened. Explain why.

Availability of professional learning

Professional learning for practitioners can take a wide range of forms. It is useful to consider professional learning under three characteristics:

- Initial qualifications vs continuing professional development.
- Practice-based/vocational vs academic/theoretical.
- Essential/core vs building skills/knowledge.

These characteristics will be explored further below. Although the contrast between each end of the spectrum is not absolute – for example, many courses include both practice and theory – identifying where a learning opportunity lies can help to inform decisions. As discussed above, reflection on current knowledge and future needs should be used, along with professional dialogue with colleagues and management.

Initial qualifications are often required by early years settings prior to employment (as discussed more fully in Chapter 16), although some settings offer apprenticeships. In line with the characteristics outlined above, initial qualifications may have more of a practice-based focus, such as Scottish Vocational Qualifications or National Vocational Qualifications, or they may focus more on theory, such as Higher National Certificates and Diplomas. The level of an initial qualification may be set by a regulator. In Scotland from 2003, this is the Scottish Social Services Council (SSSC, 2022b), while in England, the Early Years Educator qualification at Level 3 has been required since 2014 (Department for Education [DfE], 2019). Levels of accredited courses differ between Scotland and England as qualification frameworks vary (Scottish Qualifications Authority, 2021), and courses internationally are unlikely to be equivalent. However, most regulatory bodies will consider equivalence, or Recognition or Accreditation of Prior Learning (SSSC, 2022b; DfE, 2019), allowing practitioners to practise in or from other countries.

Beyond the initial qualification, both employers and regulatory bodies often require essential courses; it is your responsibility to be aware of these. These courses often address health and safety, such as first aid, child protection and food hygiene, and usually need to be repeated at regular intervals. While it may be easy to dismiss such mandatory trainings, these can be approached with a fresh outlook by reflecting on recent situations where this knowledge has been required. Interacting with other course participants to share practice and experiences is also informative, since opportunities to apply the knowledge and skills gained may not arise regularly within your own setting.

In addition to the essential courses, local authorities may offer training that aligns with their priorities for their employees and for partner providers. General child development may be a focus, such as training on language development or communication: for example, Edinburgh Council rolled out Hanen Teacher Talk training (NHS Lothian, 2021). Authority-wide training may also be aimed at children with additional support needs, whether this be on autism, managing challenging behaviour or trauma-informed practice for refugees. A final area that may be a priority is to introduce a theoretical approach more widely. The programme Froebelian Futures (Froebel Trust, 2021) aims to support early years practitioners to embed Froebelian ideas, such as in Falkirk Council (Falkirk Early Learning, 2021), while outdoor learning, including forest schools, has gained in popularity across the UK (Coates and Pimlott-Wilson, 2019). Although there are significant cost and time implications for authority-wide training, the benefits of having all practitioners following the same approach make such investment worthwhile (Jenkins et al., 2020; McKenna, 2020).

Continuing professional development goes beyond the essential courses required by employers, regulatory bodies and local authorities. Engaging in CPD offers an opportunity for practitioners at all levels to follow their own interests to develop their practice. Within settings and playrooms, having 'specialists' contributes to improved outcomes for children (Quinn and Parker, 2018). Some settings nominate 'champions', for example for literacy, numeracy, or health and wellbeing; these practitioners have dedicated responsibility for developing their area and often access to additional training (Potter, 2019). Areas such as outdoor learning offer a range of potential avenues for training, such as cooking with fire, promoting risky play, or loose parts play. Generally, such initiatives are more successful if practitioners 'opt in' to training, rather than this being dictated to them (Trotter, 2006; Day, 1999). Settings may also promote specific philosophies such as Montessori or Steiner/Waldorf (Martin, 2000), which require dedicated training.

Within settings, practitioners may also be encouraged to undertake professional learning aimed at addressing challenges relevant to particular children. While these needs may align with authority-wide approaches, such as supporting children with English as an additional language, others may be more specific. Needs could include medical training, such as monitoring the blood sugar of a diabetic child or learning to use an Epi-pen; Makaton for children with hearing or speech impairments; or the use of Boardmaker symbols to create visual timetables for children on the autism spectrum. Settings in deprived areas may benefit from training in facilitating nurture groups or a nurture approach (Hughes and Schlösser, 2014), which is suitable for all children.

For practitioners wishing to be promoted to a more senior position within a playroom or to a managerial role, further study is often required. While the theoretical aspects of university study can be intimidating for some practitioners, and they may feel underprepared for academic writing (Pollock, 2013), feedback is generally positive, for example increased confidence and improved professional relationships (Wingrave et al., 2020). In Scotland, one option is a Professional Development Award at Level 9 (SSSC, 2022b); however, it is more common for practitioners to undertake university study, for example by gaining a BA in Childhood Practice, or, for those already holding a degree, a Postgraduate Diploma (Davis, 2014). As indicated above, most universities will provide Recognition or Accreditation of Prior Learning, including informal learning experiences, to allow students to gain credit for previous study such as their practice qualification. The benefits of more highly qualified leaders in early years settings have been discussed by Wingrave and McMahon (2016), Siraj-Blatchford and Dunlop (2008), and Manni (2007).

Continuing professional development also encompasses informal learning, which is recognised by the SSSC (2022b) as well as the DfE (2019) to meet ongoing requirements for registration (Sakr and Bonetti, 2021). Informal learning can take a wide range of forms, and may result in a certificate, but is not considered a full qualification. Such learning can include independent or shared reading, attendance at conferences and other networking events, professional dialogue within and beyond staff teams, observation in other playrooms and settings, sharing good practice and partnership working with other agencies and professionals. In order to gain from these experiences, as from more formal training, reflection is essential; keeping a log of learning (an SSSC requirement) supports such reflection. Further, an open mind helps to make the most of the opportunities to learn from others.

─────────────────────── **THINKING POINT 17.3** ───────────────────────

1.   How is CPD promoted and encouraged within your setting?
2.   What is the most useful CPD you have engaged in over the past year, and how have you implemented this learning?
3.   Can you think of an example of CPD that, at the time, you felt was not relevant, but has since been helpful?

Keeping engaged

Regardless of the impetus for the professional learning experience, some key aspects to consider throughout are motivation, study skills, working with others, reflection and application of knowledge. These aspects will be considered in turn, with practical tips for how to maximise learning. Throughout this section, 'course' will be used, but this should be understood as any professional learning experience, from a webinar or conference presentation to a multi-year degree.

As implied above, the impetus for undertaking the training can have an effect on how much learning is gained. If motivation is solely extrinsic – for example, a course that is required by the local authority – engagement may be low (de Rijdt et al., 2016). However, intrinsic motivation may lead to selecting courses that lack applicability to real-world situations (Addison and Brundrett, 2008) and that are difficult to apply to practice. A blend of both types of motivation allows learners to gain the most (Hartwig and Schwabe, 2018; Gorozidis and Papaioannou, 2014). Clearly identifying the purpose of a course, both prior to committing and through the course induction, can help learners to begin to reflect on its utility to their roles. If a course does not seem relevant, reframing can be a useful tool for increasing motivation (Berkovich and Eyal, 2017; Kim and Pekrun, 2013), for example by considering whether course content might be applicable in a future role. The attitude towards engaging in a course can have a significant impact on how much knowledge is attained and retained (Narayan and Steele-Johnson, 2007; Cheng and Ho, 2001).

In addition to approaching a course with a positive attitude, using appropriate study skills also allows learners to get the most out of the course. Depending on the nature of the course, the required skills will vary; these could include active listening, effective teamwork, note-taking and synthesis (Castle, 2010). Learners may also need to develop presentation skills; such skills can have immediate benefits in practice, for example in improving communication with parents/carers. As in practice, working with others during a course is a key skill that also has benefits for increasing the impact of training (Fox and Wilson, 2015; Kennedy, 2011; McArdle and Coutts, 2010). Another way to increase impact is to apply the learning to practice as soon as possible. Too often, learners participate in a training experience only to file away their notes and not remain engaged (Pollock et al., 2015); consequently, support from management may be required in order to incorporate and sustain changes to practice.

Getting and giving support from others on the course is not only an effective study skill, but also helps to develop interpersonal or 'soft' skills (Scottish Government [SG], 2012b). Many learners identify the networking, professional dialogue and sharing of good practice that occur on courses as among the most valuable aspects of the learning experience (Carmichael et al., 2006). Even when collaboration is not an official component of the course, working together can enhance learning. In addition to other learners, support can and should be sought from the course tutor or organiser, from a mentor (whether or not this is a course requirement, as it is for SSSC-accredited courses), from colleagues and from management. In this way, more experienced practitioners can share knowledge and support professional development. Working with external partners can also provide useful insights, such as discussions with speech and language therapists if studying language development.

As argued throughout this chapter, ongoing reflection is not only a professional practice, but can also improve engagement with CPD. The process of reflection can help to identify 'next steps' in training by evaluating current practice and thinking about how future practice could be improved. Honest reflection on areas that require development can provide a more targeted approach to training, which can increase motivation (de Paor and Murphy, 2018). If undertaken with management and/or with colleagues, group reflection can also improve performance more generally (Freese, 2006; Powell et al., 2003). Once training has begun, reflection through discussion with others on the course, as outlined above, can enhance learning. Such discussions can also build confidence as they provide low-pressure opportunities to consolidate learning and make links to practice. In addition to reflecting on and evaluating your own practice during training, reflecting on and evaluating the course and course content can also deepen engagement. As confidence and experience grow, practitioners may find that certain courses, styles of delivery or methods of assessment suit them better than others. This knowledge can then be used when accessing future courses. Offering feedback to the course provider can also benefit future learners.

Perhaps the most effective way to remain engaged during any learning opportunity is to reflect throughout on how the knowledge and skills gained can be applied to practice. As mentioned above, some training may not be immediately applicable, but through professional dialogue with other learners, examples from practice in other settings may be obtained. By maintaining an open mind, and thinking beyond current challenges, any training may improve practice. These benefits affect a range of stakeholders: practitioners at all levels, management, children and young people, families/carers and external partners.

Summary

This chapter has argued that the purpose of professional learning within NCE should be not only to increase knowledge and skills, but also to build confidence in putting this learning into practice to support outcomes for children. Too often, learners do not apply new knowledge and skills (Pollock et al., 2015). This failure may be due to a lack of confidence, a lack of opportunity or a lack of initiative. Reflection can help to avoid all of these pitfalls by increasing self-awareness and therefore confidence, by identifying areas to apply new ideas, and by encouraging action.

END-OF-CHAPTER QUESTIONS

1. How has your thinking on CPD changed over time?
2. How might you influence the approach to CPD in your setting?
3. What action(s) will you take after reading this chapter with regard to your own professional learning?

18
Professional inquiry
Mike Carroll and Mary Wingrave

Key ideas

This chapter will explore:

- Professional inquiry as a form of practice-based research.
- The four key research paradigms.
- The quantitative/qualitative divide.
- The research/practice divide.
- A framework for inquiry.

Introduction

Many in professional practice see research as the domain of specialist academic researchers, usually working in universities. Arguably, practitioners faced with challenges in their professional practice tend not to go to research for answers but rather favour a more direct, 'hands-on approach' when examining aspects of practice. This 'gap' between academic research and professional practice can be explained in terms of three scripts, the:

- unidirectional script – a lack of information channels from research to practice;
- loop script – research failing to address the problems of practitioners; and
- interactive script – the absence of practitioner involvement throughout all the stages of the research process (Bauer and Fischer, 2007).

The gap between professional cultures suggests a need for researchers and practitioners to build joint communities, bringing together both research and a practical focus on the challenges faced by practitioners in their day-to-day lived professional lives (Korthagen, 2007); consequently, collaboration between academic researchers and practitioners enabling once-competing discourses to be integrated to transform practice (Sinnema et al., 2011) and 'close the gap'.

According to Holloway and Galvin (2017), the methodology or paradigm of inquiry guides the design of the study, the data collection methods and the subsequent analysis of data. In this chapter, we will use the term professional inquiry (also referred to as practitioner inquiry) to describe a distinct approach to research, where the research undertaken is located in and undertaken by those in practice. The process outlined has been defined by Menter et al. (2011) as a process of 'finding out' and it is often based on the intent to improve or evaluate current practice. According to Gilchrist (2018), professional inquiry should be viewed as a verb rather than a noun, where inquiry is an ongoing action which is continually revisited. Professional inquiry is a means of improving practice through the expansion of expertise which can offer those in practice opportunities for continued growth (Holloway and Wheeler, 2013).

The first step in the process is the identification of the issues/question which will be at the heart of the inquiry (Ratan et al., 2019). The question(s) asked will determine the process of framing the inquiry and involves identifying the paradigm (see Table 18.1) which determines the philosophical principles that underpin the choice of methods. A paradigm is 'a basic set of beliefs that guide action' (Guba, 1990: 17). The methodology, tools for data collection along with the approach to data analysis are determined by the paradigm, with the project, the paradigm and the methods for inquiry being congruent (Levers, 2013).

Research paradigms

This chapter examines four paradigms: positivist and non-positivist (i.e. interpretivist, post-positivist and critical theory) which help guide the process of inquiry (Wohlfart, 2020). Each paradigm views inquiry from a different perspective (Holloway and Wheeler, 2013). Hairston (1982) suggests that no one paradigm is better than another: different paradigms frame different but equally valid projects and issues. Identifying the appropriate paradigm allows the inquirer to start to make informed decisions about the inquiry design and to think about which strategies will help answer the question(s) being asked (Easterby-Smith et al., 2009).

Table 18.1 Key elements of a paradigm

According to Guba and Lincoln (1994), the defining features of a paradigm include:	
1. Ontology	Refers to the form and nature of reality and what can be known about it. Is there a single reality or are there multiple realities? Our ontological beliefs influence our epistemological assumptions.
2. Epistemology	Refers to the knowledge and how knowledge is acquired and validated. Our epistemological position influences our choice of methodology.
3. Methodology	Refers to the conceptual framework used to conduct the research which in turn influences the research methods (data collection instruments).
Heron and Reason (1997) advocate the inclusion of a fourth feature, namely:	
4. Axiology	Refers to principles and values ensuring that there is an ethical perspective to the research and that this applies to all those involved in the research.

Positivism

The positivist approach is premised on the belief that knowledge can be discovered (Holloway and Wheeler, 2013). Reality in this paradigm can be observed and captured, enabling possible explanations or patterns of covariation to be described. Often, the methods employed focus on observation and experiments which can be controlled and measured (Alakwe, 2017). Relationships between variables are seen as fixed, and that subjectivity or bias can be eliminated or at least controlled (Reiss and Sprenger, 2020). The inquirer is seen as an objective observer so they are not 'involved' in the outcomes, often writing in the 'third person' as results are not interpreted, they are simply recorded and presented (Kivunja and Kuyini, 2017). Park et al. (2020: 691) argue that findings can be used to disprove or 'prove' a hypothesis, and further investigations using the same methods should produce similar results, thus verifying theories. There is an emphasis on generalisability, that is, the extent to which findings can be reliably extrapolated to a broader population through the use of inferential statistical techniques.

Interpretivism

The interpretivist view is that there are multiple socially constructed realities. This approach seeks to understand how individuals understand their world (Cohen et al., 2018). There are different realities which can be understood in different ways and there is no one truth about behaviours. Even the same results can be analysed in different ways to derive different understandings (Holloway and Wheeler, 2013). The inquirer can never be completely objective, as our senses, prior experiences and knowledge all differ, resulting in various perspectives of the same event (Wellington and Szczerbinski, 2007). Therefore, inquiry and the inquirer are never value-free, with there being more than one explanation for any given finding. Experiences influence people's perspectives in interpretivist studies (Creswell, 2014). There is an emphasis on meaning making and often the inquirer will use multiple methods to gather data which reflect different aspects of the subject. Although not objective, it is necessary that the inquirer remains free of judgement when interpreting data and conducting the inquiry (Anderson, 2010). Sample sizes are often small so the inquiry makes no claims of generalisability; however, readers of the findings may find them relatable to their own contextual experience (Dzakiria, 2012). Data from interpretivist inquiry, often in the form of quotes elicited from participants, provide detailed (thick) descriptions of what is observed/discussed which are interpreted and developed into conceptual frameworks which best align with what was uncovered (Hammersley, 2013). The interpretation of the data and the tentative suggestions about what the findings might mean are often underpinned by literature and previous inquiry (Braun and Clarke, 2006). Results can produce a theory about a phenomenon, but it is contextualised and non-generalisable (Hammersley, 2013) as someone else examining the same data may view them differently.

Post-positivism

The post-positivist paradigm challenges the positivist approach. Post-positivists argue that the approaches used by the natural sciences can be applied to the social sciences (Martens, 2015). There is no claim of providing comprehensive or definitive answers; in fact, it accepts that reality can never be entirely captured. Post-positivist inquiry, according to Creswell (2014: 36), assumes that judicious study of an objective reality is 'out there'. Like positivists, post-positivists view reality as objective and constant, but they view reality as imperfect and difficult to capture (Tracy, 2013). According to Ryan (2006), post-positivists recognise the subjectivity of inquiry so that they move away from the entirely objective perspective embraced by positivists. Inquirers within post-positivism do not confine themselves to either the scientific or a social science discipline but they do share the same goals for inquiry and employ similar methods of investigation as positivist studies. The inquirer uses observations which concentrate on perceptions and recognises that these are imperfect; however, the inquirer nevertheless tries to achieve objectivity by employing numerous measures and observations in order to triangulate the data (Tracy, 2013). These approaches seek to obtain a richer understanding of what is reality but accept that human truths are subject to 'conjectures' so it is not always possible to capture the whole perspective of knowledge. Within this paradigm, bias, which ideally should be eliminated, is inevitable; the goal is to eliminate bias, which includes the inquirer examining their own values and beliefs when collecting, analysing and presenting their work (Kivunja and Kuyini, 2017).

Critical theory

According to Kivunja and Kuyini (2017: 35), critical theory relates to the use of power and seeks to uncover inequality and promote positive social change. Critical theory challenges current understandings and attempts to bring about a fair and equal society (Ferreira, 2018). Critical theory seeks to uncover and challenge structures which oppress sections of the community. Bohman (2005) suggests that critical theory should seek to clarify the existing social experience, identify what action should be taken to change it and provide a clear standard for change. The aim is to accomplish an emancipatory objective. Kincheloe and McLaren (2005) note that ontologically, critical theorists examine historical realism, where current reality has been shaped by society by factors such as cultural, ethnicity, politics, gender and religion. Further, in terms of epistemology it is assumed that all that is being examined and the inquirer will be influenced by these factors. Consequently, critical researchers acknowledge their epistemological position and accept that their own values will also be influenced. Hussain et al. (2013) note that methods of data collection can be qualitative, quantitative, or a mix of methods. Guba and Lincoln (1994) suggest that discussion and debate are often used to challenge people's views in order to bring about change. The inquirer will often adopt a collaborative approach and engage participants in the inquiry process. Richards (2003: 40) suggests that critical theory is where 'action [is] designed to redress the unequal and oppressive structures that have now been exposed'. Results are not generalisable.

———— VIEW FROM PRACTICE ————

Selecting a paradigm to guide and structure an inquiry

Peter is a head of centre of a large early years centre and an out-of-school care provision currently undertaking a Master's in Childhood Practice. As part of his studies, Peter is asked to plan an inquiry which relates to his practice. He is aware that staff have differing views towards play

(Continued)

and the various attitudes and approaches appear to result in different staff practices. Peter wants to improve the opportunities offered to children but is aware that in order to do this he needs to first understand the various staff views and approaches towards play. Peter is aware that before starting the project he must situate his inquiry in a suitable paradigm as this will help him guide and structure his inquiry. To do this, Peter examines the key elements of four paradigms: positivist, interpretivist, post-positivist and critical theory. Consider these paradigms and determine which paradigm will best help Peter to understand the different staff attitudes towards play.

The quantitative and qualitative debate

Bryman (2001: 106) argues that 'the distinction between qualitative and quantitative research perspective is really a technical matter whereby the choice between them is to do with their suitability in answering particular research questions'. According to Denzin and Lincoln (2000), qualitative methods aim to collect data which provide an understanding of an experience or event and often involve interviews, observations or photographs. The data collected provide a detailed description of the issue being examined. Quantitative methods gather numerical data which are analysed using either simple descriptive statistical or advanced inferential techniques to analyse and present findings. The data collection methods used to gather the data can involve the use of surveys, questionnaires, observations or the use of secondary data such as published government statistics.

These differences in approach result in different language being used to describe those involved and the data collected. It is important that the inquirer uses congruent language associated with the collection of data. For example, the inquirer in the positivist paradigm will not involve respondents in the inquiry in line with their methodological approach; however, the non-positivists will involve participants in the inquiry. This is because those involved will participate in the inquiry and are not separate from the process (Roller and Lavrakas, 2015). Further, positivists seek to establish the relationship between variables through formulating and testing a hypothesis, whilst those undertaking non-positivist inquiry seek to uncover or highlight theoretical constructs that emerge from an analysis of the data set (Connelly, 2015) (see Table 18.2).

Table 18.2 Contrasting positions of paradigms

	Positivist	Non-positivist
Question	Hypothesis	Issue/Question
Aim	Predict/Control	Insights/Understandings
Those involved	Respondents	Participants

	Positivist	Non-positivist
The research results	Validity/Reliability	Goodness/Trustworthy / Authenticity
You seek to	Establish causality-disprove or 'prove'	Uncover
The results	Generalisable	Not generalisable

The literature review

According to Burns and Grove (1997), the purpose of a literature review is to help delineate the area of inquiry and to find a suitable methodology and techniques for data collection. A review of literature provides background information and establishes the importance of the subject under consideration (Bloomberg and Volpe, 2012). Additionally, it demonstrates familiarity and knowledge in relation to the topic and it allows the inquirer to carve out a space which justifies the proposed inquiry. This can be done by outlining important trends, what is current in the field, the strengths and weaknesses of existing inquiry as well as allowing the inquirer to identify any potential gaps in knowledge (Fink, 2020).

A literature review is not just a list of studies, instead it should be a systematic discussion which examines what has been identified as being important in relation to the area for inquiry (Tranfield et al., 2003). Houser (2018: 109) advocates a 'critical component of the research process that provides an in-depth analysis of recently published research findings in specifically identified areas of interest'. The inquirer introduces and summarises the landscape of information relating to the topic under consideration, presenting the key arguments. Preparing a full literature review requires the inquirer to critique the sources relating to the study. This allows areas of agreement and difference between the sources examined to be established. This should enable the inquirer to demonstrate an awareness of positions adopted with respect to the area of inquiry as well as to support the inquirer's position.

Synthesising the literature lets the reader know where sources overlap and where they differ and allows the information to be pulled together to reflect the different interpretations of the landscape being examined and the inquirer's position to be presented (Foster, 2013). The novice needs to be aware of the importance (or not) of the reading undertaken and should not simply include a source because it is something to do with the topic. Careful consideration should be given to all sources and should only be included after careful evaluation. Throughout the review, the inquirer may find it useful to include short concluding statements and signposting to subsequent sections in order to help the reader understand the points being made and why this topic is worthy of investigation.

───────────────── **THINKING POINT 18.1** ─────────────────

1.   Having read about the four paradigms, consider which one is the 'best fit' for you if asked to conduct an improvement-focused inquiry in your establishment.
2.   Consider whether, and how, research evidence informs practice within your establishment.

───

A model of professional inquiry

The process of inquiry normally follows the classical spiral of cycles of planning, acting, observing and reflecting. Pedaste et al. (2015: 49) indicate that 'inquiry-based learning is not a prescribed, uniform linear process'; however, models of inquiry tend not to provide those new to inquiry with a framework to ensure that they will conduct an effective inquiry. We have developed a seven-phase model, working with groups of students and practitioners from non-compulsory care and education (NCE) settings as part of supporting them to engage in improvement-focused inquiries in their professional contexts (see Figure 18.1).

Although presented in linear format, professional inquiry is not a prescribed, uniform linear process but rather forms part of a cyclical process that contributes, at an individual level, to personal and professional development. As well as individual development, the model supports peer-to-peer development and organisational development. The model incorporates regressive and iterative loops. Regressive loops occur when a 'gap' in knowledge or understanding is detected. This requires those involved in the inquiry to revert to an earlier stage to plug the gap through additional reading, further professional dialogue and/or making adjustments to the inquiry question or methodological approach. Iterative loops are not uncommon when an inquiry is focused on introducing a change in the children's routines. Children adjust to change at different rates so it is sometimes necessary to let the change become part of the children's lived experience before data collection can take place. To forge ahead irrespective of how children have accommodated the change is likely to compromise the quality of the data gathered. The model consists of:

Phase 1: Identifying the issue

John Dewey in his seminal text *How We Think* (1910) suggested that the process of inquiry has as its initial stimulus a 'felt difficulty', a feeling that 'something is not quite right'. Unfortunately, reference to 'difficulty' and 'problems' has led to a concentration on the language of deficit and accordingly inquiry is often framed as an attempt to

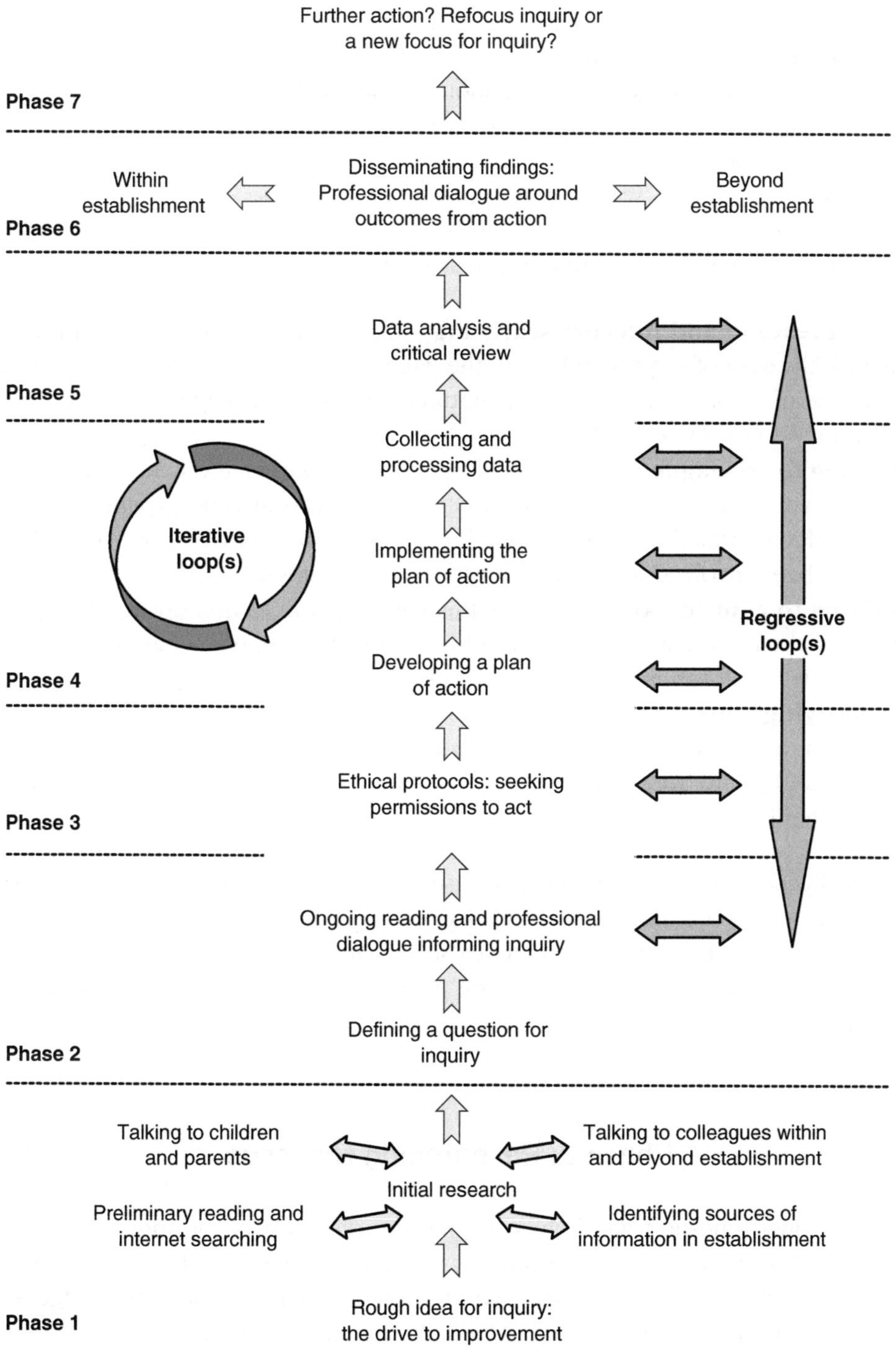

Figure 18.1 Seven-phase model of professional inquiry

improve dysfunctional practice. Thus, the 'felt difficulty' may arise with respect to seeking improvement in effective practice, albeit that this tends to be less common. It is this 'felt difficulty' that usually generates the inquirer's interest in a particular topic that starts the process of inquiry but first it is necessary to problematise the issue to be resolved by generating a question for inquiry.

A question for inquiry will help to state or describe the nature and scope of the inquiry; however, before this question can be generated it is first necessary to engage in some preliminary intelligence gathering which can involve:

- **Initial reading and internet searching** – this will help you to obtain a broad feel for the area of inquiry. What are the gaps in knowledge? Is there conflicting evidence of inconsistencies in the literature? What methodological approaches have been used to examine similar issues?
- **Talking to colleagues** – this will help you to find out what others, within and beyond your establishment, know about the issue. Has anyone experience of being involved in conducting inquires linked to your proposed issue? More generally, has anyone been involved in improvement-focused inquiries?
- **Talking to children and parents** – this will help you to find out what they think about the issue of concern. What would they like to happen? What outcomes would they wish for as a result of the inquiry?
- **Identifying sources of information** – this will help you determine if there are any resources that can be used to inform the inquiry. It is pointless to reinvent the wheel if there are existing resources that could be utilised during the course of the inquiry.

Initial intelligence gathering will increase your knowledge and understanding about the issue and as a consequence this may well generate a number of questions. Although it will become important to narrow the focus such that there is one primary question, this need not be too much of a concern during phase 1 as a more detailed literature review will be undertaken as part of phase 2.

Phase 2: Researching the issue

A clearly defined question will help you plan the direction of the inquiry. Articulating the question for inquiry is usually born out of the preliminary work that you undertake in phase 1 which will help to sensitise you to potential gaps in your knowledge as well as possible solutions to the challenge faced. An inquiry question focused on a specific aspect of practice will help to determine the methodology to be used, plan the way through the various stages of inquiry and suggest a means for analysis.

Phase 3: Seeking permissions to act

Practitioner researchers normally do not need to go through the process of seeking ethical approval in the same way as students undertaking an inquiry as part of study at university. As someone working in a professional context, it is vital to engage in professional dialogue with senior staff in order to determine what the process of seeking approval entails within your local context. Whatever the individual circumstances are, it is vital that we follow ethical protocols as outlined in the British Educational Research Association (BERA) (2018: 1) guidelines and 'apply them with integrity in [our] research activities so that [our] actions can be seen to be ethical, justifiable and sound'.

Throughout all phases of an inquiry, it is important to ensure that 'ethical decision-making becomes an actively deliberative, ongoing and iterative process of assessing and reassessing the situation and issues as they arise' (BERA, 2018: 2). The key things to consider include (BERA, 2018: 6–26):

- **Voluntary informed consent** – 'researchers should do everything they can to ensure that all potential participants understand, as well as they can, what is involved in a study' (BERA, 2018: 9).
- **Transparency** – 'Researchers should aim to be open and honest with participants and other stakeholders' (BERA, 2018: 16).
- **The right to withdraw** – 'it should be made clear to participants that they can withdraw at any point without needing to provide an explanation' (BERA, 2018: 9).
- **Incentives** – the 'use of incentives to encourage participation should be commensurate with good sense, such that the level of incentive does not impinge on the free decision to participate' (BERA, 2018: 19).
- **Harm arising from participation in research** – researchers should 'think through their duty of care in order to recognise potential risks, and to prepare for and be in a position to minimise and manage any distress or discomfort that may arise' (BERA, 2018: 19).
- **Privacy and data storage** – 'the confidential and anonymous treatment of participants' data is considered the norm for the conduct of research' (BERA, 2018: 21).
- **Disclosure** – professional practitioners engaged in research in all likelihood have a statutory duty to disclose confidential information to relevant authorities if, during the course of the inquiry, they become aware of behaviour that is 'likely to be harmful to the participants or to others' (BERA, 2018: 25).

Phase 4: Planning and implementing action

The action plan outlines the strategy for implementing the inquiry. The plan is broken down into a series of objectives which are more specific than the overall goal set by the question for inquiry. Each objective articulates a specific action step that cumulatively will enable you to accomplish the larger goal set by the question for inquiry. In many ways, objectives provide a route map that will enable you to successfully implement the inquiry. The action plan describes the:

- Overall goal.
- Specific objectives.
- Actions to be undertaken.
- Resources required.
- Who will undertake action.
- Target date for completion.
- Success criteria for the objective.

Data collection

To understand and develop practice through the process of inquiry, you need to go beyond common-sense explanations and strategies. It is important to gather evidence from a variety of perspectives:

- Children and parents.
- Activities.
- Colleagues.
- Learning plans.
- Context of establishment.
- Policy.

You need to decide what data (evidence) you are going to collect, when, how, by whom, for how long and for what reason. Childcare and educational establishments are data-rich environments so it is important that you only collect data if you have a clear rationale for why you are collecting it.

Data processing

Data can be subdivided into two broad types: namely, quantitative (numerical) and qualitative (non-numerical). It is not the case of one or the other type of evidence but rather that evidence should be checked from several different sources. Data processing involves collating the information and starting to think about presentational formats. This process inevitably leads into data analysis, particularly when processing non-numerical data, whereby the data set is examined in order to draw conclusions and how this will help to inform our understanding of the inquiry.

——————————————— **THINKING POINT 18.2** ———————————————

1. What aspects of your professional context would benefit from an improvement-focused intervention and why?
2. With a critical friend, talk through what the first four phases of such an improvement-focused intervention would involve.

Phase 5: Data analysis and critical review

Analysis starts alongside the processing of the data. Critically reviewing the outcomes of the inquiry takes the process of analysis further as it involves making judgements about both the process and the outcomes of the inquiry. A critique should touch upon the reliability (consistency of the measurement), validity (accuracy of the measurement), strengths and weakness of the inquiry. Findings are examined in terms of the question for inquiry, the literature review and the conceptual framework used.

Interpret and explain your results: What patterns and/or trends have emerged? What do the results tells us? What do they not tell us? What are the possible causes of the results? What are the possible consequences/implications of the results for theory, practice and policy? What findings/themes are concordant or discordant with previous research (i.e. themes identified in the literature review)? What new themes have emerged?

Phase 6: Disseminating findings

Wilson et al. (2010: 2) define 'dissemination as a planned process that involves consideration of target audiences and the settings in which research findings are to be received and, where appropriate, communicating and interacting with wider policy and health service audiences in ways that will facilitate research uptake in decision-making processes and practice'. Most inquiry cycles will have dissemination scheduled to take place once an overall evaluation of the outcomes of inquiry has taken place, that is, phase 6. However, dissemination can and should occur throughout all phases of the inquiry in order to promote the cross-fertilisation of professional understanding amongst participants and to assess progress at key phases of the inquiry model. This will help inform our understanding of the necessary improvement-focused alterations to ensure successful implementation.

We suggest that opportunities for dissemination are built into the inquiry model. When these occur can be determined by the inquirer, possibly in discussion with a critical friend; however, we would suggest that phases 4 and 5 are of critical importance in this regard. It is not uncommon for ad hoc dissemination events to take place during the course of the inquiry, for example through professional dialogue with critical friends, meetings with key stakeholders and/or parents, etc. The purpose may be to increase our understanding of necessary improvements or more simply to ensure that our key stakeholders are kept aware of the outcomes that the inquiry has realised and is hoping to achieve.

Phase 7: Further action?

Following completion of the inquiry, it is important to ask, 'what are your next steps?' Reflection-on-action (Schön, 1991) focuses on evaluating both the product and process of inquiry. Reflection may lead you to the conclusion that:

- it is necessary to repeat the cycle with adjustments in place;
- there are ways in which the process of inquiry could be improved; and/or
- there are issues for a new inquiry cycle.

Summary

In this chapter, we suggested that professional inquiry is a distinct approach to research, where the inquiry undertaken is located in and undertaken by those in practice. We went on to examine four commonly adopted paradigms which help guide such inquiries (Wohlfart, 2020), indicating that each paradigm views inquiry from a different perspective (Holloway and Wheeler, 2013). Finally, we outlined a seven-phase model of inquiry that may help with the structuring of an improvement-focused inquiry.

END-OF-CHAPTER QUESTIONS

1. Having read this chapter, how has your understanding of professional inquiry changed?
2. If you were considering undertaking a professional inquiry, what do you think the benefits of using the seven-phase model of inquiry would be?
3. Why do you think it is important to share with your practice community the results of any inquiry you undertake?

19
Evaluation in childcare settings
Jacqui Horsburgh and Kristina Robb

Key ideas

This chapter will explore:

- The purpose of focused self-evaluation.
- The importance of identifying and analysing reliable and valid data.
- Evaluation of the physical environment.
- Assessing how the cultural and social environment impacts on learning.
- The importance of sharing findings.

Introduction

We open this chapter by suggesting that the ability to undertake effective evaluation is a key skill required by all childcare practitioners. We will discuss the ways in which, as part of the planning process, data can be collected, analysed and used to improve provision and manage progress. As part of this discussion, we will explore what constitutes reliable and valid data and the ways in which the impact of data will depend upon the uses to which they are put. If childcare practitioners are to be asked to invest time and effort in gathering and analysing data, they must see a value in it.

We will then consider how practitioners might undertake evaluation of the physical, cultural and social/emotional environment to identify how they can support learning and teaching in their widest sense. Moving on, we discuss strategies for evaluating and recording the progress of individual children to plan for progress and recognise all aspects of achievement in a range of non-compulsory care and education (NCE) settings. In addition, through the use of a 'View from Practice', the ways in which establishments can involve stakeholders in meaningful evaluation activities will be explored. Finally, we look at the importance of disseminating the results of evaluation activities to demonstrate impact.

Over recent decades, expectations of childcare settings to demonstrate that they have effective quality assurance systems have increased. There is an expectation that all childcare settings will have robust systems in place to evaluate and improve provision. Leithwood (2001) suggests we are in the age of accountability in education; however, it could be argued that childcare practitioners, like other educators, have always been accountable. Only now, practitioners at all levels are required to play a key part in the self-evaluation and improvement process.

Variables considered when evaluating the quality of childhood settings tend to fall into the two categories of structure and process. Structural variables tend to be those that can be regulated such as adult–child ratio, group size and staff training. When discussing process variables, we tend to focus on dynamic aspects including interactions between different stakeholders within and beyond the setting. As the emphasis here is on relationships, these aspects can be more challenging to measure and evaluate. In this chapter, we explore ways in which practitioners can evaluate different aspects of a childcare environment. Some quality assurance systems will operate internally and rely on self-evaluation led by those within the establishment. At other times, evaluations will be undertaken by external agencies. In these instances, it is important that practitioners have a sound understanding of their establishment in order to engage in productive dialogue with external assessors. In this chapter, we want to focus on self-evaluation, why it is important and how practitioners can develop the skills to carry it out effectively. Unless a childcare centre has a 'sense' of how well it is doing, it is unlikely to be able to know how it can improve further.

The quality of provision in childcare settings is a multifaceted, multilevel construct that includes a variety of programme and classroom features (Mashburn et al., 2008). In some instances, quality indicators have been developed, in line with relevant policy, in order to support the evaluation of different aspects of a setting. In order to judge a setting against these indicators, we need to gather appropriate evidence. Sources of evidence will come from what we observe and from what different stakeholders tell us in addition to various data that may be available.

The ability to undertake effective evaluation is a key skill required by all childcare practitioners. In the next section, we will discuss the ways in which, as part of the planning process, data can be collected, analysed and used to improve provision and manage progress. In order to evaluate provision, we need detailed information or data about the setting.

THINKING POINT 19.1

1. What are the key purposes of self-evaluation in your setting?
2. Outline the values and beliefs that underpin the evaluation activities that you engage in.

What constitutes reliable and valid data?

Before we can evaluate the quality of childcare provision, we need to establish a shared understanding of what quality is and the instruments that would be appropriate to measure it. Practitioners can establish what constitutes quality provision through examining policy and theory and discussing what it means in the context of their establishment. In some instances, there may be quality indicators that they can refer to. The important element here is the discussion that takes place between practitioners in order that they can share their views and establish a common understanding of what would constitute high-quality provision in their setting. Once an agreement has been reached on what high-quality provision would look like then there is a need to consider how aspects of the provision can be evaluated in order to ensure best practice across the setting.

In some instances, existing tools such as How Good is Our Early Learning and Childcare? (Education Scotland [ES], 2016), Achieving Quality Scotland (Scottish Out-of-School Care Network [SOSCN], 2020), the Program for Infant and Toddler Care Program Assessment Rating Scale (California Department of Education, 2009) or the Statutory Framework for the Early Years Foundation Stage (Department for Education [DfE], 2021b) can be used to evaluate aspects of a provision. There may however be times when an establishment would want to develop their own evaluation instruments. Where this is the case, there is a need to ensure that the instruments are both valid and reliable. The validity of an assessment tool relates to the extent to which it measures what it claims to measure. For example, if we intend to evaluate the ways in which children engage with each other a simple checklist recording the number of times a child talks to someone else may not be considered to be valid. However, an observation schedule where details such as who the child engages with, who initiated the engagement, and the length and type of engagement may be considered to be more valid. This is because it measures different aspects of engagement rather than simply the frequency. For a measure to be reliable, it should yield precise and accurate results; for example, if three people use the same method to analyse data such as the age profile of children then if that method is reliable, they should all get the same result. Reliability of qualitative data is a contentious issue; some such as Lincoln and Guba (1985) suggest that better terms are credibility or dependability because qualitative data are often gathered from individual or one-off events which cannot be replicated. For example, if we are evaluating the interaction between an adult and group of children during a craft activity, the interactions occur naturally and are spontaneous. We would not be likely to get the same results if we repeated the activity even with the same group; however, this does not mean that we cannot take steps to ensure the reliability of qualitative data. We can do this by ensuring that the data we record, such as observations of outdoor activities, are as accurate and comprehensive as possible. In some instances, practitioners may use an agreed observation schedule in order to focus on specific aspects of an event.

In undertaking evaluation of childcare settings, it is important to keep the process manageable. Thus, there is a need to develop a strategic plan for evaluating and improving the provision for children. Such plans normally cover a three-year period and prioritise the focus of developments for each year. In a number of countries, there are nationally produced benchmarks or quality indicators against which establishments can evaluate their own provision. One crucial element to keep in mind is the importance of finding appropriate methods for obtaining the views of the children themselves as they are who the service is for. Once data have been collected and analysed, it is important that practitioners answer the 'So what?' question by informing stakeholders of the ways in which the intelligence will be used to improve aspects of the service. If individuals and groups have given their time to share their views and opinions, then it is important to ensure that they know that these are valued and are aware of the impact they have.

———————————————— **THINKING POINT 19.2** ————————————————

In what ways can you ensure the meaningful engagement of relevant stakeholders in evaluating aspects of your establishment?

Physical aspects of childcare settings

Purposeful evaluation requires a focus, whether it is through the lens of an established evaluation framework or a proprietary method. By evaluating the environment in which children learn, practitioners can build on the skills of reflective practice, identifying how they can best support learning and teaching in their setting. The environment in which children learn can be considered to be physical, cultural and social and emotional, with practitioners taking all these elements into account. As the context in which learning takes place, the physical environment has a profound impact on the quality of children's experiences. The physical environment is considered one of the most important aspects of the Reggio Emilia approach, referred to by Loris Malaguzzi (1920–94) as 'the third teacher', giving support to the learning through careful consideration and planning (Gandini, 2011). The provision of a child-centred environment with access to a wide range of open-ended resources encourages learning and skill development, provides those who use it with signals of our underlying pedagogy and the actions and interactions that are valued (Jarman, 2008).

Approaches to evaluation of the physical environment will vary but there is often an accepted structure to the way that settings are laid out, with defined areas such as role play, construction, sand and water, creative, home corner, small world, etc. However, these areas can become isolated spaces, with children and adults fixing their ideas of learning in that area based on provision (Daniels, 2016). By being flexible and examining the provision for diverse types of play and learning in these spaces, practitioners can offer an integrated and challenging environment which gives opportunities for choice and agency, leading to more motivated learners (Bruner, 1996).

Given that children are the users of the spaces, it would seem essential that they are involved in the evaluation of it through listening and consultation (Clark et al., 2003). Other stakeholders such as parents can, and should, be involved. Practitioners can evaluate by observing children at play in the spaces they provide. Do they play freely and without physical barriers? Do they use all the spaces? Does the layout of the space inhibit or encourage movement from one space to another and the connection of different elements such as moving blocks into the role-play area? Do the areas that are set out by adults meet the children's needs for schematic play or developmental differences? Does the provision support language, numeracy and health and wellbeing through a rich and varied provision and, importantly, does it change in line with learning and individual needs?

Some environmental toolkits such as the Early Childhood Environment Rating Scale (ECERS) address not only the physical environment as part of the assessment, but also consider other areas such as the interactions with adults, the routines, and the provision for specific areas of learning (Harms et al., 2014). This acknowledges the need for practitioners not only to examine the physical environment but also how their actions and the child's cultural, social and emotional experiences influence the use of the space.

————————————— **THINKING POINT 19.3** —————————————

1. What range of opportunities do staff have to engage in staff development to develop their understanding of how to plan for the effective use of physical aspects of your setting?
2. Consider how you could develop a shared understanding of theory underpinning the effective use of space in developing aspects of play and learning.
3. Think about ways of exploring practice in other settings, either virtually or by visiting.

Socio-cultural aspects of childcare settings

According to socio-cultural theory, interactions between children and their carers or peers shape children's development (see Chapter 5). The quantity and quality of interactions between a child and their primary caregivers, including childcare providers, are significant factors influencing development. However, because of the nature of such interactions the evaluation of this aspect of a provision can be complex. Attachment theory (Young et al., 2019; Ainsworth and Bell, 1970) argues that frequent, consistent and sensitive interactions with caregivers create a secure base for the child, promoting social-emotional adjustment and approaches to learning. To be effective, such learning and development need to be underpinned by high-quality interactions. Thus, it is important that practitioners are able to draw on theory and guidance in order to agree collegiately what constitutes high-quality interactions in their setting. This may be achieved through various types of professional development activities, including undertaking observations in their own and other establishments which are considered to offer examples of good practice.

Observations of different types may be undertaken for a range of purposes in childcare settings. These might include anecdotal records, running records and time sampling (Decker and Decker, 2001). Unfortunately, as noted earlier, some disadvantages in using qualitative methods have been identified: qualitative data may be impacted by observer bias, and may include subjective interpretation by observers (Marion, 2004; Olswang and Bain, 1994). Where qualitative data (e.g. anecdotes and ratings) and quantitative data (e.g. time sampling and event recording) are used, it is important that these complement each other to provide a holistic impression. By acknowledging the advantages and disadvantages of each type of data, the benefit of systematically collecting both quantitative and qualitative data can also be argued (Olswang and Bain, 1994).

Emotional aspects of childcare settings

A positive emotional climate in a childcare setting is important for children to feel secure enough to form relationships with both adults and each other. Factors that comprise emotional aspects of a childcare environment relate to the ways in which children and adults express emotions, both positive and negative. This may be evidenced by the ways in which successes are celebrated, inappropriate behaviours are dealt with or those experiencing upset are consoled. An important aspect to consider here is the responsiveness and sensitivity of the staff and the extent to which they are able to consider issues from the perspective of a child (Pianta et al., 2008). Responsiveness and sensitivity are evident when staff read emotional cues and respond appropriately to a child's needs (Shonkoff and Phillips, 2000). When considering how to evaluate such interactions, practitioners may want to consider how they can arrange to observe interactions in different contexts in the setting. In undertaking such observations, it will be important to consider both what they see and what they hear. In order to ensure that the information they gather is reliable, practitioners will need to ensure that they allocate sufficient time to undertake this form of data collection. In best practice, such observations would be supported by discussions with staff and children in order to obtain their perspective on the engagement.

In addition to considering the needs of individual children when evaluating the emotional climate of a setting, there is a need to consider the extent to which programmes and policies are responsive to specific cultural and family practices. Building strong relationships with all families allows parents and carers to trust providers and supports staff to understand the child's home context and routines (Sandstrom et al., 2011). In order to build such relationships, an establishment needs to ensure that it has a range of effective communication systems in place. It is important that communication strategies are reviewed regularly not only to ensure that best use is made of technology but also to ensure that no assumptions are made about parents' ability to engage with different media.

——————————— THINKING POINT 19.4 ———————————

1. What might you need to put in place in order to develop an observation schedule to evaluate emotional aspects of your setting?
2. Consider undertaking a review of your communication strategy to ensure that you are using an appropriate range of media effectively.
3. What measures could you put in place to monitor the effectiveness of the ways in which you communicate with a range of stakeholders?

'It is culture that provides the tools for organizing and understanding our worlds in communicable ways' (Bruner, 1996: 3). Children develop their understanding of the world and their self-identity through their diverse experiences in the environments in which they grow. The culture of a setting is created by the customs, beliefs, values and attitudes that are shared by the people within it (Daly and Beloglovsky, 2018: 1), and therefore influences the culture of the children who attend. The cultural capital that children bring with them must be considered when adults plan environments and experiences, not just the skills, knowledge and attitudes of the dominant culture or the team themselves.

Reid et al. (2019: 976) suggest that our understanding of culture in this context is moving from the 'food, fashions, and festivals' approach which has been pervasive in past years, to a dynamic process, individual to each child. The multicultural celebration of festivals, a type of cultural tourism, which are not necessarily relevant to the children is no longer enough and there is a precariousness in introducing cultures to children and expecting them to conform without bringing their own understandings to the situation (Banks, 2008; Connolly et al., 2002). Children will display agency as they act on their environment and create their own culture together with the adults (Corsaro, 2005). Therefore, as professionals we must be aware of our 'cultural competence' in our own cultures and those of the children we work with, as identified in Playwork settings by Else (2009).

When considering the cultural aspects of self-evaluation, the advice of Aiming High: Understanding the Needs of Minority Ethnic Pupils in Mainly White Schools – A Guide to Good Practice (Department for Education and Skills [DfES], 2004b: 20) still holds true: difference and diversity are expected to be taught about alongside commonality and sameness while the use of examples of culturally diverse achievements should be pervasive. In order to achieve this, there is a need to work closely with families and communities, valuing the contributions that can be made by a range of stakeholders with the most relevant lived experience.

———————— THINKING POINT 19.5 ————————

1. How as adults can we ensure that the needs of the children we care for are met in an appropriate cultural context?
2. Determine the extent to which evaluative strategies in your setting are up to date and in line with guidance on culture and diversity. What changes may have to be made?
3. Have we considered the changes to the cultural landscape in recent years that influence our whole community?
4. How can we upskill ourselves to ensure we are attuned to the surroundings of our settings?

Evaluating and recording progress of individual children

One key measure of the effectiveness of a childcare setting is the outcomes that are achieved for individual children. The wellbeing and learning of children are primary determinants of their later outcomes in educational attainment, socio-economic status, health, wellbeing and civic engagement in adulthood. While all aspects of children's development and wellbeing matter, some skills are more predictive of children's later outcomes than others. In addition, certain contexts may be more appropriate than others for nurturing and developing specific skills. In identifying the skills that an establishment is aiming to support children to develop, there is a need to take account of guidance at the local, national and international levels. There may be existing frameworks which help to identify relevant skills and achievements that practitioners should be supporting children to develop in specific contexts. It is important that any framework of skills and development should articulate the vision and aims of the individual centre.

Phair (2021) identified three key aspects of children's learning that have significant effects on children's development trajectories. These are cognitive skills: literacy and numeracy; self-regulation and social-emotional skills. Practitioners may want to consider the ways in which the service they provide contributes to children's development in each of these areas as this will influence the evaluation framework that they choose to use to assess and record children's progress. The ways in which tools or assessment schedules are used to measure the progress of individual children is of paramount importance. It is important to establish a baseline for each child so that their progress over time can be measured against prior achievement and attainment.

An important aspect of evaluating children's attainment and achievement is the involvement of children and their parents or carers. It is important to allocate sufficient time in order to do this effectively. As children are experts in their own lives, it would seem logical that they are given a key role in contributing to discussions about their strengths and areas for development. One way of involving children in identifying and evaluating relevant achievement goals is through the use of well-structured learning conversations. As Horsburgh (2022) notes, it is important that staff are supported to structure learning conversations effectively so that the discussions support a continuous and progressive profiling of the various ways in which a child is developing. This is important because not only is listening to children a matter of human rights but also, as Veeran (2004) suggests, interventions will be more successful if they are planned in conjunction with those they are designed to help. It is also important that these discussions are recorded in a format that is accessible to and understood by all relevant stakeholders.

Increasingly, childcare centres are developing creative strategies for involving parents and carers in evaluating both their own child's progress and the wider work of the establishment. In order for parents and carers to be comfortable and confident about contributing their ideas, they need to know that they are valued within the community. Without the establishment of positive relationships and trust, it may be more difficult for staff to approach sensitive issues related to support and development.

THINKING POINT 19.6

To what extent do your processes for evaluating and recording the progress of children reflect the core values and aims of the establishment?

VIEW FROM PRACTICE

Outcome of an external inspection

Robyn has recently taken up post as the manager of Meadowside Centre, which provides an after-school and holiday care service to a maximum of 50 children from 3 to 12 years of age. The aim of the service is to: 'Offer play and educational opportunities that are both fun and challenging. To promote the dignity, privacy, choice, safety, potential and diversity of all users and staff.' In reviewing existing documentation, it was clear that there had been limited engagement in self-evaluation activities. Robyn identified that there were a handful of staff who were proactive in developing aspects of the provision; however, there were a number of staff who appeared to lack initiative and did not engage enthusiastically with the children. From minutes of meetings and correspondence with parents, it was clear that there was a high level of engagement with a core of parents who sat on the management committee; however, there was limited engagement with the wider parent body.

A recent external inspection had evaluated the provision as follows:

- Care and support 3 – Adequate
- Environment 3 – Adequate
- Staffing 3 – Adequate
- Management and leadership 2 – Weak

The inspection report made the following recommendations:

1. Staff should review the pace of the day, taking account of the transitions children have within their sessions. Consideration should be given to children's individual needs; in particular, younger children who may have attended from breakfast club to after-school care.
2. Management and staff should review their environment, taking account of the diverse age group the service is provided for. Staff should use information on children's developmental

needs and individual needs as detailed within their written personal plans. Consultation on any changes should take place with children and their families to allow children to have ownership. Resources that include natural materials could be added to allow children to actively explore, make decisions and follow through their plans for play.

3. All areas of play would benefit from more natural resources that are open-ended to support children's curiosity and development, extending their play. The main hall had been organised with physical play space at the back of the room linked to the outdoors. Staff told us children valued this when coming in after school. Children told us they had used it to play ball games. Better recording within children's personal plans will support staff to plan resources that can offer more challenge. The manager advised that the service is at present waiting on confirmation of funding that is planned to purchase new resources to offer children choices.

4. In consultation with staff, children and their families, management should develop a Specific Measurable Agreed Realistic Time (SMART) based annual improvement plan that takes account of self-evaluations to support the service to improve. This should be reviewed on a regular basis, sharing progress with staff, children and their families. Meadowside Centre should further develop rigorous and systematic quality assurance systems and monitoring processes.

THINKING POINT 19.7

1. In what ways, if any, does this scenario reflect your experience of self-evaluation?
2. Who would you identify as key stakeholders in Meadowside Centre and how would you involve them in self-evaluation activities?
3. How would you utilise the evaluation tools, both formal and informal, that you are familiar with in order to inform improvement planning in this scenario?

Summary

In this chapter, we have discussed the importance of considering a range of variables, such as the physical, cultural and social aspects of the establishment, when evaluating the quality of childhood settings. The need to establish what constitutes quality provision before identifying and analysing reliable and valid data is highlighted. When exploring the collection of intelligence, we emphasised the need to consider a wide range of qualitative data, gathered through, for example, observations, questionnaires, focus groups and individual discussions in addition to the array of quantitative data that will be available in the establishment. Throughout, we emphasise the importance of working with a

range of stakeholders, both within and beyond the setting, in order to engage in evaluation for improvement. This is of particular importance as it helps to ensure transparency and establish trusting relationships between all parties working together to ensure
improvement and quality of provision.

END-OF-CHAPTER QUESTIONS

1. How could you work with stakeholders to establish and share the key purposes of
    self-evaluation in your establishment?
2. How confident are staff in your setting about using a range of data collection
    methods? What steps could you take to build capacity in this area?
3. In what ways could you promote the involvement of children and their parents or
    carers in planning for and evaluating individual progress?

Part VI
The wider context of non-compulsory care and education

Part VI
The wider context of non-compulsory care and education

20
Leadership and management in Childhood Practice

Mike Carroll and Craig Orr

Key ideas

This chapter will explore:

- The distinction between leadership and management.
- Management functions and skills.
- Forms and principles of leadership.
- Styles of leadership.
- Leadership in early childhood settings.

Introduction

Research on leadership within early childhood settings is sparse; consequently, leadership theory remains underdeveloped (Klevering and McNae, 2018). Early childhood practitioners wishing to develop their understanding of leadership find themselves drawing upon sources that rely heavily on business or school-based understandings of leadership, which often have limited application for early childhood settings (Murray and McDowall Clark, 2013: 291). Rodd (1997) suggests that utilising mainstream leadership theory can be problematic as these theoretical constructs do not fully take account of diverse early childhood settings with a workforce who are driven by an ethic of care, nurture and support. Krieg et al. (2014) identify the mismatch between theories that are focused on leaders in large, hierarchical product-driven organisations and the shared, collaborative, community-building approach taken in small childcare settings. This is supported by Palaiologou and Male (2019), who claim that leadership in the childcare sector is different from other educational contexts, and it is important to avoid the temptation to 'import mindscapes and models, concepts and definitions', as 'you can't borrow the character, you have to create it' (Sergiovanni, 1992: 214).

Leadership and management

Leadership is often conflated with management (Murray and McDowall Clark, 2013) so much so that Brooker and Cumming (2019: 111) contend that '"leadership" and "management" are often used interchangeably according to the context in which the leader is situated'. Various academics writing on leadership suggest that there is indeed a difference between leadership and management, where:

- leadership is 'future orientated' (visions) whereas management is 'present orientated' (day-to-day work) (Rodd, 1997);
- leadership is seen to focus on people and management is concerned with achieving results (Mistry and Sood, 2012); and
- a manager's focus is on stability and maintaining the status quo (Candy, online), whereas leaders focus more on change and development.

There is general agreement that it is difficult to separate leadership and management in the work of early childhood settings (Klevering and McNae, 2018), with both being seen as complementary and essential for organisational wellbeing and success.

Management functions

Henri Fayol (1916, cited in Belyh, 2019) developed a general theory of business management in his seminal text, *Administration Industrielle et Generale*, in which he identified several key management functions, which include:

- **Planning** – this involves taking a vision for a desired goal and breaking it down into a roadmap or plan to be followed by the team. In determining the best course of action to achieve the desired goals, planning must consider how best to utilise the human and material resources to establish who will do what by when.
- **Organising** – bringing together resources and assigning roles and responsibilities, which may well entail delegating authority, to ensure that the right people, with the necessary skills, have the necessary resources to undertake their assigned tasks.
- **Directing** – assigning tasks through meeting and connecting with colleagues as part of day-to-day interaction. Where and when necessary, supervising, motivating, communicating with and through colleagues as well as acting upon any feedback received to ensure that the work undertaken is consistent with the overall aims and purposes of the organisation.
- **Staffing** – recruiting, maintaining and retaining suitably qualified human resources such that there is sufficient capacity (the right amount of people) with the capability (the right mix of skills) to help achieve the organisation's desired goals.
- **Controlling** – evaluating whether progress is being made towards the desired goals. This involves articulating measurable objectives, monitoring performance and taking corrective action when and if required (Belyh, 2019).

Although not based on empirical evidence, Fayol's (1916) management functions are still used today to help inform our understanding of what managers do.

THINKING POINT 20.1

1. Consider establishments in which you have worked. What do you see as the distinctions between leadership and management activity?
2. Consider the management functions. As a practitioner, what do you see as your areas of strength and areas for development?

Dimensions of leadership

Early childhood leadership can take different forms due to the variety of early childhood settings, i.e. state, private and voluntary (Aubrey et al., 2012). Despite the complexity of early childhood leadership, Bush and Glover (2014: 554–5) suggest that there are three key dimensions to leadership, namely:

- **Leadership as influence** – an intentional process exerted by one person over others to bring about change.
- **Leadership and values** – actions are linked to explicit personal and professional values.
- **Leadership and vision** – the development of a preferred vision of the future is seen as a key component of effective leadership.

There are some tensions evident within these dimensions of leadership in that vision may well be one that is centrally mandated, rather than developed internally, and as such may not fully align with the values that help inform working relationships within an organisation (Bush and Glover, 2014).

Kagan and Hallmark (2001, cited in Muijs et al., 2004: 162) suggest that there are five domains of leadership activity in early childhood settings. We have added another three (Personal, Strategic and Team), giving eight, interrelated domains of leadership. These domains of leadership go beyond the personal attributes of a single person by being located in the wider professional community (see Figure 20.1):

Personal – all leadership stems from a sense of self-knowledge as one's beliefs, attitudes and assumptions can influence the trajectory of any leadership activity. Self-improvement through a commitment to career-long professional learning is also crucial to sustain effective leadership.

Pedagogic – influencing learning and development is a critical component in providing care, nurture and support. All staff need to be supported in understanding the role that they play in facilitating growth and development. The notion of best practice requires linkages to be established between research and other establishments in order that new insights can be gained to help inform improvement-focused initiatives.

Community – early childhood settings are connected to the communities that they serve so there are opportunities to influence children's learning by fostering family engagement. In addition, community leadership can make a profound contribution towards enhancing wellbeing and improvement in their communities through establishing links among families with services and resources provided by stakeholders.

Figure 20.1 Different domains of leadership in early childhood settings

Strategic – is about understanding the shared values, aims and purposes that shape early childhood settings. 'Who we are' as an organisation is set within an ever changing external environment; consequently, understanding the current context becomes the starting point in formulating a compelling vision of an improved organisational future.

Conceptual – involves making sense of the complexity inherent within broader societal change and how this will affect early childhood settings in the future. Identifying societal trends and finding ways to adapt and even capitalise on these evolving trends require innovative and creative ways of thinking.

Team – teamwork allows everyone to contribute according to their own unique strengths, which is essential to ensure that we work together to achieve our goals and is essential for early childhood settings to cope with the increased pace of change. Leadership is necessary not only to ensure that each individual is well placed to make a positive contribution to the process of change but also to coordinate individual contributions in pursuit of a shared vision.

Advocacy – involves seeking to influence the opinions and decisions of stakeholders, policy makers and the public as to the benefits of early childhood education. This includes celebrating the successes and articulating the challenges faced by the children placed in our care in order to raise their public profile amongst stakeholders and policy makers. Finally, this involves a continuous and adaptive process of taking action to meet the priorities of the communities that we serve so that the children and their families have a voice that is heard, leading to long-term, positive social change.

Operational – involves establishing and sustaining operating procedures in early childhood settings so that everyone – staff, children and families – knows what to do and, wherever possible, their needs are met. There are a range of technical activities covered under this, including recruitment and selection of staff, supporting professional learning, overseeing budgets, as well as ensuring that all paperwork is accurate and timeously processed.

Styles of leadership

There are many different styles of leadership. Rodd (2013) argues that it is important for practitioners to understand the range of theories, models and styles of leadership, selecting those most appropriate for the situation and circumstances. Rodd (2013) describes five leadership theories appropriate for Childhood Practice contexts:

- **Trait theory** focuses on the individual traits, characteristics and attributes associated with effective leadership.
- **Behavioural theory** places a greater emphasis on the ways in which leaders act and behave.
- **Contingency theory** describes the ways in which the style of leadership adopted is contingent on the situation and circumstances.
- **Transactional theory** has a greater emphasis on the use of power and influence to motivate followers and achieve goals.
- **Transformational theory** describes the ways in which shared values and vision influence and inspire, leading to new ideas, initiatives and innovative practice.

Rodd (2013: 48) argues that, given the increasing complexities within non-compulsory care and education (NCE), 'effective leadership requires capacity for flexibility, agility and diverse types of expertise'. Although early childhood practitioners may be reluctant to see themselves as leaders (Rodd, 2013), their interaction with children, colleagues, families and stakeholders, as well as their participation in implementing change-focused initiatives, may well be considered as leadership activity when viewed through the lens of leadership styles. This does not lessen the early childhood practitioners' role as 'educators and child developers' (Mistry and Sood, 2012: 28). Some of the more common styles are discussed below (see also Table 20.1).

Table 20.1 Different ways of conceptualising leadership

Giltinane (2013)	Chan (2018)	Bush and Glover (2014)	Copeland (2014)	MacBeath (2003)
Situational	Strategic	Contingent	Authentic	Authoritarian
Transactional	Technical	Distributed	Complex	Charismatic
Transformational	Transactional	Instructional	Connective	Collaborative
	Transformational	Managerial	Contextual	Dispersed
		Moral	Ethical	Distributed and distributive
		System	Self-sacrificial	
		Teacher	Servant	Heroic
		Transformational	Shared	Instructional
			Spiritual	Invitational
			Transformational	Learning-centred
			Values-based	Moral
				Principle-centred
				Professional
				Shared
				Situational
				Strategic
				Teacher
				Transactional
				Transformational
				Visionary

Distributed

Aliakbari and Sadeghi (2014) define distributed leadership as focusing on leadership practice, as opposed to structures, functions, roles and routines. Hard and Jónsdóttir (2013) state that a distributed leadership perspective recognises that leading and managing can involve multiple individuals rather than just those who are at the top of the organisation or have formal leadership titles. Practitioners who are not formal leaders may take responsibility for organisational routines and provide leadership and management (Spillane and Diamond, 2007).

To challenge notions of positional authority, Waniganayake et al. (2000) claim that leadership should not be related to roles and should be orientated towards the people and relationships involved, rather than a sole focus on the task. This is a point developed by Hard and Jónsdóttir (2013), who state that distributed leadership recognises that leadership involves multiple individuals, not only those in positions of formal authority. Moshel and Berkovitch (2020) go further, arguing that the concept of distributed leadership subverts the traditional view that leadership is held within one individual and should, instead, be distributed between multiple professionals and teams. Denee and Thornton (2021: 129) suggest that 'without the support of formal leaders, distributed leadership is unlikely to occur'. Formal leaders play an important role in promoting a culture of leadership by developing capability in practitioners through supporting ongoing professional learning. Sims et al. (2015) claim that leaders fail to see that distributed leadership should mean ongoing reflection and in-depth discussion by all parties to determine how to support the existing leadership structures as well as finding ways to flatten leadership structures within an organisation (Gronn, 2002). This collaborative approach leads to what Alvesson and Spicer (2012) call 'deliberated leadership', entailing a collaborative deliberation about authority. McDowall Clark (2012) argued that this represented a new form of leadership; one which he called catalytic leadership. This is a form of leadership where the leader inspires changes in the quality-of-service delivery from a position independent of power. The leaders in McDowall Clark's study were often unsure of their role (McDowall Clark categorised this as the 'imposter syndrome' [p. 395]) and were aware of their lack of authority to direct others.

Instructional

Instructional (curriculum) leadership is focused on supporting teachers in their key role of implementing the curriculum in order to ensure effective and efficient teaching (MacBeath, 2003); it is primarily concerned with teaching rather than learning (Bush and Glover, 2014). This approach does little to address the complexities of early Childhood Practice where learning and development are interlinked. Pedagogical or learning-centred leadership is the term more commonly used in the UK and more particularly with respect to early Childhood Practice. Murray and McDowall Clark (2013) argue that the concept of pedagogic leadership is not uniformly understood, with the term often being used to refer to an appointed role as a childcare centre leader, or to a function of teachers in relation to the curriculum, or to a style of leadership generally. Pedagogical leadership covers a wider range of activity as part of supporting learning and learning outcomes, to include advocating on behalf of children to ensure that they have access to resources and services as well fostering family engagement in order to enhance home and school learning (Heikka and Waniganayake, 2011). Siraj-Blatchford and Manni (2007) argue that the role of leadership within Childhood Practice is mainly that of 'leadership for learning', requiring a detailed understanding of the context in which the leader is working in order to effectively support outcomes for children and families. Hallet (2013) argues that Childhood Practice practitioners have a defined role as 'Leaders of Learning', leading change in pedagogy and shaping professional practice through a collaborative leadership style. Nutbrown (2012) states that pedagogical leaders are those practitioners who have extensive knowledge and understanding of child development, of play, of the individual needs of children and their families and how to support them all. Stamopoulos (2012) claims that pedagogical leadership within Childhood Practice must connect to practice, build capacity and recognise the importance of relationship building. Thus, 'pedagogical leadership is connected with not only children's learning, but also the capacity building of the early childhood profession, and values and beliefs about education held by the wider community' (Heikka and Waniganayake, 2011: 510). This is a point developed by Palaiologou and Male (2019), who argue that pedagogical leadership in the twenty-first century should extend the principle of 'leadership for learning' beyond the classroom to embrace the community.

Moral

A variety of terms have been used to describe values-based leadership (Bush and Glover, 2014). These include moral leadership, authentic leadership, ethical leadership, spiritual leadership and principle-centred leadership. They all, with subtle differences, focus on the moral purpose behind providing care, nurture and support to children and require practitioners to operate on the basis of 'what is right' or 'what is good' (Bush, 2003). Leadership is focused on constructing an organisational framework underpinned by principles such as integrity, trust, honesty, compassion, fairness, being true to your word and respect (Newman, 2000). These principles serve to inform the organisation's vision and purpose as well as to underpin decision making in addition to providing everyone linked with the organisation a modus operandi on how to conduct themselves. These models assume that leaders, both personally and professionally, consistently act in accordance with these principles: they 'bring of themselves' and they 'walk the talk'. They are authentic! Outcomes are more likely to be enhanced when there is an alignment between the principles articulated at an organisational level and the practitioners' professional practice.

Shared/collaborative

There is conceptual incoherence with respect to defining collective approaches to leadership such as participative, shared and collaborative. What they have in common is a shift from leadership being an activity carried out by someone with positional authority to a more collective approach, often in response to the pressures brought about by the ever-increasing pace of change, both professional and societal (Bush, 2019). Shared leadership is facilitated by organisational leaders when they recognise that other team members are in a position to exert influence based on the expertise they have to offer. Leadership, based on expertise rather than positional authority, is usually linked to teamwork involving the participation of colleagues and, on occasions, children, family members and stakeholders (Morrison and Arthur, 2013). This is a dynamic process with individuals moving in and out of leadership by virtue of the expertise that they have to offer at any given time. In addition to developing the breadth and density of leadership expertise (Hallinger and Heck, 2010), such an approach is more likely to lead to 'buy in' to any agreed decisions from team members as the decision-making processes rest with the group rather than an individual (Bush, 2003).

Collaborative leadership is similar to shared leadership albeit that it is often linked to inter-agency working, often including families and community groups, who come together to focus attention on a particular situation (MacBeath, 2003). VanVactor (2012: 557) defines collaboration as 'a mutually beneficial relationship with clearly defined roles among multiple parties for the attainment of a common organizational goal'. As with shared leadership, all members of collaborative teams can serve as leaders at different times and in different ways based on the expertise that they have to offer to the team. Ultimately, collaborative leadership can facilitate integrated services for children and young people and their families, so it is sometimes referred to as leadership for community (Morrison and Arthur, 2013).

--------------------------- **VIEW FROM PRACTICE** ---------------------------

Seeing oneself in the role of leader

As a practitioner in the under-2s' room in an early years setting, Evelyn had never thought of herself as a leader and so, when asked to attend a course on effective leadership and management, she had reluctantly agreed. Attending the course developed Evelyn's understanding of leadership and she began to reflect on the leadership within her current role. With a strong passion for parental engagement, Evelyn was often tasked with taking prospective families around the service, discussing the values, vision and pedagogical approaches and demonstrating the high-quality provision. On top of this, many staff would turn to Evelyn for advice on engaging with parents, considering approaches that would be most effective. Recognising the ways in which she was already an established leader developed Evelyn's confidence and she then began to actively seek out further leadership responsibilities.

Situational (or site-based leadership)

Osborn et al. (2002: 799) argue that leadership is interconnected with its context. Early childhood contexts are diverse, so a one-size-fits-all approach to educational leadership is unlikely to enable all early childhood leaders to be responsive to the array of different organisational problems encountered within early childhood settings (Bush, 2003). The situational, contextual or contingent model of leadership provides a pragmatic rather than a principled approach of adapting leadership styles to respond to the individual situations encountered in different early childhood settings (Bush and Glover, 2014). Situational leadership tends to be focused on leaders as opposed to followers (Giltinane, 2013). This approach involves the leader concentrating their attention on the situation being addressed in order to determine the best course of action to take (Giltinane, 2013). The leader provides 'directive support' (Giltinane, 2013) through clear articulation of what is expected of each member of staff, how they should proceed and what success will look like within the time frame set for completion of the task. 'Leadership is an emerging social construction embedded in a unique organization – it is contextual leadership' (Osborn et al., 2002: 832).

Strategic

MacBeath (2003) links strategic leadership to the process of development planning that will enable an organisation to realise a positive change (improvement) in its operational status: it is a future-orientated approach to leadership. The intention behind planning is to determine 'where we are going' and 'how we will get there', whilst considering the pace and scale of change that is currently possible given organisational capacity (the number of people available to undertake change) and capability (the current levels of expertise amongst people). This has sometimes been referred to as 'procedural wisdom' (Mistry and Sood, 2012). Strategic leaders are able to identify the shifts in societal and professional thinking that may present opportunities or threats to their early childhood setting at some point in the future (Chan, 2018). In developing their vision for the future, strategic leaders demonstrate 'people wisdom' as they take time to ensure that followers and stakeholders align with this vision of an improved future (Mistry and Sood, 2012). Strategic leaders engage in 'big picture thinking' whereby they see the organisation as a whole whilst at the same time being able to see how the various parts of an organisation relate to each other (Chan, 2018). In addition, strategic leaders require 'contextual intelligence' (Mistry and Sood, 2012) as they need to consider how a variety of stakeholders will respond to the proposed change and how any such change aligns with wider community issues.

Transactional

Transactional leadership does not seek to disperse power and authority throughout the organisation but rather this remains with the head of establishment by virtue of their position. Central to transactional leadership is a process of exchange whereby leaders offer rewards, such as promotion or discretionary salary increments, to staff in order to secure their short-term commitment to specific tasks (Bush, 2003). A transactional approach is task-orientated and can be effective in order to meet deadlines (Giltinane, 2013); however, it does not secure the staff's long-term commitment to the vision that the leader may have for the organisation. Leaders offer contingent rewards and inducements, that is, subject to successful completion of the task. Leaders do not seek to win the hearts and minds of staff through motivating them or seeking to improve their commitment to wider organisational goals (Chan, 2018).

Transformational

According to Bush (2003: 187), the notion of vision is a central dimension of transformational leadership, with leaders seeking to engage with staff and all stakeholders to win their hearts and minds and so secure their commitment to the vision that the leader has for the organisation (Giltinane, 2013). Transformational leaders seek to motivate, influence and develop the skills of others in order to bring about change within individuals whilst securing their commitment to organisational goals and ultimately inspire them to become leaders themselves (Boardman, 2020). Miller and Miller (2001: 182) argue that 'through the transforming process the [goals] of the leader and follower merge'. That the leader and followers are in agreement suggests a collaborative approach; however, critics of this approach argue that it can be potentially manipulative, with the underlying purpose one of implementing the leader's vision (Chan, 2018). Giltinane (2013) suggests that the main focus of transformational leaders is to influence outcomes rather than the nature or direction of these outcomes.

———————————— THINKING POINT 20.2 ————————————

Consider the establishments in which you have worked. What leadership styles have been evident and how have these manifested themselves?

Final thoughts

There is a growing body of evidence that suggests that early childhood education provides 'a good start in life' (Moshel and Berkovich, 2020: 517) by developing the potential and raising the attainment of children (Muijs et al., 2004) and that effective leadership is crucial in facilitating organisational improvement (Office for Standards in Education [Ofsted], 2000). Several writers have found a 'reluctance' amongst early childhood practitioners to take on the role of leadership. There are a variety of reasons for this, including the complexities associated with the varied early childhood settings (Klevering and McNae, 2018) and the different age ranges of the children (Murray and McDowall Clark, 2013). Diversity in the workforce, with some childminders working in isolation whereas in other contexts there are high ratios of staff, makes early childhood settings a complex arena for leadership (Rodd, 2013). For a variety of reasons, there is some ambivalence linked to the notion of 'being in authority', which is partly due to the low value placed upon early childhood education by wider society (Nicholson et al., 2020). In addition, the notion that leadership is linked to power and authority holds little appeal to practitioners who see their primary role as working with children and families (Hard and Jónsdóttir, 2013).

Furthermore, much of the work of early childhood practitioners involves working with different professionals drawn from a wide range of organisations who are in a position to provide support and services for children and families; consequently, '[t]hese multi-professional relationships need to be shaped and based on something other than authority' [*as they*] 'may not be connected in the same organisation or hierarchy and this poses challenges for exercising leadership in traditional ways' (Murray and McDowall Clark, 2013: 292). Finally, there is also the suggestion that early childhood professionals are ill prepared to take on a leadership role as this does not feature in many preparatory programmes of study (Sims et al., 2015), and this lack of leadership development is compounded by limited access to mentors who can support leadership development whilst working in early childhood settings (Klevering and McNae, 2018).

Summary

The Nutbrown Review (2012: 55) argues that there is a need for all early childhood practitioners to become leaders of practice as opposed to leaders of settings. This widens our understanding of leadership from being solely located in a person, assigned power and authority by virtue of their position in the organisation, to one that sees taking on a leadership role, when appropriate, as a professional responsibility (Campbell-Evans et al., 2014).

The latter construct no longer sees leadership as a formal role, or responsibility for task completion, but rather a form of agency whereby individual practitioners or a group of practitioners are empowered to lead improvement-focused activity based on their expertise. This is linked to growing literature linked to dispersed leadership (Spillane, 2006) in which leadership is conceptualised as a set of behaviours and practices that are undertaken collectively. It is connected to the 'professional motivation "to make a difference" and work for the well-being and education of young children and their families' (Murray and McDowall Clark, 2013: 292) and with establishing good working relationships and connections among individuals within an establishment (Muijs and Harris, 2007: 112).

Heikka and Waniganayake (2011) suggest that 'distributed' leadership is primarily focused on supporting children's learning and development as well as capacity building amongst colleagues. This fits well with the five main areas of responsibility of an early childhood leader suggested by Moshel and Berkovich (2020: 518), which are: leading care, upbringing and teaching; leading service organisation; leading work organisation; leading expertise; and being an expert in early childhood education. In addition, distributed leadership is consistent with the six dispositions of an early childhood leader suggested by Davitt and Ryder (2018: 18), which are: being a communicator; relationship focused; caring of others; supportive of the team; a leader of growth and change, and acting as a critical friend.

END-OF-CHAPTER QUESTIONS

1. Why is an understanding of leadership important to the Childhood Practice practitioner?
2. Having read this chapter, what areas of your professional activity could be considered as indicative of leadership and management activity?
3. Assuming that you wish to pursue leadership opportunities in the future, what sort of leader would you wish to become?

21
Working in partnership

Marie McQuade
and Tracey Stewart

Key ideas

This chapter will explore:

- Working with parents/carers and other professionals to ensure the best experiences for children and families.
- Effective partnership working and outcomes for children and families.
- The impact of developing relationships with parents and carers on children's social and emotional skills and wellbeing.
- Collaborating with professionals from other agencies to build a community of best practice.

Introduction

Effective partnership working is critical to ensuring that the experiences of children and families engaging with Childhood Practice services are positive and fulfilling. Throughout this chapter, we use the term Childhood Practice (CP) to describe what Orr and Wingrave term, in Chapter 1, as NCE (non-compulsory care and education). This chapter will firstly define key terms and outline the relevant legislative and policy drivers which necessitate collaborative working practices. It will then consider the importance of practitioners developing sensitive and supportive relationships with parents, discussing how this can help develop highly effective practice and deliver improved outcomes for children. Consideration will be given to the importance of relationships with colleagues in developing high-quality services before focusing on the critical role of integrated children's services (ICS), considering the facilitators that help to ensure that families are supported consistently and holistically. Finally, this chapter will consider how practitioners can build knowledge, understanding and capacity to deliver these high-quality services through engagement with continued professional learning.

The purpose of meaningful interactions

> … children's daily interactions through their ECEC (Early Childhood Education and Care) settings – with other children, staff and teachers, space and materials, their families and the wider community – reflect the quality of ECEC they experience. Together, these interactions are known as 'process quality' and are the most proximal drivers of children's development, learning and well-being.
>
> (Organisation for Economic Co-operation and Development [OECD], 2021: 9)

This quote recognises what Bronfenbrenner (1992) termed Ecological Systems Theory, which focuses on the quality and context of the child's environment, highlighting the impression that these have on the child (see Chapter 5). The theory signals that as a child develops, the interactions within the relevant environments become more complex. This complexity can arise as the child's physical and cognitive structures grow and mature. To this end, all those who impact on a child's experience – family, friends, practitioners and wider society – will have an impact on the outcomes the child experiences, and effective cross-sectoral working and family engagement can ensure the best outcomes for the child.

Benefits to effective parental relationships

Parents are the primary carer and knower of their child (note that the primary carer may well include other carers/guardians). The relationship between them is of paramount importance in both the child's and parents' lives and as such they are the most significant adult partner with whom practitioners will work. Parents' knowledge of their child is essential information that should be solicited and embraced (Moss et al., 1999). Goodall and Montgomery (2014) discuss the importance of creating active engagement between parents, the setting and their child's learning, rather than the more passive concept of 'involvement' with the setting – which tends to be in terms of fundraising and communication channels – and this highlights that whilst parents may not be involved with the childcare setting itself, they can still be positively and actively engaged in their child's learning. Within Scotland's Getting it Right for Every Child (GIRFEC) (Scottish Government [SG], 2012a), England and Wales's Every Child Matters (Department for Education and Skills [DfES], 2003) and Northern Ireland's Children and Young People's Strategy (Northern Ireland Executive, 2020a), the concept of the child at the centre of an integrated system is evidenced. Parents/carers are integral to this idea, therefore creating positive relationships with them is an essential part of the practitioner's role. The OECD (2021) highlighted family connections and continuity between the home and early learning and childcare environments as vital in contributing to children's personal, social and emotional skills and early outcomes.

Barriers to effective parental relationships

Despite the importance of close and mutually respectful working relationships, the association between professionals and parents can be of an asymmetrical nature; as a practitioner, you are working within your professional capacity within the setting. Your position as 'manager' or 'practitioner' will also indicate a professional identity to parents and carers and bring with it particular expectations and presuppositions. This may include expectations of professionalism, assumptions about knowledge, experience of child development, and that you have significant experience in the sector along with a caring and approachable manner. Ultimately, you are a professional in your place of work. Parents however are in their personal role as a parent and not entering the relationship on a professional basis. Their own 'identity' (Stets and Burke, 2020; Burke and Stets, 2009) as a parent is relevant here as whilst most will see themselves as competent, others may see themselves as failing in some way and hold insecurities about their capabilities or parenting skills. Their perceptions of their child are based around family and home life, whilst yours are based around a wider social setting, and of course their emotions towards their child are far more heightened than yours towards that child. As childcare is often a privately financed sector – prior to the child accessing statutory entitled provision – this makes parents 'clients', paying for care, and their expectations as to the social and emotional development aims of childcare may differ from yours. It is therefore important to establish positive communication channels through which you can gain a mutual understanding, for example on the benefits of outdoor play to a parent who objects to their child getting muddy.

Another challenging factor that may impact the relationship is time: you are in your place of work and communication with parents is part of your role, however parents/ carers are in transit to other destinations, thus the opportunity to interact at drop off and collection times will be limited and shared with other parents, whilst appointments have to be scheduled, and again are usually time bound. Language barriers may also come into play, as might cultural perceptions. Unconscious bias, for example, in relation to age, gender or other protected characteristics can also have an effect as practitioners may subconsciously alter their behaviour around some family members.

Whilst creating a positive relationship will initially support the child in their transition into the setting (Education Scotland [ES], 2020), it is also a bedrock should intervention initiatives be considered. Having already established a mutually respectful dialogue, it is far easier for sensitive topics to be raised such as potential emotional and behavioural issues. Considering yourself to be a knowledgeable, reflexive professional (see Chapter 17) will also support your discussion around your professional observations of the child.

Raise the barriers

Being aware of the identity issues raised here may be beneficial. Acknowledging your own subconscious attitudes to both how you are viewed as a practitioner and how you view parents is key to influencing positive relationships. Creating a genuine and supportive team ethos will help create a warm and welcoming environment for parents. Initial transition visits with a key worker to ensure continuity of support is important, as is the creation of regular opportunities for dialogue with parents.

Ensuring that multilingual resources are available for those that should need them, and where possible facilitating same-language interactions between staff and parents are necessary in creating an inclusive environment. Greeting both children and parents by their name at the start of the day and taking the time to actively listen to them; and being able to share a brief summary of the child's day verbally at the end of the day and responding quickly to concerns, are simple ways to increase rapport. Eye contact and the spoken word are considerably more personal than emails and texts. Staff are role models, and it is crucial to remember that children are observing their interactions and learning from them. Frequent opportunities for longer conversations through 'drop-in' sessions may also be encouraged. For many settings, introducing stay and play sessions whereby parents are encouraged to participate in the day-to-day life of the setting are seen as a positive mechanism to boost parent involvement, engagement and parent and staff interactions, plus the positive benefits to children from the shared experience (ES, 2020: 59–60).

However, for those parents who can't personally 'drop off', then digital solutions such as interactive journals, social media sites and private messaging apps sharing photographs and videos and other communications, can be effectively utilised to engage with them on a daily basis (Stratigos and Fenech, 2021). The advent of online video conferencing into our daily lives means that this type of interaction can also be considered as viable when time and physical constraints exist. Time will necessarily be an important factor; structuring the setting's day to enable practitioners to meet and greet all parents and children individually is not always as simple as it sounds, as the physicality of the building and the ratio of staff must be taken into account; however, these are all considerations that should be discussed with parents as well as with staff.

THINKING POINT 21.1

1. How and when do you interact with parents and carers in your service?
2. How could you improve those interactions?

Partnership with colleagues

Why?

The most obvious benefit to fostering a healthy, constructive working relationship with your colleagues is the enjoyable and smooth running of everyone's working day and the role modelling of constructive communication to the children in your care. Working within an environment of mutual respect whereby everyone is appreciated for their contributions and encouraged to voice their opinion enhances one's sense of worth and purpose (Rodd, 2006). Research shows that parents respond very positively to a warm team ethos (Vuorinen, 2021). Whilst everybody is fulfilling a professional role and has duties to attend to, there is always room for individuality, in the same way as the early years principles of individual learning are fostered, and by modelling this to the children in your care you are setting an example of the appreciation of diversity and a humanistic approach to life and learning. Creating an ethos of mutual respect, staff are more able to effectively undertake group reflective evaluations and thereby enhance outcomes for children.

Raise the barriers

Within smaller establishments, the opportunities for all-staff meetings and shared observations can be far easier and the benefits of reflexive practice are discussed in Chapter 17. However, larger settings which may have bigger staff teams and variable working patterns may find that team building is a more challenging exercise. The familiarity with online communications and virtual meeting software, which are now commonly used, allows for further opportunities to communicate with wider teams. What is most important is that the team within which you interact most frequently is a cohesive unit: a group of individuals, with a variety of interests and skills, working with a common aim. Rodd (2006: 149) describes an effective team as having:

- the pursuit of a common philosophy, ideals and values;
- commitment to working through the issues;
- shared responsibility;
- open and honest communication; and
- a support system.

Again, it is important to tackle one's own subconscious attitudes and understand that it is healthy and constructive to air disagreements, so long as it is done in a mutually respectful way. Issues of professionalism and leadership are covered elsewhere in this book (see Chapters 16 and 20), but it is important to reiterate here that the same values of acceptance and diversity that we look to instil in the children within our care should be modelled by the staff around them. Building the ability and opportunities to reflect on practice within a safe and nurturing environment and creating a strong team ethos are further discussed in Chapter 17 of this book.

─────────────── **THINKING POINT 21.2** ───────────────

What values can you model in your relationships with colleagues that will support children's learning?

VIEW FROM PRACTICE

Multi-professional collaboration in the early learning and childcare sector

As has been highlighted in Chapter 10 of this book, the early years of a child's life are crucial to their speech and language development. A landmark government-commissioned review of services for children and young people with speech, language and communication needs (SLCN) in England signalled the centrality of SLCN in early development, learning and later academic and lifelong success (Bercow, 2008). Much has been written highlighting the positive impact on speech gained from socialisation in early learning settings, and the importance of opportunities to listen, observe and interact with both children and adults (Neum, 2012; Nutbrown, 2012).

For children exhibiting speech and language delays, common practice across Scottish health care was for children to be seen individually within a speech and language (SAL) clinic. This system is reliant on parents/carers having the time and transport to attend and for them then to share the advocated feedback and suggested exercises with the staff team; rarely did time allow for the speech and language therapist (SaLT) to visit the child in the setting. However, in 2019, within one Scottish local authority, a setting had been targeted as in need of specific language development interventions, due mainly to the high numbers of children living in poverty and children for whom English was an additional language. SAL therapists spent several days in the setting, demonstrating group activities and modelling individual communication tactics that could be utilised to boost observational and listening skills amongst children. These initiatives had been discussed at collegiate meetings which included manager, senior practitioner and practitioners, where the enhanced positive outcomes for all the children within the setting were recognised. Practitioners also considered the lengthy waiting times for SaLT referrals, the lack of knowledge and confidence in practitioners in determining what constituted a speech delay and what could be indicative of other social and emotional needs. A commitment to developing greater knowledge was made by practitioners, and a collaborative approach that would ultimately benefit both sectors and better meet the required multi-agency approach was born.

A small team of SAL therapists was tasked with delivering a two-day in-service training session for practitioners across the region. It was determined that a minimum of two senior practitioners from each setting should attend, to boost the understanding of the project as an all-sector initiative and not a small-scale, local project. Practitioners were introduced to various tools for measuring the current vocabulary skills and observational/listening skills to gain a 'baseline' from which to measure the impact of interventions. Toolkits containing intervention resources were made available to all settings and the activities within them were demonstrated and discussed at the training session. The local authority subsidised the purchase of these resource packs for each setting.

Over the next few months, practitioners used the toolkits to assess children's individual abilities and put in place group exercises to boost observational and listening skills. Practitioners reported

(Continued)

feeling that the toolkit provided them with a more objective and specific way to assess children's current abilities and enjoyed having a new repertoire of activities to choose from. This allowed for an objective approach to measuring impact and enhanced outcomes for all children attending the setting. Professionals also reported a sense of achievement in their own upskilling and thus increased potential to make a difference to the children and families they worked with. At the end of term, practitioners reassessed individual children's listening and vocabulary skills using the SAL toolkit and the outcomes were universally positive.

Although there are established and effective partnerships with many professionals in the setting, the nature of this project necessitated the development of respectful working relationships and a significant commitment to a common approach. The benefits of partnership working in this scenario are clear to see: a mutually respectful community of practice was created, within which health and education professionals were able to build trusting relationships and work collaboratively, utilising evidence-based approaches to further develop their cross-sectoral understanding.

Why take a multi-agency approach to children's services?

The move towards better integrating children's services was driven by the political climate of the UK. The main drivers to legislative changes that impact on early years practitioners were often scandals and systemic failure. The Cleveland child abuse case provoked the creation of the 1989 Children's Act (UK Parliament [UKP], 1989) and placed a significantly increased focus on the development of cross-sectoral working relationships and an expectation that parental relationships would be prioritised. The subsequent 2004 Children Act (UKP, 2004) came about in response to the Laming Report (2003) on the death of Victoria Climbié. The report found that significant failures were identified of the agencies involved in her care and that there were multiple opportunities where those individuals could have prevented her death. The report criticised a systemic lack of cooperation and information sharing amongst the involved agencies, and in particular criticised senior managers involved in decisions about her care.

This resulted in the development of Every Child Matters (DfES, 2003) in England, and For Scotland's Children, in Scotland, a precursor to Getting it Right for Every Child (GIRFEC) (SG, 2012a). These frameworks set out expectations for heightened partnership working within children's services and the development of information-sharing agreements and aligned values. This was supported by a significant body of literature showing how children's physical and mental health, wellbeing, attainment and life outcomes could potentially be enhanced through better multi-agency working and the development of shared values and ways of working (Department for Education [DfE], 2021c). In all UK policy landscapes, efforts were made to look more holistically at children's services; however, systemic change takes time to embed effectively. Guidance was written on information sharing; national practice models were developed; and cross-sectoral training materials were written to support services sharing information and expertise across children's services. Children's services, including statutory Early Learning and Childcare (ELC) and non-statutory school-aged childcare services, have been encouraged to take an early intervention and prevention approach, seeking to avoid future crisis-intervention by ensuring children's wellbeing is considered, prioritised and planned for by all services in conjunction (Rose, 2012). Multi-agency working remains integral to the safeguarding of children (Sidebotham et al., 2016) and it is essential that practitioners from all services work closely together to ensure they have a full understanding of a child's life and have a coordinated approach to delivering care and support.

--------------------------- **THINKING POINT 21.3** ---------------------------

1. Outline the range of other professionals who work with your children and families.
2. Determine the extent to which you have opportunities to discuss shared approaches to working with families.
3. Identify other professionals who could be usefully invited to contribute to developments in your setting.

What is a multi-agency approach?

Integrated working with other services and professionals can be difficult to define accurately as it can mean different things to different people. Davis (2011: 13) indicates that the central feature is a 'jointness' in approach, which can be seen when agencies work closely together, when professional barriers are dismantled, and cross-sectoral relationships developed. Effective collaborative work could involve information sharing, sharing of subject knowledge or joint professional learning, but does not necessarily require the full integration of systems to work well for families (Cohen et al., 2004). Key to integrated approaches are the behaviours of individuals, services and systems that enable cooperation, collaboration, and coordination of approach. Fitzgerald and Kay (2008: 7) envisaged a spectrum that illustrated levels of integration ranging from simple multi-agency working to the most complex level of integration, transdisciplinary working. Wherever on that spectrum their work lies, all practitioners, during their professional lives, will have an involvement in integrated children's services (ICS). In addition to ensuring the delivery of better outcomes for children, practitioners in all sectors will also benefit from understanding the wider needs of children and families, collaborating to meet those needs, developing parity of esteem across sectors, understanding the vision and values of other services, and shared training and expertise.

Multi-agency working within children's services is reliant on effective leadership, well-developed systems, a shared language and a sound understanding and communication of the roles and responsibilities of all parties in the relationship (Davis, 2011; Fitzgerald and Kay, 2008). Leadbetter et al. (2007) focused on the importance of co-location of services, a shared understanding of professional identities and an agreed division of responsibilities as issues that must be planned for when defining multi-agency team roles. In analysing the effectiveness of ICS, we must consider the extent of integration, the frameworks that support children's services at national and local strategic level, operational-level processes and the access to other professionals and relevant organisations (Fitzgerald and Kay, 2008).

Barriers to multi-agency partnership working

There are however tensions within the system which can act as significant barriers to effective service integration. The attitude and empathy of a cohesive multi-agency staff team rely on the shared values and intentions created and agreed by a unified team working towards agreed outcomes. Barriers to the effective integration of children's services may include a lack of clarity of roles and responsibilities or the cultural differences between organisations and sectors. Underpinning theories used by CP staff and health care workforces are not always aligned, and the challenges of blending cultures and organisational norms from different services are among the most crucial in integrating services (Fullan, 2007). Improvement can be enabled with the publication of standards and frameworks to support multi-agency approaches; however, the drivers of effective teamworking are more likely to be the values and ethos of staff members who have the best interests of the child and family at heart (Appleby and Andrews, 2012). Seeking commonality between standards and codes of practice underpinning different professions, we can conclude that commitment to communication, relationships and interactions, children's experiences, and the creation of supportive environments are key to effective multi-agency working. While there will always be differences in policy and procedure, positive relationships and respect for professional identities will enable the best outcomes for children and families.

Enablers to multi-agency partnership working

While a commitment to interdisciplinary working is required of all parties, there remains a tension within the CP sector with regard to recognition and parity of esteem with others within the education workforce (Brock, 2011). Policy levers seek to redress this through increased professionalisation of the workforce and the creation of training and qualification frameworks that support continuous development (Wingrave and McMahon, 2016; Oberhuemer, 2005). Building collaborative practice through partnership working, the importance of good communication and information sharing and the need to support effective team building through strong leadership are key to ensuring effective multi-agency working.

Continuous professional development (CPD) is an essential aspect of workforce development within all childcare services and is linked to the quality of children's experiences (Siraj and Kingston, 2015). If the sector is expected to support a highly qualified, professional and skilled workforce with access to good quality professional learning to help deliver the best experiences for our children, then government investment must be met by workforce time and commitment. Engagement with regulators, curricular support and appropriate guidance must be available to practitioners, irrespective of their settings or grade, and a commitment to reflective practice and continual improvement must be supported within all workplaces. Managers and leaders are key to supporting the workforce to access appropriate professional learning, to meet their registration requirements and industry standards, and should ensure that they themselves and the practitioners they support have sufficient time within their working week to engage in professional learning and reflective practice. A particular challenge can be creating cross-sectoral and collaborative training and learning opportunities between the different agencies working with the child. As can be seen in the 'View from Practice' earlier in the chapter, effective cross-agency learning and development can create a strengths perspective and encourage a politics of recognition and respect that transcends professional boundaries.

Key principles to multi-agency communication

As discussed above, when working in a busy childcare environment, effective communication is vital. This is particularly important if you are sharing information that affects a child's safety and/or wellbeing. It is essential to prioritise children's needs at all times. Think about other teams working with the child and whether there is any information you can share that will help them provide appropriate support. It is particularly important to have a comprehensive handover whenever a child starts to work with a new practitioner or a different team. The National Society for the Prevention of Cruelty to Children highlights some key principles of communication (NSPCC, online-b):

- **Be clear about what you are sharing and why**

  For example, when sharing information, are you making a child protection referral which needs to be acted upon immediately, noted as a concern to be monitored, or are you simply sharing information only?

- **Follow up with written documentation**

  All verbal communication should be followed up with clear and comprehensive written documentation within your setting according to local policy.

- **Use specific language and describe risk and vulnerability in detail**

  Different teams and agencies, for example health visitors or speech and language professionals, may use different terminology, so ensure you use clear language when communicating. If there is a form for inter-agency information sharing, use it.

- **Understand roles and responsibilities**

  If you are working in a multidisciplinary or multi-agency team, make sure you understand your own and everyone else's role. Discuss how you will work together to support a child or family.

Summary

To ensure the best outcomes for children and families, it is essential that everyone involved in the child's life work together collaboratively to offer the most appropriate support where and when it is most needed. This chapter has sought to demonstrate and discuss the benefits of working with parents, colleagues and multi-agency children's services. It considers barriers to good practice and ways of overcoming these barriers. Whilst structural change has been identified by policy makers as integral to the development of effective multi-agency working, this must be implemented through effective communication and relationship building from the front-line workers who know and understand the children and families using their service and are situated within their local communities, placing the child at the centre of the multifaceted world they occupy.

END-OF-CHAPTER QUESTIONS

1. How do you communicate your vision and values to families?
2. How do you engage with parents and carers who are typically 'hard to reach'?
3. In what way can working with other professionals contribute to your learning?
4. What value might be found through taking part in shared professional learning opportunities with professionals from other disciplines?

22
International perspectives on childcare provision and practice

Cynthia Abel, Marie McQuade and Craig Orr

Key ideas

This chapter will explore:

- The importance of reflecting on international practices within childcare services, to better understand the variety of factors that impact local policy and provision.
- The benefits of looking outwards to broaden our knowledge of the landscape of the non-compulsory care and education (NCE) sector.
- The value of developing a systems perspective to both policy and practice.
- The importance of reflecting on some of the societal factors that are influenced by, and can influence, childcare service provision.
- The importance of a rights-based approach to service provision.

Introduction

In times of intense scrutiny, system change and sector growth, it is easy to become inward looking, fixed on developing our own services for children and families and focusing on identified local improvement initiatives based primarily on reflection on our own practice. However, the benefits of 'looking outward' to inform our practice can help us question our decision making and methodologies, resulting in services focused on continuous improvement. A greater awareness of systems, practices and pedagogical approaches from elsewhere in the world may help us reflect on why we do the things we do and consider what changes can improve the quality of our service and ultimately benefit the children in our care. Triangulation of personal experience, evidence-based practice and robust theory should ensure changes to our practice are grounded in evidence. To remain critically reflexive practitioners, and to lead in a volatile, complex and ever-changing sector, we must open our minds and explore the learning to be gained from the wider global context.

This chapter will explore the importance of looking outwards to broaden our knowledge. It aims to encourage consideration of the complexities of delivering early learning and care (ELC) and school-aged care (SAC) through an exploration of models of delivery developed internationally. The chapter will begin by providing a brief description of systems approaches before moving on to consider how non-compulsory care and education (NCE) is understood and valued internationally. This will be followed by an analysis of the ways in which quality provision is understood across and between different countries. The ways in which quality provision is targeted can reflect broader societal issues, which is illustrated through the various ways in which various countries' approaches to childcare provision responded in the face of the COVID-19 pandemic. The chapter will conclude with a consideration of the ways in which children's rights are situated within larger systems, and the importance of establishing a rights-based approach to ELC and SAC provision.

Understanding systems perspectives

We live in a world of systems. As we go about our daily lives, we engage with multiple systems. For example, our family physician is part of a health care system; the commuter train we take to work is part of a transit system; and the park that we walk through is part of a living ecosystem. Even our professional practice exists within a complex system of multiple players and organisations. A system is comprised of a complex set of interconnected components that work together to achieve a common purpose (Bertalanffy, 1973).

Viewing systems as machines that operate based on established rules, regulations and power relationships has been the prevailing understanding of systems during the industrial age (Senge, 2000: 54). Each component of the machine system exists independently of the others and therefore change is a mechanical process which is applied sequentially to individual isolated elements within the system. However, this approach suggests that elements within the system can only influence others if they are directly connected. By this reasoning, change that is applied at the programme leadership level would have no effect on individual educators.

A more recent trend has been to view human services, including health care, education and community support systems, as part of 'living systems' (Senge, 2000: 55). Accordingly, systems theory purports that individuals and organisations with a common purpose are interconnected within the 'system' (Senge, 2006). While individuals or organisations within a living system are independent, their interactions are dynamic and affect each other.

According to Jacobson et al. (2019: 113), this kind of complex living system can be thought of as a self-organising network, in which individual components have some behaviours that are independent of the other components within the system as well as collective behaviours that are shared across the system. The behaviour of change within a living system is analogous to dropping a stone in water. While the stone only touches a small part of the water, its impact causes a ripple of disruption across the entire body of water. Similarly, while governments may introduce new policy initiatives, change is not limited to an isolated segment of the system. Rather, the ripple effects of change permeate the entire system, affecting the daily practice of practitioners either directly or indirectly.

Orr and Wingrave argue in Chapter 1 that policy implementation must occur through a bottom-up approach, ensuring all staff and stakeholders are engaged in the process of change. Staff's engagement with the change initiative can be further supported by ensuring that related factors are considered at all levels of the system. By 'looking outward', at the policies and practices in other settings, and indeed other countries, alternative strategies for implementation may become evident. By adopting a systems approach, situating our own practice within the broader context, new perspectives and insights become available.

Wheatley (2006) explains that observing changes in this way involves simultaneously examining what is happening with individual components, while maintaining an awareness of the dynamics at play in the larger system. Using this approach can be both complex and challenging as it involves assuming a humble stance, suspending our mental models and maintaining a constant state of curious awareness (Wheatley, 2012). Developing a systems perspective in relation to NCE allows practitioners, leaders and managers to reflect on and examine the multiple systemic factors that can shape and influence their everyday practice.

International ELC and policy

Development of high-quality ELC and SAC services may help to improve outcomes for the youngest children in our society. This view is supported by recent findings (Scottish Government [SG], 2017c), which show that a highly qualified and well-supported workforce, underpinned by effective pedagogical leadership and professional collaboration, is an essential characteristic of the kind of high-quality service which can help to support enhanced outcomes for children and reduce inequalities.

Internationally, in recent years, there has been a strong focus on developing ELC services (Organisation for Economic Co-operation and Development [OECD], 2006, 2001) with the recognition that high-quality ELC not only supports the development of young children but is also a valuable long-term economic investment (Scobie and Scott, 2017; Heckman and Masterov, 2007). In parallel is the emergence of a discourse surrounding wraparound school care services and their ability to support families into work or training (Bisback and Kopf-Johnson, 2010). In recent years, throughout the United Kingdom, as a matter for devolved governments, the expansion and development of ELC services has been a priority for all administrations (SG, 2017c; Welsh Government, 2017; Department for Education [DfE], 2016). This echoes activity internationally where the design and delivery of a range of curriculum documents, wellbeing initiatives and workforce developments have been implemented (Australian Children's Education and Care Quality Authority [ACECQA], 2018; Oberhuemer, 2005).

While ELC and SAC provision cannot eliminate the impact of social and economic disadvantage, they may help mitigate against it (Siraj and Kingston, 2015; Heckman, 2012). Van Lancker (2018) argues that childcare services are increasingly identified as important policy levers to combat poverty, disadvantage and inequalities. International bodies such as the OECD (2008, 2006), the World Bank (Paes de Barros et al., 2009) and the United Nations (UN) all prioritise a focus on early childhood and childcare provision. It is recognised that children's early experiences have a profound impact on both their wellbeing and their future life opportunities. This view is corroborated also by international evidence (OECD, 2017; Melhuish et al., 2015) which reports that low-quality ELC services impact negatively on a child's wellbeing and learning.

In times of significant change in the delivery of childcare, the responsibility comes to lie on the workforce to embrace change and support the implementation of new policies and programmes. The UN Education Scientific and Cultural Organization (UNESCO, 2004) argued that in order to deliver high-quality ELC, a strong policy lead from governments must be paralleled by investment in a professional, motivated workforce. Significant research focuses on the benefit and impact of degree-level qualifications and the importance of effective and relevant career-long professional learning for the workforce (Siraj and Kingston, 2015). To this end, professional development and academic programmes have often been at the core of improvement planning.

─────────────── **VIEW FROM PRACTICE** ───────────────

Scotland's Equity and Excellence Leads

The strategic development of a new role within the early years workforce demonstrates an example of systemic change in the Scottish childcare sector. Responding to research indicating that access to highly qualified practitioners with expertise in early childhood learning and development can play a key role in realising government ambitions for the youngest children, in 2018 the Scottish Government delivered (SG, online) and evaluated (SG, 2021d) a new policy, effectively creating a new leadership post in the early learning and childcare sector. The support of graduate-level practitioners is known to be particularly effective in improving outcomes for young children who face the greatest disadvantages. In response, the government provided an additional graduate in every ELC setting located in Scotland's most deprived areas, called Equity and Excellence Leads (the Leads). These practitioners use a rights-based approach, to support the delivery of effective multi-agency working. The Leads are an additional resource in the staff team, not tied to the service's adult:child ratios like other staff and therefore they have greater flexibility to practise in a targeted fashion based on a knowledge and an understanding of local priorities and challenges. They focus on delivering an increase in evidence-based practice. They demonstrate pedagogical leadership and develop relationships with families and other professionals to support the confidence and capability of parents in the most deprived areas.

─────────────── **THINKING POINT 22.1** ───────────────

How might the childcare workforce be developed in your country?

International understandings of quality

Given the focus of ensuring high quality in the delivery of ELC and SAC, the concept of quality is a complex term full of contradictions (Urban, 2016). As Penn (2009) identified, how quality is defined and delivered varies considerably between countries. This is an issue that had also been raised by the OECD (2001) in the first of their Starting Strong reports, in which they argued that definitions of quality vary considerably across countries. Nevertheless, the OECD (2001) acknowledges that, despite the variance, there are several common characteristics and structural aspects of quality within such settings, such as group size, staff:child ratios, the environment, and staff training and development. The OECD (2021) later identified five policy levers underpinning the quality of children's experiences:

- quality standards, governance and funding;
- curriculum and pedagogy;
- workforce development;
- monitoring and data; and
- family and community engagement.

When used together, these policy levers can support governments in developing a quality agenda that focuses on whole-system change. Although acknowledging that such measures of quality need to be broad enough to enable individual settings to respond appropriately to the children, families and communities they serve (OECD, 2001), some authors, such as Dahlberg et al. (2007) and Penn (2011), argue against universal attempts to define, deliver and measure quality, claiming that such technocratic, managerial approaches are not suited to ELC. Instead, authors such as Urban (2016) argue that it is the continuous search for quality that ultimately defines it. It is by questioning, debating and evaluating practice that constitutes how the quality of ELC delivery is best understood.

──────────────── **THINKING POINT 22.2** ────────────────

In what ways are understandings of 'quality' likely to be similar and/or different in different countries?

───

Policy, provision and societal inequities

Given the five policy levers that the OECD (2021) claims underpin the quality of children's experiences, it is necessary to consider how ELC services are valued within the wider social system, to establish how these indicators of quality can be understood and embedded within wider contexts and human social systems. Tobin et al. (2009) consider that the value that societies place on children and childhood can be measured by the quality of ELC services and the level of investment therein. In its 2013 Social Investment Package, the European Commission stressed the importance of investing in early childhood through high-quality childcare provision in order to break the intergenerational chain of poverty and exclusion (European Commission, 2013). Yet, a report the following year identified that childcare providers generally prioritise working parents. Disadvantaged families with only a weak labour market attachment were often unable to secure a place in formal childcare services (European Commission, 2014). It is evident that different approaches to the delivery of childcare services have developed in response to localised political and societal agendas and that while we can learn from other approaches, it is important to be mindful that there may be local levers that may not seem relevant in our own context.

Drawing on Sen's (1999) capability approach, Yerkes and Javornik (2019) compared childcare policies across six countries: Australia, Iceland, the Netherlands, Slovenia, Sweden and the United Kingdom. Through a cross-country comparison of key aspects of policy design, including availability, accessibility, affordability, quality and flexibility, the authors identified two distinct approaches to the design of childcare policies. In Iceland, Slovenia and Sweden, childcare has historically been designed through public service provision. A key driver in such an approach was the need to support and promote gender equality (Gornick and Meyers, 2003). This was reflected in related policies, such as the attempt to challenge gendered parenting roles through shared parental leave. With a strong focus on affordability and accessibility, public service provision empowers parents, supporting them in accessing appropriate childcare.

In comparison, the Netherlands, Australia and the United Kingdom focused on the marketisation of childcare policies. Across the countries studied, the authors found that marketised childcare services were prohibitively more expensive, leading to inequal provision of childcare across social class. It is also commonly recognised that the private sector tends to establish services in affluent areas, in which both demand and purchasing power are high (Akgunduz and Plantenga, 2014; European Commission, 2014; Noailly and Visser, 2009). This approach can limit childcare opportunities for those in less affluent areas or those on lower incomes. Although Yerkes and Javornik (2019: 531) acknowledge the developments in these three countries in recent years, they argue that it remains the case that 'childcare is often not available as a continuous entitlement from birth to school'.

In comparing these approaches to childcare policy design, public service provision or marketisation, from an international perspective, Yerkes and Javornik (2019) identified not only the commonalties and differences across countries, but the impact these different approaches had in practice. By 'looking outward', the authors demonstrated how developments at one level of the system, in this case the system of childcare policy design, influenced, and in some instances exacerbated, other societal issues. Factors such as the availability, accessibility and affordability of childcare services can be unevenly distributed across lines of gender and social class.

──────────── THINKING POINT 22.3 ────────────

How do you think the childcare sector in your country may impact societal inequities, either positively or negatively?

International responses to global concerns

As seen in the study by Yerkes and Javornik (2019), the ways in which childcare services are operationalised within a given country invariably reflect the underpinning philosophies and values of the respective governments. Scheiwe and Willekens (2009: 4) identified two primary motivating factors influencing the development of the childcare sector across Europe: a 'a need of public education' and a 'reconciliation of care work and paid work'. However, Bacchi (1999) identified another motivating factor influencing the development of childcare services: the desire to mitigate social inequalities. Together, these three factors demonstrate how childcare services are understood and valued at the societal system level: the educational model, the work–care reconciliation model and the welfare model. As Blum and Dobrotić (2021) argue, these models are not mutually exclusive but can be utilised heuristically to develop our understanding of the drivers behind the development of the childcare sector and the ways in which change can be managed and understood. Senge (2000) suggests that how we define a system dictates how we view and consequently engage with it. Furthermore, when policy decisions are made through the lens of a larger, dominant system, foundational ideologies and priorities emerge. As a result, the same policy lever can manifest itself in different ways. A recent example of this concept can be found in how governments approached the closure and reopening of ELC and SAC services during the COVID-19 pandemic.

Exploring cross-country childcare policy responses to the COVID-19 pandemic, Blum and Dobrotić (2021) noted striking differences. From mid-March 2020, schools and childcare services around the globe closed as a result of the COVID-19 pandemic. The cross-country variation noted by Blum and Dobrotić (2021) was most notable as these services began to reopen. The timing and manner in which services closed and reopened evidenced two extremes: a precautionary, population-level response, involving the 'full closure' of services, and a more proportional, high-risk response, which tended to keep these services open. Between the two extremes lay a myriad of approaches, all of which attempted to balance the education and care of children with the broader public health concerns in different ways. The closure of educational and care services proved contentious, adversely impacting the economy, employment and education (OECD, 2020b). Yet, it was the reopening of these services that Blum and Dobrotić (2021) found to be increasingly reflective of each country's differing perspectives. As services gradually reopened, initial priority was frequently given to select groups. Which parties gained earlier access proved to be of particular interest to the authors. For example, the needs of working parents were linked to the decision in Denmark to reopen schools in April, demonstrating a strong focus on the reconciliation of work and family.

Exploring different countries' approaches to the closure, and importantly reopening of educational and childcare services, led Blum and Dobrotić (2021) to identify that, given the unique circumstances afforded by the pandemic, the aforementioned models of childcare service provision were extended to include another dimension. Along with the focus on education, the reconciliation of work and care responsibilities and social welfare, the reopening of childcare services was also driven by a focus on public health, which had not been a large contributory factor to childcare policy before the pandemic. Blum and Dobrotić (2021) suggest that, as evidenced in some countries' responses, the pandemic raised the importance of childcare, placing it higher on political agendas as it began to be viewed as a critical economic infrastructure. Whether public health remains a significant factor in childcare policy will come down to a number of factors, not least how the pandemic itself is managed. However, while much research focuses on the value of high-quality services for children aged 3 and 4, it is vital for policy makers and practitioners alike to understand that childcare is diverse, and that families' needs are complex, for example simultaneously requiring day care for a 1-year-old, ELC for a 4-year-old and wraparound SAC for a 7-year-old. In order that economic investment in childcare is realised and begins to impact on the closure of the poverty-related attainment gap, it is important to understand the complexity of the landscape parents and carers negotiate and to examine the systemic responses to this complexity.

—— VIEW FROM PRACTICE ——

COVID-19 essential worker childcare – Canada

In March 2020, as a result of the COVID-19 pandemic, most of the population were ordered to work from home, and schools and childcare services were closed down. This had a profound impact on almost every aspect of life. Very quickly, it was realised that to keep health services, distribution chains and food shops open, a new system of childcare needed to be created to care for the children of the essential workers employed in these areas. In the course of just a few days, staff were asked to design and implement free childcare services for eligible essential workers by making use of schools, community centres, nurseries and outdoor spaces. In some cases, staff had to learn to work with children of different ages, while supporting learning and development, mental health and play. Simultaneously, the workforce had to adapt to the challenges brought about by public health measures such as mask-wearing, social distancing and the requirement that children were kept in small, consistent groups to minimise infection risk. A focus on delivering high-quality services was maintained throughout. While delivering childcare in person, the workforce was also tasked with staying in touch with and providing learning opportunities for children who were not attending settings and instead learning at home with parents not classed as essential worker parents. These were delivered remotely through digital means, or hand-delivered to families through local networks. The role and value of the childcare sector in supporting the economy were explicitly understood across society and the importance of relationships built up by practitioners evident in delivering family support.

─────────────────── **THINKING POINT 22.4** ───────────────────

How did childcare services in your country develop in light of the COVID-19 pandemic? What factors were considered? Consider both early years and school-aged childcare.

───

Non-compulsory care and education
and children's rights

A key factor shaping childcare services and policy that is not as recognised as the focus on education, public health, social welfare or the reconciliation of work and care responsibilities, reflects the rights of the children themselves. Indeed, the two factors discussed by Bacchi (1999) and Scheiwe and Willekens (2009), the education model and the welfare model, can be understood from two different perspectives: the human capital perspective, in which the child can be seen to be a future investment, and that of the child as a citizen in the here and now, 'therefore entitled to developmental and material resources not only on the basis of their family membership' (Saraceno, 2011: 91). Designing childcare services as a right of the child does not deny the child's future worth, nor does it deny the affordances that flexible, high-quality childcare provision offer parents in establishing a 'reconciliation of care work and paid work' (Scheiwe and Willekens, 2009: 4). With the rights of the child at the centre, childcare has the potential to ensure every child has the opportunity to develop their full range of capabilities, regardless of eligibility criteria, accessibility or affordability (Saraceno, 2011).

─────────────────── **VIEW FROM PRACTICE** ───────────────────

Australia's development of a school-aged childcare framework:
My Time, Our Place

The Australian Government has produced My Time, Our Place: Framework for School Age Care in Australia (ACECQA, 2018). This practice guidance aims to support school-aged childcare practitioners to help children to reach their full potential as well as to support better outcomes in the future. The guidance recognises that SAC practitioners work in partnership with children, families and the wider community, including schools. It aims to extend and enrich children's wellbeing and development in school-aged care settings. Uncommonly, Australia has chosen to view SAC through a national policy lens, focusing on the need for high-quality and child-centred experiences. The Framework extends early learning and childcare principles and practices to the experiences of the children and young people who attend SAC settings, to ensure that the most appropriate environments, relationships and management structures are in place to allow children to flourish. Closely aligned to the UN Convention on the Rights of the Child (UNCRC) (UN, 1989), the Framework places the importance of play and leisure in children's learning and development as central to their experience of childcare, and presents a focus on the development of life skills including social and emotional strength. The Framework offers practitioners a foundation for ensuring that children attending SAC are given the opportunity to have quality experiences that enhance their learning, personal development and cohesion with their local community.

Summary

This chapter aimed to identify the importance of 'looking outwards', at international approaches to NCE. By reflecting on the international context, practitioners, leaders and managers are best situated to understand their own national approach to NCE. Building on this concept, we discussed the ways in which a reflective process can be supported by developing a systems perspective, in which changes to practice can be understood and explored at different levels of the larger system. This was further developed through considerations of some of the societal drivers relating to ELC and SAC provision, including mitigating against issues such as economic and social disadvantage. This often requires a strong policy lead from governments, paralleled by investment in a professional, motivated childcare workforce with a focus on high-quality provision. Yet, by considering how quality is understood across and between countries, the chapter explored the societal impacts quality provision can generate.

The chapter went on to explore cross-country comparisons, reflecting the value that different countries placed on childcare provision. As was demonstrated, the design of such policies and practices is often invariably reflective of larger societal issues, such as inequities in gender or social class. This is also evident when considering different countries' responses to immediate global issues. By examining how countries prioritised childcare provision during the COVID-19 pandemic, we demonstrated how change at one level of the system invariably impacted, and in some instances exacerbated, some of these issues. Finally, this chapter concluded by reflecting on the importance of developing NCE services with a core focus on children's rights. By adopting a systems perspective, practitioners, leaders and managers are better placed to understand the ways in which their own practice is influenced by a number of larger societal issues. The importance of high-quality provision, both ELC and SAC, is situated within a larger socio-political context. It is through understanding such a complex tapestry that practitioners, leaders and managers can ensure their settings and their services are grounded in the rights of the child.

END-OF-CHAPTER QUESTIONS

1. What is the value of looking outwards to understand Childhood Practice services in other societies?
2. What key similarities and differences can you identify between policies impacting settings in your country and those discussed in this chapter?
3. How might quality look different in other societies?

References

Abebe, T. (2019) 'Reconceptualising children's agency as continuum and interdependence', *Social Sciences*, 8(3): 1–16.

Action for Children (2017) *Eat better, start better: A practical guide*. Watford: Action for Children.

Addison, R. and Brundrett, M. (2008) 'Motivation and demotivation of teachers in primary schools: The challenge of change', *International Journal of Primary, Elementary and Early Years Education*, 36(1): 79–94.

Ainsworth, M. (1979) 'Infant–mother attachment', *American Psychologist*, 34(10): 932–7.

Ainsworth, M.D. and Bell, S.M. (1970) 'Attachment, exploration, and separation: Illustrated by the behavior of one-year-olds in a strange situation', *Child Development*, 41(1): 49–67.

Akgunduz, Y.E. and Plantenga, J. (2014) 'Childcare in the Netherlands: Lessons in privatisation', *European Early Childhood Education Research Journal*, 22(3): 379–85.

Akhal, A. (2019) *The early years workforce: A comparison with retail workers*. London: Education Policy Institute.

Alaimo, K. (2002) 'Historical roots of children's rights in Europe and the United States', in K. Alaimo and B. Klug (eds), *Children as equals: Exploring the rights of the child*. Lanham, MD: University Press of America, pp. 1–24.

Alakwe, K.O. (2017) 'Positivism and knowledge inquiry: From scientific method to media and communication research', *Specialty Journal of Humanities and Cultural Science*, 2(3): 38–46.

Aldemir, J., Barreto, D. and Kermani, H. (2019) 'The integration of mobile technology into curricula for early childhood preservice teachers', *Journal of Educational Technology*, 16(3): 21–33.

Alden, C. and Pyle, A. (2019) 'Multi-sector perspectives on outdoor play in Canada', *International Journal of Play*, 8(3): 239–54.

Aliakbari, M. and Sadeghi, A. (2014) 'Iranian teachers' perceptions of teacher leadership practices in schools', *Educational Management Administration & Leadership*, 42(4): 576–92.

Allen, G. (2011) *Early intervention: The next steps*. London: Cabinet Office.

Allen, M., Witt, P.L. and Wheeless, L.R. (2006) 'The role of teacher immediacy as a motivational factor in student learning: Using meta-analysis to test a causal model', *Communication Education*, 55(1): 21–31.

Allnock, D. and Miller, P. (2013) *No one noticed, no one heard: A study of disclosure of childhood abuse*. London: NSPCC.

Alsop-Shields, L. and Mohay, H. (2001) 'John Bowlby and James Robertson: Theorists, scientists and crusaders for improvements in the care of children in hospital', *Journal of Advanced Nursing*, 35(1): 50–8.

Alvesson, M. and Spicer, A. (2012) 'Critical leadership studies: The case for critical performativity', *Human Relations*, 65(3): 367–90.

Anderson, C. (2010) 'Presenting and evaluating qualitative research', *American Journal of Pharmaceutical Education*, 74(8): 141–6.

Anghileri, J. (2006) 'Scaffolding practices that enhance mathematics learning', *Journal of Mathematics Teacher Education*, 9(1): 33–52.

Appleby, K. and Andrews, M. (2012) 'Reflective practice is the key to quality improvement', in M. Reed and N. Canning (eds), *Implementing quality improvement and change in the early years*. London: SAGE, pp. 57–72.

Archard, D. (2015) *Children, rights and childhood (Third edition)*. Abingdon: Routledge.

Aries, P. (1962) *Centuries of childhood*. London: Jonathan Cape.

Arizpe, E., Farrell, M. and McAdam, J. (2013) 'Opening the classroom door to children's literature: A review of research', in K. Hall, T. Cremin, B. Comber and L. Moll (eds), *International handbook of research on children's literacy, learning, and culture*. London: John Wiley & Sons, pp. 241–57.

Ashurt, A. (2019) 'Equality and diversity training for care staff', *Nursing and Residential Care*, 21(1): 54–6.

Aubrey, C., Godfrey, R. and Harris, A. (2012) 'How do they manage? An investigation of early childhood leadership', *Educational Management Administration & Leadership*, 41(1): 5–29.

Australian Childhood Foundation (2010) *Making space for learning: Trauma informed practice in schools*. Ringwood, VIC: Australian Childhood Foundation.

Australian Children's Education and Care Quality Authority (ACECQA) (2018) *My time, our place: Framework for school age care in Australia*. Canberra: Department of Education and Training.

Bacchi, C. (1999) *Women, policy and politics: The construction of policy problems*. London: SAGE.

Bakken, L., Brown, N. and Downing, B. (2017) 'Early childhood education: The long-term benefits', *Journal of Research in Childhood Education*, 31(2): 255–69.

Bal, A., Thorious, K. and Kozelski, E. (2012) *Culturally responsive positive behaviour support matters*. Tempe, AZ: Equity Alliance at Arizona State University.

Baldry, H. and Moscardini, L. (2010) *Jeely Nursery Project final report*. Glasgow: University of Strathclyde.

Bandura, A. (1986) *Social foundations of thought and action: A social cognitive theory*. Englewood Cliffs, NJ: Prentice-Hall.

Bandura, A. (1997) *Self-efficacy: The exercise of control*. New York: W.H. Freeman.

Banks, J.A. (2008) *An introduction to multicultural education*. London: Pearson.

Banning, M. (2005) 'Approaches to teaching: Current opinions and related research', *Nurse Education Today*, 25(7): 502–8.

Banse, H.W., Clements, D.H., Sarama, J., Day-Hess, C., Simoni, M. and Joswick, C. (2021) 'Intentional teaching moments supporting executive function development and early mathematics through a geometry activity', *Young Children*, 76(3): 75–81.

Barnes, J.K., Guin, A., Allen, K. and Jolly, C. (2016) 'Engaging parents in early childhood education: Perspectives of childcare providers', *Family and Consumer Sciences Research Journal*, 44(4): 360–74.

Barron, I. (2016) 'Flight turbulence: The stormy professional trajectory of trainee early years' teachers in England', *International Journal of Early Years Education*, 24(3): 325–41.

Barrow, M. (2013) *Schools during the Victorian times*. www.primaryhomeworkhelp.co.uk/victorians/children/schools.htm (accessed 25 October 2021).

Barton, D. and Hamilton, M. (2003) *Local literacies: Reading and writing in one community*. London: Routledge.

Bates, C. (2020) 'Rewilding education? Exploring an imagined and experienced outdoor learning space', *Children's Geographies*, 18(3): 364–74.

Battram, A. (2000) *Navigating complexity: The essential guide to complexity theory in business and management*. London: The Industrial Society.

Batty, D. (2009) 'Lord Laming's recommendations on child protection', *The Guardian*, 12 March.

Bauer, K. and Fischer, F. (2007) 'The educational research–practice interface revisited: A scripting perspective', *Educational Research and Evaluation: An International Journal on Theory and Practice*, 13(3): 221–36.

BBC News (2003a) *Inquiry's key recommendations*. http://news.bbc.co.uk/1/hi/uk/2702643.stm (accessed 10 January 2022).

BBC News (2003b) *Death sparks child protection review*. http://news.bbc.co.uk/1/hi/scotland/3176668.stm (accessed 10 January 2022).

BBC News (2003c) *Huntley guilty of Soham murders*. http://news.bbc.co.uk/1/hi/uk/3312551.stm (accessed 10 January 2022).

BBC News (2021) *1.5m pupils out of school in England last week*. www.bbc.com/news/education-57820776 (accessed 10 January 2022).

BBC Newsround (2021) *Climate change: Children don't feel listened to says Unicef*. www.bbc.co.uk/newsround/59001663 (accessed 2 January 2022).

Bee, H. and Boyd, D. (2013) *The developing child (Thirteenth edition)*. London: Pearson.

Belyh, A. (2019) *Functions of management – Planning, organizing, staffing and more*. www.cleverism.com/functions-of-management-planning-organizing-staffing (accessed 9 November 2021).

Bennathan, M. and Boxall, M. (1996) *Effective intervention in primary schools: Nurture groups*. London: Fulton.

Benoit, L., Lehalle, H. and Jouen, F. (2004) 'Do young children acquire number words through subitizing or counting?', *Cognitive Development*, 19(3): 291–307.

Bentzen, N. (2019) *UN Convention on children's rights: 30 years on*. Brussels: European Commission.

Bercow, J. (2008) *The Bercow report: A review of services for children and young people (0–19) with speech, language and communication needs*. Nottingham: Department of Children, Schools and Families.

Bergin, C. and Bergin, D. (2009) 'Attachment in the classroom', *Educational Psychology Review*, 21(2): 141–70.

Berkovich, I. and Eyal, O. (2017) 'Emotional reframing as a mediator of the relationships between transformational school leadership and teachers' motivation and commitment', *Journal of Educational Administration*, 55(5): 450–68.

Bertalanffy, L. (1973) *General system theory: Foundations, development, applications*. New York: G. Braziller.

Beunderman, J. (2010) *People make play: The impact of staffed play provision on children, families and communities. A research report written by Demos for Play England*. London: National Children's Bureau.

Biaggi, C. (2020) 'Reforming education in post-partition Northern Ireland: State control and churches' interference', *History of Education*, 49(3): 379–97.

Bichard, M. (2004) *The Bichard inquiry*. London: The Stationery Office.

Bisback, K. and Kopf-Johnson, L. (2010) *An introduction to school age care in Canada*. Toronto: Pearson Education.

Björklund, C., Magnusson, M. and Palmér, H. (2018) 'Teachers' involvement in children's mathematizing – beyond dichotomization between play and teaching', *European Early Childhood Education Research Journal*, 26(4): 469–80.

Black-Hawkins, K. (2017) 'Understanding inclusive pedagogy', in V. Plows and B. Whitburn (eds), *Inclusive education: Making sense of everyday practice*. Rotterdam: Sense Publishers, pp. 13–28.

Bleach, J. (2014) 'Developing professionalism through reflective practice and ongoing professional development', *European Early Childhood Education Research Journal*, 22(2): 185–97.

Blizard, R.A. and Bluhm, A.M. (1994) 'Attachment to the abuser: Integrating object-relations and trauma theories in treatment of abuse survivors', *Psychotherapy*, 31(3): 383–90.

Bloom, A. (1987) *The closing of the American mind*. New York: Simon and Schuster.

Bloom, B.S. (1956) *Taxonomy of educational objectives: Handbook 1 – The cognitive domain*. New York: David McKay.

Bloomberg, L.D. and Volpe, M. (2012) *Completing your qualitative dissertation: A road map from beginning to end (Second edition)*. London: SAGE.

Blum, S. and Dobrotić, I. (2021) 'Childcare-policy responses in the COVID-19 pandemic: Unpacking cross-country variation', *European Societies*, 23(suppl. 1): S545–63.

Boardman, K. (2020) 'Early years teachers as leaders of change through reflexivity praxis?', *Early Child Development and Care*, 190(3): 322–32.

Bohman, J. (2005) *Critical theory: The Stanford encyclopaedia of philosophy (Spring edition)*. http://plato.stanford.edu/archives/spr2013/entries/critical-theory (accessed 29 October 2021).

Bolton, G. (2010) *Reflective practice: Writing and professional development (Third edition)*. London: SAGE.

Bond, J. and Bond, S. (1994) *Sociology and health care: An introduction for nurses and other health care (Second edition)*. New York: Churchill Livingstone.

Bonetti, S. (2019) *The early years workforce in England: A comparative analysis using the Labour Force Survey*. London: Education Policy Institute.

Bonetti, S., Vaganay, A., Bury, J., Mayer, M., Hammelsbeck, R., Bristow, T., Read, H. and Akhal, A. (2020) *The stability of the early years workforce in England*. London: Social Mobility Commission.

Borthwick, A., Gifford, S. and Thouless, H. (2021) *The power of pattern: Patterning in the early years*. Derby: Association of Teachers of Mathematics.

Bourdieu, P. and Passeron, J.C. (1977) *Reproduction in education, society and culture*. London: SAGE.

Bowlby, J. (1960) 'Separation anxiety: A critical review of the literature', *International Journal of Child Psychology and Psychiatry*, 1(4): 251–69.

Bowlby, J. (1969) *Attachment and loss, Vol. 1: Attachment*. New York: Basic Books.

Bowlby, J. (1973) *Attachment and loss, Vol. 2: Separation, anxiety and anger*. New York: Basic Books.

Bowlby, J. (1979) *The making and breaking of affectional bonds*. London: Tavistock Publications.

Bowlby, J. (1980) *Attachment and loss, Vol. 3: Loss, sadness and depression*. New York: Basic Books.

Braun, V. and Clarke, V. (2006) 'Using thematic analysis in psychology', *Qualitative Research in Psychology*, 3(2): 77–101.

Brehony, K. (2008) *Theories of play*. www.faqs.org/childhood/Th-W/Theories-of-Play.html (accessed 6 February 2022).

Bretherton, I. (1992) 'The origins of Attachment Theory: John Bowlby and Mary Ainsworth', *Developmental Psychology*, 28(5): 759–75.

Bridgeman, J. (2017) 'The provision of healthcare to young and dependant children: The principle, concepts, and utility of the Children Act 1989', *Medical Law Review*, 25(3): 363–96.

British Educational Research Association (BERA) (2018) *Ethical guidelines for educational research (Fourth edition)*. London: BERA.

Brock, A. (2011) 'Perspectives on professionalism', in C. Rankin and A. Brock (eds), *Professionalism in the interdisciplinary early years team: Supporting young children and their families*. New York: Continuum, pp. 59–78.

Bronfenbrenner, U. (1977) 'Toward an experimental ecology of human development', *American Psychologist*, 32(7): 513–31.

Bronfenbrenner, U. (1979) *The ecology of human development: Experiments by nature and design*. London: Harvard University Press.

Bronfenbrenner, U. (1989) 'Ecological systems theory', in R. Vasta (ed.), *Annals of child development, Vol. 6*. Greenwich, CT: JAI Press, pp. 187–249.

Bronfenbrenner, U. (1992) 'Ecological systems theory', in R. Vasta (ed.), *Six theories of child development*. London: Jessica Kingsley, pp. 187–249.

Bronfenbrenner, U. and Ceci, S.J. (1994) 'Nature–nurture reconceptualised: A bio-ecological model', *Psychological Review*, 101(4): 568–86.

Brooker, M. and Cumming, T. (2019) 'The "dark side" of leadership in early childhood education', *Australasian Journal of Early Childhood*, 44(2): 111–23.

Brookfield, S. (2017) *Becoming a critically reflective teacher (Second edition)*. San Francisco: Jossey-Bass.

Brown, F. (2003a) 'Compound flexibility: The role of playwork in child development', in F. Brown (ed.), *Playwork – theory and practice*. Buckingham: Open University Press, pp. 51–65.

Brown, F. (2003b) *Playwork theory and practice*. Maidenhead: Open University Press.

Brown, F. (2008a) 'Services to children's play', in P. Jones, D. Moss, P. Tomlinson and S. Welch (eds), *Childhood services and provision for children*. Harlow: Pearson Education, pp. 168–81.

Brown, F. (2008b) 'The fundamentals of playwork', in F. Brown and C. Taylor (eds), *Foundations of playwork*. Maidenhead: Open University Press, pp. 123-127.

Brown, F. and Wragg, M. (2015) 'Editorial', *International Journal of Play*, 4(3): 215–16.

Brown, F., Brock, A. and Jarvis, P. (2018) 'Three perspectives on play', in A. Brock, P. Jarvis and Y. Olusoga (eds), *Perspectives on play: Learning for life (Third edition)*. Abingdon: Routledge, pp. 2–46.

Brown, J.M. and Kaye, C. (2017) 'Where do the children play? An investigation of the intersection of nature, early childhood education and play', *Early Child Development and Care*, 187(5–6): 1028–41.

Brown, S. (2010) *Play: How it shapes the brain, opens the imagination, and invigorates the soul*. London: Penguin Books.

Browne, N. (2004) *Gender equity in the early years*. Maidenhead: Open University Press.

Bruce, C.D., Davis, B., Sinclair, N., McGarvey, L., Hallowell, D., Drefs, M., Francis, K., Hawes, Z., Moss, J., Mulligan, J., Okamoto, Y., Whiteley, W. and Woolcott, G. (2017) 'Understanding gaps in reserach networks: Using "spatial reasoning" as a window into the importance of networked educational research', *Educational Studies in Mathematics*, 95(2): 143–61.

Bruce, T. (1993) 'The role of play in children's lives', *Childhood Education*, 69(4): 237–8.

Bruce, T. (ed.) (2012) *Early childhood practice: Froebel today*. London: SAGE.

Bruckman, A. (1999) *Can educational be fun? Game Developers Conference*, March 1999, San Jose, CA.

Bruner, J.S. (1996a) *The culture of education*. Cambridge, MA: Harvard University Press.

Bruner, J.S. (1966b) Toward a theory of instruction. Cambridge, MA: Harvard University Press.

Bruner, J.S. (2006) *In search of pedagogy, Vol. 2*. Abingdon: Routledge.

Brussoni, M., Gibbons, R., Gray, C., Ishikawa, T., Sandseter, E.B.H., Bienenstock, A., Chabot, G., Fuselli, P., Herrington, S., Janssen, I., Pickett, W., Power, M., Stanger, N., Sampson, M. and Tremblay, M.S. (2015) 'What is the relationship between risky outdoor play and health in children? A systematic review', *International Journal of Environmental Research and Public Health*, 12(6): 6423–54.

Bryman, A. (2001) *Social research methods*. Oxford: Oxford University Press.

Burbules, N.C., Fan, G. and Repp, P. (2020) 'Five trends of education and technology in a sustainable future', *Geography and Sustainability*, 1(2): 93–7.

Burghardt, G. (2005) *The genesis of animal play: Testing the limits*. Cambridge, MA: The Massachusetts Institute of Technology (MIT) Press.

Burke, P.J. and Stets, J.E. (2009) *Identity theory*. Oxford: Oxford University Press.

Burns, N. and Grove, S.K. (1997) *The practice of nursing research: Conduct, critique and utilization (Third edition)*. Philadelphia: Saunders.

Bush, T. (2003) *Theories of educational leadership and management (Third edition)*. London: SAGE.

Bush, T. (2019) 'Collaborative school leadership: Can it co-exist with solo leadership in high accountability settings?', *Educational Management Administration & Leadership*, 47(5): 661–2.

Bush, T. and Glover, D. (2014) 'School leadership models: What do we know?', *School Leadership and Management*, 34(5): 553–71.

Bussey, K. (2021) *Sturgeon to include free wraparound childcare in government plans for the coming year.* https://careappointments.com/care-news/scotland/164042/sturgeon-to-include-free-wraparound-childcare-in-government-plans-for-the-coming-year (accessed 13 October 2021).

Cafiero, J.M. (2012) 'Technology supports for individuals with autism spectrum disorders', *Journal of Special Education Technology*, 27(1): 64–76.

California Department of Education (2009) *Infant/toddler learning and development program guidelines: The workbook.* Sacramento: California Department of Education.

Cameron, C. (2018) *Hands on, minds on: How executive function, motor and spatial skills foster school readiness.* New York: Teachers College Press.

Cammack, I. (2012) 'Chinese whispers: My journey towards understanding and appreciating reflection', *Reflective Practice*, 13(2): 209–22.

Campbell-Evans, G., Stamopolous, E. and Maloney, C. (2014) 'Building leadership capacity in early childhood pre-service teachers', *Australian Journal of Teacher Education*, 39(5): 42–9.

Candy, L. (online) *The leadership versus management debate: What's the difference?* www.educational-business-articles.com/leadership-versus-management (accessed 1 November 2021).

Canning, N. (2010) 'The influence of the outdoor environment: Den-making in three different contexts', *European Early Childhood Education Research Journal*, 18(4): 555–66.

Care Inspectorate (2018) Food matters: Nurturing happy, healthy children. https://hub.careinspectorate.com/media/3241/food-matters-nurturing-happy-healthy-children.pdf (accessed 19 January 2022).

Care Inspectorate Wales (2019) *Guidance handbook for inspecting care and education in regulated non-school settings eligible for funding for part-time education.* Llandudno Junction: Care Inspectorate Wales

Carl, J. (2009) 'Industrialization and public education: Social cohesion and social stratification', in R. Cowen and A.M. Kazamias (eds), *International handbook of comparative education. Springer international handbooks of education, Vol. 22.* Dordrecht: Springer, pp. 503–18.

Carmichael, P., Fox, A., McCormick, R., Procter, R. and Honour, L. (2006) 'Teachers' networks in and out of school', *Research Papers in Education*, 21(2): 217–34.

Caron, F., Plancq, M.C., Tourneux, P., Gouron, R. and Klien, C. (2020) 'Was child abuse underdetected during the COVID-19 lockdown?', *Archives de Pediatrie*, 27(7): 399–400.

Carpendale, J. and Lewis, C. (2021) *What makes us human: How minds develop through social interactions.* Abingdon : Routledge.

Carpenter, T.P., Franke, M.L., Johnson, N.C., Turrou, A.C. and Wager, A.A. (2017) *Young children's mathematics: Cognitively guided instruction in early childhood education.* Portsmouth, NH: Heinemann.

Carpentieri, J.D. (2012) *Family learning: A review of the research literature*. London: Institute of Education, University of London.

Carr, M. and Lee, W. (2019) *Learning stories in practice*. London: SAGE.

Carruthers, E. and Worthington, M. (2006) *Children's mathematics: Making marks, making meaning (Second edition)*. London: SAGE.

Casey, T. and Robertson, J. (2019) *Loose parts play: A toolkit*. Edinburgh: Inspiring Scotland.

Castle, K. (2010) *Study skills for your Masters in Teaching and Learning*. London: Learning Matters.

Central Advisory Council for Education (CACE) (1967) *The Plowden report: Children and their primary schools*. London: HMSO.

Cerna, L. (2013) *The nature of policy change and implementation: A review of different theoretical approaches*. Paris: Organisation for Economic Co-operation and Development (OECD).

Chan, C.W. (2018) 'Leading today's kindergartens: Practices of strategic leadership in Hong Kong's early childhood education', *Educational Management Administration & Leadership*, 46(4): 679–91.

Chang, S.H., Lee, N.H. and Koay P.L. (2017) 'Teaching and learning with concrete-pictorial-abstract sequence: A proposed model', *The Mathematics Educator*, 17(1): 1–28.

Charlwood, N. and Steele, H. (2004) 'Using attachment theory to inform practice in an integrated centre for children and families', *European Early Childhood Education Research Journal*, 12(2): 59–74.

Cheng, E.W.L. and Ho, D.C.K. (2001) 'The influence of job and career attitudes on learning motivation and transfer', *Career Development International*, 6(1): 20–7.

Cherry, L. (2021) *Conversations that make a difference for children and young people*. Abingdon: Routledge.

Child Poverty Action Group (2022) *What we do*. https://cpag.org.uk/about-cpag/what-we-do (accessed 30 January 2022).

Children in Scotland (online) *Access to childcare fund*. https://childreninscotland.org.uk/access-to-childcare-fund-summary (accessed 22 December 2021).

Children's Commissioner for Wales (2017) *The right way*. www.childcomwales.org.uk/wp-content/uploads/2017/04/The-Right-Way.pdf (accessed 10 April 2022).

Children's Commissioner for Wales (2019) *A plan for all children and young people, 2019–2022*. Port Talbot: Children's Commissioner for Wales.

Children's Parliament (2017) *School should be a joyful place. Learning and school life in Scotland: A Child's Parliament report*. Edinburgh: Children's Parliament.

Children's Rights Alliance for England (2022) *Laws protecting children's rights*. https://crae.org.uk/our-guide-childrens-rights-and-law/laws-protecting-childrens-rights/un-convention-rights-child (accessed 20 October 2022).

Chilton, T. (2013) *Adventure playgrounds: A brief history*. Bognor Regis: Fair Play for Children.

Choi, J. and Kang, W. (2019) 'Sustainability of cooperative professional development: Focused on teachers' efficacy', *Sustainability in Leadership and Education*, 11(3): 585–99.

Christensen, P. and Prout, A. (2005) 'Anthropological and sociological perspectives on the study of children', in S. Greene and D. Hogan (eds), *Researching children's experiences: Approaches and methods*. London: SAGE, pp. 41–60.

Clark, A., McQuail, S. and Moss, P. (2003) *Exploring the field of listening to and consulting with young children: Research report No. 445*. Nottingham: Department for Education and Skills (DfES).

Clements, D.H. and Sarama, J. (2017) *Play, mathematics, and false dichotomies*. https://dreme.stanford.edu/news/play-mathematics-and-false-dichotomies (accessed 10 November 2021).

Clements, D. and Sarama, J. (2019) *Learning and teaching with learning trajectories [LT]2*. www.learningtrajectories.org (accessed 3 November 2021).

Clements, D. and Sarama, J. (2021) *Learning and teaching early math (Third edition)*. New York: Routledge.

Clements, D., Sarama, J. and Germeroth, C. (2016) 'Learning executive function and early mathematics: Directions of causal relations', *Early Childhood Research Quarterly Review*, 36: 79–90.

Clements, D., Sarama, J., Layzer, C., Unlu, F. and Fesler, L. (2020) 'Effects on mathematics and executive function of a mathematics and play intervention versus mathematics alone', *Journal for Research in Mathematics Education*, 51(3): 301–33.

Clements, R. (2004) 'An investigation of the status of outdoor play', *Contemporary Issues in Early Childhood*, 5(1): 68–80.

Clifton, J. and Cook, W. (2012) *A long division: Closing the attainment gap in England's secondary schools*. London: Institute for Public Policy Research.

Coates, J.K. and Pimlott-Wilson, H. (2019) 'Learning while playing: Children's Forest School experiences in the UK', *British Educational Research Journal*, 45(1): 21–40.

Coban, A. (2020) 'On pandemics, technology, and early childhood education: An opinion piece', *Childhood Education*, 96(6): 66–9.

Cohen, B., Moss, P., Petrie, P. and Wallace, J. (2004) *A new deal for children? Re-forming education and care in England, Scotland and Sweden*. Bristol: Policy Press.

Cohen, C.P. (2002) 'United Nations Convention on the Rights of the Child: Developing international norms to create a new world for children', in K. Alaimo and B. Klug (eds), *Children as equals: Exploring the rights of the child*. Lanham, MD: University Press of America, pp. 49–72.

Cohen, L., Manion, L. and Morrison, K. (2018) *Research methods in education*. London: Taylor and Francis.

Colton, M. and Roberts, S. (2006) 'Factors that contribute to high turnover among residential child care staff', *Child & Family Social Work*, 12(2): 133–42.

Comber, B. (2001) 'Critical literacy: Power and pleasure with language in the early years', *Australian Journal of Language and Literacy*, 24(3): 168–81.

Comber, B. (2003) 'Critical literacy: What does it look like in the early years?', in N. Hall, J. Larson and J. Marsh (eds), *Handbook of early childhood literacies*. London: SAGE, pp. 355–68.

Conkbayir, M. (2021) *Early childhood and neuroscience: Theory, research and implications for practice (Second edition)*. London: Bloomsbury Academic.

Connelly, L.M. (2015) 'Research questions and hypotheses', *Medsurg Nursing Journal*, 24(6): 435–6.

Connolly, P., Smith, A. and Kelly, B. (2002) *Too young to notice? The cultural and political awareness of 3–6-year-olds in Northern Ireland*. Belfast: Northern Ireland Community Relations Council.

Cook, D.T. (2019) 'Panaceas of play: Stepping past the creative', in S. Spyrou, R. Rosen and D.T. Cook (eds), *Reimagining childhood studies*. London: Bloomsbury Academic, pp. 123–36.

Cooke, G. and Lawson, K. (2008) *For love or money: Pay, progression and professionalisation in the 'early years' workforce*. London: Institute for Public Policy Research.

Copeland, M.K. (2014) 'The emerging significance of values based leadership: A literature review', *International Journal of Leadership Studies*, 8(2): 105–135.

Coppock, V. and Gillett-Swan, J.K. (2016) 'Children's rights in a 21st century digital world: Exploring opportunities and tensions', *Global Studies of Childhood*, 6(4): 369–75.

Cornelius-White, J. (2007) 'Learner-centred teacher–student relationships are effective: A meta-analysis', *Review of Educational Research*, 77(1): 113–43.

Correia, N., Aguair, C. and Amaro, F. (2021) 'Children's participation in early childhood education. A theoretical overview', *Contemporary Issues in Early Childhood*, Published online: 1–20. https://repositorio.iscte-iul.pt/bitstream/10071/21288/1/2021%20POS-PRINT_Childrens%20participation%20in%20early%20childhood%20education%20A%20theoretical%20overview.pdf9 (accessed 07 November 2022).

Corsaro, W.A. (1997) *The sociology of childhood*. Thousand Oaks, CA: Pine Forge Press.

Corsaro, W.A. (2005) *The sociology of childhood (Second edition)*. Thousand Oaks, CA: Pine Forge Press.

Corsaro, W.A. (2012) 'Interpretive reproduction in children's play', *American Journal of Play*, 4(4): 488–504.

Corsaro, W.A. (2017) *The sociology of childhood* (Fifth edition). Thousand Oaks, CA: Pine Forge Press.

Council for the Curriculum, Examinations and Assessment (CCEA) (2007) *The Northern Ireland curriculum primary*. Belfast: CCEA.

Council for the Curriculum, Examinations and Assessment (CCEA) (2018) *Curricular guidance for pre-school education*. Belfast: CCEA.

Council for the Curriculum, Examinations and Assessment (CCEA) (online) *Curriculum*. Belfast: CCEA. https://ccea.org.uk/about/what-we-do/curriculum (accessed 3 November 2021).

Council of Europe (2013) *European Convention on Human Rights*. Strasbourg: Council of Europe.

Council of Europe (2021) *Child participation*. www.coe.int/en/web/children/participation (accessed 19 October 2021).

Cousin, G. (2011) 'Rethinking the concept of "western"', *Higher Education Research & Development*, 30(5): 585–94.

Cowan, K. (2020) 'Tracing the ephemeral: Mapping young children's running games', *Designs for Learning*, 12(1): 81–93.

Cozolino, L. (2013) *The social neuroscience of education*. New York: W.W. Norton.

Creative Commons (online) *Participation models: Citizens, youth online*. Mountain View, CA: Creative Commons.

Creswell, J.W. (2014) *Research design: Qualitative, quantitative and mixed methods approaches (Fourth edition)*. London: SAGE.

Crittenden, P. (2017) 'Gifts from Mary Ainsworth and John Bowlby', *Clinical Child Psychology*, 22(3): 436–42.

Croke, R. and Hoffman, S. (2021) *ENOC synthesis report: Mapping the impact of emergency measures introduced in response to the COVID-19 pandemic on children's rights in ENOC member states*. Strasbourg: European Network of Ombudspersons for Children (ENOC).

Cruess, R., Johnston, S. and Cruess, R.L. (2004) '"Profession": A working definition for medical educators', *Teaching and Learning in Medicine*, 16(1): 74–6.

Cunningham, H. (2006) *The invention of childhood*. London: BBC Books.

Cunningham, H. (2020) *Children and childhood in western society since 1500 (Third edition)*. Abingdon: Routledge.

Dahlberg, G., Moss, P. and Pence, A. (2007) *Beyond quality in early childhood education and care: Languages of evaluation*. Abingdon: Routledge.

Daly, L. and Beloglovsky, M. (2018) *Loose parts 3: Inspiring culturally sustainable environments*. St Paul, MN: Redleaf Press.

Daniels, K. (2016) 'Exploring enabling literacy environments: Young children's spatial and material encounters in early years classrooms', *English in Education*, 50(1): 12–34.

Daniels, K., Bower, K., Burnett, C., Escott, H., Hatton, A., Ehiyazaryan-White, E. and Monkhouse, J. (2019) 'Early years teachers and digital literacies: Navigating a kaleidoscope of discourses', *Education and Information Technologies*, 25(2): 2415–26.

Dasborough, M., Lamb, P. and Suseno, Y. (2015) 'Understanding emotions in higher education change management', *Journal of Organizational Change Management*, 28(4): 579–90.

Daus, C.S., Dasborough, M.T., Jordan, P.J. and Ashkanasy, N.M. (2012) 'We are all mad in Wonderland: An organizational culture framework for emotions and emotional intelligence research', *Research on Emotion in Organizations*, 8(2): 375–99.

Davidson, E., Critchley, A. and Wright, L. (2020) 'Making Scotland an ACE-informed nation', *Scottish Affairs*, 29(4): 451–5.

Davies, S. (2012) 'Embracing reflective practice', *Education for Primary Care*, 23(9): 9–12.

Davis, B., Rea, T. and Waite, S. (2006) 'The special nature of the outdoors: Its contribution to the education of children aged 3–11', *Journal of Outdoor and Environmental Education*, 10(2): 3–12.

Davis, J.M. (2011) *Integrated children's services*. London: SAGE.

Davis, J.M. (2014) *Taking the first steps – is Childhood Practice working?* Dundee: Scottish Social Services Council.

Davis, J.M., Bell, A. and Pearce, M. (2014) *Taking the first steps – is Childhood Practice working? An investigation by the University of Edinburgh for the SSSC*. Dundee: Scottish Social Services Council.

Davis, R. (2018) *Education, literature and the paradox of 'the whole child'*. https://researched.org.uk/2018/09/26/education-literature-and-the-paradox-of-the-whole-child (accessed 9 December 2021).

Davitt, G. and Ryder, D. (2018) 'Dispositions of a responsible early childhood education leader: Voices from the field', *Journal of Educational Leadership, Policy and Practice*, 33(1): 18–31.

Day, C. (1999) *Developing teachers: The challenges of lifelong learning*. London: Falmer Press.

Day, C. (2017) 'Competence-based education and teacher professional development', in M. Mulder (ed.), *Competence-based vocational and professional education. Technical and vocational education and training: issues, concerns and prospects, Vol. 23*. Dordrecht: Springer, pp. 165–82.

De Mause, L. (1995) *The evolution of childhood*. Northvale, NJ: Jason Aronson.

de Paor, C. and Murphy, T.R.N. (2018) 'Teachers' views on research as a model of CPD: Implications for policy', *European Journal of Teacher Education*, 41(2): 169–86.

de Rijdt, C., Dochy, F., Bamelis, S. and van der Vleuten, C. (2016) 'Classification of staff development programmes and effects perceived by teachers', *Innovations in Education and Teaching International*, 53(2): 179–90.

Decker, C.A. and Decker, J.R. (2001) *Planning and administering early childhood programs (Seventh edition)*. Upper Saddle River, NJ: Prentice-Hall.

DeLeon, P. and DeLeon, L. (2002) 'What ever happened to policy implementation? An alternative approach', *Journal of Public Administration Research and Theory*, 12(4): 467–92.

Demie, F. and McLean, C. (2016) 'Tackling disadvantage: What works in narrowing the achievement gap in schools', *Review of Education*, 3(2): 138–74.

Denee, R. and Thornton, K. (2021) 'Distributed leadership in ECE: Perceptions and practices', *Early Years*, 41(2–3): 128–43.

Denzin, N.K. and Lincoln, Y.S. (2000) 'Introduction: The discipline and practice of qualitative research', in N.K. Denzin and Y.S. Lincoln (eds), *The SAGE handbook of qualitative research (Third edition)*. Thousand Oaks, CA: SAGE, pp. 1–29.

Department for Education (2010) United Nations Convention on the Rights of the Child (UNCRC): how legislation underpins implementation in England. https://assets.publishing.service.gov.uk/government/uploads/system/uploads/attachment_data/file/296368/uncrc_how_legislation_underpins_implementation_in_england_march_2010.pdf (accessed 17 October 2022).

Department for Education (DfE) (2016) *30 hours free childcare entitlement: Delivery model*. London: DfE.

Department for Education (DfE) (2018a) *Working together to safeguard children*. London: DfE.

Department for Education (DfE) (2018b) *Early years entitlements: Operational guidance. For local authorities and providers*. London: DfE.

Department for Education (DfE) (2019) *Early years educator level 3: Qualifications criteria*. www.gov.uk/government/publications/early-years-educator-level-3-qualifications-criteria/early-years-educator-level-3-qualifications-criteria (accessed 17 October 2021).

Department for Education (DfE) (2021a) *Keeping children safe in education 2021: Statutory guidance for schools and colleges*. London: DfE.

Department for Education (DfE) (2021b) *Statutory framework for the early years foundation stage*. London: DfE.

Department for Education (DfE) (2021c) *Multi-agency reform: Key behavioural drivers and barriers. Summary report.* London: DfE.

Department for Education (DfE) (online) *National curriculum.* www.gov.uk/national-curriculum (accessed 3 November 2021).

Department for Education and Skills (DfES) (2003) *Every child matters.* Norwich: HMSO.

Department for Education and Skills (DfES) (2004a) *Every child matters: Change for children.* London: DfES.

Department for Education and Skills (DfES) (2004b) *Aiming high: Understanding the needs of minority ethnic pupils in mainly white schools. A guide to good practice.* London: DfES.

Department of Agriculture, Environment and Rural Affairs (DoAERA) (Northern Ireland) (online) *Eco-schools: Outdoor learning.* www.eco-schoolsni.org/eco-schoolsni/documents/007123.pdf (accessed 23 November 2021).

Department of Education (Northern Ireland) (DfE (NI)) (2018) *Curriculum guidance for pre-school education.* www.education-ni.gov.uk/sites/default/files/publications/education/PreSchool_Guidance_30May18_Web.pdf (accessed 30 January 2022).

Department of Health and Children (2020) *Food and nutrition guidelines for pre-school services.* Dublin: Department of Health and Children. www.gov.ie/en/publication/0252ea-food-and-nutrition-guidelines-for-pre-school-services (accessed 1 April 2022).

Department of Health and Social Policy Unit: Northern Ireland (DHSS NI) (1999) *Children first: The Northern Ireland childcare strategy.* Belfast: DHSS NI.

Department of Health, Northern Ireland (2018) *Childminding and day care for children under age 12: Minimum standards.* Belfast: Department of Health. www.health-ni.gov.uk/sites/default/files/publications/dhssps/early-years-standards-full-version.pdf (last accessed 10 October 2022)

Destination Unknown (2020) *Child trafficking during the pandemic.* https://destination-unknown.org/news-and-events/child-trafficking-during-the-pandemic (accessed 10 January 2022).

Dewey, J. (1910) *How we think.* Boston: D.C. Heath & Company.

Dewey, J. (1933) *How we think: A reinstatement of the relation of reflective thinking to the educative process.* Chicago: Henry Regnery Co.

Di Lemma, L.C.G., Davies, A.R., Ford, K., Hughes, K., Homolova, L., Gray, B. and Richardson, G. (2019) *Responding to adverse childhood experiences: An evidence review of interventions to prevent and address adversity across the life course.* Cardiff and Wrexham: Public Health Wales and Bangor University.

Diamond, A. (2016) 'Why improving and assessing executive functions early in life is critical', in J. Griffin, P. McCardle and L. Freund (eds), *Executive function in preschool-age children: Intergrating measurement, neurodevelopment, and translational research.* Washington DC: American Pschological Association, pp. 11–43.

Diaz, R.M., Neal, C.J. and Amaya-Wiliams, M. (1992) 'The social origins of self-regulation', in L.E. Moll (ed.), *Vygotsky and education: Instructional implication and applications of sociohistorical society.* Cambridge: Cambridge University Press, pp. 127–54.

Dillon, J., Morris, M., O'Donnell, L., Reid, A., Rickinson, M. and Scott, W. (2005) *Engaging and learning with the outdoors.* Slough: National Foundation for Educational Research.

Disclosure Services (online) *What is a PVG scheme?* www.disclosureservices.com/products-services/pvg-scheme/ (accessed 10 January 2022).

Donson, A. (2014) *Children and youth.* https://encyclopedia.1914-1918-online.net/pdf/1914-1918-Online-children_and_youth-2014-10-08.pdf (accessed 12 September 2021).

Doucet, A., Netolicky, D., Timmers, K. and Tuscano, F.J. (2020) *Thinking about pedagogy in an unfolding pandemic: An independent report on approaches to distance learning during COVID19 school closures.* Brussels: Education International.

Dowling, M. (2014) *Young children's personal, social and emotional development.* London: SAGE.

Dunlop, A.-W. (2008) *A literature review on leadership in the early years.* Glasgow: Learning and Teaching Scotland.

Dunn, J., Gray, C., Moffett, P. and Mitchell, D. (2018) '"It's more funner than doing work": Children's perspectives on using tablet computers in the early years of school', *Early Child Development and Care*, 188(6): 819–31.

Duschinsky, R. (2012) 'Tabula rasa and human nature', *Philosophy*, 87(34): 509–29.

Dzakiria, H. (2012) 'Theory of relatability as a possible alternative to the issue of generalising of research findings: The case of open and distance learning (ODL) at Universiti Utara Malaysia', *Malaysian Journal of Distance Education*, 14(1): 41–58.

Early Childhood Maths Group (2021a) *Early years mathematics pedagogy: Exploration, apprenticeship and making sense.* file:///C:/Users/user/Downloads/Early-Childhood-Mathematics-Pedagogy-illustrated-ECMG.pdf (accessed 7 December 2021).

Early Childhood Maths Group (2021b) *The development of spatial reasoning.* https://earlymaths.org/wp-content/uploads/2021/05/ECMG-Spatial-Reasoning-DEVELOPMENT.pdf (accessed 20 January 2022).

Early Childhood Mathematics Group (2021c) *Supporting children's spatial reasoning.* https://earlymaths.org/wp-content/uploads/2021/05/ECMG-Spatial-Reasoning-SUPPORT.pdf (accessed 20 January 2022).

Early Education (2021) *Birth to five matters.* St Albans: Early Education.

Early Years Scotland (online) *Young children affected by parental imprisonment.* https://earlyyearsscotland.org/about-us/services/working-with-children-and-families/young-children-affected-by-imprisonment (accessed 30 January 2022).

Easterby-Smith, M., Li, S. and Bartunek, J. (2009) 'Research methods for organizational learning: The transatlantic gap', *Management Learning*, 40(4): 439–47.

Education and Training Inspectorate (2017) *Inspection and self-evaluation framework: Effective practice and self-evaluation questions for pre-school.* Bangor: Education and Training Inspectorate.

Education Scotland (2016) *How good is our early learning and childcare?* Livingston: Education Scotland.

Education Scotland (2018a) *Child protection and safeguarding policy.* Livingston: Education Scotland.

Education Scotland (2018b) *Nurture, adverse childhood experiences and trauma informed practice: Making the links between these approaches.* Livingston: Education Scotland.

Education Scotland (2020) *Realising the ambition: Being me. National practice guidance for early years in Scotland.* Livingston: Education Scotland.

Education Scotland (online-a) *What is curriculum for excellence?* https://education.gov.scot/education-scotland/scottish-education-system/policy-for-scottish-education/policy-drivers/cfe-building-from-the-statement-appendix-incl-btc1-5/what-is-curriculum-for-excellence/ (accessed 20 January 2022).

Education Scotland (online-b) *Review of family learning.* https://education.gov.scot/improvement/Research/review-of-family-learning (accessed 30 January 2022).

Edwards, C. (2012) 'Teacher and learner, partner and guide: The role of the teacher', in C. Edwards, L. Gandini and G. Forman (eds), *The hundred languages of children (Third edition)*. Santa Barbara, CA: Praeger, pp. 147–72.

Edwards, C., Gandini, L. and Forman, G. (eds) (1998) *The hundred languages of children: The Reggio Emilia approach – advanced reflections (Second edition)*. Greenwich, CT: Ablex.

Edwards, S. (2003) 'New directions: Charting the paths for the role of sociocultural theory in early childhood education and curriculum', *Contemporary Issues in Early Childhood*, 4(3): 251–66.

Elfer, P. (2006) 'Exploring children's expressions of attachment in nursery', *European Early Childhood Education Research Journal*, 14(2): 81–95.

Elfer, P., Goldschmied, E. and Selleck, D.Y. (2011) *Key persons in the early years: Building relationships for quality provision in early years settings and primary schools (Second edition)*. London: Taylor and Francis Group.

Ellenbogen, S., Klein, B. and Wekerle, C. (2014) 'Early childhood education as a resilience intervention for maltreated children', *Early Childhood Development and Care*, 184(9–10): 1364–77.

Ellis, S. and Rowe, A. (2020) 'Literacy, social justice and inclusion: A large-scale design experiment to narrow the attainment gap linked to poverty', *Support for Learning*, 35(4): 418–39.

Else, P. (2009) *The value of play*. London: Continuum International Publishing Group.

Emotion Works (2021) *Welcome to our story*. www.emotionworks.org.uk/home/our-story (accessed 26 October 2021).

ENABLE Scotland (2021) *About us*. www.enable.org.uk/aboutus (accessed 30 January 2022).

Ephgrave, A. (2018) *Planning in the moment with young children: A practical guide for early years practitioners and parents*. Abingdon: Routledge.

Erikson, E.H. (1963a) *Childhood and society (Second edition)*. New York: Norton.

Erikson, E.H. (1963b) *Youth: Change and challenge*. New York: Basic Books.

European Commission (2013) *Commission recommendation of 20.2.2013: Investing in children: breaking the cycle of disadvantage*. Brussels: European Commission.

European Commission (2014) *Key data on early childhood education and care in Europe (2014 Edition), Eurydice and Eurostat Report*. Luxembourg: Publications Office of the European Union.

European Commission (2019) *Review of the social situation and the development in the social protection policies in the Member States and the Union*. Luxembourg: Publications Office of the European Union.

Falch-Ericksen, A., Toros, K., Sindi, I. and Lehtme, R. (2019) 'Children expressing their views in child protection casework: Current research and their rights going forward', *Child and Family Social Work*, 26(3): 485–97.

Falkirk Early Learning (2021) *Falkirk Froebel family*. https://blogs.glowscotland.org.uk/fa/falkirkearlyyears/falkirk-froebel-family (accessed 22 January 2022).

Falloon, G. (2020) 'From digital literacy to digital competence: The teacher digital competency (TDC) framework', *Education Technology Research Development*, 68: 2449–72.

Feldman, D. (2016) 'Honoring the child's right to respect: Janusz Korczak as holocaust educator', *The Lion and the Unicorn*, 40(2): 129–43.

Felitti, V.J., Anda, R.F, Nordenberg, D., Williamson, D.F., Spitz, A.M., Edwards, V., Koss, M.P. and Marks, J.S. (1998) 'Relationship of childhood abuse and household dysfunction to many of the leading causes of death in adults: the Adverse Childhood Experiences (ACE) study', *American Journal of Preventive Medicine*, 14(4): 245–58.

Ferreira, M.F. (2018) *Introducing critical theory in international relations*. www.e-ir.info/2018/02/18/introducing-critical-theory-in-international-relations (accessed 15 November 2021).

Fink, A. (2020) *Conducting research literature reviews: From the internet to paper (Fifth edition)*. London: SAGE.

Fitzgerald, D. and Kay, J. (2008) *Working together in children's services*. Abingdon: Routledge.

Flavell, J.H. (1963) *The developmental psychology of Jean Piaget*. New York: Van Nostrand.

Fleer, M. (2021) 'Conceptual playworlds: The role of imagination in play and learning', *Early Years*, 41(4): 353–64.

Ford, J.D., Ford, L.W. and D'Amelio, A. (2008) 'Resistance to change: The rest of the story', *The Academy of Management Review*, 33(2): 362–77.

Foreman, M. (2017) *Hello, Mr World*. London: Walker Books.

Forman, G. and Fyfe, B. (2012) 'Negotiated learning through design, documentation and discourse', in C. Edwards, L. Gandini and G. Forman (eds), *The hundred languages of children (Third edition)*. Santa Barbara, CA: Praeger, pp. 247–71.

Foster, R.L. (2013) 'Extracting and synthesizing information from a literature review', *Journal for Specialists in Paediatric Nursing*, 18(2): 85–8.

Fotakopoulou, O., Hatzigianni, M., Dardanou, M., Unstad, T. and O'Connor, J. (2020) 'A cross-cultural exploration of early childhood educators' beliefs and experiences around the use of touchscreen technologies with children under 3 years of age', *European Early Childhood Education Research Journal*, 28(2): 272–85.

Foucault, M. (2009) *Security, territory, population. Lectures at the Collège de France, 1977–1978* (Trans. G. Burchell). London: Palgrave Macmillan.

Fox, A.R.C. and Wilson, E.G. (2015) 'Networking and the development of professionals: Beginning teachers building social capital', *Teaching and Teacher Education*, 47(1): 93–107.

Freebody, P. and Luke, A. (1990) 'Literacies programs: Debates and demands in cultural context', *Prospect: Australian Journal of TESOL*, 5(7): 7–16.

Freeman, M. (1998) 'The sociology of childhood and children's rights', *International Journal of Children's Rights*, 6(4): 433–44.

Freeman, M. (2020) *A magna carta for children? Rethinking children's rights.* Cambridge: TJ International Ltd.

Freeman, N.K. (2007) 'Preschoolers' perceptions of gender appropriate toys and their parents' beliefs about genderized behaviors: Miscommunication, mixed messages, or hidden truths?', *Early Childhood Education Journal*, 34(5): 357–66.

Freese, A.R. (2006) 'Reframing one's teaching: Discovering our teacher selves through reflection and inquiry', *Teaching and Teacher Education*, 22(1): 100–19.

Freire, P. (1984) *Pedagogy of the oppressed.* London: Penguin Books.

Froebel Trust (2021) *Froebelian futures.* www.froebel.ed.ac.uk/frobelian-futures (accessed 21 October 2021).

Frones, I. (1993) 'Changing childhood', *Childhood*, 1(1): 1–2.

Fuchs, E. (2007) 'Children's rights and global civil society', *Comparative Education*, 43(8): 393–412.

Fullan, M. (2004) *Leading in a culture of change.* San Francisco: John Wiley & Sons.

Fullan, M. (2007) *The new meaning of educational change.* New York: Routledge.

Fuson, K. (2009) 'Avoiding misinterpretations of Piaget and Vygotsky: Mathematical teaching without learning, learning without teaching, or helpful learning-path teaching?', *Cognitive Development*, 24(4): 343–63.

Fyfe, B. (2012) 'The relationship between documentation and assessment', in C. Edwards, L. Gandini and G. Forman (eds), *The hundred languages of children (Third edition).* Santa Barbara, CA: Praeger, pp. 273–91.

Gandini, L. (2011) 'Play and the hundred languages of children: An interview with Lella Gandini', *American Journal of Play*, 4(1): 1–18.

Gaunt, C. (2021) *Parents 'will be turned away' due to Level 3 staffing crisis.* www.nurseryworld.co.uk/news/article/parents-will-be-turned-away-due-to-level-3-staffing-crisis (accessed 13 October 2021).

Geddes, H. (2003) 'Attachment and the child in school: Part 1', *Emotional and Behavioural Difficulties*, 8(3): 231–42.

Geddes, H. (2017) 'Attachment behaviour and learning', in D. Colley and P. Cooper (eds), *Attachment and emotional development in the classroom.* London: Jessica Kingsley, pp. 37–48.

Gee, J. (2012) *Social linguistics and literacies: Ideology in discourses (Fourth edition).* New York: Routledge.

Gelman, R. and Gallistel, C. (1978) *The child's understanding of number.* Cambridge, MA: Harvard University Press.

General Teaching Council for Scotland (GTCS) (2021) *The standard for full registration.* Edinburgh: GTCS.

Gerin, M.I., Hanson, E., Viding, E. and McCrory, E.J. (2019) 'A review of childhood maltreatment, latent vulnerability and the brain: Implications for clinical practice and prevention', *Adoption and Fostering*, 43(3): 310–28.

Gesell, A. (1934) *An atlas of infant behavior: A systematic delineation of the forms and early growth of human behavior patterns.* New Haven, CT: Yale University Press.

Ghazinoory, S., Esmail Zadeh, A. and Memariani, A. (2007) 'Fuzzy SWOT analysis', *Journal of Intelligent & Fuzzy Systems*, 18(1): 99–108.

Gianoutsos, J. (2006) 'Locke and Rousseau: Early childhood education', *The Pulse*, 4(1): 1–23.

Gibbs, G. (1988) *Learning by doing: A guide to teaching and learning methods*. Oxford: Oxford Brookes University.

Gibbs, S., Beckmann, J.F., Elliott, J., Metsäpelto, R.-L., Vehkakoski, T. and Aro, M. (2020) 'What's in a name: The effect of category labels on teachers' beliefs', *European Journal of Special Needs Education*, 35(1): 115–27.

Gibson, J.J. (1979) 'The theory of affordances', in R. Shaw and J. Branford (eds), *Perceiving, acting, and knowing: Toward an ecological psychology*. Hillsdale, NJ: Erlbaum, pp. 127–37.

Gifford, S. (2005) *Teaching mathematics 3 – 5: Developing learning in the foundation stage*. Maindenhead: Open University Press.

Gilchrist, G. (2018) *Practitioner enquiry: Professional development with impact for teachers, schools and systems*. London: Taylor and Francis.

Gill, T. (2007) *No fear: Growing up in a risk averse society*. London: Calouste Gulbenkian Foundation.

Gillard, D. (2018) *Education in England: A history*. www.educationengland.org.uk/history (accessed 29 October 2021).

Gilster, P. (1997) *Digital literacy*. New York: Wiley.

Giltinane, C.L. (2013) 'Leadership styles and theories', *Nursing Standard*, 27(41): 35–9.

Ginsburg, H. (2006) 'Mathematical play and playful mathematics: A guide for early education', in D. Singer, R. Golinkoff and K. Hirsh-Pasek (eds), *Play = learning: How play motivates and and enhances children's cognitive and social-emotional growth*. Oxford: Oxford University Press, pp. 145–65.

Ginsburg, H. (2016) 'Helping early childhood educators to understand and assess young children's mathematical minds', *ZDM Mathematics Education*, 48(7): 941–6.

Glasgow Centre for Population Health (GCPH) (2014) *Nurture corners in nurseries: Exploring perspectives on nurture approaches in preschool provision in Glasgow*. Glasgow: GCPH.

Goddard, C. (2020) *Play – Children's workforce guide to qualifications and training*. www.cypnow.co.uk/other/article/play-children-s-workforce-guide-to-qualifications-and-training (accessed 13 October 2021).

Goddard, C. (2021) *Early years – Children's workforce guide to qualifications and training*. www.cypnow.co.uk/other/article/early-years-children-s-workforce-guide-to-qualifications-and-training-1 (accessed 12 October 2021).

Goldschmied, E. and Selleck, D. (1996) *Communication between babies in their first year*. London: National Children's Bureau.

Goodall, J. and Montgomery, C. (2014) 'Parental involvement to parental engagement: A continuum', *Educational Review*, 66(4): 399–410.

Goodhall, N. and Atkinson, C. (2019) 'How do children distinguish between "play" and "work"? Conclusions from the literature', *Early Child Development and Care*, 189(10): 1695–708.

Goouch, K. (2009) 'Forging and fostering relationships in play: Whose zone is it anyway?', in T. Papatheodorou and J. Moyles (eds), *Learning together in the early years: Exploring relational pedagogy*. Abingdon: Routledge, pp. 139–51.

Gornick, J.C. and Meyers, M. (2003) *Families that work: Policies for reconciling parenthood and employment*. New York: Russell Sage Foundation.

Gorozidis, G. and Papaioannou, A.G. (2014) 'Teachers' motivation to participate in training and to implement innovations', *Teaching and Teacher Education*, 39(1): 1–11.

Gray, P. (1994) *Psychology (Second edition)*. Boston: Worth Publishers.

Gray, P. (2011) 'The decline of play and the rise of psychopathology in children and adolescents', *American Journal of Play*, 3(4): 443–63.

Gronn, P. (2002) 'Distributed leadership', in K.A. Leithwood and P. Hallinger (eds), *Second international handbook of educational leadership and administration*. Dordrecht: Springer, pp. 653–96.

Guba, E.G. (1990) 'The alternative paradigm dialog', in E.G. Guba (ed.), *The paradigm dialog*. London: SAGE, pp. 17–31.

Guba, E.G. and Lincoln, Y.S. (1994) 'Competing paradigms in qualitative research', in N.K. Denzin and Y.S. Lincoln (eds), *The SAGE handbook of qualitative research*. Thousand Oaks, CA: SAGE, pp. 163–94.

Gunderson, E.A., Ramirez, G., Beilock, S.L. and Levine, S.C. (2012) 'The relation between spatial skill and early number knowledge: The role of the linear number line', *Developmental Psychology*, 48(5): 1229–41.

Gunkel, D.J. (2003) 'Second thoughts: Toward a critique of the digital divide', *New Media & Society*, 5(4): 499–522.

Guy-Evans, O. (2020) *Bronfenbrenner's ecological systems theory*. www.simplypsychology. org/Bronfenbrenner.html (accessed 9 December 2021).

Hadley, E., Newman, K. and Mock, J. (2020) 'Setting the stage for TALK: Strategies for encouraging language-building conversations', *The Reading Teacher*, 74(1): 39–48.

Haines, A.M. (2000) 'Montessori in early childhood: Positive outcomes among social, moral, cognitive and emotional dimensions', *NAMTA Journal*, 25(2): 27–59.

Hairston, M. (1982) 'The winds of change: Thomas Kuhn and the revolution in teaching of writing', *College Composition and Communication*, 33(1): 76–88.

Hallet, E. (2013) '"We all share a common vision and passion": Early years professionals reflect upon their leadership of practice role', *Journal of Early Childhood Research*, 11(3): 312–25.

Hallinger, P. and Heck, R.H. (2010) 'Leadership for learning: Does collaborative leadership make a difference in school improvement?', *Educational Management Administration & Leadership*, 38(6): 654–78.

Hammersley, M. (2013) *What is qualitative research?* London: Bloomsbury.

Hannula-Sormunen, M., Lehtinen, E. and Räsänen, P. (2015) 'Preschool children's spontaneous focusing on numerosity, subitizing and counting skills as predictors of their mathematical performance seven years later at school', *Mathematical Thinking and Learning*, 17(2–3): 155–77.

Hannula-Sormunen, M., Nanu, C., Luomaniemi, K., Heinonen, M., Sorariutta, A., Södervik, I. and Mattinen, A. (2020) 'Promoting spontaneous focusing on numerosity and cardinality-related skills at day care with one, two, how many and count, how many programs', *Mathematical Thinking and Learning*, 22(4): 312–31.

Hard, L. and Jónsdóttir, A.H. (2013) 'Leadership is not a dirty word: Exploring and embracing leadership in ECEC', *European Early Childhood Education Research Journal*, 21(3): 311–25.

Harding, F.M.L. (1991) 'The Children Act 1989 in context: Four perspectives in child care law and policy (I)', *The Journal of Social Welfare and Family Law*, 13(3): 179–93.

Hargreaves, A. (2005) 'The emotions of teaching and educational change', in A. Hargreaves, *Extending educational change: International handbook of educational change*. Dordrecht: Springer, pp. 278–95.

Harmon, M. (2018) *'I'm a Catholic Buddhist': The voice of children on religion and religious education in an Irish Catholic primary school classroom*. https://doras.dcu.ie/22639/ (accessed 27 January 2022).

Harms, T., Clifford, R.M. and Cryer, D. (2014) *Early childhood environment rating scale (Third edition)*. New York: Teachers College Press.

Harper, N.J. (2017) 'Outdoor risky play and healthy child development in the shadow of the "risk society": A forest and nature school perspective', *Child and Youth Services*, 38(4): 318–34.

Harris, F. (2018) 'Outdoor learning spaces: The case of forest school', *Area*, 50(2): 222–31.

Harste, J., Woodward, V. and Burke, C. (1984) *Language stories and literacy lessons*. Portsmouth, NH: Heinemann.

Hart, R.A. (1992) *Children's participation: From tokenism to citizenship (Innocenti essays No. 4)*. Florence: UNICEF International Child Development Centre.

Hart, S.N. (1991) 'From property to person status: Historical perspective on children's rights', *American Psychologist*, 46(1): 53–9.

Hartman, H. (2002) *Scaffolding and co-operative learning: Human learning and instruction*. New York: City College of the City University of New York Press.

Hartwig, S.J. and Schwabe, F. (2018) 'Teacher attitudes and motivation as mediators between teacher training, collaboration, and differentiated instruction', *Journal for Educational Research Online*, 10(1): 100–22.

Health and Safety Executive (2012) *Children's play and leisure – Promoting a balanced approach*. www.hse.gov.uk/entertainment/childrens-play-july-2012.pdf (accessed 1 April 2022).

Heckman, J. (2012) *Invest in early childhood development: Reduce deficits, strengthen the economy*. Ann Arbor, MI: The Heckman Equation.

Heckman, J. and Masterov, D. (2007) 'The productivity argument for investing in young children', *Review of Agricultural Economics*, 29(3): 446–93.

Heft, H. (1988) 'Affordances of children's environments: A functional approach to environmental description', *Children's Environmental Quarterly*, 5(3): 29–37.

Heikka, J. and Waniganayake, M. (2011) 'Pedagogical leadership from a distributed perspective within the context of early childhood education', *International Journal of Leadership in Education*, 14(4): 499–512.

Hendrick, H. (2008) 'The child as a social actor in historical sources: Problems of identification and interpretation', in P. Christensen and A. James (eds), *Research with children's perspectives and practices (Second edition)*. Abingdon: Routledge, pp. 40–65.

Hendrick, H. (2015) 'Constructions and reconstructions of British childhood: An interpretative survey, 1800 to the present', in A. James and A. Prout (eds), *Constructing and reconstructing childhood: Contemporary issues in the sociological study of childhood* (Second edition). London: Falmer Press, pp. 34–62.

Heron, J. and Reason, P. (1997) 'A participatory inquiry paradigm', *Qualitative Inquiry*, 3(3): 274–94.

Hillman, J. and Williams, T. (2015) *Early years education and childcare: Lessons from evidence and future priorities*. London: Nuffield Foundation.

Hodson, D. and Hodson, J. (1998) 'From constructivism to social constructivism: A Vygotskian perspective on teaching and learning science', *School Science Review*, 79(289): 33–41.

Hoffman, S. (2019) 'The UN Convention on the Rights of the Child, decentralisation and legislation integration: A case study from Wales', *The International Journal of Human Rights*, 23(3): 374–91.

Hogg, N. (2019) *The UNCRC: In our stride, or a giant leap*. www.lawscot.org.uk/members/journal/issues/vol-64-issue-06/the-uncrc-in-our-stride-or-a-giant-leap (accessed 25 February 2022).

Holden, J. (2006) *Cultural value and the crisis of legitimacy*. London: Demos.

Holloway, I. and Galvin, K. (2017) *Qualitative research in nursing and healthcare (Fourth edition)*. London: Wiley Blackwell.

Holloway, I. and Wheeler, S. (2013) *Qualitative research in nursing and healthcare (Third edition)*. London: Wiley.

Holmes, H. and Burgess, G. (2021) *New horizons: Digital exclusion and the importance of getting online*. Cambridge: Cambridge Centre for Housing & Planning Research, University of Cambridge.

Holmqvist, M. and Lelinge, B. (2021) 'Teachers' collaborative professional development for inclusive education', *European Journal of Special Needs Education*, 36(5): 819–33.

Horppu, R. and Ikonen-Varila, M. (2004) 'Mental models of attachment as a part of kindergarten student teachers' practical knowledge about caregiving', *International Journal of Early Years Education*, 12(3): 231–43.

Horsburgh, J. (2022) *Improving outcomes for looked after children*. Bingley: Emerald.

Houser, J. (2018) *Nursing research: Reading, using, and creating evidence (Fourth edition)*. Burlington, MA: Jones and Bartlett.

Houston, G. (2019) *Inclusion – My story*. www.nurseryworld.co.uk/features/article/inclusion-my-story (accessed 15 January 2022).

Howard, J. and McInnes, K. (2013) *The essence of play*. Abingdon: Routledge.

Hoyle, E. (2001) 'Teaching: Prestige, status and esteem', *Educational Management Administration & Leadership*, 29(2): 139–52.

Hughes, B. (1996) *Play environments: A question of quality*. London: Playlink.

Hughes, B. (2002) *A playworker's taxonomy of play types (Second edition)*. London: Playlink.

Hughes, B. (2012) *Evolutionary playwork (Second edition)*. Abingdon: Routledge.

Hughes, N.K. and Schlösser, A. (2014) 'The effectiveness of nurture groups: A systematic review', *Emotional and Behavioural Difficulties*, 19(4): 386–409.

Human Rights Watch (2021) *Years don't wait for them: Increased inequalities in children's right to education due to the Covid-19 pandemic.* www.hrw.org/report/2021/05/17/years-dont-wait-them/increased-inequalities-childrens-right-education-due-covid (accessed 17 January 2022).

Humanist UK (2021) *Success! Scotland enshrines UN Convention on Children's Rights into law.* https://humanists.uk/2021/03/17/success-scotland-enshrines-un-convention-on-childrens-rights-into-law (accessed 10 January 2022).

Humes, W. and Priestley, M. (2021) 'Curriculum reform in Scottish education: Discourse, narrative and enactment', in M. Priestley, D. Alvunger, S. Philippou and T. Soini (eds), *Curriculum making in Europe: Policy and practice within and across diverse contexts.* Bingley: Emerald, pp. 175–98.

Hussain, M.A., Elyas, T. and Naseef, O.A. (2013) 'Research paradigms: A slippery slope for fresh researchers', *Life Science Journal*, 10(4): 2374–81.

Hutchinson, J., Bonetti, S., Creena-Jennings, W. and Akhal, A. (2019) *Education in England: Annual report 2019.* London: Education Policy Institute.

I CAN (2021) *About us.* https://ican.org.uk/about-us/ (accessed 26 October 2021).

Ihmeideh, F.M. and Al-Qaryouti, I.A. (2016) 'Exploring kindergarten teachers' views and roles regarding children's outdoor play environments in Oman', *Early Years*, 36(1): 81–96.

Ingleby, E. (2015) '"We don't just do what we're told to do!" Exploring pedagogical technology development needs', *International Journal of Early Education*, 24(1): 36–48.

Inkeles, A. (1968) *Social change in Soviet Russia.* Cambridge, MA: Harvard University Press.

Institute of Learning (IoL) (2021) *About outdoor learning.* www.outdoor-learning.org/Good-Practice/Research-Resources/About-Outdoor-Learning (accessed 26 October 2021).

International Council of Education Advisers (ICEA) (2020) *International Council of Education Advisers: Report 2018–2020.* Edinburgh: Scottish Government.

International Play Association (IPA) (2013) *Summary of United Nations general comment No. 17.* http://ipaworld.org/wp-content/uploads/2013/11/IPA-Summary-of-UN-GC-article-31_FINAL1.pdf (accessed 6 February 2022).

Jacobson, M.J., Levin, J.A. and Kapur, M. (2019) 'Education as a complex system: Conceptual and methodological implications', *Educational Researcher*, 48(2): 112–19.

James, A. and James, A. (2004) *Constructing childhood: Theory, policy and social practice.* Basingstoke: Palgrave Macmillan.

James, A. and Prout, A. (2015) 'A new paradigm for the sociology of childhood: Provenance, promise and problems', in A. James and A. Prout (eds), *Constructing and reconstructing childhood: Contemporary issues in the sociological study of childhood (Second edition).* London: Falmer Press, pp. 1–7.

James, A., Jenks, C. and Prout, A. (1998) *Theorizing childhood.* Cambridge: Polity.

Jans, M. (2004) 'Children as citizens: Towards a contemporary notion of child participation', *Childhood*, 11(1): 27–44.

Janssen, I. (2015) 'Hyper-parenting is negatively associated with physical activity among 7–12-year-olds', *Preventive. Medicine*, 73(April): 55–9.

Janssen, J., Stoyanov, S., Ferrari, A., Punie, Y., Pannekeet, K. and Sloep, P. (2013) 'Experts' views on digital competence: Commonalities and differences', *Computers & Education*, 68: 473–81.

Jarman, E. (2008) 'Creating spaces that are "communication friendly"', *Mathematics Teaching*, 209: 31–3.

Jarvis, M. (2005) *The psychology of effective learning and teaching*. Cheltenham: Nelson Thornes.

Jarzabkowski, P., Balogun, J. and Seidle, D. (2007) 'Strategizing: The challenges of a practice perspective', *Human Relations*, 60(1): 55–61.

Jellesma, F.C. and Vingerhoets, J.J.M. (2012) 'Crying in middle childhood: A report on gender differences', *Sex Roles*, 67(1): 412–21.

Jenkins, P., Finlay, J. and Cameron, J. (2020) *Reducing mental health stigma and discrimination in schools – the benefits of a local authority approach*. Glasgow: Mental Health Foundation Scotland.

Jenks, C. (2002) 'A sociological approach to childhood development', in P.K. Smith and C.H. Hart (eds), *Blackwell handbook of childhood social development*. London: Blackwell Publishers, pp. 78–94.

Jones, J. (2005) *Management skills in schools: A resource for school leaders*. London: Paul Chapman.

Jordan, A., Carlile, O. and Stack, A. (2008) *Approaches to learning*. Maidenhead: Open University Press.

Kalpogianni, D.E. (2019) 'Why are the children not outdoors? Factors supporting and hindering outdoor play in Greek public day-care centres', *International Journal of Play*, 8(2): 155–73.

Kamii, C. (1996) 'Piaget's theory and the teaching of arithmetic', *Prospects*, 26(1): 99–111.

Karami-Akkary, R., Mahfouz, J. and Mansour, S. (2019) 'Sustaining school-based improvement: Considering emotional responses to change', *Journal of Educational Administration*, 57(1): 50–67.

Karkhaneh, M., Clark, B., Ospina, M.B., Seida, J.C., Smith, V. and Hartling, L. (2010) 'Social stories to improve social skills in children with autism spectrum disorder: A systematic review', *Autism*, 14(6): 641–62.

Karsten, L. (2005) 'It all used to be better? Different generations on continuity and change in urban children's daily use of space', *Children's Geographies*, 3(3): 275–90.

Kashin, D. (2019) *A provoking post on provocations*. https://tecribresearch.wordpress.com/2019/09/28/a-provoking-post-on-provocations (accessed 19 January 2022).

Kelly, P., Watt, L. and Giddens, S. (2020) 'An attachment aware schools programme: A safe space, a nurturing learning community', *Pastoral Care in Education*, 38(4): 335–54.

Kelly, S. (2019) *Reflective practice vs reflexive practice*. www.parenta.com/2019/05/01/reflective-practice-vs-reflexive-practice (accessed 30 January 2022).

Kemple, K.M., Oh, J., Kenney, E. and Smith-Bonahue, T. (2016) 'The power of outdoor play and play in natural environments', *Childhood Education*, 92(6): 446–54.

Kendrick, A. (2004) *Recent developments in child protection policy and practice in Scotland and the UK*. https://strathprints.strath.ac.uk/1988/6/strathprints001988.pdf (accessed 1 April 2022).

Kennedy, A. (2011) 'Collaborative continuing professional development (CPD) for teachers in Scotland: Aspirations, opportunities and barriers', *European Journal of Teacher Education*, 34(1): 25–41.

Kennedy, J.H. and Kennedy, C.E. (2004) 'Attachment theory: Implications for school psychology', *Psychology in the Schools*, 41(2): 247–59.

Kerber-Ganse, W. (2015) 'Eglantyne Jebb – a pioneer of the Convention on the Rights of the Child', *International Journal of Children's Rights*, 23(2): 272–82.

Khanlou, N. and Wray, R. (2014) 'A whole community approach toward child and youth resilience promotion: A review of resilience literature', *International Journal of Mental Health and Addiction*, 12(1): 64–79.

Kiley, T.J. and Jensen, R.A. (2003) 'Assessing the climate of an early childhood centre by using key features of organisational culture', *European Early Childhood Research Journal*, 11(2): 77–100.

Kilkelly, U. (2001) 'The best of both worlds for children's rights: Interpreting the European CRC on Human Rights in the light of the UN Convention on the Rights of the Child', *Human Rights Quarterly*, 23(2): 308–26.

Kilvington, J. and Wood, A. (2018) *Reflective playwork: For all who work with children (Second edition)*. London: Bloomsbury.

Kim, C. and Pekrun, R. (2013) 'Emotions and motivation in learning and performance', in J. Spector, M. Merrill, J. Elen and M. Bishop (eds), *Handbook of research on educational communities and technology*. New York: Springer, pp. 65–75.

Kimmons, R. and Hall, C. (2017) 'How useful are our models? Pre-service and practicing teacher evaluations of technology integration models', *Tech Trends*, 62(1): 29–36.

Kinard, T., Gainer, J., Valdez-Gainer, N., Volk, D. and Long, S. (2021) 'Interrogating the "gold standard": Play-based early childhood education and perpetuating white supremacy', *Theory into Practice*, 60(3): 322–32.

Kincheloe, J.L. and McLaren, P. (2005) 'Rethinking critical theory and qualitative research', in N.K. Denzin and Y.S. Lincoln (eds), *The SAGE handbook of qualitative research (Third Edition)*. Thousand Oaks, CA: SAGE, pp. 303–32.

King, P. and Newstead, S. (2018) *Researching play from a playwork perspective*. Abingdon: Routledge.

King, P. and Newstead, S. (2019) 'Childcare worker's understanding of the Play Cycle Theory: Can a focus on "process not product" contribute to quality childcare experiences?', *Child Care in Practice*. https://cronfa.swan.ac.uk/Record/cronfa51697 (accessed 28 February 2022).

King, P. and Newstead, S. (2020) 'Re-defining the play cycle: An empirical study of playworkers' understanding of playwork theory', *Journal of Early Childhood Research*, 18(1): 99–111.

Kivunja, C. and Kuyini, A.B. (2017) 'Understanding and applying research paradigms in educational contexts', *International Journal of Higher Education*, 6(5): 26–41.

Klegon, D. (1978) 'The sociology of professions: An emerging perspective', *Work and Occupations*, 5(3): 259–83.

Klerfelt, A. and Haglund, B. (2014) 'Presentation of research on school-age Educare in Sweden', *International Journal for Research on Extended Education*, 2(1): 45–62.

Klevering, N. and McNae, R. (2018) 'Making sense of leadership in early childhood education: Tensions and complexities between concepts and practices', *Journal of Educational Leadership, Policy and Practice*, 33(1): 5–17.

Kluczniok, K. and Schmidt, T. (2020) 'Socio-cultural disparities in the quality of children's interactions in preschools', *European Early Childhood Education Research Journal*, 28(4): 519–33.

Knopf, H.T. and Swick, K.J. (2007) 'How parents feel about their child's teacher/school: Implications for early childhood professionals', *Early Childhood Education Journal*, 34(4): 291–6.

Kokko, A.K. and Hirsto, L. (2021) 'From physical spaces to learning environments: Processes in which physical spaces are transformed into learning environments', *Learning Environments Research*, 24(3): 71–85.

Kolb, D. (1984) *Experiential learning: Experience as the source of learning and development*. Englewood Cliffs, NJ: Prentice-Hall.

Kolb, D. (2015) *Experiential learning: Experiences as the source of learning and development (Second edition)*. Upper Saddle River, NJ: Pearson Education.

Kolkman, M.E., Kroesbergen, E.H. and Leseman, P.P. (2013) 'Early numerical development and the role of non-symbolic and symbolic skills', *Learning and Instruction*, 25: 95–103.

Korthagen, F.A. (2007) 'The gap between research and practice revisited', *Educational Research and Evaluation: An International Journal on Theory and Practice*, 13(3): 303–10.

Kosher, H., Ben-Arieh, A. and Hendelsman, Y. (2016) *Children's rights and social work*. Cham: Springer.

Kotter, J.P. (1995) 'Leading change: Why transformation efforts fail', *Harvard Business Review*, March–April: 59–67.

Krieg, S., Smith, K.A. and Davis, K. (2014) 'Exploring the dance of early childhood educational leadership', *Australasian Journal of Early Childhood*, 39(1): 73–80.

Kuperminc, G., Chan, W.Y., Hale, K.E. and Joseph, H. (2019) 'The role of school-based group mentoring in promoting resilience among vulnerable high school students', *American Journal of Community Psychology*, 65(1–2): 136–48.

Kuschner, D. (2012) 'Play is natural to childhood but school is not: The problem of integrating play into the curriculum', *International Journal of Play*, 1(3): 242–9.

Kyttä, M. (2003) *Children in outdoor contexts: Affordances and independent mobility in the assessment of environmental child friendliness*. PhD thesis, Helsinki University of Technology.

Lacey, R.E. and Minnis, H. (2020) 'Practitioner review: Twenty years of research with adverse childhood experience scores – advantages, disadvantages and applications to practice', *The Journal of Child Psychology and Psychiatry*, 61(2): 116–30.

Ladson-Billings, G. (2014) 'Culturally relevant pedagogy 2.0: a.k.a the remix', *Harvard Educational Review*, 84(1): 74–84.

Lahikainen, A.R. and Arminen, I. (2017) 'Family, media and the digitalization of childhood', in A.R. Lahikainen, T. Mälakä and K. Repo (eds), *Media, family and the digitalization of childhood*. Northampton, MA: Edward Elgar, pp. 185–93.

Laming, W.H. (2003) *The Victoria Climbié inquiry: Report of an inquiry by Lord Laming*. London: HMSO.

Lansdown, G. (2006) 'International developments in children's participation: Lessons and challenges', in K. Tisdall, J. Davis, M. Hill and A. Prout (eds), *Children, young people and social inclusion: Participation for what?* Bristol: Policy Press, pp. 140–56.

Lansdown, G. (2014) '25 years of UNCRC: Lessons learned in children's participation', *Canadian Journal of Children's Rights*, 1(1): 172–90.

le Roux, J. (2002) 'Effective educators are culturally competent communicators', *Intercultural Education*, 13(1): 37–48.

Leadbetter, J., Daniels, H., Edwards, A., Martin, D., Middleton, D., Popova, A., Warmington, P., Apostlov, A. and Brown, S. (2007) 'Professional learning within multi-agency children's services: Researching into practice', *Educational Research*, 49(1): 83–98.

Learning and Teaching Scotland (2010) *Curriculum for excellence through outdoor learning.* Glasgow: Learning and Teaching Scotland.

Leeson, C. and Bamsey, V. (2015) 'In praise of reflective practice', in R. Parker-Rees and C. Leeson (eds), *Early childhood studies: An introduction to the study of children's lives and children's worlds (Fourth edition).* London: SAGE, pp. 251–64.

Lefrancois, G. R. (2000) *Theories of human learning: What the old man said (Fourth edition).* London: Thomson Learning Berkshire House.

Leithwood, K. (2001) 'School leadership in the context of accountability policies', *International Journal of Leadership in Education*, 4(3): 217–35.

Leonard, M (2016) *The sociology of children childhood and generation.* London: SAGE.

Lester, S. (2008) 'Play and the play stage', in F. Brown and C. Taylor (eds), *Foundations of playwork.* Maidenhead: Open University Press, pp. 55–58.

Lester, S. (2018) 'Playwork and the co-creation of play spaces: The rhythms and refrains of a play environment', in F. Brown and B. Hughes (eds), *Aspects of playwork: Play and culture studies, Vol. 14.* London: Rowman and Littlefield, pp. 75–92.

Lester, S. and Russell, W. (2008a) *Play for a change – Play policy and practice: A review of contemporary perspectives.* London: Play England.

Lester, S. and Russell, W. (2008b) *Summary report. Play for a change. Play, policy and practice: A review of contemporary perspectives.* London: National Children's Bureau.

Levers, M.J.D. (2013) 'Philosophical paradigms, grounded theory, and perspectives on emergence', *Research Methodology and Design*, 3(4): 1–6.

Levine, S.C., Ratliff, K.R., Huttenlocher, J. and Cannon, J. (2012) 'Early puzzle play: A predictor of preschoolers' spatial transformation skill', *Developmental Psychology*, 48(2): 530–42.

Lillard, A.S. (2017) *Montessori: The science behind the genius (Third edition).* New York: Oxford University Press.

Lillard, A.S., Lerner, M.D., Hopkins, E.J., Dore, R.A., Smith E.D. and Palmquist, C.M. (2013) 'The impact of pretend play on children's development: A review of the evidence', *Psychological Bulletin*, 139(1): 1–34.

Lincoln, Y. and Guba, E.G. (1985) *Naturalistic inquiry.* Newbury Park, CA: SAGE.

Lindahl, M.G. and Folkesson, A. (2012) 'ICT in preschool: Friend or foe? The significance of norms in a changing practice', *International Journal of Early Years Education*, 20(4): 422–36.

Lindon, J. and Webb, J. (2020) *Safeguarding and child protection (Fifth edition)*. London: Hodder Education.

Lindsay, G., Strand, S. and Davis, H. (2011) 'A comparison of the effectiveness of three parenting programmes in improving parenting skills, parent mental well-being and children's behaviour when implemented on a large scale in community settings in 18 English local authorities: The parenting early intervention pathfinder (PEIP)', *BMC Public Health*, 11(1): 1–13.

Linting, M., Groeneveld, M.G., Vermeer, H.J. and van Ijzendoorn, M.H. (2013) 'Threshold for noise in daycare: Noise level and noise variability are associated with child wellbeing in home-based childcare', *Early Childhood Research Quarterly*, 28(4): 960–71.

Little, H. and Wyver, S. (2008) 'Outdoor play: Does avoiding the risks reduce the benefits?', *Australian Journal of Early Childhood*, 33(2): 33–40.

Liu, C., Solis, S.L., Jensen, H., Hopkins, E.J., Neale, D., Zosh, J.M., Hirsh-Pasek, K. and Whitebread, D. (2017) *Neuroscience and learning through play: A review of the evidence (research summary)*. Billund: The LEGO Foundation.

Local Government Association (2022) *The Equality Act and protected characteristics*. https://local.gov.uk/equality-act-and-protected-characteristics (accessed 17 June 2022).

Locke, J. (1996) *Some thoughts concerning education, and of the conduct of the understanding, 1693* (R.W. Grant and N. Narcov, eds). London: Clarendon Press.

Loebach, J. and Cox, A. (2020) 'Tool for Observing Play Outdoors (TOPO): A new typology for capturing children's play behaviors in outdoor environments', *International Journal of Environmental Research and Public Health*, 17(15): 1–34.

Louv, R. (2005) *Last child in the woods: Saving our children from nature-deficit disorder*. Chapel Hill, NC: Algonquin Books.

Lui, C. and Audran, J. (2017) 'Analysis of young children's technology difficulties and challenges in operating and using educational application in tablet', *International Journal of Information and Education Technology*, 7(12): 893–9.

Lund, A., Furberg, A., Bakken, J. and Engelien, K. (2014) 'What does professional digital competence mean in teacher education?', *Nordic Journal of Digital Literacy*, 9(4): 281–99.

Lundy, L. (2007) 'Voice is not enough: Conceptualising Article 12 of the United Nations Convention on the Rights of the Child', *British Educational Research Journal*, 33(6): 927–42.

Lundy, L. (2018) 'In defence of tokenism? Implementing children's right to participate in collective decision-making', *Childhood*, 25(3): 340–54.

Lundy, L., Kilkelly, U., Byrne, B. and Kang, J. (2012) *The UN Convention on the Right of the Child: A study of legal implementation in 12 countries*. Belfast: Queen's University Belfast.

Lundy, L., Kilkelly, U. and Byrne, B. (2013) 'Incorporation of the United Nations Convention on the Rights of the Child in law: A comparative review', *International Journal of Children's Rights*, 21(3): 442–63.

Lynch, J. and Redpath, T. (2014) '"Smart" technologies in early years literacy education: A meta-narrative of paradigmatic tensions in iPad use in an Australian preparatory classroom', *Journal of Early Childhood Literacy*, 14(2): 147–74.

Lyons, S. (2017) *The repair of early trauma: A 'bottom up' approach*. Littlehampton: Beacon House.

Lyttleton-Smith, J. (2019) 'Objects of conflict: (Re) configuring early childhood experiences of gender in the preschool classroom', *Gender and Education*, 31(6): 655–72.

MacBeath, J. (2003) *The alphabet soup of leadership*. Cambridge: Leadership for Learning, University of Cambridge.

Madanipour, P. and Cohrssen, C. (2020) 'Augmented reality as a form of digital technology in early childhood education', *Australasian Journal of Early Childhood*, 45(1): 5–13.

Main, M. and Solomon, J. (1986) 'Discovery of a new, insecure-disorganized/disoriented attachment pattern', in T.B. Brazelton and M. Yogman (eds), *Affective development in infancy*. Norwood, NJ: Ablex, pp. 95–124.

Maller, C., Townsend, M., Pryor, A., Brown, P. and St Leger, L. (2006) 'Healthy nature healthy people: "Contact with nature" as an upstream health promotion intervention for populations', *Health Promotion International*, 21(1): 45–54.

Malone, K. (2007) 'The bubble-wrap generation: Children growing up in walled gardens', *Environmental Education Research*, 13(4): 513–27.

Manches, A. and Plowman, L. (2017) 'Computing education in children's early years: A call for debate', *British Journal of Educational Technology*, 48(1): 191–201.

Manning-Morton, J. and Thorp, M. (2006) *Key times: A framework for developing high quality provision for children from birth to three*. Maidenhead: Open University Press.

March, S. and Kearney, M. (2017) 'A psychological service contribution to nurture: Glasgow's nurturing city', *Emotional and Behavioural Difficulties*, 22(3): 237–47.

Marion, M. (2004) *Using observation in early childhood education*. Upper Saddle River, NJ: Pearson Education.

Marsh, J., Plowman, L., Yamada-Rice, D., Bishop, J. and Scott, F. (2016) 'Digital play: A new classification', *Early Years*, 36(3): 242–53.

Martens, D.M. (2015) *Research and evaluation in education and psychology (Fourth edition)*. London: SAGE.

Martin, R.A. (2000) *An introduction to educational alternatives*. www.educationrevolution. org/store/resources/alternatives/introtoalternatives (accessed 20 October 2021).

Martin, R.B., Cirino, P.T., Sharp, C. and Barnes, M. (2014) 'Number and counting skills in kindergarten as predictors of grade 1 mathematical skills', *Learning and Individual Differences*, 34: 12–23.

Mashburn, A.J, Pianta, R.C., Hamre, B.K., Downer, J.T., Barbarin, O.A., Bryant, D., Burchinal, M., Early, D.M. and Howes, C. (2008) 'Measures of classroom quality in prekindergarten and children's development of academic language, and social skills', *Child Development*, 79(3): 732–49.

Massey, D. (2005) *For space*. London: SAGE.

May, W. (2001) *Beleaguered rulers: The public obligation of the professional*. Louisville, KY: John Knox Press.

Mayall, B. (1994) *Children's childhoods: Observed and experienced*. London: Falmer.

Maynard, T., Waters, J. and Clement, J. (2013) 'Child-initiated learning, the outdoor environment and the "underachieving" child', *Early Years*, 33(3): 212–25.

McArdle, K. and Coutts, N. (2010) 'Taking teachers' continuous professional development (CPD) beyond reflection: Adding shared sense-making and collaborative engagement for professional renewal', *Studies in Continuing Education*, 32(3): 201–15.

McCaslin, M. Vega, R.I., Anderson, E.E., Calderon, C.N. and Labistre, A.M. (2011) 'Tabletalk: Navigating and negotiating in small-group learning', in D.M. McInerney, R.A. Walker and G.A.D. Liem (eds), *Sociocultural theories of learning and motivation: Looking back, looking forward.* Charlotte, NC: Information Age Publishing, pp. 191–222.

McDonald, J.L., Milne, S., Knight, J. and Webster, V. (2012) 'Developmental and behavioural characteristics of children enrolled in a child protection pre-school', *Journal of Paediatrics and Child Health*, 49(2): E142–6.

McDowall Clark, R. (2012) '"I've never thought of myself as a leader but…": The early years professional and catalytic leadership', *European Early Childhood Education Research Journal*, 20(3): 391–401.

McKendrick, J.H. (2021) *Holiday out of school provision in Scotland: Case study analyses of claims to impact and drivers of success.* Glasgow: Scottish Poverty and Inequality Research Unit.

McKenna, M. (2020) 'Improving educational outcomes through Getting it Right for Every Child in Glasgow', *European Review*, 28(suppl. 1): S86–92.

McLeod, S.A. (2018) *Erik Erikson's stages of psychosocial development.* www.simplypsychology.org/Erik-Erikson.html (accessed 18 December 2021).

McLeod, S.A. (2020) *Jean Piaget's stages of cognitive development.* www.simplypsychology.org/piaget.html (accessed 25 October 2021).

McNamara, L., Colley, P. and Franklin, N. (2017) 'School recess, social connectedness and health: A Canadian perspective', *Health Promotion International*, 32(2): 392–402.

Meek, M. (1988) *How texts teach what readers learn.* Stroud: Thimble Press.

Melhuish E., Ereky-Stevens, K. and Petrogiannis, K. (2015) *A review of research on the effects of Early Childhood Education and Care (ECEC) upon child development.* CARE Project, Utrecht University.

Menter, I., Elliot, D., Hulme, M., Lewin, J. and Lowden, K. (2011) *A guide to practitioner research in education.* London: SAGE.

Meredith, R. (2021) *Covid-19 having 'devastating effect' on children.* www.bbc.com/news/uk-northern-ireland-55698214 (accessed 9 April 2022).

Mersky, J.P., Janczewski, C.E. and Topitzes, J. (2017) 'Rethinking the measurement of adversity: Moving toward second-generation research on adverse childhood experiences', *Child Maltreatment*, 22(1): 58–68.

Mertala, P. (2019) 'Teachers' beliefs about technology integration in early childhood education: A meta-ethnographical synthesis of qualitative research', *Computers in Human Behaviour*, 101: 334–49.

Meyer, R. and Whitmore, K. (2017) 'Reclaiming early childhood literacies', in R. Meyer and K. Whitmore (eds), *Reclaiming early childhood literacies: Narratives of hope, power and vision.* New York: Routledge, pp. 1-12.

Miller, L., Nelson, F.P., Yun, C., Bennett, L. and Phillips, E.L. (2019) '"Am I doing what I think I'm doing?": The importance of a theoretical frame when integrating tablets in teacher education', *Educational Renaissance*, 8(1): 20–9.

Miller, T.W. and Miller, J.M. (2001) 'Educational leadership in the new millennium: A vision for 2020', *International Journal of Leadership in Education*, 4(2): 181–9.

Mishra, P. and Koehler, M.J. (2006) 'Technological pedagogical content knowledge: A framework for teacher knowledge', *Teachers College Record*, 108(6): 1017–54.

Mishra, P., Koehler, M.J. and Kereluik, K. (2009) 'The song remains the same: Looking back to the future of educational technology', *Tech Trends*, 53(5): 48–53.

Mistry, M. and Sood, K. (2012) 'Challenges of early years leadership preparation: A comparison between early and experienced early years practitioners in England', *Management in Education*, 26(1): 28–37.

Molloy, E.J. (2019) 'Dr Janusz Korczak: Paediatrician, children's advocate and hero', *Pediatric Research*, 86(6): 783–4.

Moloney, M. and Pope, J. (2020) 'Changes and challenges in school age childcare in Copenhagen', *Education 3–13*, 48(1): 76–86.

Montessori, M. (2002) *Basic ideas of Montessori's educational theory: Extracts from Maria Montessori's writings and teachings*. Oxford: Clio Press.

Montgomery, H. (2009) *An introduction to childhood: Anthropological perspectives on children's lives*. Chichester: Wiley-Blackwell.

Monti, F., Farné, R., Crudeli, F., Agostini, F., Minelli, M. and Ceciliani, A. (2019) 'The role of outdoor education in child development in Italian nursery schools', *Early Child Development and Care*, 189(6): 867–82.

Mooney, G. and McCafferty, T. (2005) '"Only looking after the weans"? The Scottish nursery nurses' strike, 2004', *Critical Social Policy*, 25(2): 223–39.

Moore, D., Morrissey, A.-M. and Robertson, N. (2021) '"I feel like I'm getting sad there": Early childhood outdoor playspaces as places for children's wellbeing', *Early Child Development and Care*, 191(6): 933–51.

Moran-Ellis, J. (2010) 'Reflections on the sociology of childhood in the UK', *Current Sociology*, 58(2): 186–205.

Morris, P., Millenky, M., Raver, C.C. and Jones, S.M. (2013) 'Does a preschool social and emotional learning intervention pay off for classroom instruction and children's behavior and academic skills? Evidence from the Foundations of Learning Project', *Early Education and Development*, 24(7): 1020–42.

Morrison, M. and Arthur, L. (2013) 'Leadership for inter-service practice: Collaborative leadership lost in translation? An exploration', *Educational Management Administration & Leadership*, 41(2): 179–98.

Moshel, S. and Berkovich, I. (2020) 'Navigating ambiguity: Early childhood leaders' sense-making of their identity in a new mid-level role', *Educational Management Administration & Leadership*, 48(3): 514–31.

Moss, P., Petrie, P. and Poland G. (1999) *Rethinking school: Some international perspectives*. Leicester: Youth Work Press.

Mowat, J. (2015) '"Inclusion – that word!" Examining some of the tensions in supporting pupils experiencing social, emotional and behavioural difficulties/needs', *Emotional and Behavioural Difficulties*, 20(2): 153–72.

Mowat, J. (2019) 'Exploring the impact of social inequality and poverty on the mental health and wellbeing and attainment of children and young people in Scotland', *Improving Schools*, 22(3): 204–23.

Muijs, D. and Harris, A. (2007) 'Teacher leadership in (in)action', *Educational Management Administration & Leadership*, 35(1): 111–34.

Muijs, D., Aubrey, C., Harris, A. and Briggs, M. (2004) 'How do they manage? A review of the research on leadership in early childhood', *Journal of Early Childhood Research*, 2(2): 157–69.

Mulligan, J. and Mitchelmore, M. (2009) 'Awareness of pattern and structure in early mathematical development', *Mathematics Education Research Journal*, 21(2): 33–49.

Munn, P. (1994) 'The early development of literacy and numeracy skills', *European Early Childhood Education Research Journal*, 2(1): 5–18.

Murray, J. (2019) 'Introduction: Young children's rights to protection', in J. Murray, B.B. Swadener and K. Smith (eds), *The Routledge international handbook of young children's rights*. Abingdon: Routledge, pp. 79–84.

Murray, J. and McDowall Clark, R. (2013) 'Reframing leadership as a participative pedagogy: The working theories of early years professionals', *Early Years*, 33(3): 289–301.

MyGovScot (2021) *Funded early learning and childcare.* www.mygov.scot/childcare-costs-help/funded-early-learning-and-childcare (accessed 28 October 2021).

Nachmanovitch, S. (1990) *Free play: Improvisation in life and art.* New York: Penguin.

Nah, K. and Waller, T. (2015) 'Outdoor play in preschools in England and South Korea: Learning from polyvocal methods', *Early Child Development and Care*, 185(11–12): 2010–25.

Narayan, A. and Steele-Johnson, D. (2007) 'Relationships between prior experience of training, gender, goal orientation and training attitudes', *International Journal of Training and Development*, 11(3): 166–80.

National Assembly for Wales (2014) *Social Services and Well-being (Wales) Act 2014 (anaw4).* www.legislation.gov.uk/anaw/2014/4/contents (accessed 3 November 2021).

National Autistic Society (2022) *Who we are and how we work.* www.autism.org.uk/what-we-do/who-we-are (accessed 13 March 2022).

National Centre for Excellence in the Teaching of Mathematics (NCETM) (2021) *Cardinality and number sense.* www.ncetm.org.uk/features/cardinality-and-number-sense (accessed 1 November 2021).

National Council for Curriculum and Assessment (2015) *Learning and developing through interactions.* https://curriculumonline.ie/getmedia/e50a42c4-24ab-4998-82a5-c897ed0974f1/Learning-through-Interactions_EN.pdf (accessed 16 January 2022).

National Day Nurseries Association (NDNA) (2019) NDNA 2018/19 Workforce Survey England. https://ndna.org.uk/wp-content/uploads/2021/12/NDNA-Full-Workforce-Survey-Report-2018-2019-1.pdf (accessed 10 October 2022).

National Education Association (NEA) (2012) *An educator's guide to the 'Four Cs': Preparing 21st century students for a global society.* Washington, DC: NEA.

National Occupational Standards (NOS) (online) *Repository for all approved National Occupational Standards.* www.ukstandards.org.uk (accessed 26 October 2021).

National Scientific Council on the Developing Child (2004) *Children's emotional development is built into the architecture of their brains: Working paper No. 2.* Cambridge, MA: Harvard University Press.

National Society for the Prevention of Cruelty to Children (NSPCC) (2020a) *How safe are our children? 2020: An overview of data on abuse of adolescents.* London: NSPCC Learning.

National Society for the Prevention of Cruelty to Children (NSPCC) (2020b) *Nominated child protection lead or designated safeguarding officer*. https://learning.nspcc.org.uk/research-resources/templates/nominated-child-protection-lead-role (accessed 10 January 2022).

National Society for the Prevention of Cruelty to Children (NSPCC) (2021) *History of child protection in the UK*. https://learning.nspcc.org.uk/child-protection-system/history-of-child-protection-in-the-uk (accessed 2 November 2021).

National Society for the Prevention of Cruelty to Children (NSPCC) (2022a) *Safeguarding children and child protection*. https://learning.nspcc.org.uk/safeguarding-child-protection (accessed 20 March 2022).

National Society for the Prevention of Cruelty to Children (NSPCC) (2022b) *What is child abuse?* www.nspcc.org.uk/what-is-child-abuse (accessed 10 January 2022).

National Society for the Prevention of Cruelty to Children (NSPCC) (2022c) *Types of abuse*. www.nspcc.org.uk/what-is-child-abuse/types-of-abuse (accessed 10 January 2022).

National Society for the Prevention of Cruelty to Children (NSPCC) (2022d) *Child protection plan and register statistics*. https://learning.nspcc.org.uk/research-resources/child-protection-plan-register-statistics (accessed 10 January 2022).

National Society for the Prevention of Cruelty to Children (NSPCC) (online-a) *Safeguarding children and child protection*. https://learning.nspcc.org.uk/safeguarding-child-protection (accessed 10 January 2022).

National Society for the Prevention of Cruelty to Children (NSPCC) (online-b) *Multi-agency working*. https://learning.nspcc.org.uk/child-protection-system/multi-agency-working-child-protection (accessed 1 April 2022).

Neenan, E.E., Roche, J. and Bell, L. (2021) 'Time to listen: Children's voice in geoscience education research', *Frontiers in Environmental Science*, 9(669430): 1–6. https://doi.org/10.3389/fenvs.2021.669430 (accessed 25 February 2022).

Neum, S. (2012) *Language and literacy for the early years*. Los Angeles: SAGE.

Neumann, M.M., Hood, M., Ford, R.M. and Neumann, D.L. (2013) 'Letter and numeral identification: Their relationship with early literacy and numeracy skills', *European Early Childhood Education Research Journal*, 21(4): 489–501.

Newman, L. (2000) 'Ethical leadership or leadership in ethics?', *Australasian Journal of Early Childhood*, 25(1): 40–5.

NHS Education for Scotland (2017) *Transforming psychological trauma: A knowledge and skills framework for the Scottish workforce*. Edinburgh: NHS Education for Scotland.

NHS Health Scotland (2019) *Adverse childhood experiences in context*. Edinburgh: NHS Health Scotland.

NHS Lothian (2021) *Training: supporting communication in the early years*. www.lets-talk.scot.nhs.uk/early-years-professionals/local-early-years-information/edinburgh (accessed 10 October 2022).

NI Direct Government Services (2022) *Childcare benefits and other help for working parents*. www.nidirect.gov.uk/information-and-services/childcare/childcare-benefits-and-other-help-working-parents (accessed 13 March 2022).

NI Direct Government Services (online) *AccessNI: Criminal record checks*. www.nidirect.gov.uk/articles/using-criminal-record-check (accessed 3 April 2022).

Nicholson, J., Perez, L. and Kurtz, J. (2018) *Trauma-informed practices for early childhood educators: Relationship-based approaches that support healing and build resilience in young children*. Abingdon: Routledge.

Nicholson, J., Kuhl, K., Maniates, H., Lin, B. and Bonetti, S. (2020) 'A review of the literature on leadership in early childhood: Examining epistemological foundations and considerations of social justice', *Early Child Development and Care*, 190(2): 91–122.

Nicholson, S. (1971) 'How not to cheat children: The theory of loose parts', *Landscape Architecture*, 62(1): 30–5.

Nikolajeva, M. (2013) 'Picturebooks and emotional literacy', *The Reading Teacher*, 67(4): 249–54.

Noailly, J. and Visser, S. (2009) 'The impact of market forces on child care provision: Insights from the 2005 Child Care Act in the Netherlands', *Journal of Social Policy*, 38(3): 477–98.

Noddings, N. (2012) 'The caring relation in teaching', *Oxford Review of Education*, 38(6): 771–81.

Northern Ireland Assembly (1995) *The Children (Northern Ireland) Order 1995 (755)*. London: HMSO.

Northern Ireland Assembly (2003) *The Education and Libraries (Northern Ireland) Order*. London: HMSO.

Northern Ireland Assembly (2015) *Children's Services Co-operation Act (Northern Ireland) 2015 (c.10)*. London: HMSO.

Northern Ireland Executive (2020a) *Children and young people's strategy 2020–2030 for Northern Ireland*. Belfast: Department of Education.

Northern Ireland Executive (2020b) *New decade, new approach*. Belfast: UK Government.

Northern Ireland Social Care Council (NISCC) (2019) *Social Care Council: Standards of conduct and practice*. Belfast: NISCC.

Norwich, B. (2014) 'Changing policy and legislation and its effects on inclusive and special education: A perspective from England', *British Journal of Special Education*, 41(4): 403–25.

Nursery Resources (2007) *The early years foundation stage effective practice: Outdoor learning*. www.nurseryresources.org/resources/eyfs-effective-practise-outdoor-learning (accessed 07 November 2022).

Nussbaum, M. (1993) 'The use and abuse of philosophy in legal education', *Stanford Law Review*, 45(6): 1627–45.

Nutbrown, C. (2012) *Foundations for quality: Review of early education and childcare qualifications (final report)*. London: Department for Education.

Nutbrown, C. (2019) *Early childhood educational research: International perspectives*. London: SAGE.

Oberhuemer, P. (2005) 'Conceptualising the early childhood pedagogue: Policy approaches and issues of professionalism', *European Early Childhood Education Research Journal*, 13(1): 5–16.

O'Brien, J. (1994) 'Show mum you love her: Taking a new look at junk mail', *Reading*, 28: 43–6.

O'Brien, J. and Comber, B. (2001) 'Negotiating critical literacies with young children', in C. Barratt-Pugh and M. Rohl (eds), *Literacy learning in the early years*. Buckingham: Open University Press, pp. 152–71.

Oetzel, J., Ting-Toomey, S., Chew-Sanchez, M.I., Harris, R., Wilcox, R. and Stumpf, S. (2003) 'Face and facework in conflicts with parents and siblings: A cross-cultural comparison of Germans, Japanese, Mexicans, and U.S. Americans', *Journal of Family Communication*, 3(2): 67–93.

Office for Standards in Education (Ofsted) (2000) *Improving city schools*. London: Ofsted.

Office for Standards in Education (Ofsted) (2008) *Learning outside the classroom: How far should you go?* London: Ofsted.

Office for Standards in Education (Ofsted) (2020) *Ofsted warns of risk to children 'out of sight' during pandemic*. www.gov.uk/government/news/ofsted-warns-of-risk-to-children-out-of-sight-during-pandemic (accessed 10 January 2022).

Office for Standards in Education (Ofsted) (2021) *Early years inspection handbook for Ofsted-registered provision*. www.gov.uk/government/publications/early-years-inspection-handbook-eif/early-years-inspection-handbook-for-ofsted-registered-provision-for-september-2021 (accessed 26 March 2022).

Oldman, D. (1994) 'Adult child relations as class relations', in M. Bardy, G. Sgritta and H. Wintersberger (eds), *Childhood matters: Social theory, practice and politics*. Avebury: Ashgate, pp. 43–58.

Oliveira, P. (2018) 'True then, truer now', *National Association for the Education of Young Children (NAEYC)*, 73(3): 87–9.

Olsen, H. and Smith, B. (2017) 'Sandboxes, loose parts, and playground equipment: A descriptive exploration of outdoor play environments', *Early Child Development and Care*, 187(5–6): 1055–68.

Olson, M.H. and Hergenhahn, B.R. (2009) *An introduction to theories of learning (Eighth edition)*. Upper Saddle River, NJ: Pearson-Prentice Hall.

Olswang, L.B. and Bain, B. (1994) 'Data collection: Monitoring children's treatment progress', *American Journal of Speech-Language Pathology*, 3(3): 55–66.

Opie, I. and Opie, P. (1969) *Children's games in street and playground*. Chichester: Wiley-Blackwell.

Oreg, S., Vakola, M. and Armenakis, A. (2011) 'Change recipients' reactions to organizational change: A 60-year review of quantitative studies', *The Journal of Applied Behavioral Science*, 47(4): 461–524.

Organisation for Economic Co-operation and Development (OECD) (2000) *Early childhood education and care policy in the United Kingdom*. Paris: OECD.

Organisation for Economic Co-operation and Development (OECD) (2001) *Starting strong: Early childhood education and care. Education and skills*. Paris: OECD.

Organisation for Economic Co-operation and Development (OECD) (2006) *Starting strong II: Early childhood education and care*. Paris: OECD.

Organisation for Economic Co-operation and Development (OECD) (2008) *Growing unequal: Income distribution and poverty in OECD countries*. Paris: OECD.

Organisation for Economic Co-operation and Development (OECD) (2015) *Starting strong IV: Monitoring quality in early childhood education and care*. Paris: OECD.

Organisation for Economic Co-operation and Development (OECD) (2017) *Starting strong 2017: Key OECD indicators on early childhood education and care.* Paris: OECD.

Organisation for Economic Co-operation and Development (OECD) (2020a) *Early childhood education and care: Equity, quality and transitions. Report for the G20 Education Working Group.* Paris: OECD.

Organisation for Economic Co-operation and Development (OECD) (2020b) *Combatting COVID-19's effect on children.* www.oecd.org/coronavirus/policy-responses/combatting-covid-19-s-effect-on-children-2e1f3b2f (accessed 14 June 2021).

Organisation for Economic Co-operation and Development (OECD) (2021) *Starting strong VI: Supporting meaningful interactions in early childhood education and care.* Paris: OECD.

Organisation for Economic Co-operation and Development (OECD) and Education International (2021) *Effective and equitable educational recovery: 10 principles.* Paris: OECD.

Orrock, A. (2012) 'Homo ludens: Pieter Bruegel's children's games and the humanist educators', *Journal of Historians of Netherlandish Art*, 4(2): 1–42.

Osborn, R.N., Hunt, J.G. and Jauch, L.R. (2002) 'Toward a contextual theory of leadership', *The Leadership Quarterly*, 13(6): 797–837.

Osgood, J. (2006) 'Deconstructing professionalism in early childhood education: Resisting the regulatory gaze', *Contemporary Issues in Early Childhood*, 7(1): 5–14.

Osgood, J., Elwick, A., Robertson, L., Sakr, M. and Wilson, D. (2017) *Early years teacher and early years educator: A scoping study of the impact, experiences and associated issues of recent early years qualifications and training in England.* London: Middlesex University.

O'Sullivan, J. (2019) *Why are we so afraid of talking about early years pedagogy?* www.teachearlyyears.com/learning-and-development/view/why-are-we-so-afraid-of-talking-about-early-years-pedagogy (accessed 6 February 2022).

Out-of-School Care Alliance (OSCA) (2021) *Funding.* www.outofschoolalliance.co.uk/funding (accessed 13 October 2021).

Paas, F. and Sweller, J. (2012) 'An evolutionary upgrade of cognitive load theory: Using the human motor system and collaboration to support the learning of complex cognitive tasks', *Educational Psychology Review*, 24(1): 27–45.

Paes de Barros, R., Ferreira, F.H.G., Molinas Vega, J.R. and Saavedra Chanduvi, J. (2009) *Measuring inequality of opportunities in Latin America and the Caribbean.* Washington, DC: World Bank.

Page, J. (2018) 'Characterising the principles of Professional Love in early childhood care and education', *International Journal of Early Years Education*, 26(2): 125–41.

Page, J. and Elfer, P. (2013) 'The emotional complexity of attachment interactions in nursery', *European Early Childhood Education Research Journal*, 21(4): 553–67.

Palaiologou, I. (2016) 'Children under five and digital technologies: Implications for early years pedagogy', *European Early Childhood Education Research Journal*, 24(1): 5–24.

Palaiologou, I. and Male, T. (2019) 'Leadership in early childhood education: The case for pedagogical praxis', *Contemporary Issues in Early Childhood*, 20(1): 23–34.

Paliwal, V. and Baroody, A.J. (2018) 'How best to teach the cardinality principle?', *Early Childhood Research Quarterly*, 44: 152–60.

Paliwal, V. and Baroody, A.J. (2020) 'Cardinality principle understanding: The role of focusing on the subitizing abaility', *ZDM Mathematics Education*, 52(4): 649–61.

Papatheodorou, T. (2009) 'Exploring relational pedagogy', in T. Papatheodorou and J. Moyles (eds), *Learning together in the early years: Exploring relational pedagogy*. Abingdon: Routledge, pp. 3–17.

Park, Y.S., Konge, L. and Artino, A.R. (2020) 'The positivism paradigm of research', *Academic Medicine*, 95(5): 690–4.

Parks, L. (2018) 'Sensory overload: Quieting the noise in early childhood classrooms', *Texas Child Care Quarterly*, 41(4): 1–5.

Parsons, K.J. and Traunter, J. (2020) 'Muddy knees and muddy needs: Parents' perceptions of outdoor learning', *Children's Geographies*, 18(6): 699–711.

Parten, M.B. (1933) 'Social play among preschool children', *The Journal of Abnormal and Social Psychology*, 28(2): 136–47.

Pedaste, M., Mäeots, M., Siiman, L.A., de Jong, T., van Riesen, S.A.N., Kamp, E.T., Manoli, C.C., Zacharia, Z.C. and Tsourlidaki, E. (2015) 'Phases of inquiry-based learning: Definitions and the inquiry cycle', *Educational Research Review*, 14(1): 47–61.

Peeple (online) *Peep learning together programme*. www.peeple.org.uk/ltp (accessed 30 January 2022).

Peleg, N. (2013) 'Reconceptualising the child's right to development: Children and the capability approach', *The International Journal of Children's Rights*, 21(3): 523–42.

Pellegrini, A.D. and Blatchford, P. (2000) *The child at school: Interactions with peers and teachers*. London: Edward Arnold.

Pellegrini, A.D., Kato, K., Blatchford, P. and Baines, E. (2002) 'A short-term longitudinal study of children's playground games across the first year of school: Implications for social competence and adjustment to school', *American Educational Research Journal*, 39(4): 991–1015.

Penn, H. (2009) 'International perspectives on quality in mixed economies of childcare', *National Institute Economic Review*, 207: 83–9.

Penn, H. (2011) *Quality in early childhood services: An international perspective*. Maidenhead: Open University Press.

Perry, B. (2009) 'Examining child maltreatment through a neurodevelopmental lens: Clinical applications of the neurosequential model of therapeutics', *Journal of Loss and Trauma*, 14(4): 240–55.

Perry, B. and Pollard, D. (1997) *Altered brain development following global neglect in early childhood*. Proceedings from Annual Meeting, Society for Neuroscience, New Orleans, LA.

Petersen, P. (2015) '"That's how much I can do!": Children's agency in digital tablet activities in a Swedish preschool environment', *Nordic Journal of Digital Literacy*, 10(3): 145–69.

Petrie, P., Boddy, J., Cameron, C., Heptinstall, E., McQuail, S., Simon, A. and Wigfall, V. (2009) *Pedagogy – a holistic, personal approach to work with children and young people, across services: European models for practice, training, education and qualification*. London: Thomas Coram Research Unit.

Petty, G. (2014) *Teaching today (Fifth edition)*. Oxford: Oxford University Press.

Phair, R. (2021) *International early learning and child well-being study assessment framework; OECD educational working paper No. 246*. Paris: OECD.

Piaget, J. (1952) *The origins of intelligence in children*. New York: W.W. Norton and Co.

Piaget, J. (1960) The psychology of intelligence. Paterson, New Jersey: Littlefield, Adams and Co.

Piaget, J. (1964) 'Cognitive development in children: Development and learning', *Journal of Research in Science Teaching*, 2(1): 176–86.

Pianta, R.C. (2001) *Student–teacher relationship scale: Professional manual*. Lutz, FL: Psychological Assessment Resources.

Pianta, R.C., Steinberg, M.S. and Rollins, K.B. (1995) 'The first two years of school: Teacher–child relationships and deflections in children's classroom adjustment', *Development and Psychopathology*, 7(2): 298–312.

Pianta, R.C., Hamre, B. and Stuhlman, M. (2003) 'Relationships between teachers and children', in W.M. Reynolds, G.E. Miller and I.B. Weiner (eds), *Handbook of psychology: Volume 7 – Educational psychology*. Hoboken, NJ: Wiley, pp. 199–234.

Pianta, R.C., Belsky, J., Vandergrift, N., Houts, R. and Morrison, F.J. (2008) 'Classroom effects on children's achievement trajectories in elementary school', *American Educational Research Journal*, 45(2): 365–97.

Pilcher, J. (1995) *Age and generation in modern Britain*. Oxford: Oxford University Press.

Plantenga, J. and Remery, C. (2017) 'Out-of-school childcare: Exploring availability and quality in EU member states', *Journal of European Social Policy*, 27(1): 25–39.

Platt, D. (2012) 'Understanding parental engaging with child welfare services: An integrated model', *Child and Family Social Work*, 17(2): 138–48.

Play England (2020) *Charter for play*. www.playengland.org.uk/charter-for-play (accessed 30 January 2022).

Play Scotland (2021) *Progress review of Scotland's play strategy 2021: Play in a Covid 19 context*. Edinburgh: Play Scotland.

Play Scotland (2022) *Guidance on Playwork*. www.playscotland.org/play/playful-learning/information-on-playwork (accessed 3 January 2022).

Play Wales (2015) *The playwork principles – An overview*. Cardiff: Play Wales.

Play Wales (2021) *Practising playwork. Playwork guides – volume 2*. Cardiff: Play Wales.

PlayBoard NI (online) *Why play?* www.playboard.org/why-play (accessed 30 January 2022).

Playwork Principles Scrutiny Group (PPSG) (2005) *Playwork principles*. Cardiff: Play Wales.

Pollock, I. (2013) *Perceptions of academic readiness among BA Childhood Practice students*. Unpublished MEd dissertation, University of Glasgow.

Pollock, R.V.H., Jefferson, A.M. and Wick, C.W. (2015) *The six disciplines of breakthrough learning: How to turn training and development into business results (Third edition)*. Hoboken, NJ: John Wiley & Sons.

Postman, N. (1994) *The disappearance of childhood (Revised edition)*. New York: Vintage.

Potter, J. (2019) 'We are champions', *BDJ Team*, 6: 19017. https://doi.org/10.1038/bdjteam.2019.17 (accessed 30 January 2022).

Powell, C. (2011) *Safeguarding and child protection for nurses, midwives and health visitors: A practical guide*. Maidenhead: Open University Press.

Powell, E., Furey, S., Scott-Evans, A. and Terrell, I. (2003) 'Teachers' perceptions of the impact of CPD: An institutional case study', *Journal of In-Service Education*, 29(3): 389–404.

Prochner, L. (2000) *Early childhood care and education in Canada: Past, present, and future*. Vancouver: University of British Columbia Press.

Professional Association for Childcare and Early Years (2022) *Training and qualifications*. www.pacey.org.uk/training-and-qualifications (accessed 30 January 2022).

Prout, A. (2005) *The future of childhood*. Abingdon: Routledge.

Prout, A. (2011) 'Taking a step away from modernity: Reconsidering the new sociology of childhood', *Global Studies of Childhood*, 1(1): 4–14.

Public Health Scotland (2022) *Child and adolescent mental health services (CAMHS) waiting times: Quarter ending 30 June 2022*. Edinburgh: Public Health Scotland. https://publichealthscotland.scot/publications/child-and-adolescent-mental-health-services-camhs-waiting-times/child-and-adolescent-mental-health-services-camhs-waiting-times-quarter-ending-june-2022 (accessed 9 October 2022).

Puentedura, R. (2006) *Transformation, technology, and education: A model for technology and transformation*. http://hippasus.com/resources/tte/puentedura_tte.pdf (accessed 18 January 2022).

Puentedura, R. (2013) *Paths to technology integration: SAMR & TPCK in context*. www.hippasus.com/rrpweblog/archives/2013/05/29/PathsToTechnologyIntegration.pdf (accessed 18 January 2022).

Pyle, A. and Danniels, E. (2017) 'A continuum of play-based learning: The role of the teacher in play-based pedagogy and the fear of hijacking play', *Early Education and Development*, 28(3): 274–89.

Qualification and Credit Framework (QCF) (online) *Accredited qualifications*. www.accreditedqualifications.org.uk/qualifications-and-credit-framework-qcf.html (accessed 14 October 2021).

Quality Assurance Agency for Higher Education (QAA) Scotland (2007) *Scottish subject benchmark statement: Standard for childhood practice*. Glasgow: QAA Scotland.

Quigley, M. and Blashki, K. (2003) 'Beyond the boundaries of the sacred garden: Children and the internet', *Information Technology in Childhood Education Annual*, 2003(1): 309–16.

Quinn, S.F. and Parker, L. (2018) 'How do twenty-first century teacher trainees connect their practice to Froebel's pedagogic principles?', in T. Bruce, P. Elfer, S. Powell and L. Werth (eds), *The Routledge international handbook of Froebel and early childhood practice*. Abingdon: Routledge, pp. 191–200.

Qvortrup, J. (1994) 'Childhood matters: An introduction', in J. Qvortrup, M. Bardy, G. Sgritta and H. Wintersberger (eds), *Childhood matters: Social theory, practice and politics*. Aldershot: Avebury Press, pp. 1–24.

Qvortrup, J. (2009) 'Are children human beings or human becomings? A critical assessment of outcome thinking', *Rivista Internazionale di Scienze Sociali*, 117(3/4): 631–53.

Ralph, R. (2018) 'Media and technology in preschool classrooms: Manifesting prosocial sharing behaviours when using iPads', *Technology, Knowledge and Learning*, 23(2): 199–221.

Ranson, K. and Urichuk, L. (2008) 'The effect of parent–child attachment relationships on child biophysical outcomes: A review', *Early Child Development and Care*, 178(2): 129–52.

Ratan, S.K., Anand, T. and Ratan, J. (2019) 'Formulation of research question: Stepwise approach', *Journal of Indian Association of Paediatric Surgeons*, 24(1): 15–20.

Reid, J.L., Kagan, S.L. and Scott-Little, C. (2019) 'New understandings of cultural diversity and the implications for early childhood policy, pedagogy, and practice', *Early Child Development and Care*, 189(6): 976–89.

Reiss, J. and Sprenger, J. (2020) 'Scientific objectivity', in E.N. Zalta (ed.), *The Stanford encyclopedia of philosophy (Winter 2020 Edition)*. https://plato.stanford.edu/cgi-bin/encyclopedia/archinfo.cgi?entry=scientific-objectivity&archive=win2020 (accessed 20 December 2021).

Reynaert, D., Bouverne-De Bie, M. and Vandevelde, S. (2009) 'A review of children's rights literature since the adoption of the United Nations Convention on the Rights of the Child', *Childhood*, 16(4): 518–34.

Richards, K. (2003) *Qualitative inquiry in TESOL*. New York: Palgrave Macmillan.

Riggs, N.R. and Greenberg, M.T. (2004) 'After-school youth development programs: A developmental-ecological model of current research', *Clinical Child and Family Psychology Review*, 7(3): 177–90.

Riley, P. (2013) 'Attachment theory, teacher motivation and pastoral care: A challenge for teachers and academics', *Pastoral Care in Education*, 31(2): 112–29.

Robinson, K. (2010) *Changing education paradigms*. www.ted.com/talks/sir_ken_robinson_changing_education_paradigms (accessed 25 October 2021).

Rodd, J. (1997) 'Learning to be leaders: Perceptions of early childhood professionals about leadership roles and responsibilities', *Early Years*, 18(1): 40–4.

Rodd, J. (2006) *Leadership in early childhood (Third edition)*. Maidenhead: Open University Press.

Rodd, J. (2013) *Leadership in early childhood: The pathway to professionalism (Fourth edition)*. Maidenhead: Open University Press.

Rogers, S. (2011) 'Play and pedagogy: A conflict of interests?', in S. Rogers (ed.), *Rethinking play and pedagogy in early childhood education: Concepts, contexts and cultures*. Abingdon: Routledge, pp. 5–18.

Rogoff, B. (2003) *The cultural nature of human development*. New York: Oxford University Press.

Rolfe, H., Metcalfe, H., Anderson, T. and Meadows, P. (2003) *Recruitment and retention of childcare, early years and play workers: Research study National Institute of Economics and Social Research*. Nottingham: Department for Education and Skills.

Rolfe, S. (2004) *Rethinking attachment for early childhood practice: Promoting security, autonomy and resilience in young children*. Abingdon: Routledge.

Roller, M.R. and Lavrakas, P.J. (2015) *Applied qualitative design: A total quality framework approach*. New York: Guilford Press.

Romanou, E. and Belton, E. (2020) *Isolated and struggling: Social isolation and the risk of child maltreatment, in lockdown and beyond*. London: NSPCC.

Rosa, E.M. and Tudge, J.R.H. (2013) 'Urie Bronfenbrenner's theory of human development: Its evolution from ecology to bioecology', *Journal of Family Theory and Review*, 5(4): 243–58.

Rose, J. and Rogers, S. (2012) *The role of the adult in early years settings*. Maidenhead: Open University Press.

Rose, J., McGuire-Snieckus, R., Gilbert, L. and McInnes, K. (2019) 'Attachment aware schools: The impact of a targeted and collaborative intervention', *Pastoral Care in Education*, 37(2): 162–84.

Rose, W. (2012) 'Incorporating safeguarding and well-being in universal services: Developments in early years multi-agency practice in Scotland', in L. Miller and D. Hevey (eds), *Policy issues in the early years*. London: SAGE, pp. 153–68.

Rowe, D. (2010) 'Directions for studying early literacy as social practice', *Language Arts*, 88(2): 134–43.

Rubin, K.H. (2001) *The play observation scale (revised)*. College Park, MD: University of Maryland.

Russell, W. (2018) 'Nomadic wonderings on playwork research', in P. King and S. Newstead (eds), *Researching play from a playwork perspective*. Abingdon: Routledge, pp. 39–55.

Ryan, A.B. (2006) 'Methodology: Analysing qualitative data and writing up your findings', in M. Antonesa (ed.), *Researching and writing your thesis: A guide for postgraduate students*. Maynooth: National University of Ireland, pp. 92–108.

Ryan, P.J. (2008) 'How new is the "new" social study of childhood? The myth of a paradigm shift', *Journal of Interdisciplinary History*, 38(4): 553–76.

Saitadze, I. and Lalayants, M. (2021) 'Mechanisms that mitigate the effects of child poverty and improve children's cognitive and social-emotional development: A systematic review', *Child & Family Social Work*, 26(3): 289–308.

Sakr, M. and Bonetti, S. (2021) 'Continuing professional development for the early years workforce in England since 2015: A synthesis of survey data highlighting commonalities, discrepancies and gaps', *Early Years: An International Research Journal*. https://doi.org/1 0.1080/09575146.2021.1959524

Salvato, C. and Vassolo, R. (2018) 'The sources of dynamism in dynamic capabilities', *Special Issue: New Theory in Strategic Management*, 39(6): 1728–52.

Sanders, M.R. and Mazzucchelli, T.G. (eds) (2017) *The power of positive parenting: Transforming the lives of children, parents, and communities using the Triple P system*. Oxford: Oxford University Press.

Sandseter, E.B.H. (2009) 'Characteristics of risky play', *Journal of Adventure Education and Outdoor Learning*, 9(1): 3–21.

Sandseter, E.B.H. (2010) '"It tickles in my tummy!" Understanding children's risk-taking in play through reversal theory', *Journal of Early Childhood Research*, 8(1): 67–88.

Sandstrom, H., Moodie, S. and Halle, T. (2011) 'Beyond classroom-based measures for preschoolers: Addressing the gaps in measures for home-based care and care for infants and toddlers', in M. Zaslow, I. Martinez-Beck, K. Tout and T. Halle (eds), *Quality measurement in early childhood settings*. Baltimore, MD: Brookes, pp. 317–43.

Saraceno, C. (2011) 'Childcare needs and childcare policies: A multidimensional issue', *Current Sociology*, 59(1): 78–96.

Sarnecka, B.W. and Carey, S. (2008) 'How counting represents number: What children must learn and when they learn it', *Cognition*, 108: 662–74.

Satchwell-Hirst, M. (2017) 'Neuroscience and emotional development', in D. Colley and P. Cooper (eds), *Attachment and emotional development in the classroom*. London: Jessica Kingsley, pp. 49–63.

Saunders, R., Brack, M., Renz, B., Thomson, J. and Pilling, S. (2020) 'An evaluation of parent training interventions in Scotland: The Psychology of Parenting Project (PoPP)', *Journal of Child and Family Studies*, 29(1): 3369–80.

Save the Children (2021) *COVID-19 crisis has pushed child traffickers online and out of sight – Save the Children*. www.savethechildren.net/news/covid-19-crisis-has-pushed-child-traffickers-online-and-out-sight-%E2%80%93-save-children (accessed 10 January 2022).

Sayre, R.K., Devercelli, A.E., Neuman, M.J. and Wodon, Q. (2014) *Investing in early childhood development: Review of the world's bank's recent experiences*. Washington, DC: World Bank.

Scheiwe, K. and Willekens, H. (2009) *Child care and preschool development in Europe: Institutional perspectives*. Basingstoke: Palgrave Macmillan.

Schön, D. (1991) *The reflective practitioner: How professionals think in action*. London: Temple Smith.

Scobie, G. and Scott, E. (2017) *Rapid evidence review: Childcare quality and children's outcomes*. Edinburgh: NHS Health Scotland.

Scottish Adverse Childhood Experiences Hub (2017) *Tackling the attainment gap by preventing and responding to ACEs*. Edinburgh: NHS Health Scotland.

Scottish Credit and Qualification Framework (SCQF) (online) *About the framework*. https://scqf.org.uk/about-the-framework (accessed 14 October 2021).

Scottish Executive (2002) *National care standards: A guide*. Edinburgh: Scottish Executive.

Scottish Executive (2004) *National review of the early years and childcare workforce: Investing in children's futures*. Edinburgh: Scottish Executive.

Scottish Government (2008a) *The early years framework*. Edinburgh: Scottish Government.

Scottish Government (2008b) *Curriculum for excellence*. Edinburgh: Scottish Government.

Scottish Government (2009) *Curriculum for excellence: Literacy across learning: Principles and practice*. https://education.gov.scot/Documents/literacy-across-learning-pp.pdf (accessed 30 January 2022).

Scottish Government (2012a) *Getting it right for children and families: A guide to getting it right for every child*. Edinburgh: Scottish Government.

Scottish Government (2012b) *Common core of skills, knowledge and understanding and values for the 'children's workforce' in Scotland*. Edinburgh: Scottish Government.

Scottish Government (2013a) *Play strategy for Scotland: Our vision*. Edinburgh: Scottish Government.

Scottish Government (2013b) *Play strategy for Scotland: Our action plan*. Edinburgh: Scottish Government.

Scottish Government (2015) *Tackling inequalities in the early years: Key messages from 10 years of the Growing Up in Scotland study*. Edinburgh: Scottish Government.

Scottish Government (2017a) *ELC for two year old children.* www.gov.scot/policies/early-education-and-care/elc-for-two-year-old-children (accessed 30 January 2022).

Scottish Government (2017b) *Health and social care standards: My support, my life.* Edinburgh: Scottish Government.

Scottish Government (2017c) *A blueprint for 2020: An expansion for early education and childcare.* Edinburgh: Scottish Government.

Scottish Government (2018) *Out to play: Practical guidance for creating outdoor play experiences in early learning and childcare.* Edinburgh: Scottish Government.

Scottish Government (2019) *Out of school care in Scotland: Draft framework 2019 executive summary.* Edinburgh: Scottish Government.

Scottish Government (2021a) *A fairer, greener Scotland: Programme for government 2021–22.* Edinburgh: Scottish Government.

Scottish Government (2021b) *National guidance for child protection in Scotland 2021.* Edinburgh: Scottish Government.

Scottish Government (2021c) *Connecting Scotland: A year in view.* Edinburgh: Scottish Government.

Scottish Government (2021d) *Equity and excellence leads: Report on the Care Inspectorate special inspection focus and update on development of the role.* Edinburgh: Scottish Government.

Scottish Government (online) *Early education and care.* www.gov.scot/policies/early-education-and-care/early-learning-support-for-deprived-communities (accessed 2 February 2022).

Scottish Out-of-School Care Network (SOSCN) (2020) *Achieving quality Scotland.* https://soscn.org/quality (accessed 15 January 2021).

Scottish Parliament (2000) *Standards in Scotland's Schools etc (Scotland) Act 2000 (c.6).* London: HMSO.

Scottish Parliament (2001) *Regulation of Care (Scotland) Act 2001.* London: HMSO.

Scottish Parliament (2003) *Official report: Plenary, 13 Nov 2003.* https://archive2021.parliament.scot/parliamentarybusiness/report.aspx?r=4472&mode=html (accessed 10 January 2022).

Scottish Parliament (2006) *Scottish Schools (Parental Involvement) Act 2006 (asp. 8).* London: HMSO.

Scottish Parliament (2007) *Protection from Vulnerable Groups (Scotland) Act 2007 (asp. 14).* London: HMSO.

Scottish Parliament (2014) *Children and Young People (Scotland) Act 2014 (asp. 8).* London: HSMO.

Scottish Parliament (2020) *Children (Scotland) Act 2020 (asp. 16).* London: HSMO.

Scottish Qualifications Authority (2021) *Comparing qualification levels.* www.sqa.org.uk/sqa/64561.html (accessed 21 October 2021).

Scottish Social Services Council (SSSC) (2003) *Registration.* www.sssc.uk.com/registration www.sssc.uk.com/registration (accessed 10 October 2022).

Scottish Social Services Council (SSSC) (2015) *A trusted, skilled and valued social service workforce: The work of the Scottish Social Services Council in 2015.* Dundee: SSSC.

Scottish Social Services Council (SSSC) (2016a) *The codes of practice for social service workers and employers*. Dundee: SSSC.

Scottish Social Services Council (SSSC) (2016b) *The standard for childhood practice. Revised 2015*. Dundee: SSSC.

Scottish Social Services Council (SSSC) (2022a) *Registration*. www.sssc.uk.com/registration/ (accessed 10 January 2022).

Scottish Social Services Council (SSSC) (2022b) *Help with register parts, fees and qualifications*. www.sssc.uk.com/registration/help-with-register-parts-fees-and-qualifications (accessed 30 January 2022).

Scottish Social Services Council (SSSC) (online) *Workforce information and planning – role of Skills for Care & Development*. https://www.sssc.uk.com/knowledgebase/article/KA-01710/en-us (accessed 10 October 2022).

Seddighi, H., Salmani, I., Javadi, H.M. and Seddighi, S. (2021) 'Child abuse in natural disasters and conflicts: A systematic review', *Trauma, Violence and Abuse*, 22(1): 176–85.

Sen, A. (1999) *Commodities and capabilities*. Oxford: Oxford University Press.

Senge, P.M. (2000) 'Systems change in education', *Reflections*, 1(3): 52–60.

Senge, P.M. (2006) *The fifth discipline: The art and practice of the learning organization*. New York: Doubleday.

Serafini, F. (2012) 'Expanding the Four Resources Model: Reading visual and multi-modal texts', *Pedagogies: An International Journal*, 7(2): 150–64.

Sergiovanni, T.J. (1992) *Moral leadership: Getting to the heart of school improvement*. San Francisco: Jossey-Bass.

Shackell, A., Butler, N., Doyle, P. and Ball, D. (2008) *Play England: Making space for play*. Nottingham: DCSF Publications.

Sheridan, C. (2001) 'Children's literature and literacy learning', in C. Barratt-Pugh and M. Rohl (eds), *Literacy learning in the early years*. London: Routledge, pp. 105–28.

Sheridan, S., Giota, J., Han, Y.-M. and Kwon, J.-Y. (2009) 'A cross-cultural study of preschool quality in South Korea and Sweden: ECERS evaluations', *The Early Childhood Research Quarterly*, 24(1): 142–56.

Shier, H. (2001) 'Pathways to participation: Openings, opportunities and obligations: A new model for enhancing children's participation in decision-making in line with Article 12.1 of the United Nations Convention on the Rights of the Child', *Children & Society*, 15(2): 107–17.

Shirvanian, N. and Michael, T. (2017) 'Implementation of attachment theory into early childhood settings', *The International Education Journal: Comparative Perspectives*, 16(2): 97–115.

Shonkoff, J.P. and Phillips, D.A. (2000) *From neurons to neighborhoods: The science of early childhood development*. Washington, DC: National Academies Press.

Short, K.G. (2009) 'Critically Reading The Word And The World: Building intercultural understanding through literature', *Bookbird: A Journal of International Children's Literature*, 47(2): 1–10.

Siann, G. (1994) *Gender, sex and sexuality (Contemporary psychology)*. Bristol: Taylor and Francis.

Sidebotham, P., Brandon, M., Bailey, S., Belderson, P., Dodsworth, J., Garstang, J., Harrison, E., Retzer, A. and Sorensen, P. (2016) *Pathways to harm, pathways to protection: A triennial analysis of serious case reviews 2011 to 2014: final report*. London: Department for Education.

Sims, M., Forrest, R., Semann, A. and Slattery, C. (2015) 'Conceptions of early childhood leadership: Driving new professionalism?', *International Journal of Leadership in Education*, 18(2): 149–66.

Sims-Bishop, R. (1990) 'Mirrors, window and sliding glass doors', *Perspectives: Choosing and Using Books for the Classroom*, 6(3): n.p. https://scenicregional.org/wp-content/uploads/2017/08/Mirrors-Windows-and-Sliding-Glass-Doors.pdf (accessed 25 October 2022).

Sinclair, R. (2004) 'Participation in practice: Making it meaningful, effective and sustainable', *Children & Society*, 18(2): 106–18.

Sinnema, C., Sewell, A. and Milligan, A. (2011) 'Evidence-informed collaborative inquiry for improving teaching and learning', *Asia-Pacific Journal of Teacher Education*, 39(3): 247–61.

Siraj, I. and Kingston, D. (2015) *An independent review of the Scottish early learning and childcare (ELC) workforce and out of school care (OSC) workforce*. London: University College London, Institute of Education.

Siraj-Blatchford, I. and Manni, L. (2007) *Effective leadership in the early years sector: The ELEYS study*. London: Institute of Education Press.

Siraj-Blatchford, I. and Sylva, K. (2004) 'Researching pedagogy in English pre-schools', *British Educational Research Journal*, 30(5): 713–30.

Siraj-Blatchford, I., Sylva, K., Muttock, S., Gilden, R. and Bell, D. (2002) *Researching effective pedagogy in the early years. Research report No. 356*. London: Department for Education and Skills.

Skinner, B.F. (1938) *The behaviour of organisms*. New York: Appleton-Century-Crofts.

Skinner, B.F. (1972) *Beyond freedom and dignity*. Harmondsworth: Pelican Books.

Skolnick, A. (1975) 'The limits of childhood: Conceptions of child development and social context', *Law and Contemporary Problems*, 39(3): 38–77.

Smilansky, S. (1968) *The effects of sociodramatic play on disadvantaged preschool children*. New York: John Wiley & Sons.

Smith, F. (1988) *Joining the literacy club: Further essays into education*. London: Heinemann Educational Books.

Smith, K. (2011) 'Producing governable subjects: Images of childhood old and new', *Childhood*, 19(1): 24–37.

Smith, M. (2012) 'Social pedagogy from a Scottish perspective', *International Journal of Social Pedagogy*, 1(1): 46–55.

Smith, M. (2021) *What is pedagogy?* https://infed.org/mobi/what-is-pedagogy (accessed 30 January 2022).

Smith-Brennan, H. (2018) 'Researching children's play as a playworker-ethnographer', in P. King and S. Newstead (eds), *Researching play from a playwork perspective*. Abingdon and New York: Routledge, pp. 56–72.

Snider, S. and Hirschy, S. (2009) 'A self-reflection framework for technology use by classroom teachers of young learners', *He Kupu*, 2(1): 30–44.

Social Care Wales (2021) Codes of practice and guidance. https://socialcare.wales/dealing-with-concerns/codes-of-practice-and-guidance (accessed 10 October 2022)

Sosu, E. and Ellis, S. (2014) *Closing the attainment gap in Scottish education*. York: Joseph Rowntree Foundation.

Spillane, J.P. (2006) *Distributed leadership*. San Francisco: Jossey-Bass.

Spillane, J.P. and Diamond, J.B. (eds) (2007) *Distributed leadership in practice*. New York: Teachers College, Columbia University.

Spodek, B. and Saracho, O.N. (1999) 'The relationship between theories of child development and the Early Childhood Curriculum', *Early Child Development and Care*, 152(1): 1–15.

Sserwanja, Q., Kawuki, J. and Kim, H.J. (2020) 'Increased child abuse in Uganda amidst COVID-19 pandemic', *Journal of Paediatrics and Child Health*, 57(2): 188–91.

Stack, J. and Nikiforidou, Z. (2021) 'Preschoolers' possession-based disputes during indoor and outdoor play', *Early Child Development and Care*, 191(6): 847–60.

Stamopoulos, E. (2012) 'Reframing early childhood leadership', *Australasian Journal of Early Childhood*, 37(2): 42–8.

Stangor, C. (2012) *Social psychology principles*. https://2012books.lardbucket.org/pdfs/social-psychology-principles.pdf (accessed 25 February 2022).

Starkey, P. and Cooper, R. (1995) 'The development of subitizing in young children', *British Journal of Developmental Psychology*, 13(4): 399–420.

Stein, M. (2008) 'Resilience and young people leaving care', *Child Care in Practice*, 14(1): 35–44.

Stephen, C. (2010) 'Pedagogy: The silent partner in early years learning', *Early Years*, 30(1): 15–28.

Stets, J. and Burke, P. (2000) 'Identity theory and social identity theory', *Social Psychology Quarterly*, 63(3): 224–37.

Stone, K. (2017) *Reconsidering primary literacy: Enabling children to become critically literate*. Abingdon: Routledge.

Stratigos, T. and Fenech, M. (2021) 'Early childhood education and care in the app generation: Digital documentation, assessment for learning and parent communication', *Australasian Journal of Early Childhood*, 46(1): 19–31.

Sturrock, G. (2003) 'Towards a psycholudic definition of playwork', in F. Brown (ed.), *Playwork theory and practice*. Buckingham: Open University Press, pp. 81–98.

Sturrock, G. and Else, P. (1998) *The playground as therapeutic space: Playwork as healing*. Proceedings from the IPA/USA Triennial National Conference, Play in a Changing Society: Research, Design, Application, Colorado, USA, June 1998. https://ipaewni.files.wordpress.com/2016/05/colorado-paper.pdf (accessed 13 February 2022).

Sutton-Smith, B. (1997) *The ambiguity of play*. Cambridge, MA: Harvard University Press.

Sutton-Smith, B. (2003) 'Play as a parody of emotional vulnerability', in D.E. Little (ed.), *Play and educational theory and practice: Play and culture studies, Vol. 5*. Westport, CT: Praeger, pp. 3–17.

Sydney Playground Project (2017) *Sydney playground project*. www.sydneyplaygroundproject. com (accessed 17 January 2022).

Takhvar, M. and Smith, P.K. (1990) 'A review and critique of Smilansky's classification scheme and the "nested hierarchy" of play categories', *Journal of Research in Childhood Education*, 4(2): 112–22.

Talat, U. (2017) *Emotion in organizational change: An interdisciplinary exploration*. Cham: Palgrave.

Teale, W.H. and Sulzby, E. (1986) *Emergent literacy: Writing and reading*. Norwood, NY: Ablex.

Tembo, S. (2021) '"Hang on, she just used that word like it's totally easy": Encountering ordinary racial affects in early childhood education and care', *Ethnicities*, 21(5): 875–92.

Teo, S.S.S. and Griffiths, G., (2020) 'Child protection in the time of COVID-19', *Journal of Paediatrics and Child Health*, 56(6): 838–40.

Thomas, Y.E., Anurudran, A., Robb, K. and Burke, F.T. (2020) 'Spotlight on child abuse and neglect response in the time of COVID-19', *The Lancet: Correspondence*, 5(7): e371.

Thornton, C. and Underwood, K. (2013) 'Conceptualisations of disability and inclusion: Perspectives of educators of young children', *Early Years*, 33(1): 59–73.

Tisdall, E.K.M. and Punch, S. (2012) 'Not so "new"? Looking critically at childhood studies', *Children's Geographies*, 10(3): 249–64.

Tisdall, K. and Bell, R. (2006) 'Included in governance? Children's participation in "public" decision making', in K. Tisdall, J. Davis, M. Hill and J. Prout (eds), *Children, young people and social inclusion: Participation for what?* Bristol: Policy Press, pp. 104–19.

Tisdall, K. and Davis, J. (2004) 'Making a difference? Bringing children's and young people's views into policy-making', *Children & Society*, 18(2): 131–42.

Tisdall, K., Davis, J., Hill, M. and Prout, J. (eds) (2006) *Children, young people and social inclusion: Participation for what?* Bristol: Policy Press.

Tobin, J. (2015) 'Understanding children's rights: A vision beyond vulnerability', *Nordic Journal of International Law*, 84(2): 155–82.

Tobin, J., Hsueh, Y. and Karasawa, M. (2009) *Preschool in three cultures revisited: China, Japan, and the United States*. Chicago: University of Chicago Press.

Tobin, M. (2016) *Childhood trauma: Developmental pathways and implications for the classroom*. Camberwell, Melbourne: Australian Council for Educational Research.

Together (Scottish Alliance for Children's Rights) (2021) *Supreme Court judgment: Here's what you need to know*. https://togetherscotland.blog/2021/10/06/supreme-court-judgment-heres-what-you-need-to-know (accessed 9 April 2022).

Together (Scottish Alliance for Children's Rights) (2022) *UN Convention on the Rights of the Child: About the convention*. www.togetherscotland.org.uk/about-childrens-rights/un-convention-on-the-rights-of-the-child/#:~:text=The%20USA%20is%20the%20only%20country%20that%20has%20not%20ratified%20the%20Convention (accessed 9 April 2022).

Tomlinson, J. (2020) *DfE announces £11.8 million boost to school breakfast club programme*. www.theschoolbus.net/news/featured-article/dfe-announces-118-million-boost-to-school-breakfast-club-programme/7472 (accessed 13 October 2021).

Tovey, H. (2017) *Bringing the Froebel approach to your early years practice (Second edition)*. Abingdon: Routledge.

Tracy, S.J. (2013) *Qualitative research methods: Collecting evidence crafting analysis communicating impact*. Oxford: John Wiley & Sons.

Tranfield, D., Denyer, D. and Smart, P. (2003) 'Towards a methodology for developing evidence-informed management knowledge by means of systematic review', *British Journal of Management*, 14(1): 207–22.

Trawick-Smith, J. (1989) 'Play is not learning: A critical review of the literature', *Child and Youth Care Quarterly*, 18(3): 161–70.

Trawick-Smith, J. (2014) *Early childhood development: A multicultural perspective (Sixth edition)*. London: Pearson.

Treaty Bodies (online) *Complaints about human rights violations*. www.ohchr.org/en/treaty-bodies/complaints-about-human-rights-violations (accessed 9 April 2022).

Tremblay, M.S., Gray, C., Babcock, S., Barnes, J., Bradstreet, C.C., Carr, D., Chabot, G., Choquette, L., Chorney, D., Collyer, C., Herrington, S., Janson, K., Janssen, I., Larouche, R., Pickett, W., Power, M., Sandseter, E.B.H., Simon, B. and Brussoni, M. (2015) 'Position statement on active outdoor play', *International Journal of Environmental Research and Public Health*, 12(6): 6475–505.

Trotter, Y.D. (2006) 'Adult learning theories: Impacting professional development programs', *Delta Kappa Gamma Bulletin*, 72(2): 8–13.

Trundley, R. (2008) 'The value of two', *Mathematics Teaching*, 211: 17–21.

Turnbull, J. and Jenvey, V.B. (2006) 'Criteria used by adults and children to categorize subtypes of play', *Early Child Development and Care*, 176(5): 539–51.

Tyler, K. and Price, D. (2016) *Gender diversity and inclusion in early years education*. Abingdon: Routledge.

Uhlenberg, J. and Geiken, R. (2021) 'Supporting young children's spatial understanding: Examining toddlers' experiences with contents and containers', *Early Childhood Education Journal*, 49(1): 49–69.

UK Government (2003) *Every child matters*. London: The Stationery Office.

UK Government (2015) *Policy paper. 2010 to 2015 government policy: Childcare and early education*. www.gov.uk/government/publications/2010-to-2015-government-policy-childcare-and-early-education (accessed 7 January 2022).

UK Government (2018) *Early years self-evaluation form*. www.gov.uk/government/publications/early-years-online-self-evaluation-form-sef-and-guidance-for-providers-delivering-the-early-years-foundation-stage (accessed 30 January 2022).

UK Government (UKG) (2021) *Guidance: Check early years qualifications*. www.gov.uk/guidance/early-years-qualifications-finder#qualification-requirements (accessed 28 October 2021).

UK Government (2022) *30 hours free childcare*. www.gov.uk/30-hours-free-childcare (accessed 13 March 2022).

UK Government (online) *Require a basic DBS check*. www.gov.uk/request-copy-criminal-record (accessed 3 April 2022).

UK Parliament (1870) *Elementary Education Act 1870*. London: HMSO.

UK Parliament (1872) *Education (Scotland) Act 1872*. London: HMSO.

UK Parliament (1889) *Prevention of Cruelty to, and Protection of, Children Act 1889*. London: HMSO.

UK Parliament (1891) *Factory and Workshop Act, 1891*. London: HMSO.

UK Parliament (1899) *An Act for the Prevention of Cruelty to, and better Protection of, Children 1889 (c.44)*. London: HMSO.

UK Parliament (1933) *An Act to Consolidate Certain Enactments Relating to Persons Under the Age of Eighteen Years 1933 (c.12)*. London: HMSO.

UK Parliament (1989) *Children Act 1989*. London: HMSO.

UK Parliament (1995a) *The Children (Northern Ireland) Order 1995*. London: HMSO.

UK Parliament (1995b) *Children (Scotland) Act 1995 (c.36)*. London: HMSO.

UK Parliament (2000) *Care Standards Act 2000 (c.14)*. London: HMSO.

UK Parliament (2002) *Education Act 2002 (Chapter 32)*. London: HSMO.

UK Parliament (2003) *Health and Social Care (Community Health and Standards) Act 2003 Commencement (Wales: 43) (c.12)*. London HMSO.

UK Parliament (2004) *Children Act 2004 (Chapter 31)*. London HMSO.

UK Parliament (2006) *The Childcare Act 2006 (c.21)*. London: HMSO.

UK Parliament (2010) *Equality Act 2010*. London HMSO.

UK Parliament (2011) *Safeguarding Board Act (Northern Ireland) 2011 (Chapter 7)*. London: HMSO.

UK Parliament (2014) *Children and Families Act 2014 (Chapter 6)*. London: HMSO.

UK Parliament (2015) *Children's Services Co-operation Act (Northern Ireland) 2015 (Chapter 10)*. London: HMSO.

UK Parliament (2017) *Children and Social Work Act 2017 (c.16)*. London: HMSO.

UK Parliament (2021a) *Later factory legislation*. www.parliament.uk/about/living-heritage/transformingsociety/livinglearning/19thcentury/overview/laterfactoryleg (accessed 27 October 2021).

UK Parliament (2021b) *The 1870 Education Act*. www.parliament.uk/about/living-heritage/transformingsociety/livinglearning/school/overview/1870educationact (accessed 28 October 2021).

UK Parliament (2022) *The 1833 Factory Act*. London: HMSO. www.parliament.uk/about/living-heritage/transformingsociety/livinglearning/19thcentury/overview/factoryact (accessed 25 January 2022).

UN General Assembly (1959) *Declaration of the Rights of the Child*, 20 November 1959, A/RES/1386(XIV): Resolutions adopted on the reports of the Third Committee. www.refworld.org/docid/3ae6b38e3.html (accessed 17 October 2022).

United Nations (1989) *The United Nations Convention on the Rights of the Child*. London: UNICEF.

United Nations (2013) *Youth in action on climate change: Inspirations from around the world. Joint framework initiative on children, youth and climate change*. Bonn: United Nations Framework Convention on Climate Change Secretariat.

United Nations (online-a) *Education for all*. www.un.org/en/academic-impact/education-all (accessed 30 January 2022).

United Nations (online-b) *The United Nations Convention on the Rights of the Child*. https://downloads.unicef.org.uk/wp-content/uploads/2016/08/unicef-convention-rights-child-uncrc.pdf (accessed 9 April 2022).

United Nations (online-c) *Committee on the Rights of the Child*. www.ohchr.org/en/treaty-bodies/crc (accessed 9 April 2022).

United Nations (online-d) *Functions and powers of the general assembly*. www.un.org/en/ga/about/background.shtml (accessed 17 October 2022).

United Nations Committee on the Rights of the Child (UNCRC) (2003) *General comment No. 5*. Geneva: Committee on the Rights of the Child.

United Nations Committee on the Rights of the Child (UNCRC) (2009) *General comment No. 12: The right of the child to be heard*. Geneva: Committee on the Rights of the Child.

United Nations Committee on the Rights of the Child (UNCRC) (2013) *General comment No. 17*. Geneva: Committee on the Rights of the Child.

United Nations Educational, Scientific and Cultural Organization (UNESCO) (1994) *The Salamanca statement and framework for action on special needs education*. Paris: UNESCO.

United Nations Educational, Scientific and Cultural Organization (UNESCO) (2004) *EFA global monitoring report 2005: Education for all – The quality imperative*. Paris: UNESCO.

United Nations Educational, Scientific and Cultural Organization (UNESCO) (2020) *With one in five learners kept out of school, UNESCO mobilizes education ministers to face the COVID-19 crisis*. https://en.unesco.org/news/one-five-learners-kept-out-school-unesco-mobilizes-education-ministers-face-covid-19-crisis (accessed 10 December 2021).

United Nations International Children's Emergency Fund (UNICEF) (2015) *Education 2030: Incheon Declaration and Framework for Action for the Implementation of Sustainable Development Goal 4: Ensure inclusive and equitable quality education and promote lifelong learning opportunities for all*. https://unesdoc.unesco.org/ark:/48223/pf0000245656 (accessed 31 January 2022).

United Nations International Children's Emergency Fund (UNICEF) (2020a) *Global status report on preventing violence against children 2020*. Geneva: World Health Organization.

United Nations International Children's Emergency Fund (UNICEF) (2020b) *Child friendly cities celebrating the 30th anniversary of the Convention on the Rights of the Child*. https://childfriendlycities.org/wp-content/uploads/2020/01/CFCI-CRC@30-Report.pdf (accessed 11 January 2022).

United Nations International Children's Emergency Fund (UNICEF) (2021a) *Scotland votes to incorporate children's rights in law*. www.unicef.org.uk/press-releases/scotland-votes-to-incorporate-childrens-rights-in-law (accessed 20 January 2022).

United Nations International Children's Emergency Fund (UNICEF) (2021b) *Guidance of child and adolescent participation: As part of Phase III of the preparatory action for a European Child Guarantee*. www.unicef.org/eca/media/19426/file/Child%20and%20Adolescent%20Participation%20in%20the%20CG%20Phase%20III_Version%201.0-Dec2021.pdf (accessed 21 January 2022).

United Nations International Children's Emergency Fund (UNICEF) (online-a) *Convention on the Rights of the Child*. www.ohchr.org/en/professionalinterest/pages/crc.aspx (accessed 28 December 2020).

United Nations Children's Fund (online-b) *The state of the world's children 2021: On my mind – promoting, protecting and caring for children's mental health*. www.unicef.org/lac/media/28726/file/SOWC2021-full-report-English.pdf (accessed 17 October 2022).

United Nations International Children's Emergency Fund (UNICEF) (online-c) About the rights respecting schools award: Putting children's rights at the heart of schools. https://www.unicef.org.uk/rights-respecting-schools/the-rrsa/about-the-rrsa (accessed 17 October 2022).

United Nations International Children's Emergency Fund (UNICEF) (online-d) *Child rights and why they matter: Every right, for every child*. www.unicef.org/child-rights-convention/child-rights-why-they-matter (accessed 2 November 2021).

United Nations International Children's Emergency Fund (UNICEF) (online-e) *Convention on the Rights of the Child: The children's version*. www.unicef.org/media/60981/file/convention-rights-child-text-child-friendly-version.pdf (accessed 6 February 2022).

Urban, M. (2016) 'Starting wrong? The trouble with a debate that just won't go away', in G.S. Cannella, M.S. Pérez and I.-F. Lee (eds), *Critical examinations of quality, regulation, disqualification and erasure*. New York: Peter Lang, pp. 85–104.

Uscianowski, C., Oppenzato, C. and Ginsburg, H.P. (2019) *Using picture books: Counting*. https://prek-math-te.stanford.edu/counting/using-picture-books-counting (accessed 7 December 2021).

Uttal, D.H., Meadow, N.G., Tipton, E., Hand, L.L., Alden, A.R., Warren, C. and Newcombe, N.S. (2013) 'The malleability of spatial skills: A meta-analysis of training studies', *Psychological Bulletin*, 139(2): 352–402.

van der Kolk, B. (2014) *The body keeps the score*. London: Penguin.

van der Ven, S., Boom, J. and Leseman, P. (2012) 'The development of executive functions and early mathematics: A dynamic relationship', *British Journal of Educational Psychology*, 82(1): 100–19.

van Dijk, J. (2020) *The digital divide*. Cambridge: Polity Press.

van Lancker, W. (2018) 'Reducing inequality in childcare service use across European countries: What (if any) is the role of social spending?', *Social Policy & Administration*, 52(1): 271–92.

van Oers, B. (1996) 'Are you sure? Stimulating mathematical thinking during young children's play', *European Early Childhood Education Research Journal*, 4(1): 71–87.

van Oers, B. (2010) 'Emergent mathematical thinking in the context of play', *Educational Studies in Mathematics*, 74(1): 23–37.

van Oers, B. and Duijkers, D. (2013) 'Teaching in a play-based curriculum: Theory, practice and evidence of developmental education for young children', *Journal of Curriculum Studies*, 45(4): 511–34.

vanVactor, J.D. (2012) 'Collaborative leadership model in the management of health care', *Journal of Business Research*, 65(4): 555–61.

Vasquez, V. (2014) *Negotiating critical literacies with young children*. New York: Routledge.

Veeran, V. (2004) 'Working with street children: A child-centred approach', *Child Care in Practice*, 10(4): 359–66.

Veerman, P. (1992) *The rights of the child and the changing image of childhood*. London: Martinus Nijhoff.

Veerman, P. and Levine, H. (2000) 'Implementing children's rights on a local level: Narrowing the gap between Geneva and the grassroots', *International Journal of Children's Rights*, 8(4): 373–84.

Venken, M. and Röger, M. (2015) 'Growing up in the shadow of the second world war: European perspective', *European Review of History: Revue Européenne d'Histoire*, 22(2): 199–220.

Verdine, B.N., Golinkoff, R.D., Hirsh-Pasek, K., Newcombe, N.S., Filipowicz, A.T. and Chang, A. (2014) 'Deconstructing building blocks: Preschoolers' spatial assembly performance relates to early mathematical skills', *Child Development*, 85(3): 1062–76.

Verschueren, K. and Koomen, H.M.Y. (2012) 'Teacher–child relationships from an attachment perspective', *Attachment and Human Development*, 14(3): 205–11.

von Glaserfeld, E. (1982) 'Subitizing: The role of figural patterns in the development of numerical concepts', *Archives de Psychologie*, 50(194): 191–218.

Vuorinen, T. (2021) '"It's in my interest to collaborate … " – Parents' views of the process of interacting and building relationships with preschool practitioners in Sweden', *Early Child Development and Care*, 191(16): 2532–44.

Vygotsky, L. (1962) *Thought and language*. Boston, MA: Massachusetts Institute of Technology Press.

Vygotsky, L. (1978) *Mind in society: The development of higher psychological processes*. Cambridge, MA: Harvard University Press.

Vygotsky, L.S. (2004) 'Imagination and creativity in childhood' *Journal of Russian & East European Psychology*, 42(1): 7–97.

Wales Council for Outdoor Learning (WCOL) (2018) *High quality outdoor learning for Wales*. https://evolve.edufocus.co.uk/evco/assets/conwy/high_quality_outdoor_learning_welshenglish.pdf (accessed 28 November 2021).

Walker, S.P., Wachs, T.D., Grantham-McGregor, S., Black, M.M., Nelson, C.A., Huffman, S.L., Baker-Henningham, H., Chang, S.M., Hamadani, J.D., Lozoff, B., Gardner, J.M.M., Powell, C.A., Rahman, A. and Richter, L. (2011) 'Inequality in early childhood: Risk and protective factors for early child development', *The Lancet*, 378(97–99): 1325–38.

Walsh, G., McMillan, D. and McGuinness, C. (2017) *Playful teaching and learning*. London: SAGE.

Walsh, G., Sproule, L., McGuinness, C. and Trew, K. (2011) 'Playful structure: A novel image of early years pedagogy for primary school classrooms', *Early Years*, 31(2): 107–19.

Waniganayake, M., Morda, R. and Kapsalakis, A. (2000) 'Leadership in childcare centres: Is it just another job?', *Australian Journal of Early Childhood*, 25(1): 13–19.

Ward, C. (1978) *The child of the city*. London: Architectural Press.

Watkins, C., Carnell, E., Lodge, C., Wagner, P. and Whalley, C. (2000) *Learning about learning: Resources for supporting effective learning*. London: Routledge.

Waugh, M.J., Robbins, I., Davies, S. and Feigenbaum, J. (2007) 'The long-impact of war experiences and evacuation on people who were children during World War Two', *Aging and Mental Health*, 11(2): 168–74.

Weiten, W. (1992) *Psychology: Themes and variations (Second edition)*. New York: Thomson Brooks/Cole Publishing Co.

Wellington, J. and Szczerbinski, M. (2007) *Research methods for the social sciences*. London: Bloomsbury.

CHILDHOOD PRACTICE

Wells, G. (1986) *The meaning makers: Children learning language and using language to learn*. Portsmouth, NH: Heinemann.

Wells, K. (2021) *Childhood in a global perspective (Third edition)*. Cambridge: Polity Press.

Welsh Assembly Government (2002) *Welsh Assembly Government play policy*. Cardiff: Welsh Assembly Government.

Welsh Assembly Government (2004) *Children and young people: Rights to action*. Cardiff: Welsh Assembly Government.

Welsh Government (2015) *Foundation phase framework*. Cardiff: Welsh Government.

Welsh Government (2016) *National minimum standards for regulated childcare for children up to the age of 12 years*. Cardiff: Welsh Government.

Welsh Government (2017) *Childcare, play and early years workforce plan*. Cardiff: Welsh Government.

Welsh Government (2019) *Food and nutrition for childcare settings*. https://gov.wales/food-and-nutrition-childcare-settings-full-guidance (accessed 1 April 2022).

Welsh Government (2020) *Languages, literacy and communication*. https://hwb.gov.wales/curriculum-for-wales/languages-literacy-and-communication/statements-of-what-matters (accessed 20 January 2022).

Welsh Government (2021a) *Introduction to curriculum for Wales guidance*. https://hwb.gov.wales/curriculum-for-wales/introduction (accessed 20 January 2022).

Welsh Government (2021b) *Flying start health programme guidance*. Cardiff: Welsh Government.

Welsh Government (2022a) *Policy and strategy: Children's rights in Wales*. https://gov.wales/childrens-rights-in-wales (accessed 20 October 2022).

Welsh Government (2022b) *Childcare for 3 and 4 year olds*. https://gov.wales/childcare-3-and-4-year-olds (accessed 13 March 2022).

Welsh Government (2022c) *A curriculum for funded non-maintained nursery settings*. https://hwb.gov.wales/curriculum-for-wales/curriculum-for-funded-non-maintained-nursery-settings (accessed 6 February 2022).

Welsh Government (online) *Curriculum for Wales*. https://hwb.gov.wales/curriculum-for-wales (accessed 22 November 2021).

West, A., O'Kane, C. and Hyder, T. (2008) 'Diverse childhoods: Implications for childcare, protection, participation and research practice', in A. Leira and C. Saraceno (eds), *Childhood: Changing contexts*. Bingley: Emerald, pp. 265–92.

Wheatley, M.J. (2006) *Leadership and the new science: Discovering order in a chaotic world (Third edition)*. San Francisco: Berrett-Koehler.

Wheatley, M.J. (2012) *So far from home: Lost and found in our brave new world*. San Francisco: Berrett-Koehler.

White, J. (2017) *Evidence summary: Reducing the attainment gap – the role of health and wellbeing interventions in schools*. Edinburgh: NHS Health Scotland.

Whitters, H. (2020) *Adverse childhood experiences, attachment and the early years learning environment*. Abingdon: Routledge.

Who Cares? Scotland (2022) *Participation of care experienced people*. www.whocaresscotland.org/what-we-do/participation (accessed 30 January 2022).

Wild, M., Silberfeld, C. and Nightingale, B. (2015) 'More? Great? Childcare? A discourse analysis of two recent social policy documents relating to the care and education of young children in England', *International Journal of Early Years Education*, 23(3): 230–44.

Wilding, K. (2020) *Let's go on a subitising walk!* www.youtube.com/watch?v=bX3i6g7in0M (accessed 1 November 2021).

Wilson, P. (2010) *The playwork primer*. College Park, MD: Alliance for Childhood.

Wilson, P.M., Petticrew, M., Calnan, M.W. and Nazareth, I. (2010) 'Disseminating research findings: What should researchers do? A systematic scoping review of conceptual frameworks', *Implementation Science*, 5(91): 1–16.

Wiltshire Council (2020) *Calming techniques for early years*. Trowbridge: Wiltshire Council.

Wingrave, M. (2015) *SCEL scoping exercise: Early learning and childcare sector in Scotland. Project report*. Glasgow: Scottish College for Educational Leadership.

Wingrave, M. and McMahon, M. (2016) 'Professionalisation through academicisation: Valuing and developing the early years sector in Scotland', *Professional Development in Education*, 42(5): 710–31.

Wingrave, M., Boyle, S., Black, E. and Orr, C. (2020) 'The standard for childhood practice – 10 years on', *Researching Education Bulletin*, 9: 5–9.

Winnicott, D.W. (2005) *Playing and reality*. Abingdon: Routledge.

Wohlfart, O. (2020) 'Digging deeper? Insights from a novice researcher', *International Journal of Qualitative Methods*, 19(1): 1–5.

Wolfe, S. and Flewitt, R. (2010) 'New technologies, new multimodal literacy practices and young children's metacognitive development', *Cambridge Journal of Education*, 40(4): 387–99.

Woll, L. (2001) 'Organizational responses to the Convention on the Rights of the Child: International lessons for child welfare organizations', *Child Welfare*, 80(5): 668–79.

Wood, D., Bruner, J.S. and Ross, G. (1976) 'The role of tutoring in problem solving', *Journal of Child Psychology and Psychiatry*, 17(2): 89–100.

Wood, E. (2014) 'Free choice and free play in early childhood education: Troubling the discourse', *International Journal of Early Years Education*, 22(1): 4–18.

Wood, E. (2015) 'The capture of play within policy discourses: A critical analysis of the UK frameworks for early childhood education', in J.L. Roopnarine, M.M. Patte, J.E. Johnson and D. Kuschner (eds), *International perspectives on children's play*. Maidenhead: Open University Press/McGraw-Hill Education, pp. 187–98.

Woodhead, M. (1996) *In search of the rainbow: Pathways to quality in large scale programmes for young, disadvantaged children (Early childhood development: practice and reflections 7)*. The Hague: Bernard van Leer Foundation.

Woodrow, C. and Press, F. (2018) 'The privatisation/marketisation of ECEC debate: Social versus neoliberal models', in L. Miller, C. Cameron, C. Dalli and N. Barbour (eds), *The SAGE handbook of early childhood policy*. London: SAGE, pp. 537–50.

Woolfolk, A. (2007) *Educational psychology (Tenth edition)*. Boston: Allyn and Bacon.

Wragg, M. (2013) 'Towards an inversion of the deficit model of intervention in children's play', *European Early Childhood Education Research Journal*, 21(2): 283–91.

Wyness, M. (2006) *Children and society: An introduction to the sociology of childhood.* London: Palgrave.

Wyness, M. (2015) *Childhood (Polity key concepts in the social sciences series).* London: Palgrave.

Xu, Y. (2010) 'Children's social play sequence: Parten's classic theory revisited', *Early Child Development and Care*, 180(4): 489–98.

Yanez, R.E., Fees, B.S. and Torquati, J.C. (2017) 'Preschool children's biophilia and attitudes toward nature: The effect of personal experiences', *The International Journal of Early Childhood Environmental Education*, 5(1): 57–67.

Yelland, N. (2015) 'Young children as multimodal learners in the information age', in K.L. Heider and M. Renck Jalongo (eds), *Young children and families in the information age: Applications of technology in early childhood.* Dordrecht: Springer, pp. 151–63.

Yelland, N. and Gilbert, C. (2018) 'Transformative technologies and play in the early years: Using tablets for new learning', *Global Studies of Childhood*, 8(2): 152–61.

Yerkes, M.A. and Javornik, J. (2019) 'Creating capabilities: Childcare policies in comparative perspective', *Journal of European Social Policy*, 29(4): 529–44.

Young, E.S., Simpson, J.A., Griskevicius, V., Huelsnitz, C.O. and Fleck, C. (2019) 'Childhood attachment and adult personality: A life history perspective', *Self and Identity*, 18(1): 22–38.

Zabatiero, J., Straker, L. Mantilla, A., Danby, S. and Edwards, S. (2018) 'Young children and digital technology: Australian early childhood education and care sector adults' perspectives', *Australasian Journal of Early Childhood*, 43(2): 14–22.

Zeedyk, S. (2020) *Sabre tooth tigers and teddy bears: The Connected Baby guide to attachment (Second edition).* Dundee: Connected Baby Ltd.

Zosh, J.M., Hirsh-Pasek, K., Hopkins, E.J., Jensen, H., Liu, C., Neale, D., Solis, S.L. and Whitebread, D. (2018) 'Accessing the inaccessible: Redefining play as a spectrum', *Frontiers in Psychology*, 9: 1124.

Index